A
HISTORY OF ENGLAND

UNDER THE

ANGLO-SAXON KINGS.

VOL. I.

A

HISTORY OF ENGLAND

UNDER THE

ANGLO-SAXON KINGS,

TRANSLATED FROM

THE GERMAN

OF

Dr. J. M. LAPPENBERG, For. F.S.A.,
KEEPER OF THE ARCHIVES OF THE CITY OF HAMBURG,

BY

BENJAMIN THORPE, F.S.A.

WITH ADDITIONS AND CORRECTIONS BY THE AUTHOR

AND THE TRANSLATOR.

IN TWO VOLUMES.

VOL. I.

KENNIKAT PRESS
Port Washington, N. Y./London

A HISTORY OF ENGLAND UNDER THE ANGLO-SAXON KINGS

First published in 1845
Reissued in 1971 by Kennikat Press
Library of Congress Catalog Card No: 70-118482
ISBN 0-8046-1231-5

Manufactured by Taylor Publishing Company   Dallas, Texas

PREFACE.

By many it will, without doubt, be thought singular that the history of a state, which has always been of prominent, and often of paramount importance in the affairs of the world, should have been undertaken by one who cannot, in the vocation or position of a professor, have found either an excuse for venturing on a task, however desirable, yet of difficult execution, or superior means of accomplishing it. As unfitting too, and even obnoxious to the charge of presumption, an individual must appear, who, in addition to the above-mentioned objections, has not unlimited leisure to bestow on so great a theme, but, on the contrary, has for many years been attached to a practical calling, which, though favourable to particular historical and juridical investigations, and to the elaboration of his native history, is, nevertheless, wont to stand opposed to a susceptibility for the more general views, to a conception of the more agitated life, and to the poetic and moral elements of general history, and at the same time adverse to every attempt at vivid powerful description and individual feeling, as foreign and obstructive to the matter. These considerations seem to render a few words

necessary regarding the personal circumstances of the
author in reference to his work.

The editors of ' The History of the European States[1] '
had for some years been seeking for a person willing
and qualified to undertake the History of England, but
had generally found that the external as well as internal
difficulties attending that study had held German scholars
aloof. The first historical inquirer of our time, to whom
the affairs of England were familiar from his youth,
whose premature loss we have never ceased to deplore,
had, it is said, at an early period, fostered the hope of
being one day enabled to undertake such a work.   The
most acute also of living historians had, at a later period,
actually undertaken it, when another direction given to
his investigations withdrew him from all thoughts of
England. May both names remain concealed, in order
not to excite unfavourable comparisons and vain regrets
for that which is denied to us![2] The question when
put to me, ' What is to be done?' I could at the time
answer only by naming certain German scholars, but
whose limited leisure and other circumstances proved
unfavourable to the undertaking, or Englishmen inclined to devote themselves to the later centuries only
of English history.   Influenced by these considerations,
and as a resolution must be taken—some volumes of
' The History of the European States' having already
appeared—I accepted the honourable invitation to com-

[1] Geschichte der europäischen Staaten, herausgegeben von A. H. L.
Heeren und F. A. Ukert.

[2] The literary reader will hardly fail to recognise in the one the celebrated historian of Rome, BARTHOLD GEORGE NIEBUHR, and in the other,
the learned and enlightened LEOPOLD RANKE.—T.

pose the history of a country rendered estimable to me by long residence there in early days. Having completed the arrangement of the archives of this city[1], and consequently possessed of a larger share of leisure, I had commenced several historical and juridical works, of which some are, either complete or in part, in the hands of the friends of German history; but the time consumed in the elaboration of records and other ancient documents was not at the moment sufficiently taken into account, while too much reliance was placed on a bodily frame by no means possessing the vigour of youth; though the unimpaired consciousness of what England and many of its worthiest natives had been to me, together with the magic of other unobliterated delightful recollections, had inspired me with sentiments well befitting him who should recount to his dear native land the advantages and defects, and so many to us extraordinary phenomena in the political existence of the English people.

The abode of the author in the city of his birth, the libraries of which, in works relative to the insular kingdom, are richer than most others of Germany; the valuable community of possession there in knowledge relative to the commerce, the industry and other circumstances of the present England; the proximity to that country, alike favourable to literary intercourse and personal observation; the illustrations of the Anglo-Saxon tongue which in common life offer themselves even at this day to the Lower Saxon,—such were the points urged against the doubts of the author as to

[1] They perished in the calamitous fire in May 1842.--T.

whether he should or should not devote himself to the
undertaking, while various occupations connected with
the history of the commerce of the middle age, the use
of valuable records, of which some are[1] preserved at
Hamburg, which city, previously to the great elevation
of England in the latter years of Queen Elizabeth, was
frequently in intimate connexion with the English court,
might tend to foster the hope of being useful, even to
the scholar, through some new disclosures.

When, however, the wished-for leisure for forming
the plan of the new undertaking arrived, greater difficulties than had been anticipated presented themselves,
more particularly with reference to the earlier part of the
history. The defects of the edited authorities are not
unknown in England, and the conviction of the necessity of a thorough revisal of them had been expressed
by Gibbon, who, in his great work, could apply only a
very partial remedy to the evil. Of modern writers, the
greater number, though industrious, were wanting both
in criticism and in knowledge of general history ; while
to the German it could not be difficult to gather new
views with regard to old English history, on the paths
opened to him by some honoured countrymen and pro-
fessors, in which the lovers of that study are but too apt
to feel delighted and consider themselves rich ; but for
the confirmation and establishment of such views, even
in cases where they could be proved indisputably just,
all authorities and preliminary labours were wanting.
Even the simple work of procuring the most important
original authors demanded much time, which should

---

[1] For *are* we may now substitute, *were before the conflagration.*—T.

rather have been devoted to the work itself. A welcome and stimulating phenomenon, therefore, while my volume was in progress, was the work of SIR FRANCIS PAL-GRAVE[1], which, by the novelty of its views, and the variety and abundance of its matter, both imparted instruction and invited to a completer establishment of the notions it set forth. Not less propitious to my undertaking was a correspondence accidentally established with CHARLES PURTON COOPER, ESQ., the Secretary of the Parliamentary Commission on the Public Records, who not only made me acquainted with some new sources, but afforded me an opportunity of applying more conformably to the objects of that Commission many historic and literary notices, which must otherwise have found a place only as a sort of literary ballast in my work.

That the progress of my labour has been less rapid than could be wished, is partly to be ascribed to the necessity of a new verification and reference of the accounts to their first sources, which will henceforth, in consequence of the better materials at hand, be more rarely requisite ; and partly also to the interest, never yet sufficiently considered, which the history of the unmixed German race in Britain, before their Romanizing by the Normans, must possess among their continental brethren. Of everything, therefore, which could contribute to the groundwork of a history of the Anglo-Saxon period, and which admitted of historic proof, I deemed it right not to be sparing. Much other matter relative to the Anglo-Saxon myths, the old Britons, and the historic sagas

---

[1] Rise and Progress of the English Commonwealth. See Literary Introduction, p. lxviii.—T.

connected with the north of England, will probably be communicated in another work. The genealogic tables[1], which I have drawn up of the Anglo-Saxon royal houses, will be found at the end of the volume.

My earnest endeavour to know and make known those sources of old English history, which are at present accessible, would have been far from successful, had not the chiefs of the libraries at Göttingen, Hanover, Kiel and Wolfenbüttel most kindly favoured me with the long and uninterrupted use of many rare works and manuscripts necessary for such investigations. While feeling it my duty to express to these estimable friends my sincerest gratitude for the confidence and benevolence shown me, I feel myself called on again to mention my valued friend MR. COOPER, to whose influential mediation I am indebted not only for many highly interesting and important works for the Norman and later portions of English history, but also for the communication, before the completion of the present work, of several valuable materials, prepared under the Record Commission, for Anglo-Saxon history, which he granted to the then personally unknown foreigner, for his particular use, previously to their publication. May that which is here given appear not wholly unworthy of such honourable confidence!

J. M. L.

Hamburg, 16th September, 1833.

---

[1] These, in the present translation, have not only been revised by me throughout, but also augmented by—1. a table of the ancestors of Woden, showing also the descents from his several sons; 2. the ancestors up to Woden of the founders of the Germanic states in Britain; 3. the genealogy of the princes or ealdormen of Lindisse (Lindsey).—T.

TRANSLATOR'S PREFACE.

FOLLOWING the example of my worthy and learned friend, the author, and in compliance with the general usage on such occasions, I will endeavour, as briefly as possible, to lay before the few who will honour this history with a perusal, an account of the part I have taken in it beyond that of a mere translator.

Having been presented by Dr. Lappenberg with a copy of his work immediately on its publication at Hamburg in 1834, the interest excited in me by its perusal was such that I resolved on attempting a version of it into English; for although histories of the same period in the mother-tongue and of good repute were not wanting, yet it appeared to me that in this were contained many particulars, especially with reference to chronological criticism, and to what may be called the German portion of Anglo-Saxon history, not elsewhere to be found in a condensed form, as well as much other information, which the author's pursuits in the field of old Teutonic literature had enabled him to introduce almost as matter of course, at a time when that field was a sort of *terra incognita* to most lovers of historic literature in England.

My resolve was partly executed, a translation to the end of the so-called Heptarchy was completed, when, to my mortification, I found that not one of the booksellers to whom it was offered would risk anything in its publication : nor indeed were they to blame, for it seemed at the time that few persons in the country interested themselves much about old history, a study which, from some unknown cause, had unfortunately never found that favour among us with which it has for ages been regarded in Italy, France, and Germany ; though the fruits of the Record Commission, and more especially the hope of the immediate publication of a volume of the late Mr. Petrie's ' CORPUS HISTORICUM,' certainly justified the expectation of better days. Discouraged by this somewhat discreditable state of things, and far from satisfied with my translation (which was a translation in the strictest sense of the word, without the slightest attempt at addition or rectification by reference to the sources of our early history), I destroyed the labour of many months ; and it was not till the winter of 1842 that circumstances induced me again to think of a translation of Lappenberg's Anglo-Saxon History.

During the intermediate time I had laboured sedulously in the field of Anglo-Saxon literature, and having, while editing for the Government the ' ANCIENT LAWS AND INSTITUTES OF ENGLAND,' been put in possession of Mr. Petrie's unfinished volume and other authorities, I could not withstand the temptation thus thrown in my way to test and enlarge the text of Dr. Lappenberg's history by the help of the original writers so fortunately placed within my reach. This task led ultimately to a new

translation of the whole, with many alterations and corrections, and such additions as appeared indispensable
to the original, in which the narrative had been abridged
and several facts unnoticed, in compliance with the necessity of conciseness imposed on the author by the circumstance, that his volume, forming one of a collection,
could not be extended beyond a certain limit.

On the first notice of my intention to translate his
work, Dr. Lappenberg most kindly supplied me with a
considerable quantity of matter, both as additions to and
corrections of the original, the substance of which will
be chiefly found in the text, in new annotations, or
embodied with the old ones ; while my own additions
and modifications have more especial reference to the
text, though a few notes by me[1] will be met with occasionally scattered throughout the volumes. In fulfilling
this part of my task it has been my endeavour to impart
our early story as faithfully as possible, and as fully as
the bounds which good taste forbids us to transgress
would allow. The passages from the ancient historians,
occasionally interwoven into the text, I have rendered,
not from the author's German version, but directly from
the originals.

Should it be objected by any one, that unnecessary
pains have sometimes been bestowed in recording, from
charters and other sources, the names of petty kings
(subreguli), of whom little or nothing, beyond the fact
that they once existed, is known to us, an answer is at
hand, that the knowledge of a name, especially if in
combination with a date, may, in the progress of in-

---

[1] These are distinguished by the initial T.

quiry, lead to the knowledge of a fact, and, for numismatic pursuits, such notices are often of the highest utility. Even legends are not to be indiscriminately rejected, as void of value, in recording the history of times, of which it may be said, that the germ of many an important event, connected with the establishment and progress of religion, as well as many a main spring of action, may sometimes be found in a legend.

In conclusion, I will venture to express a hope that, when a new edition of the original shall be called for in Germany—as I trust will ere long be the case—the author will not reject, as unworthy of his notice, some at least of the variations and additions introduced by me into this translation. I am here reminded of the kind interest taken in my labour by my old and much-esteemed friend MR. RICHARD TAYLOR, who has not only supplied me with several works of reference, but also obliged me with some judicious observations while the volumes were in the press—services which claim and have my best thanks.

Should this translation meet with a favourable reception, it is my intention, if life be granted me, to communicate to English readers the author's ' HISTORY OF ENGLAND UNDER THE NORMAN KINGS,' or to the accession of the house of Plantagenet. This will be comprised in a single volume.

B. T.

CONTENTS.

VOL. I.

NORMAN AUTHORITIES.

ENGLISH METRICAL CHRONICLERS.

LATER CHRONICLERS, ETC.

MODERN HISTORIANS.

BRITAIN UNDER THE ROMANS.

PART I.

FROM THE LANDING OF HENGEST AND HORSA TO THE ACCESSION OF ECGBERHT.

ERRATA.

P. xiii l. 12, *dele* chiefly.
— xlvi l. 19, *for* Athelm *read* Æthelm.
— 83 l. 16, *for* preceding *read* following.
— 83 l. 17, *for* same *read* preceding.

LITERARY INTRODUCTION.

~~~~~~~~~~~~~~~~~

As all our knowledge of ancient times necessarily depends on an acquaintance with the original sources of history, it is only when such sources are supposed to be already sufficiently known, that an accurate specification of them can be dispensed with. The want of such a specification for the History of England is felt even in the literature of England itself[1], but is more particularly disadvantageous to the natives of other countries, where the most extensive libraries are too often but sparingly supplied with these original authorities. But if it be the object of an historic work to promote a critical knowledge of history, and to aid the solitary student in his researches, mere literary or bibliographic notices will be found wholly inadequate; and, as a basis for such researches, an accurate review of the several authorities, of their peculiarities and deviations from each other, must be set forth. Among no historic writers are we more to seek for such information than among those of England, with the exception, perhaps,

---

[1] The work of Nicolson (English, Scotch and Irish Historical Libraries, 3rd edit. Lond. 1736. fol.) is not sufficient for the wants of the present day. On the chronicles of the Anglo-Saxons may be consulted with advantage a very sensible article in ' Hermes,' Bd. xxx., by Dr. Reinhold Schmid.

of Lingard and Palgrave, and even these seem to have been
guided rather by a correct, though not always followed, tact,
than by a scientifically founded view.   Hence by English historians, chroniclers are not unfrequently adduced as authorities, who in the present work are either not cited at all, or in
those rare cases only when their original sources cannot be
traced : such are Matthew of Westminster, Roger of Hoveden,
John Bromton, William Knyghton, and others. With correct
and critical editions of the several authorities, which might
serve as a compass whereby to steer on the dark ocean of history, England is but ill provided.   An analysis of the chronicles, for the purpose of separating that which is verbally
borrowed, and that which is remodelled, from that which is
original communication ; the comparison of the latter with,
and confirmation by, contemporary records and other authorities ; the illustration of the political position of the author ;
the examination of his language—all this in England, as in
other countries, belongs to the rarely possessed requisites for
historic research ; so that historic composition, like other
arts, must continue far behind its theory.

The following notices and critical remarks are given with
due regard to brevity, and have reference solely to the most
important sources of Anglo-Saxon history, to the exclusion of
Greek, Roman, Northern, and German authorities, as well as
of separate biographies, which will be found cited under the
several periods with which they are connected.

The study of English history would have been exceedingly
facilitated, had the edition of the English historians to the
year 1500, commenced under the authority of the late Parliamentary Commission, appointed for the preservation and
publication of British historical and legal monuments, been
carried on to completion ; there being not only many excellent
manuscripts still unused of the chronicles already—though
for the most part very indifferently—edited, but also a considerable number of important historic sources that have never

yet appeared in print[1]. Had this design been carried on in
a way commensurate with the means possessed by the Commission, England might, at no distant period, have exulted in
a collection of historical and legal monuments excelling those
of other countries in as great a degree as her present printed
chronicles are inferior to the historical collections of Italy,
France, Germany and Denmark.

The larger printed collections of English chroniclers belong
for the most part to the seventeenth, and some even to the
sixteenth century. The earliest is that of Dr. Matthew Parker,
archbishop of Canterbury[2], containing the British History of
Jeffrey of Monmouth, his epitomiser Ponticus Virunnius,
Beda's Ecclesiastical History, Gildas, William of Newburgh,
and an extract translated into Latin from Froissart. Besides
the above, Parker, as early as 1570, had caused Matthew of
Westminster, and, in the following year, Matthew Paris to be
printed; and, in 1574, Walsingham, and Asser's Life of Ælfred,
the latter with Anglo-Saxon types. This collection was followed by that of Sir Henry Savile, under the title of ʻ Rerum
Anglicarum Scriptores post Bedam Præcipui[3],' containing the
three principal works of William of Malmesbury, Henry of
Huntingdon, Roger of Hoveden, Ethelwerd and Ingulf—a
great acquisition for history, though so uncritically edited, that
a considerable portion of Henry of Huntingdon is reprinted
verbatim in Hoveden. The chronicles of Matthew of Westminster and Florence of Worcester were printed separately in
the same year. A few years later that unrivalled antiquary
William Camden (ob. 1623) increased the number of collections with his ʻ Anglica, Normannica, Hibernica, Cambrica,
a Veteribus Scripta[4],' containing a new but faulty edition of

---

[1] For the plan of this collection and the preliminary labours of the Commission, see Cooper's ʻ Account of the most important public Records of
Great Britain, and the publications of the Record Commissioners,' vol. ii.
pp. 144–178 and 365–370.

[2] Rerum Britannicarum Scriptores Vetustiores et Præcipui. Lugd. 1587. fol.

[3] Londini 1596. Francofurti 1601. fol.   [4] Francof. 1603. fol.

Asser's Life of Ælfred, William of Jumièges, Walsingham
(to which is needlessly appended an extract from the same
work, the Hypodigma Neustriæ), Giraldi Cambrensis Itinerarium, Descriptio Cambriæ, Topographia Hiberniæ, and
Hibernia Expugnata. As a proof of the little interest taken
in England for fundamental historic knowledge, it may be
mentioned, that so far from other and more effective editions
being there produced, these collections could only be reprinted
in Germany; nor till a lapse of fifty years was an edition of
the Saxon Chronicle brought forth, though next after Beda
the most important source of Anglo-Saxon history, and the
basis of the portion relating to that period of the principal of
the before-mentioned Latin chronicles.

The 'Historiæ Anglicanæ Scriptores Decem,' edited by
Sir Roger Twysden[1], is chiefly useful for the Anglo-Saxon
period on account of Simeon of Durham contained in it (who
not only frequently supplies the deficiencies of Florence, but
also gives many particulars not to be found elsewhere), also
the abbot of Rievaux, 'De Genealogia Regum Anglorum,'
and his Life of Edward the Confessor. Of greater interest
for the ante-Norman period are the collections printed at
Oxford, of which that by Dr. Fell, bishop of that city, contains the best edition of Ingulf, the History of Peter of Blois,
and the Chronicle of the Abbey of Melrose[2]. In the other,
edited by Dr. Gale, are comprised Gildas, Nennius, Ædde's
Life of Wilfrith, John Wallingford, the valuable Chronicles
or Histories of the Abbeys of Ely and Ramsey, besides other
works of importance for the Anglo-Saxon period of English
history[3]. From this time no similar collection has appeared,

---

[1] Londini 1652. fol.

[2] Rerum Anglicarum Scriptorum Veterum t. i. Oxon. 1684. fol. Of
this collection no more appeared. As Fell's name is not mentioned in the
volume, the work is frequently confounded with the similarly printed one
of Gale.

[3] Historiæ Britannicæ, Saxonicæ, Anglo-Danicæ Scriptores xv. opera
Thomæ Gale. Oxon. 1691. This volume, containing the earlier writers,

unless we may include in the list that of Sparke, under the title of ' Historiæ Anglicanæ Scriptores varii [1],' the chief portion of which has reference to the abbey of Peterborough, or to the Life of Thomas a Becket. Of greater interest for us, though exclusively confined to church history, is the ' Anglia Sacra' of Wharton [2], a valuable collection of the chronicles of various dioceses and monasteries, as well as Lives of celebrated ecclesiastics. Many English chronicles were, in the beginning of the last century, edited by the indefatigable Thomas Hearne, though less critically and carefully than could be wished. His publications being detached and independent of each other, are consequently not easily collected [3]. For our present purpose the Scottish chronicle of Fordun [4] is perhaps the only one of them possessing any interest.

The wish for a complete collection of the English historians of the middle age was first publicly expressed by Gibbon [5] : that his wish was not carried into effect is matter of deep regret, except in the case that no other individual than the object of his choice, John Pinkerton, had been selected for that purpose.

The unfinished first volume of the edition of English Historians [6], to have been published under the Record Com-

is usually regarded as the first, though the second, containing some writers of the Norman period, is dated 1687.

[1] Londini 1723, in two small folios.   [2] Londini 1691, ii. tom. folio.

[3] The collection sometimes cited under his name, ' Collectio Scriptorum,' etc., contains of the chronicles only the most unimportant—that of William of Worcester.

[4] Johannis de Fordun Scotichronicon genuinum, edit. Th. Hearne, v. tom. 8vo. Oxon. 1722.   [5] See his Miscellaneous Works.

[6] Just as the manuscript of this work was about to be sent to press (1833), the author had the pleasure, through the particular kindness of his highly respected friend, C. P. Cooper, Esq., to receive the first volume of Mr. Petrie's ' Materials for English History,' or ' Corpus Historicum,' as far as that work was printed ; the execution of which, it is hoped, will satisfy all reasonable expectations. Though it is to be regretted that the Introduction, containing an account of and remarks on the work, the several authors and manuscripts, is not yet printed, its present contents enable us, nevertheless, to place greater confidence in our views regarding the con-

mission, contains—after extracts from the Greek and Latin
geographers and historians—Gildas, Nennius, Beda's Chronicon and Ecclesiastical History, the Saxon Chronicle with
an English translation, Asser's Life of Ælfred, the Chronicles
of Ethelwerd, Florence of Worcester[1], Simeon of Durham,
and Henry of Huntingdon, L'Estorie des Engles of Geffrei
Gaimar, the Annales Cambriæ, the Brut y Tywysogion, or
Chronicle of the Princes of Wales (with an English translation), ascribed to Caradoc of Llancarvan (all down to the
year 1066), and the 'Carmen de Bello Hastingensi.' Four
volumes were destined to comprise all the chronicles (omitting in the later all matter copied verbatim from the earlier
ones), and whatever could be found illustrative of English
history to the period of the Norman conquest.

The hope once fostered by the historic inquirer, of deriving
considerable information respecting the earliest history of
Britain from Welsh sources, has not been realized. The history of Wales and Cornwall has undoubtedly received illustration : highly interesting is it also to have determined the
very great antiquity of the poems of the bards Aneurin,
Taliesin, Llywarch Hên and Merddyn, some of which may
probably be assigned to the sixth century[2]. Yet do these
poetic spirits set before us the subject rather than an illustration of the history of their time. We find in their glowing love
of country, in their intense hatred of the Anglo-Saxons, in
the outbreak of strong enthusiasm exulting in its subject, in
the vain-glory ever exhibiting itself more pompously with the

nexion of the known sources of English history, and to avail ourselves of
some hitherto unused authorities.

[1] The genealogies given at the end of Florence are from a MS. belonging
to C. C. Coll. Oxford, collated for the purpose by the translator of the present work.—T.

[2] This estimable treasure of old British literature is, with other relics,
published in the Myvyrian Archaiology of Wales, a collection of historical
documents from ancient MSS. 3 voll. 8vo. Lond. 1801–7. Compare
Turner's Dissertation on the age of those poems in his History of the
Anglo-Saxons.

fall of former greatness—we find in all this the germ of that world of fiction, which the Welsh of after-ages have passed off for a History of Britain. When we think of these and of similar Scandinavian compositions, the full worth of the love of truth pervading our modest monkish chronicles cannot fail most forcibly to strike us. Servile as that faithfulness may appear, easily as the earnestness and the strength of belief may be mistaken, which, by the old chroniclers, were esteemed as the greatest virtues; absurd as the accuracy is with which they copy, without the omission of a syllable, every word of a predecessor, and although, as from virtue a vice may spring, so from their dull fidelity the most insipid pedantry and grossest falsehood may grow and often has grown, yet to that schoolboy fidelity alone are we indebted for a chronological clew through the labyrinth of the middle age, the bridge, as it were, which connects the old with the new world over the rushing, ever-agitated, sparkling waves of the stream of time.

The historic Triads of the Welsh contain considerable information, but require much illustration for the satisfactory understanding of them. Adherence to an originally perhaps well-adapted form, can, in its later wholly unfitting application, only counteract the object of the composition, and cause it to degenerate into insipidity[1].

The oldest known British historian—if his work, 'Liber querulus de Excidio Britanniæ,' called also 'Historia,' can give him any pretension to that title—is Gildas[2], born A.D. 516, a scholar of St. Iltut and monk of Bangor, who, after a life spent partly in travel or pilgrimages, partly in solitude, is said to have died and been buried in the abbey of Glaston-

---

[1] See, besides the Myvyrian Archaiology, Edw. Lhuyd, Archæologia Britannica. Oxon. 1707. Davies, Celtic Researches. Lond. 1804. 8vo. Edw. Williams, Lyrical and Pastoral Poems. Lond. 1794. 12mo. vol. ii.

[2] See p. 133. He was born in the year of the battle of Bath, which Beda, from a misconception of the text of Gildas, places in 493.

bury.   To Gildas is also ascribed an 'Epistola,' wherein he
pours forth the bitterest lamentations over the corruption
and general wickedness of his time.   The History must have
been composed in the year 560, the Epistle before 547[1], in
which Maglocun, king of Gwynedd, who is mentioned in it,
died[2].   Beda, Alcwine and Lupus cite Gildas, surnamed the
Wise[3].   Jeffrey of Monmouth appeals to a larger historical
work of Gildas, which is no longer extant, unless it be latent
in the 'Historia Britonum,' bearing the name of Nennius[4].

This last-mentioned work, entitled also 'Eulogium Britanniæ,' is usually ascribed to Nennius, abbot of Bangor, a
pupil of Elbod, archbishop of Gwynedd[5].   The year 688, assigned as that of its composition, can, therefore, have reference only to the work in its original form, that which has
reached our time having many additions and interpolations.
The preface to the common manuscripts places its composition in the year 858[6], a date reconcileable with 809, that of
the death of Elbod.   A valuable manuscript of this work in
the Vatican, of the tenth century, in which the greater part
of those additions are wanting, names Mark the Hermit as
the author or, perhaps, the copier only, in the year 945.   An
edition from this manuscript, with learned and excellent remarks, was published by the Rev. W. Gunn[7].   Nennius names
as his authorities the Annales Romanorum, Chronica S. S.

---

[1] Both works are printed in Gale, t. i.; the first also in C. Bertrami
Britannicarum Gentium Historiæ antiquæ Scriptores III.   Havniæ, 1758.
8vo.   Since the first edition by Polydore Vergil (Lond. 1526. 8vo), Gildas
has been frequently printed.

[2] Annales Cambriæ h. a.   King Constantine, who is likewise mentioned
by Gildas, was living in the year 589.   See Annal. Camb.

[3] See also Will. Malmesb. de Antiq. Glaston. ap. Gale, t. i. p. 296.   A
Life of Gildas, " scripta a monacho Ruyensi," is printed in the ' Bibliotheca
Floriacensis.' Lugd. 1645. 8vo. [See Stevenson's edition, printed uniformly
with Gildas, for the English Historical Society.—T.]

[4] This is Turner's opinion.   History of the Anglo-Saxons, vol. i. p. 201.

[5] See Stevenson's edit. pref. p. viii.

[6] Also in cap. xi., and at the conclusion of the work.

[7] Historia Britonum by Mark the Hermit. Lond. 1819. 8vo.

Patrum, and Scripta Scotorum Anglorumque et Traditio
Veterum. The Welsh Triads are undoubtedly comprised in
the last, as his work abounds in trilogies[1]. An important
circumstance for criticism seems to have been overlooked,
viz. that a considerable portion of this work has been inserted,
and often verbatim, by Henry of Huntingdon into his Chronicle, though without mention of the name either of Nennius
or of Mark the Hermit. Thus (p. 695, edit. Petrie), " apud
quendam auctorem (Nenn. ix.) reperi." (Ib. p. 707) " dicitur
a quibusdam " (Nenn. xxxviii. xxxix.). In one place (p. 712)
he quotes him under the name of " Gildas historiographus[2]."
The chronology followed by Nennius is that of Eusebius,
though, in the manuscripts, particularly in that of Mark,
much corrupted.

Jeffrey ap Arthur, born at Monmouth in 1152, bishop of
St. Asaph, is the English foster-brother of the Danish Saxo
Grammaticus. In the choicest Latin of his time he has composed a history of the Britons[3], consisting of the grossest
fables, interspersed with some historic traditions. In later
times authors seem to have unanimously agreed in an unqualified rejection of the entire work, and have therefore failed
to observe, that many of his accounts are supported by narratives to be found in writers wholly unconnected with and
independent of Jeffrey[4]. He professes to have merely translated his work from a chronicle in the British tongue, called

---

[1] Cap. vii. "Venerunt tres filii cujusdam militis Hispaniæ cum xxx.
chiulis apud illos, cum xxx. mulieribus in unaquaque chiula;" Cap. xxv.
" Nonus (3 × 3) fuit Constantinus;" Cap. xxvii. "Tribus vicibus occisi
sunt duces Romanorum a Brittannis;" Cap. xxviii. "tres chiulæ;"
Cap. xlvii. three battles with the Saxons; Cap. xlviii. "Hengistus elegit
ccc. milites," etc.

[2] The passages from Nennius to be found in Henry of Huntingdon are
particularly from cc. 2–4, 9, 10, 16, 23, 28, 36, 38, 47–49, 51, 54, 61, 62.
Some passages in Huntingdon accord most closely with the Vatican MS.
e. g. p. 712, ed. Petrie, " Arthurus belliger."

[3] Editio princeps ab Ascensio, 1508, 4to, from three Parisian MSS.

[4] See p. 45, note [2].

'Brut y Brenhined,' or 'History of the Kings of Britain,' found in Brittany, and communicated to him by Walter, archdeacon of Oxford[1]. The 'Brut' of Tysilio[2] has, with some probability, been regarded as the original of Jeffrey's work, though it is doubtful whether it may not itself be rather an extract from Jeffrey[3]. The Latin elaboration of the British original seems to have been completed about the year 1128. That the whole is not a translation, appears from passages interpolated, in many places verbatim, from the existing work of Gildas[4], of whom (lib. iv. 20, vi. 13, xii. 6) he cites another work, 'De Victoria Ambrosii,' no longer extant. From Beda, of whom he speaks (lib. xii. 14), Jeffrey has rarely extracted verbatim, though he seems, in many places, to have had before him either Nennius or his original[5], where the similarity of thought and expression can hardly be accidental[6].

Among the writers who copy from Jeffrey of Monmouth, we must not reckon either William of Malmesbury or Henry of Huntingdon, both of whom he mentions at the end of his own work. Ordericus Vitalis is probably the first who (though without naming him) has excerpted from him, viz. lib. xii., the prophecy of Merlin (Galfr. lib. vii. 3). After him is Alfred of Beverley, who cites the 'Historia Britonum,' without mention of the author, and does not conceal his doubts as to its credibility. The 'Historia Britonum,' cited in the Chronicle

---

[1] Not Walter Mapes, as is generally supposed, but an earlier Walter Calenius. See Douce in Warton, H. E. P. vol. i. p. 60, edit. 1840.

[2] Translated by P. Roberts, and printed in the Welsh Archaiology, vol. ii., under the title of 'A Chronicle of British Kings.' See Dissertation on the origin of Romantic fiction in Europe, in Warton, H. E. P.

[3] Turner, H. of the A.-SS. vol. i. p. 159.

[4] All doubt will vanish on comparing Jeffrey vi. 3. with Gildas cc. xiv–xvi. Cf. also Jeffrey v. 5. with Gildas viii. Jeffrey v. 3, 14. with Gildas x., and xii. 6. with Gildas xix.

[5] Compare particularly Jeffrey vi. 12–15, 17,40–42, with Nennius xxxvi., xlv., xlvii., l.–lii.

[6] The edition of Jeffrey of Monmouth in Parker's collection is extremely faulty. An edition from the excellent MS. in the library of the Prince of Schaumburg-Lippe at Bückeburg would remove many critical doubts.

of Albericus, is probably that of Jeffrey[1]. Gervase of Tilbury gives copious extracts from him, and is said to have written four books of Illustrations of his work; and Ponticus Virunnius of Treviso[2], who lived at the close of the fifteenth century, made an epitome of it in six books.

Several writers, even contemporaries of Jeffrey, have expressed themselves strongly against his propagation of the sagas about Arthur[3], under the guise of authentic history, among whom William of Newburgh and Giraldus are the most conspicuous; and at an earlier period William of Malmesbury had also declared himself against the British traditions of Arthur. On the other hand, the welcome reception given to this garb and embellishment of the old favourite traditions was greatly promoted by the policy of Henry the First; the composition of Jeffrey's work might indeed have been occasioned by it[4]. In conclusion, we will venture to express the hope of one day seeing what is historical in Jeffrey of Monmouth separated from that which is fabulous; the latter honoured as a pleasing relic of the times of old, and the rest exalted into useful matter for the national history.

' Le Brut d'Angleterre' of Robert Wace[5] appears to be a French imitation of Jeffrey[6], an old English translation of which, made in the thirteenth century by Layamon, a priest dwelling on the banks of the Severn[7], proves the delight taken by the people in these traditions. In his preface,

[1] See p. 5, and aa. 434, 442, etc.; also about Merlin's prophecies, aa. 717, 1136, 1139.

[2] In Parker's collection.

[3] A sensible defence of Jeffrey is prefixed to Wynne's Caradoc.

[4] This supposition is rendered very probable by Turner. See History of England, vol. iv. pp. 339–355.

[5] An edit. of this work, by M. Le Roux de Lincy, has been printed at Rouen, in 2 voll. 8vo. 1836, 1838.

[6] Cf. Warton, H. E. P. vol. i. p. 58, edit. 1840; also the Abbé de la Rue's papers in the Archæologia, voll. xii.–xiv.

[7] Of this translation, so important for the old language of England, an edition, accompanied by a prose version in modern English, is in preparation by Sir F. Madden, for the Society of Antiquaries.

Layamon informs us that he did not merely translate Wace, but made use of other historic sources.

The chronicle of Caradoc, a monk of Llancarvan, has been estimated too highly with reference to English history. This work, which reaches to the year 1156, has been translated and edited, first in 1584 by H. Llwyd and Dr. Powell, and secondly in 1697 by H. Wynne[1]. Its chief basis is the Anglo-Saxon Chronicle and a Welsh chronicle, into which the author has interwoven many British traditions, though very uncritically and unchronologically. It is believed to have been composed in the monastery of Strata Florida. Some manuscripts are as early as the year 1410[2]. A similar work by John Brechfa is likewise much esteemed by inquirers into Welsh history, an edition of which, as well as of other British monuments hitherto little known, or possibly wholly unknown to us, would, without doubt, shed considerable light on the history of the remnant of a great people, which has, with remarkable tenacity, preserved its nationality throughout a period of two thousand years.

The Welsh chronicle used by Caradoc is probably the ' Chronicon Walliæ,' from the year 444 to 954, together with the beginning of the continuation of the same, or the ' Chronicon Cambriæ,' to the year 1286. An edition of both is given in the ' Corpus Historicum' under the title of ' Annales Cambriæ.' The chronology followed in these Annals is not reckoned from the birth of Christ, but begins with a year which may possibly be intended for that of the coming of the Saxons, but which would indicate an adherence to the Anglo-Saxon chronology, while among the Welsh we might rather expect to find a continuation of the Roman annals. The uncertainty arising from this mode of calculating is the more to be regretted, as these few pages, notwithstanding their brevity of detail, contain valuable notices of the rulers and of the

---

[1] A new edition was published at Shrewsbury in 1832.
[2] See Cooper on the Public Records, vol. ii. p. 457.

military history of all the British tribes ; and the general history of the Britons, as it has hitherto been known to us from Caradoc, acquires from them numerous as well as important additions and rectifications. 'The Chronicle of the Princes of Wales,' written in Welsh, entitled 'Brut y Tywysogion,' begins with the abdication of Cadwaladyr, in the year 681, in which Tysilio and Jeffrey of Monmouth terminate, and is continued to the conquest of Wales by Edward the First. This work (which, to the end of the ninth century, appears to have been translated from the 'Annales Cambriæ') has been erroneously attributed to Caradoc of Llancarvan. The Welsh text, to the year 1066, accompanied by an English version, is comprised in the ' Corpus Historicum.' The ' Brut y Saeson' is merely a manuscript, somewhat varying from the ' Brut y Tywysogion,' interpolated with passages from the Annals of Winchester (ascribed without sufficient reason to Richard of Devizes) and other chronicles.

The oldest Irish chronicles, written partly in Irish and partly in Latin, contain but little useful matter for Anglo-Saxon history, though they report some circumstances illustrative of the battles of the inhabitants of Scotland and Wales with the Anglo-Saxons, with a few otherwise unknown particulars and some variations, which cannot, however, shake our faith in Beda and the Anglo-Saxon chroniclers, but deserve attention as originating from other records of history. Dr. Charles O'Connor published a collection of these Annals under the auspices of the late duke of Buckingham and Chandos, entitled 'Rerum Hibernicarum Scriptores Veteres, auctore Carolo O'Connor, S.T.D. Buckinghamiæ,' 1814–1826. iv. tom. The first volume contains introductions, giving very instructive accounts of Irish manuscripts, the chronology of the Irish kings, the oldest proofs of the history of Ireland from the Greek and Roman authors, as well as from native historians and poets. The second contains—I. Annales Tigernachi ab anno 305 a. C. ad 1088 p. C. II. Annales Inisfalenses ab anno

428 ad 1088. III. Annales Buelliani ab anno 420 ad 1245. The third volume contains the Quatuor Magistrorum Annales Hibernici usque ad annum 1172, collected about the year 1634 by Michael O'Clery, a Franciscan friar, and other learned Irishmen. In the fourth volume is given a complete edition of the Annales Ultonienses ab anno 431 ad 1131, previously known only from some printed fragments. The General Index to the whole, which closes the last volume, can hardly be said to correspond to the industry displayed in the work itself.

Beda's great work, 'The Ecclesiastical History of the Angles,' must be reckoned among the most complete, and, for posterity, most important works of that age. The first twenty-two chapters of the first book are chiefly verbatim extracts from Orosius, Gildas, a legend of St. Germanus, with a few others, the sources of which cannot with certainty be indicated. In the greater and more important portion of his history, Beda confirms the credibility of his narrative by naming the experienced archbishops, bishops and abbots among his countrymen and contemporaries, who had supplied him with all necessary information from their own and even from the papal archives. Many other individuals were also questioned by him, the substance of whose testimony, with regard to contemporary events and credible tradition, is embodied in his admirable work[1].

The other historical writings of Beda are—two Lives of St. Cuthberht (one in hexameters), and the History of the

---

[1] Cf. Schmid, l. cit., and his Introduction to the Laws of the Anglo-Saxons. See also p. 209 of this volume. The best edition of the Latin text, and of the A.-S. version of Beda's history, as well as of the smaller historical pieces, is that of John Smith, Cantab. 1722. folio. Regarding a MS. of the church history of the eighth century, and a projected edition by the Archivarius de Ram at Mechlin, see Mone, 'Quellen und For-schungen,' Th. i. [An excellent edition of Beda's historical works has been published by Mr. Stevenson, in 2 voll. 8vo, for the English Historical Society. An edition of all Beda's works has also been recently published by the Rev. Dr. Giles.—T.]

Abbots of Wearmouth, viz. Benedict, Ceolfrith, Eosterwine, Sigefrith and Hwætberht. His 'Chronicon' also contains some historic notices, which have been used by Paul Warnefrid in his History of the Lombards, and at a later period have been transferred into the numerous works to which Beda's Chronicle has served as a foundation.

Meritorious and comprehensive works have often been prejudicial to historic research, by casting into oblivion the materials out of which they have been formed. This observation applies particularly to the History of Beda, and we feel its truth the more acutely, as it is evident that he must have found much recorded matter relative to the history of his country, which the plan of his work did not permit him to insert: hence our information with regard to Wessex, the most important of the Anglo-Saxon states, is extremely scanty. Among such records may be enumerated, Genealogies of the royal races, Lists of the successions of kings and eminent ecclesiastics, Necrologies or Obituaries, and Dionysian tables.

Of the oldest genealogies, that deserves especial notice which is given at the end of a manuscript of Nennius, written in a British hand, containing some important matter relating to the eastern and northern kingdoms of England. Others, hitherto incompletely printed, are inserted into the texts of the Saxon Chronicle and Florence of Worcester, whence they have passed into other chronicles[1]. With reference to Northumbria, much matter of this kind is to be found in Simeon of Durham.

Many regal tables are blended with the genealogies. Such a table of the West Saxon kings has been repeatedly printed[2], and because it concludes with Ælfred, has, without sufficient ground, been attributed to that monarch. It not only deviates

---

[1] See Textus Roffensis, cc. xxxvi. xxxvii.

[2] Prefixed to Wheelocke's edit. of Beda, p. 5 ; after Spelman's Vita Ælfredi, p. 199. Inserted by Gibson and Ingram in the Sax. Chron. a. 495.

materially from the common accounts, with respect to the regnal years of the West Saxon kings, in assigning to Cerdic a reign of sixteen years only instead of thirty-six, but is also inconsistent with itself, by placing the accession of Ælfred 396 years after the year 494, i. e. in 890, instead of A.D. 871. The primitive custom of dating public documents from the regnal years of the kings must have made an accurate knowledge of those years a matter of general necessity, as Beda also testifies, when speaking of many recorders of royal reigns, who, by a judicial sentence, blotted from their list the names of two unworthy kings[1], adding the year of their reign to those of their worthier successor.

The Necrologies contain, besides the day of the death of those for whose souls masses were to be celebrated, an account of the donations whereby they rendered themselves worthy of that benefit, also the names of the kindred with whom the patronage of the foundations remained, and other particulars often of general interest[2]. The old English Calendar is a large necrology, consisting for the most part of the names of Anglo-Saxon saints and pious benefactors, bearing evident signs of its origin from the obituaries of several metropolitan churches.

From what we are able to ascertain, small chronicles were composed before the time of Beda, though probably not founded on the Dionysian nineteen-yearly Easter tables, but rather on the regnal years[3].

[1] Osric of Deira and Eanfrith of Bernicia. See p. 156.—T.

[2] See such a one from the cathedral of Canterbury in 'Anglia Sacra,' t. i. p. 52 sq.

[3] It has already been remarked by others, that the Annales Majores Juvavienses (or Annals of Salzburg, printed in Mon. Germ. Histor. t. i.) bear on their face signs of their Anglo-Saxon origin. Their real or presumed errors will be discussed in another place; here we shall merely remark, that they alone supply us with the day of the death of Eadbald, king of Kent, viz. xiii. Kal. Feb. a. 640. More important, however, in a similar respect are the Annales Lauresham. Alamannici et Nazariani, though for their just appreciation requiring illustration: we must, therefore, in the first place, observe, that "a. 713 mors Alfrede et Adulfi regis," is not an

Although the very probable origin of the oldest German annals, to be found written on the margins of the Dionysian tables in the Scottish cloisters of Germany, may tend to show that this usage was carried thither from Britain, still the practice of Scottish monks would prove nothing for the Anglo-Saxons, and sufficient traces are, moreover, to be found, that among the latter an era was in use dating from their coming into Britain, which, at least in secular matters, they had not laid aside in the time of Beda. This chronology, combined with the record of the regnal years, has, to the exclusion of the Christian era, been used by Henry of

---

erroneous memorial of the death of king Ealdfrith (Aldfrith), who died in 705, but of Ælflæd, the daughter of Oswiu of Northumbria, born in 654, who died in her 59th year as abbess of Whitby, consequently in 713 (see Beda, iii. 24), and of Ealdwulf or Aldulf, king of the E. Angles, who succeeded to the crown in 664, the year of whose death was hitherto unknown. In the 'Annales Petav.' also his death is recorded in 713, under the name of Agledulfus. Under the name of the abbot Domnanus, whose death is placed in 705, hardly any other can be meant than the celebrated abbot of Hii or Iona, Adamnan, who, as we know from Beda, v. 1, 15, died about that time. The year 702 adopted by the editors is, as Smith himself confesses, arbitrary. Tigernach, Annal. and Fabricius (Bibl. Med. Ævi) nearly approximate to the above date, viz. ix. Kal. Oct. 704. Disguised as this name is, as well as those of other bishops and abbots, yet their sound enables us to recognise their Irish origin. Anno 729, Macflatheus is probably the same name as the abbot of Bangor's, Machlaisreus, in the ancient antiphoner of that cloister (Muratori Anect. t. iv. p. 159). In Dubdecris abbas, ob. 726, may perhaps be concealed a successor of Adamnan at Hii, who lived between 716 and 729, by Beda (v. 22) named Duunchadus. Anno 707, "Dormitio Tigermal," probably Tigernoth or Tigernach, bishop and confessor, whose death-day was celebrated in the Anglo-Saxon church on the 5th April. Anno 705, "Canani episcopi" we must not seek in Caman, abbot of Bangor, or the later Cronan, but is perhaps bishop Colman, who had left Lindisfarne in 664 and returned to Hii. An abbot is mentioned to have died in 716 in Tigernach, Annal. h. a. Also in the ancient 'Annales breves Fuldenses' (Monum. Germ. Hist. ii. 237) are given, besides the years of the death of the Northumbrian kings Ecgfrith and Osred, those of the Scottish bishops of Lindisfarne, Aidan, Finan and Colman : the year of the last is, however, to be referred to that of his above-mentioned departure. In the 'Fasti sive Annales Corbeienses' (ap. Pertz, Monum. t. iii.) are likewise to be found notices of Finan, Colman and Ecgfrith.

Huntingdon and other later chroniclers, and justifies the inference of sources no longer in existence.

The oldest of these small chronicles known is a Northumbrian one, ending shortly after the death of Beda[1]. Of some others, mentioned in catalogues of manuscripts in the libraries of England, we are without the means of judging, whether they are earlier than Beda and the Saxon Chronicle, or epitomes of them. Some larger ancient chronicles also still exist in manuscript in the English libraries ; among them may possibly one day be found the ' Gesta Anglorum,' cited by Adam of Bremen[2], which work I am unable to recognise in any of the known authorities.

An important work for a most interesting period of English history is the Life of King Ælfred by his friend Asser, bishop of Shireburn. Though this biography itself has not reached our times in any good manuscript, we are fortunately enabled to restore it in many places from Florence of Worcester, who has inserted a considerable portion of it verbatim into his Chronicle. In the Cottonian library there was a manuscript of Asser of the tenth century, which was slighted because it was wanting in several passages to be found in the other manuscripts, though they were also wanting in Florence. It was, consequently, pronounced defective, though the genuineness of the greater number of these passages is extremely questionable : as an instance may be cited the celebrated one relative to the antiquity of the University of Oxford, which first appeared in Camden's edition, and the non-appearance of which in the best manuscripts has, in the judgement of party-spirit, rendered them obnoxious to suspicion. These

---

[1] Printed in Wanley's Catalogue, p. 288 ; in Smith's preface to Beda ; and in Petrie, Corpus Historicum, p. 290.

[2] Lib. i. c. 35, and ii. 15.

[3] Edit. Parker, 1570. Camden, 1600 and 1603. Annales Rerum Gestarum Ælfredi, auct. Asserio, rec. F. Wise. Oxon. 1722. 8vo, containing a collation with the Cottonian MS. Printed also in the Corpus Historicum.

passages have at a later period been inserted into Asser's Life
of Ælfred from a work to which the name of Asser's Annals
has erroneously been given[1], but which is a compilation from
the Saxon Chronicle, Dudo's Norman History, several legends,
Asser's Life of Ælfred, and other sources, and can hardly be
earlier than the eleventh century.   To these Annals the title
of ' Chronicon Fani Sancti Neoti ' was given by Leland, from
his having found them in that place[2].

After Beda, the chief source of the early history of England,
and one of the most important in the whole historiography of
northern Europe, is the Anglo-Saxon Chronicle[3], composed
in the language of the country, and, in the later centuries,
abounding in contemporaneous narratives.   A thorough critical examination of its authorities, manuscripts and versions
would be a work of the highest utility for English history,
but which has hitherto been but very partially attempted,
and without any great result.   Such an examination is the
more difficult, as the texts of the manuscripts, or rather the
elaborations of them, which have been written in various
monasteries, often differ from each other, and have, in the
printed editions, been by their editors blended together without regard either to dialect or locality.   Of the Latin elaborations, some still exist only in manuscript.

The oldest known manuscript of the Saxon Chronicle is
that in the library of Corpus Christi, or Bene't, College,
Cambridge, written to the year 891 in the same hand, which
is not later than the tenth century[4].   The dialect in which it
is composed seems to be the Mercian, while the other copies
are in that of Wessex.   It is continued in Anglo-Saxon to the

---

[1] In Gale's collection, t. i.

[2] See Wise's preface to his edit. of Asser.

[3] In the present translation, the edition constantly cited is that in Petrie,
' Corpus Historicum.'—T.

[4] Accounts of the several MSS. are given in Ingram's edition, and in
Cooper on the Public Records, ii. p. 167.

year 1070, and in Latin to 1075. This manuscript, which
should serve as the basis of a text, has hitherto been only
partially used by the editors[1].

The other manuscripts are—1. One formerly belonging to
the abbey of St. Augustine at Canterbury, now in the Cottonian library, where it is marked, Tiberius A. vi. It extends
to the year 997. Another copy (Otho, B. xi.), continued to
the year 1001, perished in the fire at Ashburnham House in
1731. This was the basis of Wheelocke's edition[2]. 2. A
manuscript presented to the Bodleian library by archbishop
Laud, marked Laud E. 80[3]. This manuscript, originally
brought down to the year 1122, has been continued (with
many Normanisms in language and orthography) to 1154.
It was written in the abbey of Medeshamstede (Peterborough), and contains many demonstrably false documents
relative to that foundation. From which circumstance—
though its text indisputably belongs to the more recent ones
—it has sometimes, though rather rashly, been concluded,
that the monks of Peterborough were the original authors of
the Saxon Chronicle. 3. Greatly abridged and Normanized,
though enriched with some accounts wanting in the other
copies, is a manuscript originally perhaps from Canterbury,
but now in the Cottonian library (Domitian A. viii.). Both
this manuscript and the one last mentioned have been particularly used in Gibson's edition[4]. Gibson used also a Peterborough manuscript, brought down to the year 1016, and
thence continued beyond 1080, but now lost. 4. Of greater
importance are two manuscripts used by Ingram in his edi-

---

[1] In the edition of the Chronicle in the Corpus Historicum, the text to
the year 975 is from the C. C. MS.—T.

[2] Cantab. 1643. folio, printed at the end of his edition of Beda's history.

[3] Literal translations into Latin from the Laudian MS. are contained in
the Annales Waverleienses (ap. Gale, t. ii.), which we know, however, only
from the year 1066. Less exact, but not to be mistaken, is the use made
of this MS. by Henry of Huntingdon.   [4] Oxon. 1692. 4to.

tion of the Chronicle[1], one containing the annals of the abbey of Abingdon to the year 1066, the other those of the cathedral of Worcester to the year 1079, both in the Cottonian library (Tiber. B. i. and B. iv.). These are nearly allied to each other, and in the later years have many valuable accounts, which in the other more strictly Saxon Chronicles are given more briefly or differently. 5. A transcript from an unknown original, made by Lambarde in 1563, containing the history from A.D. 1043 to 1079. It is printed in the Appendix to Lye's Dictionary, and agrees verbatim with what Ingram gives from the Worcester copy.

This slight review may serve to call the attention of every one familiar with such studies, who are desirous to use the Anglo-Saxon Chronicle—on the several copies of which the oldest Latin chronicles of England are based—in any original or derived form, to the difficulties attending an exact critical examination of that estimable relic.

As from the time of Beda to that of William of Malmesbury—a space of near four hundred years—England possessed no chronicler who recorded independently of the Saxon Chronicle the history of the whole country, an inquiry into the sources and authors of that work is the more desirable.

For the earliest centuries of the Christian era to the year 449, Beda's work ' De sex hujus mundi ætatibus,' his Church History, Gildas and some others are regarded as the sources. I find, however, that it is only in the accounts of the ancient inhabitants of Britain and Ireland that Beda (H. E. lib. i. c. 1.) is used. For all the rest, Eusebius and some unimportant ecclesiastical history have been excerpted, Beda being tacitly used only where the Chronicle completes or deviates from his narrative. (Compare Sax. Chron. aa. 189, 435, 443, with

---

[1] London,.1823. 4to, with an English translation and critical remarks. An English translation also by Miss Gurney was printed but not published: it is highly commended.

Beda, lib. i. cc. 4, 11, 13.)   The calculation of the years from the creation is according to that of Eusebius and Orosius, who from that epoch to the birth of Christ reckon 5198 years.

From the year 449 to 597 the Chronicle contains, with some Kentish accounts, matter almost exclusively relating to Wessex, in which Beda is unfortunately so deficient. In confirmation of the general veracity of the Chronicle is the correct notice of two eclipses of the sun, in the years 538 and 540, and again in 664 and 733, though of the two last mentioned the day and the hour, which are given by Florence, are omitted in the Chronicle. In the following time to the year 731, when Beda's History terminates, the events are probably for the most part derived from that source; the accounts which are not to be found in Beda being but few, and chiefly derived from the late Laudian manuscript (as in the years 603, 616, 617), though the better manuscripts have also some additions, with the sources of which we are unacquainted (as in the years 693 and 710), together with some accounts which, as Florence has remarked, deviate from Beda.   From 732 to 845 the Chronicle is the primeval source, though during this period unquestionable errors are observable in the manuscripts; for instance, the eclipse of the moon in 796, correctly given by Simeon of Durham, is in the Chronicle placed under the year 795.   From 851 to 887 extracts from Asser's Life of Ælfred, with a few variations, are transferred into the Chronicle.

In the following part the frequently inaccurate chronology might excite a doubt as to the historic fidelity of the Chronicle (as in the years 915—922), but we ought not to charge it with errors originating in the misconceptions of editors, and which may often be rectified by the various readings which they have themselves collected, though more frequently by comparison with Florence of Worcester and Simeon of Durham.

The year 977 forms a section in the Anglo-Saxon Chronicle, as with this year not only two ancient manuscripts conclude, but also their oldest Latin copier Ethelwerd. From this time, but more particularly from the year 1001, which is also remarkable for the ending of some manuscripts, the deviations become more considerable, particularly in the Abingdon and Worcester Chronicles; and even these, though agreeing together much more closely than with other manuscripts, yet in some places differ considerably from each other, as in the years 1046, 1048, 1049, 1053, the former has Mercian accounts which are wanting in the latter.

With respect to the origin of these Chronicles, the first question to be decided seems to be, whether they, like so many other chronicles of other nations, written in the language of the country, have not been originally composed by ecclesiastics in the language of the church, and afterwards translated into Anglo-Saxon. When we call to mind that Ælfred translated, or caused to be translated, into Anglo-Saxon the Church History of Beda, the History of Orosius, etc., and that before Beda's time the language possessed the poetry of Cædmon, little doubt can be entertained of the probability, that these Annals were also composed in the Latin tongue, which till Ælfred's time are written with extreme simplicity, and even to be pronounced meagre. Florence of Worcester repeatedly cites the ' Chronica Saxonica ' (aa. 672, 674, 734), by which it appears on comparison that he means our Saxon Chronicle. Whether, besides the well-known Latin elements of the Chronicle, a West Saxon one, written in the language of the country, may have contributed to form its basis, it is now impossible either to assert or contradict : luckily the credibility of its scanty notices is not affected by our ignorance of that point. The continuations of the Chronicle are often written by contemporaries, to identify whom, however desirable for criticism, would with our present means be an impracticable task. Even in such a research, the question might not be unimportant, whether it really was or was not first written in the language of the country. On comparing Florence with the Chronicle, we find that the former bears the nearest resemblance to the Worcester manuscript; though Florence has many details wanting in the latter, as in the years 1040, 1041 and 1049; while *vice versâ*, the former has some notices, viz. under the years 693 and 710, and even 1044, relative to King Eadward's marriage, which in the latter are wanting.

Notwithstanding the variations existing among the several manuscripts, their general resemblance, particularly a striking agreement in many chronological errors, both in the Anglo-Saxon and Latin texts, must appear very remarkable. In explanation of this, Gibson refers to an account, that in the monasteries of royal foundation in England, whatever worthy of remembrance occurred in the neighbourhood was committed to writing, that such records were at the next synod compared with each other, and that from them the Chronicles were composed. It must, however, be remarked, that this account given by Walter Bower, the continuator of Fordun's Scotichronicon[1], who wrote in the beginning of the fifteenth century, cannot, without further authority, be applied to the portion of the Anglo-Saxon Chronicles in which we are at present interested.

Till the year 1036 poetical fragments are occasionally inserted into the Chronicle, viz. in the years 937, 941, 958, 973, 975, 1011, 1036 and 1065. That these verses were not composed in the years under which they stand is sometimes manifest from their words, as in the year 958, on the accession of Eadgar, where allusion is made to his conduct and character; and under 975, where the year of his death is spoken of, which it is said took place, according to the calculation of those skilled in numbers, in the month of July.

Of the Latin elaborations of the Saxon Chronicle the oldest is that of Ethelwerd, in four books, to the year 975, in which,

---

[1] Edit. Hearne, t. iv. p. 1348.

as we have observed, some manuscripts of the Chronicle itself also terminate. With the pompousness characteristic of the Anglo-Saxons he gives (and often incorrectly [1]) an epitomised version of the Chronicle, and would without the aid of the original be the more difficult to understand, as the only ancient manuscript of the work perished in the fire at the Cottonian library, and is made known to us solely through the printed text in Savile's collection. The fourth book, however, contains some valuable information relative to the reigns of Æthelred and Ælfred, not to be found in Asser and the other chroniclers, and not to be ascribed to some lost manuscript of the Saxon Chronicle, but rather to Ethelwerd himself, whose adherence to the Chronicle is, nevertheless, to be continually recognised; and even the verses inserted in that record under the year 975, are by him very indifferently imitated in Latin.

Ethelwerd was not an ecclesiastic, but an ealdorman descended from king Æthelred the First. He calls himself, in true Anglo-Saxon style, Patricius Consul Fabius Quæstor Ethelwerdus. He is generally supposed to have been the ealdorman of that name [2] who died in the year 1090, a supposition which appears even more erroneous than that which makes him a son of king Ælfred, who died in 922. Ethelwerd dedicates his work to a relation (consobrina) named Mathilda, who was descended from king Ælfred, the brother of his ancestor (abavus) Æthelred, through his granddaughter Eadgyth, the wife of the emperor Otto the First. Some, on the strength of the words, "Eadgyde, ex qua tu principium tenes nativitatis," and "vera Christi ancilla [3]," have supposed this Mathilda to have been the daughter of Otto, who became abbess of Quedlinburg; but this abbess was not his daughter by Eadgyth, who died in 947, but by his second wife Adel-

---

[1] Sax. Chron. a. 710. "gefuhton wið Gerente" he renders "bellum gesserunt contra Uuthgirente." Malmesbury (lib. i.) severely blames his style.

[2] Nicolson, Engl. Hist. Library, p. 48.   [3] Prolog. lib. i.

heid, born in 955[1]; nor can the relationship intimated be by a daughter, but only by a granddaughter of Eadgyth, as Ælfred is called not the *abavus*, but the *atavus* of Mathilda[2]. Now this person I find in the daughter of Liudolf[3], the son of Otto and Eadgyth, by Ida, a daughter of Hermann duke of Allemannia, born in 949, and married to Obizzone of Milan, the ancestor of the Visconti family; a conjecture which finds corroboration in the request of Ethelwerd to Mathilda, that she would inform him to what king in the neighbourhood of the Great St. Bernard (juxta Jupitereos montes) the sister of Eadgyth had been given in marriage, and what offspring they had; to learn which would to her be an easy matter, both by reason of her influence[4], and of the proximity of her abode. From Mathilda's place of habitation it appears why a layman came to render such a work into Latin for a lady. According to our hypothesis, the period when Ethelwerd lived is also determined, who must have composed his work about the year 1000. Which, however, of the two sons of Æthelred, whether Athelm or Æthelwold,—who married a nun whom he had carried off, and in 905 fell in an insurrection in East Anglia, against Eadward,—was the great-grandfather of Ethelwerd, appears no longer ascertainable. Three eminent men of his name died about that time—in 1001 the heah-gerefa of the king, in 1016 the son of Æthelwine, and in 1017 the son of Æthelmære the Great. Of Æthelwine's mother, Ælfwen, the wife of the under-king Æthelstan of East Anglia, we know that she was of royal lineage, and that the education of king

---

[1] She died in 999. Cf. Annal. Quedlinburg. a. 955 sq. ap. Leibnitz, Script. Rer. Brunsvic. t. i., and Pertz, t. iii.   [2] Lib. iv. c. 2 f.

[3] She also became abbess of Quedlinburg, and died in 1011. Annal. Quedl. " Abstulit (sæva mors) et de regali stemmate gemmam Machtildam abbatissam, Liudolfi filiam." Her birth is registered by Annalista Saxo, a. 949.

[4] Prolog. lib. i. " Quæ non solum affinitate, sed et potestate videris obpleta, nulla intercapedine prohibente."

Eadgar was entrusted to her: she may possibly be the link wanting in the descent of Ethelwerd from king Æthelred.

Soon after the establishment of the Norman dynasty on the throne of England the Anglo-Saxon tongue rapidly became corrupt, and fell into disuse among the clergy, who, not from any parade of learning, but from necessity, wrote the annals of the kingdom in the only to them intelligible language of the church. Of their works, several composed in the first half of the twelfth century or earlier have reached our time.

The most estimable translator of the Saxon Chronicle is Florence, a monk of Worcester, called also Bavonius, who has inserted into the Universal Chronicle of Marianus Scotus, an Irishman, who passed his life in the abbey of Fulda (ob. 1086), besides a translation either of a manuscript of the Saxon Chronicle resembling the existing Worcester manuscript, or of a text emended and enlarged by himself[1], extracts from Beda, the greater part of Asser's Life of Ælfred, and many valuable genealogical and other notices down to 1118, the year of his death. Florence had not only excellent manuscripts before him, but has translated the Anglo-Saxon more correctly than the other chroniclers. That he made use of the Historia Eliensis or its sources seems highly probable, from the close agreement of his account of the murder of the ætheling Ælfred with that in the History (lib. ii. c. 32.), which deviates from that in the Saxon Chronicle (a. 1036)[2]. Florence's Chronicle is continued by another monk of his monastery to the year 1141. His work was printed at London in 1592 in 4to, and at Frankfurt o. M. in 1601 in folio, after the 'Flores Historiarum' of Matthew of Westminster.

Marianus himself has but few special accounts relative to Britain, and these refer chiefly to Scotland and to certain ecclesiastics. Florence had apparently a much completer manuscript of Marianus than that from which Pistorius

---

[1] Cf. both under the year 988.
[2] Cf. Florence a. 1070 with the Hist. Eliensis, lib. ii. c. 44.

printed; hence we find in him many accounts relating to Germany, even to the abbey of Fulda, by Marianus, an examination into which would be an indispensable preliminary labour to a better edition of this chronicle.

The work of Florence forms in great measure, word for word, the basis of a chronicle of events from the year 848 to 1129, compiled about the last-mentioned year by Simeon, precentor of St. Cuthberht's at Durham, but which contains also some special Northumbrian and Scottish accounts[1]. Of such, however, more are to be found in another work of the same author, entitled 'Historia de Gestis Regum Anglorum,' from the year 616 to 957. In the latter he makes use of Beda, the 'Historia vel Chronica hujus patriæ,' and some legends of saints. The narrative of Harold's visit to duke William, inserted in his Chronicle under the year 1066, is also given in Eadmer's 'Historia Novorum,' lib. i., though somewhat abridged; whence it is evident that the latter cannot have been Simeon's source. The 'Historia Dunelmensis Ecclesiæ,' also under the name of Simeon, in three books, contains much interesting matter for the history of the north of England. Of this work it is supposed that Simeon, to the year 1097, was only the transcriber, and that the author was the prior Turgot[2], who after 1108 became bishop of St. Andrew's.

The Chronicle of the abbey of Melrose (Mailros)[3], from the year 735 to 1270, is for the Anglo-Saxon period merely an extract, with a few unimportant additions, from Simeon of Durham. Its value has been much overrated.

Henry, archdeacon of Huntingdon, compiled an 'Historia Anglorum' from the year of Julius Cæsar's landing to 1135,

---

[1] The notices relative to Normandy, aa. 876 and 906, agree literally with the Chronicle of Rouen (Chronicon Rothomagense), which deserves to be noticed on account of the chronology.

[2] Simeon is printed in Twysden's collection, and to 1066 in Petrie, C. H. Respecting Turgot see Twysden's preface.

[3] Printed in Fell's collection, t. i.

which is continued to 1154. The first six books embrace the period in which we are concerned, for which, besides the usual sources, Henry has availed himself of many traditions; while for the later period he has recorded either what he had witnessed himself or received from eye-witnesses[1]. Some of his few principal sources are still undiscovered : the more important of the known ones, exclusive of Eutropius, Paulus Diaconus, etc., are Beda's Chronicon and Ecclesiastical History, Nennius (whom he calls Gildas), and the Saxon Chronicle, which he sometimes misinterprets, though perhaps less often than has been supposed. His chronology is extremely confused and frequently inaccurate, as are also his genealogical notices. Particularly attractive, however, are his accounts of battles, which often appear borrowed from old poems[2]. A very close agreement with the more copious Ailred of Rievaux, which leads to the conclusion of a common, though to us unknown source, is manifest in his account of Eadmund Ironside. A striking contrast to the other monastic chroniclers, who cannot bestow sufficient praises on Dunstan, appears in his commendation of king Eadwy : and in general, throughout all which this author relates or suppresses may be recognised the patriotic Anglo-Saxon, equally averse both to temporal and ecclesiastical oppressors. That he availed himself of Norman sources may, perhaps, be inferred from his narrative of the sons of Emma, which agrees so closely with the Roman de Rou ; as well as from accounts strictly Norman given by him alone of all the English chroniclers, as A.D. 1047, of the battle of Val des Dunes, also William's speech before the battle of Hastings. From similar works he has probably derived his old British stories, as that of the princess Helena and others, which are not to be traced either to Nennius or Jeffrey of Monmouth, according to our manuscripts[3].

---

[1] See Prolog. ad lib. i.   [2] e. g. The battle of Brunanburh.—T.
[3] He is copied literally by Rob. du Mont, Wallingford, Hoveden, the Annal. Waverl., R. de Diceto, Matt. Paris, Bromton, Gervasius, Robert of Gloucester, etc.

Henry's work is dedicated to the same Alexander bishop of Lincoln whom Jeffrey addresses in his 'Historia Britonum.' A continuation of Henry of Huntingdon from 1042 to 1275 is extant in manuscript[1].

Roger of Hoveden in Yorkshire, chaplain to king Henry the Second, a jurist and professor of divinity at Oxford, was living in the year 1204. This writer has been much too often quoted, as, even to the last year of his Annals, he has (excepting a few trifling additions) copied from chronicles known to us, and, for the Anglo-Saxon period, from Simeon of Durham and Henry of Huntingdon. The beginning of his work, including the 'Prologus,' to the year 803 (edit. Frankf. pp. 401–407), is from Simeon (pp. 90–119); the following to the year 849 (p. 414) is from Huntingdon (pp. 341–348); hence to the year 1122 (pp. 414–477) is from Simeon's second work (pp. 137–245); after which, from 1122 to 1148 (p. 490), Roger returns to Henry of Huntingdon.

Alured, or Ælfred, treasurer of the monastery of Beverley, has in his Annals excerpted from Beda, Jeffrey of Monmouth and Simeon of Durham. He ends with the year in which the last-mentioned terminates; but we are not thence justified in concluding that he wrote in that year, or in inferring that the work of Jeffrey, which is known to have followed those of Henry of Huntingdon and William of Malmesbury, had already appeared in 1129. Traces of an immediate use of the Saxon Chronicle are occasionally discernible in Alured, as a. 879 (883), relative to king Ælfred's mission to India. The lists of Anglo-Saxon kings, contained in the sixth book, are, with the exception of the introduction, from the Appendix to Florence of Worcester : the author's own additions are very short and unimportant[2].

These are the principal works which, on account of their close adherence to the earliest sources of Anglo-Saxon history,

---

[1] Cooper on the Public Records, ii. p. 165.
[2] Alured was edited by Thomas Hearne, Oxon. 1716.

must here be cited. In the first centuries after the Norman
conquest several other English historic writers appeared, who,
devoted to the new dynasty, excite our attention chiefly by
reason of the baneful influence which, through their Norman
prejudices and false criticism, they have exercised on the
early history.

The work ascribed to Ingulf, an Englishman, born about
the year 1030, secretary to William of Normandy, and afterwards abbot of Croyland (ob. 1109), is the first to be noticed[1].
In this composition almost all the charters are forgeries[2], a circumstance which of itself, perhaps, might not invalidate the
general credibility of the rest of the work—which consists of
a history of Croyland abbey, interspersed with matter relating
to the kingdom of Mercia, and, at a later period, to all England;—but the narrative of Ingulf not only abounds in gross
errors and anachronisms with regard to contemporary events,
but contains matter demonstrably fabulous; such is the
account of his having studied Aristotle at Oxford[3]. Even in
the Life of abbot Thurketul, which, though composed by his
relative, the younger abbot Egelric, is said to have been continued by Ingulf, it is erroneously stated, that Constantine
king of Scotland fell in the battle of Brunanburh, in 938
(erroneously for that king's son), by the hand of Thurketul,
and that the emperor Henry the First (who it is well known
died in 936), after that battle sought the hand of Æthelstan's
daughter for his son Otto. In the accounts of Ælfred and
Eadward the Elder, the so-called Ingulf agrees so frequently,
both in erroneous matter and words, in chronology and facts,
with William of Malmesbury, that it will be difficult not to
regard this part of his chronicle as an interpolation from that

---

[1] Cf. Ingulf. a. 1075, where an account of his life is inserted.

[2] See Hickes, t. iii. p. 73.

[3] "Primum Westmonasterio, postmodum Oxoniensi studio traditus
eram. Cumque in Aristotele arripiendo," etc. For a judicious and interesting notice of Ingulf see Biographia Britannica Literaria, vol. ii., composed by Mr. Wright for the Royal Society of Literature.—T.

author, since a source common to both cannot be indicated. The account too of the interment of two relations of Thurketul in the abbey of Malmesbury is to be found in both writers[1], for which the latter cites as his authority an historic work in Latin hexameters. A charter also of Malmesbury of the year 974 is given more fully in Ingulf than in the printed work of the monk of that cloister. Even in that part of his chronicle in which contemporary events are recorded, Ingulf, as we have already observed, is not trustworthy : as in the years 1056 and 1062, where he calls count Radulf, instead of the son, the husband of Goda. The contemporary abbots of Croyland are confounded by him. He seems to have made use of Ailred of Rievaux. At the same time it must be allowed that the continuation of Ingulf's work by Peter of Blois seems to impress it with a stamp of genuineness. From the foundation of his abbey till its destruction by the Danes in 870, Ingulf appeals to five older chroniclers, viz. Aio, Thurgar, Swetman, etc.[2] By whom the history from 871 to 948 has been supplied we are not informed. Hence it seems not unreasonable to suppose that the true history of Ingulf has not reached us, but that in the work before us we possess a compilation made at an early period, into which portions of the real Ingulf are interwoven, and in the use of which the utmost caution is to be observed. It is printed in Savile's collection, and in that of Fell; no manuscript is known to exist.

Ailred (Æthelred), abbot of Rievaux in Yorkshire, has collected genealogical notices of the Anglo-Saxon kings. Of his other writings, none need be mentioned except his Life, or rather Legend of Eadward the Confessor[3]. His praise of Eadgar and account of Godwine's death remind us strongly of Alured of Beverley.

---

[1] Ingulf, p. 39; W. Malm. lib. ii. 6. Cf. also in both the passages about Eadwine.

[2] Ib. a. 974, and at the close of the work.

[3] Printed in Twysden's collection.

The works of William, a monk and librarian of Malmesbury[1] abbey (ob. about 1142), are remarkably attractive, both
from the manner in which he treats his subject and from his
arrangement, which deviates from the usual chronological
order.   These are, ' De Gestis Regum Anglorum ' lib. v.; ' Historiæ Novellæ ' lib. ii.; ' De Gestis Pontificum Anglorum '
lib. v.   From the ' Prologus ' to the first book of his principal
work it appears, that Malmesbury was unacquainted with the
invaluable historic productions of his contemporaries.   The
authors named by him are Beda, Ethelwerd, and Eadmer.
In the words, " quædam vetustatis indicia chronico more et
patrio sermone, per annos Domini ordinata," he evidently
alludes to the Saxon Chronicle.   Together with many interesting narratives preserved by Malmesbury, is to be found an
abundance of insipid tales quite irrelevant to his subject, but
to which his work is mainly indebted for much of the approbation which it has received ; for after Beda and Jeffrey of
Monmouth, no old English historic writer has been more
resorted to by chroniclers, both of his own country and of
the continent, than William of Malmesbury.   Among the
more ancient of the latter may be named Alberic des Trois-
fontaines and Vincent of Beauvais.

To Matthew, a monk of Westminster abbey, is ascribed an
historic work, compiled in the fourteenth century from various
chronicles, entitled ' Flores Historiarum[2].'   From a kind of
inadvertence this chronicle has been much used, because it
has not been noticed that almost all his sources (for the
Anglo-Saxon period) have been preserved, extracts from
which have by him only been abridged and often unskilfully
brought together, and, when dates were wanting, not un-

---

[1] Printed in Savile's collection, excepting the fifth book ' De Gestis
Pontificum,' which is to be found in Gale and Wharton. [Of the two first-
mentioned works, an excellent edition with English notes, etc. has been
published by T. D. Hardy, Esq. for the English Historical Society.—T.]

[2] Francofurti, 1601. fol.

frequently inserted under wrong years. Of his sources with which we are concerned may be mentioned Nennius, Beda, Asser, the Saxon Chronicle, Florence of Worcester, Jeffrey of Monmouth, William of Jumièges (e. g. a. 887, from lib. i. cc. 6–11 relative to Hæsting, and later about Rollo), Marianus Scotus, and William of Malmesbury, whom he occasionally mentions by name (as aa. 979, 1035). To the foregoing Henry of Huntingdon might perhaps be added, though some passages in him, chiefly concerning the north of England, on which that supposition is founded, are more fully given in Matthew, and may therefore have been more circumstantially taken from a source common to both. The account of the single combat between Eadmund Ironside and Cnut seems to have been extracted from Ailred of Rievaux (p. 364). Many legends are recounted, and narratives from monastic chronicles inserted by Matthew; hence several notices are to be found scattered throughout his work which the future gatherer of materials for English history may deem it worth his while to collect.

To John Wallingford, abbot of St. Albans (ob. 1214), Gale ascribes a chronicle published by him of events from the year 449 to 1036[1]. This author makes some attempts at historic criticism, in which, however, he is eminently unsuccessful. For the history of the northern Anglo-Saxon provinces, he gives us some accounts not to be found elsewhere. He makes great use of the first six books of William of Jumièges, and also, though not immediately, of Dudo of St. Quentin; as we find in Wallingford the narratives of the latter, together with the additions and continuations of the former of these two writers (as pp. 532 and 533, from Guil. Gemet. lib. i. cc. 3–5; also p. 548, from lib. v. c. 8; pp. 549, 550, from lib. vi. cc. 10–13). He also makes mention of Jeffrey of Monmouth, Henry of Huntingdon and William of Malmesbury, and excerpts the Lives of the saints Guthlac, Cuthberht, Neot and Eadward,

[1] Printed in Gale's collection, t. i.

also Britferth's Life of St. Dunstan. His quotation from the
' Historia Gothorum ' is copied from William of Jumièges.

We have now to mention, in a few words, those Norman
writers who have touched on this portion of English history.
In this respect Dudo, dean of St. Quentin, is but rarely of immediate interest, though, for the history of the ancestors of
king William the Conqueror, he is not only the source of
several chronicles generally more noticed, but is also, notwithstanding his many poetical ornaments and chronological
errors, much richer in undoubted facts than the learned editors of the ' Materials for French History' have been aware
of [1].

More immediately interesting to us is William, a monk of
Jumièges, whose ' Historia Normannorum' reaches to the
conquest of England by the Normans. His work being dedicated to the Conqueror, it follows that what forms the end
of the seventh and the eighth book, which is continued to the
year 1137, cannot have been written by him [2]. He has, as we
have seen, been excerpted by many English chroniclers.
Both these writers are contained in Du Chesne's collection
of ' Scriptores Rerum Normannicarum;' the latter also in
Camden's 'Anglica Normannica,' etc., an edition much inferior to that of Du Chesne, which is founded on two manuscripts from the library of De Thou.

Of much importance for historic research, notwithstanding
its poetic garb, is the ' Roman de Rou [3],' a history of the
dukes of Normandy, interwoven with many traditions, by
Robert Wace, a native of Jersey, bred at Caen, and afterwards, by appointment of Henry the Second, a prebendary
of Bayeux.   Of his ' Brut,' written about the year 1155,

---

[1] See Bouquet, t. x. Preface, and p. 141. The proofs of my assertion
cannot be given here, but will appear in a chapter on the history of Normandy before the year 1066, prefixed to the ' History of England under the
Norman Kings.'

[2] Bouquet, t. xi. Pref. No. xii., and t. xii. Pref. No. xlix.

[3] Written after 1170. See v. 16538 sq.

mention has already been made. In the 'Roman de Rou' is to be found much exclusive and credible matter for the history of the eleventh century, in the use of which, however, due allowance is to be made for the national prejudices of the Norman. This work also seems to have served as a source to some of the English chroniclers. It has for the first time been printed by M. Pluquet[1].

Anterior to Wace was Bénoît de Ste More, or, as he is styled by Wace, Maistre Beneit, who wrote in French a metrical chronicle of the dukes of Normandy, consisting of 48,000 verses. The only ancient manuscript known of this work is in the British Museum (Harl. 1717). It has recently been published at Paris from a transcript made by M. Francisque Michel, by the direction of M. Guizot, while Minister of Public Instruction[2]. Further notice of this work is reserved for 'The History of England under the Norman Kings.'

In the language of the Gallo-Normans, but written in England for the lords of the land a century after the Conquest, is 'L'Estorie des Engles solum la translation Maistre Geffrei Gaimar,' a metrical chronicle of England from the landing of Cerdic in the year 495 to the death of William Rufus in 1099. It seems to have been composed about the middle of the twelfth century, and follows the Saxon Chronicle, which the author frequently misunderstands. It contains, however, many, though not always historic additions, by which Gaimar, as the oldest known authority—though he refers to an earlier—is rendered of importance. This work,

[1] Rouen, 1827. 2 voll. 8vo, and 'Remarques' by Le Prevost and Raynouard, 1829. [For a very able prose version of the portion of the Roman de Rou relating to the conquest of England, with highly valuable and interesting illustrations, the public are indebted to a most worthy and amiable man and excellent scholar lately deceased, under the title : 'Master Wace his Chronicle of the Norman Conquest from the Roman de Rou, translated with notes and illustrations by Edgar Taylor, Esq., F.S.A.' London, 1837. 8vo.—T.]

[2] Chroniques des Ducs de Normandie, 2 tom. 4to. 1836, 1838.

to the year 1066, appears for the first time in the 'Corpus Historicum[1].'

Of great moment for the illustration of the downfall of the Anglo-Saxon dynasty in England is the biography of William the Conqueror by William of Poitiers, archdeacon of Lisieux. Though valuable for his matter, this author is objectionable on account of his style, in which he is an imitator of the Roman classics, particularly Sallust, and not only inserts fabricated speeches into his narrative, but not unfrequently sacrifices a part of the truth for the sake of sparkling antitheses and oratorical pomp. He is sometimes copied by William of Jumièges, but more copiously by Ordericus Vitalis; so much so indeed, that some defective passages in our manuscript of William of Poitiers can be supplied from Ordericus with tolerable security. His work is printed in Du Chesne's collection, and in a separate edition by Baron Maseres[2].

Ordericus Vitalis, born in the year 1075 at Attingesham on the banks of the Severn, a monk in the monastery of St. Evroult en Ouche (Uticum), has but few details relative to Anglo-Saxon history in his 'Historia Ecclesiastica,' though his extracts from William of Poitiers are not without some additional information.

Mention must also be made of the 'Carmen de Bello Hastingensi' discovered at Brussels by Dr. Pertz, and printed for the first time in the English Corpus Historicum[3]. Several gallicisms in the poem prove the author to have been a Frenchman, such as 'ter quinque dies,' *quinze jours*, for a fortnight, etc. I have no doubt that this is the poem spoken of by

---

[1] See also extracts in Depping, Histoire des expéditions maritimes des Normands, and Corpus Historicum, p. 764 *note*; and Michel, Chron. Anglo-Norm., t. i. Cf. also Wiener Jahrb. Th. 76. p. 259 sq.

[2] Historiæ Anglicanæ circa tempus Conquestus Angliæ a Gulielmo Notho, Normannorum Duce, Selecta Monumenta, etc. London 1807. 4to.

[3] It is also printed in Mr. Cooper's unpublished Report on Rymer, and in the Chroniques Anglo-Normandes par M. Michel, t. iii.

William of Jumièges (lib. vii. c. 44) and Ordericus Vitalis
(lib. iii. p. 504), as the composition of Guy (Wido) bishop of
Amiens (ob. 1075), who lived for some time at the court of
Mathilda, the queen of the Conqueror. The first verses of
this poem may therefore be supplied thus:

> Quem probitas celebrat, sapientia munit et ornat,
> Erigit et decorat, L(anfrancum) W(ido) salutat.

To these Norman writers appears to have belonged the
author of the 'Chronicon Danorum in Anglia regnantium,'
mentioned by Thomas Rudborne in the 'Historia Major
Wintoniensis' (ap. Wharton, A. S. t. i.), for the purpose of
quoting from him a tradition respecting the birth of William
the Conqueror.

Of English metrical chronicles, that of Robert of Gloucester, written about the year 1280, is one of the most valuable[1]. It begins with the tales of Jeffrey of Monmouth,
but in the Anglo-Saxon portion follows chiefly William of
Malmesbury, and sometimes Henry of Huntingdon, as in the
story of Cnut on the sea-shore, the speech of William before
the battle of Hastings, etc. His relation of the single combat
between Eadmund and Cnut, with the prolix speech, is apparently an imitation of Ailred of Rievaux.

A similar chronicle, written in French verse[2], by Peter
Langtoft, a canon regular of the order of St. Augustine, at
Bridlington in Yorkshire, whence he is also called Pers of
Bridlynton, though extant in manuscript, is known to us
only through the English metrical version of Robert Man-
nyng, or, as he is more usually called, Robert de Brunne[3].
The editor has omitted the part copied from ' Le Brut.' This
chronicle, which ends with the death of Edward the First in
1307, was without doubt composed and translated not long
after that time. The little contained in it of Anglo-Saxon

---

[1] Edited by Thomas Hearne. Oxon. 1724. 2 voll. 8vo.
[2] Extracts from the French text are printed in the Chron. Anglo-Norm. t. i.
[3] Edited by Thomas Hearne. Oxon. 1725. 2 voll. 8vo.

history, for which Gildas, Beda, Henry of Huntingdon, and William of Malmesbury are cited, are old English sagas inserted by Robert de Brunne, of which that of Havelok, king Gunter's son[1], he says expressly is not to be found in Pers of Bridlynton.

It is a remarkable circumstance that the majority of the later chroniclers are from Yorkshire or the neighbouring counties, which may, perhaps, be attributed to a longer preserved nationality in those parts. Their chief sources are rarely the Saxon Chronicle and Florence, but rather Henry of Huntingdon and William of Malmesbury, whose traditions and fables are by them generally transcribed in greater breadth. This remark is particularly applicable to the work, too often appealed to, ascribed to John Bromton, abbot of Jorvaulx in Yorkshire, who lived towards the end of the fourteenth century. It comprises the period from the year 588 to 1198, whence it might be suspected to be the production of some earlier writer, did it not contain mention of the marriage-contract of Johanna, sister of Edward the Third, with David, afterwards king of Scotland. Besides the chroniclers just enumerated, Bromton also copies Florence and the Flores Historiarum : he likewise mentions the chronicle of Walter of Giseborne. Norman anecdotes he relates in the same order as Wace in the Roman de Rou.

The only merit, with reference to Anglo-Saxon history, hitherto possessed by Bromton—that of being the earliest source of many interesting sagas, is now effaced, as we find the same sagas in Gaimar ; and they are also to be found, though in an abridged form, in the unprinted chronicle of Douglas of Glastonbury, the Hamburg vellum manuscript of which reaches to the time of Edward the Third, in which the names, disguised like those in Gaimar, sufficiently betray the use of a Norman source[2]. In the earlier part of his chro-

---

[1] See p. 116.
[2] Thus, cap. iii. Renaude for Reginald ; cap. cxii. Estrilde for Ælfthryth,

nicle Douglas follows Jeffrey of Monmouth; in the later portion he has accounts exclusively his own, relating to the wars between England and Scotland in the thirteenth and fourteenth centuries, which are valuable through the communication of contemporary ballads.

We have occasionally, in the course of our researches, made use of smaller historic works, but of which many monastic histories and Lives of Saints are still in manuscript only. Letters also, homilies and other documents have been but partially brought to light, of which several, connected with later times, will be noticed hereafter.

Of other helps to Anglo-Saxon history, the first to be mentioned are the Charters, a complete collection of which is now in course of publication by the English Historical Society. Of these important documents two volumes have already appeared[1], containing charters of Anglo-Saxon kings, ealdormen and prelates to the year 966. To the first volume is prefixed an Introduction by the learned editor, embracing an ample fund of information illustrative of the use and nature of those instruments, their dates, tests of their genuineness, etc., indispensable to those who have not made such monuments a particular branch of study. Older collections, which are in great measure superseded by this highly useful publication, are—the Textus Roffensis, belonging to the cathedral of Rochester, containing, besides many valuable charters, etc., the only copy extant of the Laws of the Kentish kings. This manuscript, compiled by bishop Ernulphus in the twelfth century, was communicated to the world by that laborious and meritorious antiquary Thomas Hearne : also Hemming's Chartulary of the church of Worcester. Many charters are

the queen of Eadgar ; cap. cvii. in " Alured that Dolphynes was called " it is not *Dauphin*, but Gaimar's (v. 3023 sq.)......" Elueret, Edelwolfing ert apelez ;" also, cap. cvii. "a Dane that me called Roynt," from Gaimar, v. 3016, "un Daneis, un tyrant, ki Sumerlede ont nun le *grant*."

[1] Codex Diplomaticus Ævi Saxonici. Opera Johannis M. Kemble, tom. i. and ii.

also to be found dispersed in Hickes's Thesaurus, Smith's edition of the historic works of Beda, the monastic histories of Ely and Glastonbury, etc. The greater number, however, of these documents having reference to churches and convents, those of the latter description are consequently collected in the 'Monasticon Anglicanum,' originally edited by William Dugdale and Roger Dodsworth, in 3 voll. folio, 1682, continued by J. Stevens in 2 voll. folio, and lastly edited anew by John Cayley, Esq., Henry Ellis, Esq., and the Rev. B. Bandinel[1].

The edition of the Anglo-Saxon Laws, commenced by the late Mr. Price, under the authority of the Commission on the Public Records, but continued and completed by the translator of the present work[2], exhibits a purer text, accompanied by collations from every known manuscript, than that of the earlier editions. In the ecclesiastical portion of the work is printed for the first time the Penitential of archbishop Theodore, the prototype of most of the later penitentials, particularly that of archbishop Ecgberht. In this work also some interesting secular documents are given for the first time in print. Before the appearance of this edition, that of Dr. Wilkins was the most complete, though abounding in errors of no trivial character. An edition of much merit, and highly useful to the German scholar, was begun by Dr. Reinhold Schmid, of which the first volume only has hitherto appeared[3]. The

---

[1] London, 1817–1830. 8 voll. folio.

[2] Ancient Laws and Institutes of England; comprising Laws enacted under the Anglo-Saxon Kings from Æthelbirht to Cnut, with an English translation of the Saxon; the Laws called Edward the Confessor's; the Laws of William the Conqueror, and those ascribed to Henry the First: also Monumenta Ecclesiastica Anglicana, from the seventh to the tenth century; and the Ancient Latin Version of the Anglo-Saxon Laws. With a compendious Glossary, &c. Printed by command of His late Majesty King William IV., under the direction of the Commissioners on the Public Records of the Kingdom. MDCCCXL. 1 vol. fol., or 2 voll. royal 8vo.

[3] Die Gesetze der Angelsachsen. In der Ursprache mit Uebersetzung und Erläuterungen herausgegeben von Dr. Reinhold Schmid, Professor der Rechte zu Jena. Leipzig, 1832. 8vo.

Anglo-Saxon ecclesiastical laws, the councils, and other church documents, are also contained in the collection of Sir Henry Spelman, though more completely in the later one of Dr. Wilkins.

The Welsh Laws, viz. those of Howel Dda and other princes, have also been recently communicated to the world under the same authority, in an excellent edition by Aneurin Owen, Esq.[1], containing the original text founded on several manuscripts with an English translation. The Welsh Laws had been previously edited by Dr. Wotton, with a Latin translation, and subsequently by Probert with an English one[2].

For the study of Anglo-Saxon numismatics, the work of Ruding on the coinage[3] is to be recommended, as containing much useful information on that ample subject; also the valuable works of Mr. Akerman[4], and several papers in the Archæologia.

On casting a glance at the labours of later historic writers since the introduction of printing, we are carried back to Douglas of Glastonbury, whose work forms the basis of the oldest printed chronicle of England,—that by the printer William Caxton, in the year 1480. Nowhere does it appear more evidently than in English historic literature, how slowly

[1] Ancient Laws and Institutes of Wales; comprising Laws supposed to be enacted by Howel the Good, modified by subsequent regulations under the native Princes prior to the conquest by Edward the First: and Anomalous Laws, consisting principally of Institutions which, by the Statute of Ruddlan, were admitted to continue in force: with an English translation of the Welsh text. To which are added a few Latin transcripts, containing Digests of the Welsh Laws, principally of the Dimetian Code. With Indexes and Glossary. Printed by command, etc. MDCCCXLI.

[2] The Ancient Laws of Cambria, translated from the Welsh by William Probert. London, 1823. 8vo, from a MS. of the year 1685.

[3] Annals of the Coinage. 4 voll. 4to.

[4] Particularly 'Coins of the Romans relating to Britain.' 8vo, 2nd edit. enlarged.

that study has, from faith in arbitrary fictions, turned to the
contemporary writers, ancient laws and other authentic monuments. From the Norman tales of Gaimar and Le Brut, in
the extract of Douglas, historians turned to Bromton, Matthew of Westminster, William of Malmesbury, and Henry of
Huntingdon, till the further the lapse of ages removed them
from us, the more zealously has historic research striven to
revert to the oldest authorities, to the great work of Beda and
other trustworthy sources. The memory of the Anglo-Saxons
seems almost to have been effaced in England by the splendour of the Norman aristocracy; and Shakspere himself,
whose muse sought a subject in every region of Europe and
in every age, and immortalized even the Lear of British tradition, the Scot and the Dane, found—while, unconsciously
to himself, his language reverted to them,—no subject in the
eventful history of the Anglo-Saxons whereby to attract his
countrymen. It was not until the fall of the Stuarts and the
rise of the commons of England that the country first gained
a tolerable history of the Anglo-Saxons in the mother-tongue,
by the hand of him who, above all others, successfully employed the Germanic element of his language,—the exalted
John Milton[1].

Unimportant as Milton's work may appear at the present
day, we must, nevertheless, praise the careful examination it
evinces of the genuine sources of our early history, so highly
laudable in one blind, verging on his seventieth year, a poet
of the highest order, an energetic statesman, to whom the
dryness of the chronicles was so distasteful, that he could not
withhold the public expression of his sentiments to that effect.
The 'Chronicon Regum Angliæ' of David Langhorne[2] is a
very useful work, evincing considerable critical judgement in
its compilation from numerous and the best authorities known

---

[1] First printed in 1671. It is reprinted in the several editions of his
Prose Works, and also in Kennet's Complete History of England, vol. i.
[2] London, 1679, 8vo.

at the time for the history of kings and wars to the reign of
Ælfred.   The Life also of that king by Spelman forms an
epoch in the historic literature of England.   In 1724 the
work of Rapin de Thoyras appeared, who, however, did very
little for the Anglo-Saxon period, and even seems to have
been ignorant of the existence of many sources then already
in print.   In the notes of his translator, Tindal, many rectifications and additions are to be found.   A considerable advance is manifest in the portion dedicated to the Anglo-Saxon
period of Carte's History of England[1], the earlier part of
which has served as a storehouse to David Hume, who was
lamentably deficient in fundamental knowledge of the early
middle age.   In praising Hume for his lively picture of the
history of the Stuarts, and for some portions of that of the
Tudors, as the most acute of modern investigators, as an unrivalled perfect model for historic composition, in whom was
united with English strength and Scottish perspicuity, the
grace of the land of his mental cultivation, his much-loved
France,—in this very praise is implied the cause why Hume,
who at first had occupied himself only on the history of the
Revolution (from which, not till a later period, he carried back
his work to the beginning of the history[2]), could not evince
in his account of the middle age either the enthusiasm or
even the industry of Milton.   It is not, therefore, surprising
that Gibbon, with his widely comprehensive studies, and who
in acuteness and powers of combination was the equal of his
great contemporary, is, in his notices of the Anglo-Saxons,
contained in his immortal work, more instructive than Hume.
After these another star of the first magnitude in the British horizon remains to be named,—though, as in the case of
Milton, as the author of a work of no great estimation,—
Edmund Burke, who wrote an Abridgment of English Hi-

---

[1] London, 1747–1755, 4 voll. folio.

[2] The History of the Stuarts appeared in 1755, that of the Tudors in
1759, that of the earlier period some years later.

story to the year 1216, in which the part relating to the jurisprudence of the Anglo-Saxons has considerable merit. From this specimen, which, though not printed until after his death, was probably the labour of his earlier years[1], we may reasonably suppose, that had this most talented of British statesmen more seriously devoted himself to the subject, the story of England would have been told in a work not inferior to those through which the enviable states of antiquity, as well as that revival of the Periclean Athens, the Tuscan city, stand in never-fading colours before the wondering eyes of after-ages.

It might almost appear as though it were intended to be shown that the greatest geniuses among a people devoted to freedom have felt themselves irresistibly drawn to the study of their native history, when we yet mention the History of England by Sir James Mackintosh, the apparent antagonist, though in fact the intellectual son of Edmund Burke. The study of philosophy and of the laws of Europe and Asia, a high judicial post at Calcutta, a truly considerable share in European politics, through the engendering and spread of creative, promoting, wide-forming ideas in internal national life, as well as of retrospective, preserving views, well founded in the policy and public law of both hemispheres ; the favour of the sportive muse, the acknowledged possession of a noble, graceful, courtly demeanour, an intercourse,—which while it much received no less distributed,—with the ablest of his contemporaries ; all this, more than Sir Walter Raleigh and the illustrious Bacon ever compassed, satisfied not the son of needy Scottish parents : even the aversion so hard to over-come, by a genius ever glowing with its own fires, for the toil-some working up of a given raw material, did not withhold this extraordinary man from labouring during several years

[1] It was written in his twenty-seventh year, and appears in the collection of his works. Eight sheets of it were printed by Dodsley in 4to, in 1757, which with the author's corrections are now in the British Museum.

on a history of England, to which his contemporaries had
already beforehand willingly awarded the palm. Indisposition
and the pressure of unwelcome age induced Mackintosh to
contract the plan of his undertaking, and death interrupted
that which he had still hoped to publish. Of what he has accomplished the excellences will be mentioned hereafter; for
the short section on Anglo-Saxon history, the praise of spirited
and just conception, as well as of worthy representation may
suffice.

But would not Mackintosh with more vigorous powers have
accomplished more? Let us freely confess that neither he
nor any other equally gifted man can in our days satisfy the
requisites of a history of any country in the middle age,
and least of all of England, where new sources spring forth
daily, where the divining rod inclines over many a deep-hidden
treasure without yet finding it. Generations must pass away
before all this matter will be found arranged and divided, in
order one day to be illustrated by the master. The Germanic
race must first have more completely investigated its old traditions, its old language, its old laws, through the labours of
antiquarians, philologists and legal historians, before an in-
controvertible answer can be given to some of the most important questions. The history of one state will always be
defective without commensurate advances in that of the neighbour states. The difficult duty of a modern investigator of
history, which requires almost endless researches, splitting
themselves in all directions into various others, and often
widely remote from each other, is little compatible with that
of an historian in the highest sense, who shall also have
learned from life, and desires to understand the past by and
for the sake of the present. History, moreover, often requires
a renewed form, as well for the purpose of appropriating to
itself the fruits of investigation, to set them in their true light,
and bestow on them their just value, as also on account of
the ever variable undeveloped necessity of the present. The

representer of past times, mindful of this duty, will not, therefore, be always anxious only to give demonstrable certainty,
but will rather often draw attention to the defects of our historic knowledge, and will even gain much by a clear glance
over the history apparently lost: he will not lull the reader
into a mere sluggish conception of what is recorded, but must
frequently draw him along with him in his investigations ; he
will consider himself as a prophet looking backwards, and
often leave the interpretation of his well-weighed judgements
to the intelligent, and probably to the more gifted or more
fortunate inquirer.

A few respected investigators of old English history remain
yet to be noticed, and first Whitaker, who, under the title of
a History of the Town of Manchester, has given a very learned
account of the country under the Romans[1].   A similar work
is his Genuine History of the Britons asserted against J.
Macpherson[2].   In the highly esteemed work of Dr. Robert
Henry[3], the Roman period is treated with predilection and
success ; to praise the Anglo-Saxon portion, it must be on
comparison with his predecessors.

To Sharon Turner, for his labours on the history of the
Anglo-Saxons[4], students are under a lasting obligation, particularly for his profounder investigation of their state of culture, his unprejudiced application of Welsh literature, and
the use which he has made of many unprinted sources.   At
the same time it must be acknowledged that this meritorious
collection of materials is charged with many unnecessary di-
gressions, and that the author has often preferred giving much
to a critical discrimination in his narratives.

Lingard's representation of Anglo-Saxon history[5] is di-

---

[1] Second edition corrected. London, 1773. 2 voll. 8vo.

[2] Second edit. Lond. 1773.

[3] History of Great Britain. 6 voll. Edinb. 1771–1793. 4to, often reprinted.

[4] History of the Anglo-Saxons, 1799–1805. 2 voll. 4to, frequently reprinted in 3 voll. 8vo.   The 6th edit. is the last that has appeared.

[5] The last edit. in 13 voll. 12mo with corrections.

stinguished for its just arrangement, as well as by the clear-
ness and solidity of its expression; though he has generally
confined himself to a repetition of the facts related by his
latest predecessors; and only in rare cases, where catholicism
prompted him to a refutation of some narrow views of English protestantism, has exhibited independent and new investigations.

Sir Francis Palgrave has, in an elaborate work[1], endeavoured,
and not unsuccessfully, to supply the existing want.   The
political institutions of the Anglo-Saxons are examined by
him with much acuteness; he has also given, in great part
from sources hitherto but little used for the purpose, a very
valuable chronological view of the larger states, as well as of
the provinces dependent on them; though in the application
of some modern hypotheses, chiefly with regard to the deri-
vation of several historical phenomena in the institutions of
the Anglo-Saxons from Roman elements, he probably goes
too far.   While the present work bears evident proofs for
how much multifarious information its author is indebted to
this learned inquirer, yet several of his principal notions cannot be acknowledged by us as new, but as an ancient common
property of the continental investigators of the history of
nations and laws.   Palgrave has likewise published, in a small
volume[2], principally designed for youth, and embellished with
maps and other engravings, a History of the Anglo-Saxons,
containing some of the results of his inquiries.

----

[1] The Rise and Progress of the English Commonwealth. Anglo-Saxon
Period. II Parts. London, 1832. 4to.

[2] History of England, vol. i. Anglo-Saxon Period. London, 1831. 12mo.
forming volume xxi. of the 'Family Library.'

A

HISTORY OF ENGLAND

UNDER THE

ANGLO-SAXON KINGS.

———◆———

INTRODUCTION.

BRITAIN UNDER THE ROMANS.

FOR the earliest notice of its existence among nations, Britain is indebted to that spirit of commerce, through which it was itself one day to become so great. More than a thousand years before the birth of our Saviour, Gades and Tartessus had been founded by the Phœnicians, whose fearless traders we behold, in our dim vision of those remote times when tin was brought in less abundance from the ports of Spain, after a tedious coasting-voyage of four months, fetching that metal from the islands which Herodotus[1] denominates the Cassiterides, or islands producing tin (κασσίτερος), and which now bear the name of the Scilly islands[2]. Herodotus was unable to ascertain the position of these islands, nor does he even mention the name of Britain. It is probable that the Phœnicians never sailed thither direct from their own coast[3],

[1] Lib. iii. § 115.

[2] Camden's Britannia. Cf. Heerens Ideen, ii. 191. Beckmann's Hist. of Inventions, vol. iv.

[3] Strabo, lib. iii., relates, that a Phœnician shipmaster, being chased by some Roman vessels, ran his ship upon a shoal, leading his pursuers into destruction, while he escaped on a fragment of the wreck, and received from the state the value of the cargo he had sacrificed.—T.

though Midacritus[1], the individual who is recorded as having
first brought tin from the Cassiterides, seems by his name to
have been a Phœnician.   The earliest mention of the British
islands by name is made by Aristotle[2], who describes them
as consisting of Albion and Ierne.   The Carthaginian Himilco, who, between the years 362 and 350 A.C., had been
sent by his government on a voyage of discovery, also found
the tin islands, which he calls Oestrymnides, near Albion,
and two days' sail from Ierne[3], in Mount's Bay[4].   His example was some years after followed by a citizen of the celebrated colony of the Phocians, the Massilian Pytheas, to the
scanty fragments of whose journal, preserved by Strabo and
other ancient authors, we are indebted for the oldest accounts
concerning the inhabitants of these islands[5].   The Massilians
and Narbonnese traded at an early period (by land-journeys
to the northern coast of Gaul[6]) with the island Ictis (Wight,
or St. Michael's Mount[7]) and with the coasts of Britain.
This early commerce was carried on both for the sake of the
tin—an article of great importance to the ancients—and of
lead; though these navigators extended their commerce to
other productions of the country, such as slaves, skins, and a

---

[1] Plin. Hist. Nat., lib. vii. c. 57.

[2] De Mundo, c. iii.   Ireland, under the name of Iernis, is mentioned by
the author of the Argonautica, v. 1179.

[3] On this geographic conclusion see the Metropolitan for January 1832.

[4] Of his diary, which was extant in the fifth century, we possess fragments in the poem of Festus Avienus, ' Ora Maritima.'   If, with Ukert and
Lelewel (Entdeckungen der Carthager und Griechen auf dem atlantischen
Ocean), we place Himilco in the middle of the fifth century A.C., the honour
of having discovered Britain must be denied to the Phœnicians and given
to the Carthaginians.

[5] Murray de Pythea Massiliensi, in Nov. Comment. Götting. tom. vi.

[6] Diod. Sic. lib. v. c. 38.

[7] The near resemblance between the names is in favour of the first supposition; while to the second the account of Diodorus, lib. v. c. 22, is alone
applicable, who, describing this island, says, that at flood-tide it appears
as an island, and at ebb as a peninsula.   The proximity to Cornwall, the
British tin country, likewise favours this interpretation.

superior breed of hunting-dogs, which the Celts made use of in war[1]. British timber was employed by Archimedes for the mast of the largest ship of war which he had caused to be built at Syracuse[2]. Gold and silver are said to have been found there; also an inferior sort of pearl, which is still to be met with[3]. This country and its metals soon became an object of scientific inquiry to the Greeks, as is proved by a work upon the subject by Polybius, the loss of which must be painfully felt by every one acquainted with the acuteness and sound judgement of that historian[4].

The Romans first became acquainted with Britain through their thirst after universal dominion. Scipio, to his inquiries concerning it among the merchants of the three most distinguished Celtic cities, Massilia, Narbo, and Corbelo, had received no satisfactory answer[5]; and Publius Crassus is named as the first Roman who visited the Cassiterides, and who observing that the metals were dug out from but a little depth, and that his men at peace were voluntarily occupying themselves on the sea, pointed out this course to such as were willing to take it[6]. This was probably the officer of that name who, by Cæsar's command, had achieved the conquest of the Gaulish nations inhabiting along the shores of the British Channel[7].

Through Cæsar's conquest of the South of England, and the later sway held over it by the Roman emperors, we are first enabled to form an idea of the country. Well might the goddess of science and of war appear to the Greeks and Romans under one form (for it was the Macedonian and Roman

---

[1] Strabo, lib. iii. Oppiani Cyneg. lib. i. *v.* 468. Nemesiani Cyneg. *v.* 123 sq.

[2] Athen. Deipn. lib. v. c. 10.

[3] Cf. Strabo, lib. iv. Tac. de Vita Agric. c. xii. Pomp. Mela, lib. iii. c. 6. Sol. Polyh. c. liii. Suet. lib. i. c. 46. Plin. H. N. ix. c. 57, and the contrary testimony of Cicero, ad Fam. vii. 7, ad Att. iv. 16.

[4] Polyb. lib. iii. c. 37. [5] Strabo, lib. iv.

[6] Strabo, lib. iii. [7] Cæsar, B. G. ii. 34.

swords that fixed for antiquity the limits both of the earth
and of historic knowledge), though their idea of Britain is, it
must be confessed, a very obscure one, and stands much in
need of the reflecting light of modern scientific research. To
Strabo, as well as to Cæsar and Ptolemy, even the figure and
relative position of the British islands were uncertain. According to Strabo, Ireland lies to the north of Britain[1]; while
to the last, the northern coasts of Ireland and Scotland
appear in the same latitude[2]. These errors must necessarily
occasion numberless mistakes with regard to the positions of
tribes and territories, when given according to the degrees of
longitude and latitude. Our knowledge too with regard to
the inhabitants is rendered extremely unsatisfactory by the
circumstance, that in the islands and their several districts
very different degrees of civilization were met with, which
have by authors been too generally applied, and in the most
opposite senses. The inhabitants of the Cassiterides, whose
position even Strabo seeks off Gallicia[3], are described by
Pytheas in almost the same words as the Iberians are in other
passages. Besides mining of a very simple description, they
applied themselves to the rearing of cattle, and exchanged
tin, lead, and hides with the traders, against salt, pottery, and
brass wares. They appeared rambling about their ten islands
with long beards like goats, clad in dark garments reaching
to their heels, and leaning upon staves[4]. It is not improbable

[1] Geogr. lib. ii.
[2] B. G. v. 13. Geogr. lib. ii. c. 2. See also the excellent disquisitions of
Mannert in his ' Geographie der Griechen und Römer,' Abth. ' Britannia.'
The Nüremberg Globe of 1520 has still the map of Ptolemy. In Edit.
Überlin. of Ptolemy Britain first appears in an upright position.
[3] Geogr. lib. ii. If the existence of these islands were not a fiction in-
vented by the traders of Gades for the purpose of misleading their commercial rivals, and inducing them to undertake fruitless expeditions, they
must be looked for only on the coast of Cornwall. The ignorance or
silence of later writers concerning them may perhaps be explained by the
supposition that the hazardous passage by sea was forgotten after the way
by land through Gaul became the usual route.
[4] Strabo, lib. iii.

that these accounts are also applicable to the neighbouring coast of Cornwall, perhaps even to the tribe of the Silures in South Wales; but it is uncertain whether in these mountaineers we are to recognise Iberian settlers[1], or an original native population identical with that of the rest of South Britain. Navigation along the coasts, though only in small boats of twisted osier covered with leather, had, for a length of time, been very lively[2]. The tin, formed into square blocks, was brought to the Isle of Wight, where it was purchased by merchants and carried over to Gaul, and then, in a journey of about thirty days, conveyed on horses to Marseilles, Narbonne, and the mouths of the Rhone[3]. A commerce of this kind, by exciting individual industry, had long rendered the inhabitants of the southern coast of Britain active, docile, and friendly to strangers; yet was their spirit sunk in a slumber which held them to their native soil, until, through the calamity of a most unjust hostile invasion, from being a country not reckoned among the nations of Europe[4], the land of British barbarians, known only to a few daring mariners, became a province closely connected with imperial Rome, and at length that state which, more than any other of the European nations, has impressed the stamp of its character and institutions not only upon this portion of the globe, but also upon lands and regions not discovered till after a long course of ages.

[1] Tac. Agric. c. xi. The opinion of Tacitus is much contested from having been made to apply to all Britain. Dionysius Periegetes, *v.* 563, also declares the inhabitants of the Cassiterides, descendants of the Iberians. On the difference between the Iberian and the old British languages, see W. v. Humboldt's ' Prüfung der Untersuchungen über die Urbewohner Hispaniens vermittelst der vaskischen Sprache,' p. 163.

[2] Lucani Phar. lib. iv.*v.* 134. Plin. H. N. lib. iv.c. 30, vii. 57. Sol. Polyh. c. xxii. F. Avien. *v.* 104 sq. We find vessels of the same description in use at a later period among the Saxon pirates. Isid. Orig. lib. xix. c. 1.

[3] Diod. lib. v. 22. Strabo, lib. iii.

[4] Even Diodorus speaks of the neighbouring islands lying between *Europe* and Britain.

The inhabitants of Britain, with the exception, perhaps, of those above mentioned as Iberian colonists, belonged to the same great national family which we find in Gaul and in Belgium, and which commonly bears the name of Celts. The supposition of Tacitus[1] of a difference between the northern and the southern race, and that the former, from its strong bodily structure and red hair, was of Germanic origin, is by other accounts shown to be groundless. The language still living, particularly in Wales and Brittany, as well as the druidic worship, which, though blended with Christianity, survived to a late period in the former country, supplying it, during a thousand years, with energy to withstand the English invaders, form the leading characteristics of this once great race, and which, being its intellectual portion, have been preserved the longest.

In treating of the primitive history of the Britons, a writer must use their native traditions with great caution. Like those of the other European nations, they appear only in that Romanized garb which was fashioned in the modern world by the last rays of the setting Roman sun. Though at every step in the region of British tradition we meet with traces of an eastern origin, yet the tales of the destruction of Troy and of the flight of Brutus, a great-grandson of Æneas, to Britain[2], are, in the unnational travestie in which alone they have been transmitted to us, wholly devoid of historic value, and the simple truth seems lost to us beyond recovery. The vain Britons gratified their pride in adorning themselves with the faded tinsel, and appropriating to themselves the fabulous national tradition of Rome.

The name of Kymry or Cumry, by which the Welsh still

[1] Vita Agric. c. xi.

[2] The oldest authority for this tradition is Nennius, who professes to have derived his information "partim majorum traditionibus, partim scriptis, partim etiam monumentis veterum Brittaniæ incolarum." Jeffrey of Monmouth is several centuries later, as is also the poem of Robert Wace, ' Le Brut d'Angleterre.'

distinguish themselves, as well as that of the north-west
county of England, Cumberland; the similarity of the words
that have been preserved of the language of the old Kimmerians or Cimbrians to the Welsh; the traditions of the
Welsh Triads, as well as the Roman narratives,—all justify
the assumption, that the race existing in Britain in the time
of Cæsar belonged to those Kimmerians who had gradually
moved forward out of Western Asia. Though the obscurity
attending the name of that people envelopes also the epoch
of their immigration, yet we may conclude, from Cæsar's own
account, that it took place long before the time of that conqueror. Hw Cadarn, or Hu the Powerful, as the Triads relate,
led the nation of the Kymry from Deffrobany, or the Land of
Summer, where Constantinople now is, over the misty ocean,
to the uninhabited island Britain, and to Llydaw (Armorica
or Brittany), where they established themselves. They delivered the country, which had previously been called Clas
Merddin (the land of sea-cliffs), and afterwards Fel Theis
(the island of honey), from the possession of bears, wolves,
and buffaloes. Prydain, son of Ædd the Great, became ruler
of the land, which, through the wisdom of his government,
enjoyed a Saturnian age, and retained his name; but later
expeditions of Lloegrwys from Gwasgwy or Gascony, and of
Brythones from Llydaw, are said to have joined their kindred
on the island, and to have settled in the south-east parts[1].

A language resembling that of the Britons was, according
to Tacitus[2], in use among the Æstii on the shores of the
Baltic, the inhabitants on the western coast of which long
retained the name of Cimbri. The Britannic Moorland on the
Ems[3] seems to owe this ancient appellation to the same Cimbric race. In Belgic Gaul, between Boulogne and Amiens,
dwelt a people bearing the name of Britanni[4]; an early example of the constant intercourse between both shores, and

---

[1] Archæology of Wales.   [2] Germania, c. xlv.
[3] In Groningen, now called the Bourtanger Moor.   [4] Plinii H. N. iv. 17.

a striking proof how little even the greatest separation by
water, however convenient a boundary for objects of state,
avails in dividing nations.   That the Belgæ inhabiting the
British coasts came hither from the Belgium of the continent
we know from Cæsar[1], who speaks of the aboriginal inhabitants, that is the Albiones, (whose name we recognise in the
Scottish Alpin, Albany), as dwelling in the interior of the
country.   But, besides the Belgæ, there dwelt also in the
thickly peopled island of Britain, the Atrebates on the Thames,
the Cenimagni on the Stour, and the Parisi on the Humber,
whose relationship to the Gaulish tribes of the same name
seems unquestionable.   The names of places also, particularly those with the Celtic termination *dunum*, equally prove
the identity of these peoples.

This state of the population plainly shows us to what class
of nations Britain belonged when the foot of Cæsar first trod
its shores, by which event the tales of mariners about the tin
islands soon fell into oblivion, the veil was withdrawn from
Britain, and the land, won for civilization by Roman arms,
had the rare fortune to find her first historian in one, for
whose thirst of knowledge, penetration, and ambition, neither
science nor the world were too extensive.

The continental Gauls, to whom the Channel formed no
intellectual barrier, were yet more closely united with the
natives of Britain by the common religion of druidism.   The
important information given us by Cæsar, that the Gauls,
though in general possessing a higher degree of culture than
the Britons, were, nevertheless, accustomed to seek their more
profound knowledge among the druids of the latter[2], together
with the account of the same observer respecting the density
of the British population, leads to the inference that migra-

---

[1] B. G. v. 12.
[2] B. G. vi. 13.   " Disciplina in Britannia reperta atque inde in Galliam
translata esse existimatur : et nunc, qui diligentius eam rem cognoscere
volunt, plerumque illo discendi caussa proficiscuntur."—T.

tions had taken place from the North to the southern lands, which had slowly and by piecemeal been conquered by their countrymen. The several mysteries of the druidic doctrines are the more obscure to us, as the transmission of them is not from the most ancient sources, but from times in which the severe religious spirit of druidism had yielded to the purer doctrines of Christianity, and the desecrated, secret lore of the druids been made subservient to scientific, patriotic, and often impure purposes. The accounts of the bardic oxstall, the mystic cauldron, and similar traditions of the Welsh, are to us either unintelligible, or void of historic value. The simple old monuments of British faith,—the cromlechs, huge stones set perpendicularly with a transverse; cairs, or concentric circles of stones; rocking stones; carns, or mounds of stone covered with earth, &c.; numbers of which, in the West of England, and in the other British islands, offer themselves at the present day to the contemplation of the antiquary,—while they indicate but a rude state of external worship, yet prove that a vast exertion of physical and mechanical power was applied to the purposes of religion[1]. To a later age those places of old religious veneration were often rendered of importance by being dedicated to Christian worship[2], a case which in Britain may have happened the more frequently, as no obstinate resistance appears to have been made by druidism to the introduction of Christianity. The oak and mistletoe were objects of profound veneration among the druids. With oak leaves they adorned their sacrifices; and if the mistletoe was found growing on a tree, a priest, ascend-

---

[1] An appeal to Hecatæus (Diod. lib. ii.) cannot, it is true, prove that Stonehenge (Chorea gigantum, *Brit.* Cor Gawr) is there alluded to, but which is, however, mentioned by the bards of the sixth century, and may with confidence from this be applied to older heathen monuments and customs. Regarding such monuments, see Mone's 'Geschichte des nordischen Heidenthumes,' Th. ii. p. 435–454, where also the religious tenets of the Britons are treated with acuteness, and with a comprehensive knowledge of the heathenism of the other Celtic nations.

[2] Mone, Th. ii. p. 457.

ing the tree, severed the sacred plant with a golden knife. A festival on the happy occasion was held under its branches, attended with the sacrifice of two white bulls[1].

With respect to the doctrines and learning of these western Brahmins, what Cæsar ascertained was very similar to that which Alexander had formerly found among those on the Ganges. They taught the immortality of the soul, its transmigration from one body to another, and—founded on this belief—inculcated a contempt of life[2]. They professed a considerable knowledge of the heavenly bodies and their motions; discoursed on the magnitude of the world, and of its countries; the nature of things; the virtues and power of the immortal gods[3].

In the druidic order, and in that of the knights or equestrian order, was vested the chief authority of the country. The druids were subordinate to a high-priest chosen by themselves, though arms occasionally decided the fate of the Celtic pontificate. Through the administration of the judicial functions they became accurately versed in temporal affairs, and thus secured worldly influence to themselves, and to justice the sanction of religious awe. Their human sacrifices[4], which

---

[1] Plinii H. N. xvi. c. 95. Max. Tyr. Dissert. xxxviii.

[2] Lucan. lib. i. v. 460. A Triad of the druids—(Davies's Celtic Researches, p. 182) "The three first principles of wisdom are obedience to the laws of God, care for the welfare of man, and fortitude under the accidents of life"—is found also as the principle of the gymnosophists, in Diogenes Laertius (Procem. § 5), Σέϭειν θεοὺς, καὶ μηδὲν κακὸν δρᾶν, καὶ ἀνδρείαν ἀσκεῖν.

[3] Cæsar, B. G. vi. 14. [Of their gods, the chief was one to whom Cæsar (vi. 17.) gives the name of Mercurius : "Deum maxime Mercurium colunt : hujus sunt plurima simulacra." Tacitus (Germ. ix.) says in the same words of the Germans : "Deorum maxime Mercurium colunt;" thereby meaning Wodan, the chief god of the Germanic nations. Hence Wodensdæg (Wednesday) = dies Mercurii. See Grimm's 'Deutsche Mythologie,' p. 76 sq. On other deities of the Britons Cæsar bestows the names of Apollo, Mars, Jupiter, and Minerva.—T.]

[4] From Cæsar, vi. 16, it appears that the human sacrifices of the Britons were not limited to public occasions. "Qui sunt adfecti gravioribus morbis, quique in prœliis periculisque versantur, aut pro victimis homines immolant, aut se immolaturos vovent, administrisque ad ea sacrificia drui-

were usually limited to criminals and captured foes, we look on with horror ; yet should posterity not too severely judge them, which, without the plea of religious infatuation, had for two thousand years deliberately persisted in similar sacrifices, before doubts as to the lawfulness of capital punishments became a subject of national consideration. As the knight by military followers, so was the druid surrounded by studious disciples, to whom twenty years seemed not too long a period for the acquisition of the required knowledge,—astrology and magic, as well as acuteness in judicial decisions,—together with the privilege of directing the sacrifices, and of proclaiming the dreaded excommunication, and the temporal advantage of exemption from taxes and military service[1]. Their precepts, which were in verse, were delivered orally, it being forbidden to commit them to writing; though in recording the common concerns of life they are said to have used the Greek letters[2].

With the druids the bards (beirdd) were closely connected[3]. They wrote in verse on the descent of their princes, and, together with didactic and epic, had also lyric poetry, which was sung to the sound of the *chrotta*[4]. Though none of the productions, nor even the names of the more ancient bards have been transmitted to us, yet all that is related of them allows us to suppose that their works resembled those still extant of the bards of the sixth and following centuries, from

dibus utuntur." For the larger sacrifices he informs us that they framed immense images of twisted osier, the members of which they filled with living beings, and then set the mass on fire. The victims were generally criminals, but when these could not be supplied, innocent persons were taken : " etiam ad innocentium supplicia descendunt."—T.

[1] Cæsar, B. G. vi. 13–16. Plinii H. N. xxx. cc. 3, 4. Tac. Ann. xiv. 30.

[2] A hieroglyphic bardic writing is also said to have been in use, consisting of sixteen characters, and formed from the figures of plants. See Davies, p. 245 sq.

[3] Diod. v. 31. Strabo, iv. Lucani Phars. i. *v.* 447 sq. Athenæus, vi. Ammian. Mar. lib. xv. 24.

[4] " Crotta Britanna." Venant. Fortun. lib. vii. c. 8. [The crowd (rote) of later minstrelsy. See Graff, Althochdeutscher Sprachschatz, ii.col. 487.—T.]

which, when treating of later times, we must not withhold our attention. That bards were known to Posidonius and Lucan[1], is a convincing proof of the antiquity of the Celtic settlement in Britain, for wandering people carry no poems about with them, scarcely even the most meagre traditions. The Anglo-Saxons and Northmen brought no poetic store from their ancient home to their new country. The peace, leisure, and prosperity of a nation, seated in its old native abode, are indispensable to the cultivation of national song[2].

Together with the druids, the ruling order was, as before said, that of the chieftains or knights. In Cæsar's time, both these noble orders had reduced to a state of dependence the greater part of the rest of the people of Gaul, who were oppressed by debts, taxes, and the tyranny of the powerful, exercising towards them all the rights of masters over slaves[3]. The Roman conquest itself might also have contributed to the completion of an already existing state of clientship of the indigent class to the opulent, such as is still to be found in the very pure patriarchal customs of the clans in the Scottish highlands and isles.

The land was divided among many tribes and their kings[4], who, slightly connected through the priesthood, lived independently near each other, cherishing their love of strife, and training up their youth in civil quarrels, without manifesting at a later period, in the days of the destruction of the common liberty, the judgement and energy necessary for a general resistance[5]. The power of these princes was much limited by the before-mentioned castes, and consisted chiefly in military command.

In the southern parts of England, which had become more

---

[1] Athen. lib. iv. c. 37.   Pharsal. lib. i. v. 447 sq.

[2] May not an instance to the contrary possibly exist in the original saga of Beowulf?—T.   [3] Cæsar, B. G. vi. 13.

[4] The royal authority and even military command could also be exercised by a female, as in the instances of Cartismandua and Boudicea.

[5] Diod. lib. v. 21.   Tac. Agric. c. xii.

civilized through commerce, the cultivation of grain, to which the mildness of the climate was favourable, had been greatly improved by the art of marling[1]. The daily consumption was taken from the unthrashed corn, preserved in caves, which they prepared for food, but did not bake as bread[2]. Horticulture was not in use among them, nor the art of making cheese[3]; yet the great number of buildings, of people, and of cattle appeared striking to the Romans. Copper and bits of iron, according to weight, served as money[4]. Their custom of painting themselves with blue and green, for the purpose of terrifying their enemies, as well as that of tattooing[5], was retained till a later period by the Picts of the North. At certain sacrifices, even the women, painted in a similar manner, resembling Ethiopians, went about without clothing[6]. Long locks and mustachios were general. Like the Gauls, they decorated the middle finger with a ring[7]. Their round simple huts of reeds or wood resembled those of that people[8], and the Gaulish checquered, coloured mantles are still in common use in the Scottish Highlands. Their clothing, more especially that of the Belgic tribes of the South, enveloped the whole body; a girdle encircled the waist, and chains of metal hung about the breast[9]. The hilts of their huge pointless swords were adorned with the teeth of marine animals[10]; their shields were small[11]. The custom of fighting in chariots (called by them esseda, covini[12]), on the axles of which scythes were fastened, and in the management of which they showed great skill, was peculiar to this and some other of the Celtic nations, in a generally level country, and where the horses were not

[1] Plin. H. N. xvii. 4.　Tac. Agric. xii.　Diod. v. 21.
[2] Diod. v. 21.　　　　[3] Strabo, lib. iv.　　　　[4] Cæsar, B. G. v. 12.
[5] Cæsar, B. G. v. 14.　"Virides Britanni." Ov. Amor. lib. ii. 16.　"Cærulei Britanni." Mart. Epig. liv.　Plin. H. N. lib. xxii. 2.　Claud. Prim. Cons. Stil. lib. ii. v. 247.　Pomp. Mela, iii. 6.　Sol. Polyh. c. xxii.
[6] Plin. H. N. xxii. 2.　　　　[7] Plin. H. N. xxxiii. 6.
[8] Strabo, iv.　Diod. v. 21.　　　　[9] Dio ap. Xiph. lxii.
[10] This was rather the custom of the inhabitants of Ireland.　Sol. Polyh. c. xxii.—T.　　　[11] Tac. Agric. xxxvi.　　　　[12] Pomp. Mela, iii. 6.

sufficiently powerful to be used for cavalry. The charioteer was the superior person, the servant bore the weapons. They begun their attacks with taunting songs and deafening howls[1]. Their fortresses or towns consisted in the natural defence of impenetrable forests[2]. In the interior of the country were found only the more rugged characteristics of a people engaged in the rearing of cattle, which, together with the chase, supplied skins for clothing, and milk and flesh for food[3]. The northern part of the country seems in great measure to have been abandoned to the shaft and javelin of the roving hunter, as skilful as he was bold[4]. That every ten or twelve men of near relationship possessed their wives in common, but that the one earliest married was regarded as the father of all the children, is probably a mere Roman fable[5]. Simplicity, integrity, temperance, with a proneness to dissension, are mentioned as the leading characteristics of the nation[6]. The reputation of bravery was more especially ascribed to the northern races[7].

A much more favourable picture of the social condition of the ancient Britons may be drawn from the Triads of Dyvnwal Moelmud, who is said to have lived several centuries before the Christian era[8], if those Triads have even the slightest claim

[1] Cæsar, B. G. iv. 33, v. 16. Strabo, iv. Tac. Agric. xii. Diod. v. 21. Dio ap. Xiph. lxii. Pomp. Mela, iii. 6.

[2] Cæsar, B. G. v. 21. Strabo, iv.

[3] Cæsar, B. G. v. 14. The abundance of milk and skins is mentioned in Eumenii Panegyr. ad Constan. Aug. c. ix. Cf. eund. ad Constan. Cæs. c. xi.

[4] Dio ap. Xiph. lxxvi. 12.

[5] Cæsar, B. G. v. 14. Diodorus does not mention this custom.

[6] Diod. v. 21, 22. Pomp. Mela, iii. 6. Tac. Agric. xii.

[7] Dio ap. Xiph. lxxvi.

[8] ["Before the crown of London and the supremacy of this island were seized by the Saxons, Dyvnwal Moelmud, son of Clydno, was king over this island, who was son to the earl of Cernyw, by a daughter of the king of Lloegyr. And his laws continued in force until the time of Howel the Good, son of Cadell." 'Ancient Laws and Institutes of Wales,' pp. 89 and 630. In a note the learned editor, Mr. A. Owen, adds, "Dyvnwal, according to the Chronicle of the Kings, in the book of Basingwerke (a

to be considered genuine which have reached us only in a very modern manuscript, and exhibit not only traces of Roman and Saxon influence, but also of numerous interpolations subsequent to the introduction of Christianity.

Of the British tribes, the first to be mentioned are the Cantii, or men of Kent. They were governed by four princes[1]. Northward of the Thames, as far as the river Stour, in the present counties of Middlesex and Essex, dwelt the Trinobantes, whose capital, London, was already a considerable emporium. To the north of the Stour, in Suffolk, dwelt the Cenimagni, a tribe of the Iceni; in Norfolk, Cambridgeshire and Huntingdonshire, the rest of the Iceni, whose chief town bore the common Celtic appellation of Venta. The Catuvellani, or Katyeuchlani of Ptolemy, inhabited the present counties of Hertford, Bedford and Buckingham.

The Coritavi (Coriniaidd), who, as the Triads relate, had migrated from a Teutonic marshland, possessed the present counties of Northampton, Leicester, Rutland, Lincoln, Nottingham and Derby. Beyond them, in the eastern part of Yorkshire, dwelt the Parisi.

The most powerful people were the Brigantes, who held the country to the north of the Humber and the Mersey, comprising the counties of York, Durham, Lancaster and Westmoreland. The Caer, or city Luel (Luguvallum, Lugubalia, or Carlisle), in the country of the Cumbri, on this side of the Picts' wall, remained long the seat of its original inhabitants. Cataractonium and Vinnovium may here also be

Welsh version of Geoffrey of Monmouth's compilation), flourished from anno B.C. 694 to 667." Of these triads Mr. Owen says (Pref. p. vii), "Their antiquity is very dubious, but in their present form and phraseology they may be attributed to the sixteenth century."—T.] See also ' The Ancient Laws of Cambria ' translated by W. Probert, 1823. Cf. Gervinus in den Heidelberg. Jahrbüchern 1831, Ss. 46–49, and Palgrave's ' Rise and Progress of the English Commonwealth,' vol. i. c. ii.

[1] Cæsar, B. G. v. 22. Ptolemy places London in the territory of the Cantii. [See also Anc. Laws and Instt. of Engl., p. 14, fol. ed.—T.]

distinguished as having evidently preserved themselves under the names of Catterick and Binchester. To this people belonged also the Jugantes and the Cangi.

The ancestors of the Welsh were the Ordovices, whose territory comprised the counties of Montgomery, Merioneth, Caernarvon, Anglesea, Denbigh and Flint; the Dimetæ in Caermarthen, Pembroke and Cardiganshire, and the most powerful tribe of those parts, the Silures, inhabiting the present shires of Hereford, Radnor, Brecknock, Monmouth and Glamorgan.

Hampshire, Somersetshire and Wiltshire, from the English to the Bristol channel, were occupied by the Belgæ, where a city, Venta, is still to be recognised in the modern Winchester.

The ancient tin country, the Bretland of the Northmen, now Cornwall and Devonshire, was inhabited by the Dumnonii or Damnonii. The Roman incursions not having reached this south-west corner of the province, we consequently possess the fewest accounts of the period relative to that part of the country which was first known to the three ancient divisions of the globe.

Between the Dumnonii and the Belgæ, in the present Dorsetshire, dwelt the Durotriges : in the counties of Gloucester and Oxford, the Dobuni. The Atrebates, whose chief city was Calleva[1], were settled in Berkshire. In the vicinity of these we are to look for the small tribes mentioned by Cæsar, of the Segontiaci, Ancalites, Bibroci (Bibracte in Bray Hundred, on the Thames, below Windsor), and the Cassi[2].

[1] Anton. Itin., Ric. Corin. p. 148, edit. 1809.

[2] For the geography of Britain under the Romans, Camden's 'Britannia' is especially to be consulted. See also the works of Horsley and Stukeley. The appendix to the first book of Henry's History of Great Britain contains a very useful illustration and comparison of the texts of Ptolemy and Antoninus, and of the extracts relative to Britain in the 'Notitia Imperii Occidentalis.' The itineraries of Antoninus and of Richard of Cirencester, with the illustrations by Gale, Horsley, and Stukeley, are given by Whitaker

The Cornabii, or Carnabii, inhabited the present counties of Warwick, Worcester, Stafford, Salop and Chester, and probably a part of Flint. In the last-mentioned county, or in that of Chester, the monastery of Bangor (Banchor Iscoed) was seated, the most celebrated religious foundation in the island, till its destruction and the slaughter of its inmates by Æthelfrith of Northumbria[1].

The Scottish and Irish races (for a knowledge of whose names we are chiefly indebted to Ptolemy) form matter exclusively for the separate history of those nations. Here it is only necessary to observe, that to the north of the Brigantes dwelt the Mæatæ, consisting of five tribes, and beyond them the Caledonians[2].

The Britons had lived hitherto without intercourse with the south of Europe, except, as before mentioned, through the medium of a few travellers, and an inconsiderable commerce, carried on for the most part by intermediate agents, when they learned that the mighty Roman people from the South had already advanced upon, and subdued many of their Gaulish brethren. Valiant, and mindful of their own danger, the Britons endeavoured, though vainly, by sending succours to the Veneti, to support the Gauls against their victorious foe[3]; but this inefficient help served only as a ground for Roman policy, or a pretext to the Roman general for risking an attack on the unsubdued island. Its inhabitants soon received intelligence from foreign traders, that the Roman commander was making preparations for an invasion, and they beheld a Roman captain, C. Volusenus, in a ship of war re-

---

at the end of his ' History of Manchester.' The notions of the ancients regarding the form of Britain, and its coasts as given by Ptolemy, are most ably illustrated by Mannert. [The localities of the several tribes given in this translation are from Petrie's ' Corpus Historicum.'—T.]

[1] Beda, ii. 2. Sax. Chron. a. 607. Ric. Corin. lib. i. c. 6. § 27. "Banchorium monasterium totius insulæ celeberrimum, quod in contentione Augustini eversum, non postea resurrexit."—T.

[2] Dio ap. Xiph. lib. lxxvi. 10.   [3] Cæsar, B. G. iii. 9.

connoitring their coast[1]. Some of the British tribes, either
terrified by the fame of the conquerors of more regions than
they had ever heard of, or with the view of amusing the enemy
by negotiations, sent ambassadors across the sea to the Roman
camp, promising hostages and submission.

They were received in the kindest manner by their ambitious enemy, whom they assured of the early fulfilment of
those promises, and were accompanied on their return by a
chieftain named Commius, whom the Romans favoured, on
account of his valour, his judgement, and his reputation, and
had placed as king over the Gaulish Atrebates, and who now
undertook the commission of persuading the Britons into a
reliance on the Roman people, and of announcing the early
arrival of their general. Scarcely, however, had Commius
made known his commission in the public assembly, when—
although it was the duty of their princes to protect the sacred
character of an ambassador—the enraged people, divining the
drift of the deceitful words, seized on the speaker, and loaded
him with chains. The Britons collected their hordes, which
they skilfully posted on the eminences along the shore[2]. The
Romans, of whom the infantry of two legions had crossed over
from the country of the Morini[3], did not at first venture upon
landing, but observing the moment of the ebb, they attempted
it upon a level tract of shore about seven miles distant[4].
Here were British cavalry and war-chariots arrayed before the
foot, who for some time skilfully and boldly held the invaders
in check: but the eagle-bearer of the tenth legion, after ex-
horting his comrades, leaped into the sea, and rushed to the
onset, when the missiles of the enemy, Roman valour, enthusiasm for their leader, the great Caius Julius Cæsar—under
whom it was regarded a greater disgrace to see the glory of
victory even slightly tarnished, than to be beaten under any

---

[1] A.C. 55.
[2] Where Dover now is.—T.
[3] Orosius, vi. 9.
[4] Near the present Deal.—T.

other general—but above all, superior discipline, effected the hostile landing[1].

In these encounters, the war-chariots of the Britons called forth the admiration of their invaders. Their manner of fighting from chariots was this:—At first they rode in all directions, casting their darts, and with the dread of their horses and noise of their wheels generally succeeded in disturbing the ranks of the enemy. Having made an opening in the bodies of cavalry, they would leap from the chariots and fight on foot: meanwhile the charioteers gradually withdrawing from the battle, would post the chariots so that, if pressed on by numbers, their comrades might find a certain retreat; thus evincing both the rapidity of cavalry and the firmness of infantry. From constant exercise they could drive their horses at full speed down a declivity, or along a precipice, checking and turning them instantaneously; and would run along the pole, sit on the yoke, and thence in an instant reseat themselves in their chariots.

The Britons, in their first consternation, imagining the danger greater than it really was, sent ambassadors to Cæsar, accompanied by the prince of the Atrebates, Commius, offering to give hostages, to place themselves under the protection of the Romans, and entreating forgiveness for the outrage committed on his ambassador.

In his glad surprise Cæsar could not do otherwise than lend a willing ear to these proposals; the British warriors were therefore sent back to their fields, and their princes came to Cæsar, for the purpose of commending themselves to his protection. They soon, however, remarked that the valour of their enemy had deceived them with regard to his numbers, and moreover learned that the ships, which had been expected with the cavalry and grain, were dispersed in a storm. Hereupon the resolution soon ripened among them of freeing for ever their native land from this daring

[1] Aug. 26. Anno u.c. 699. A.C. 55. Cæsar, B. G. iv. 21-23.

foe. They withdrew from the Roman camp, gathered their warriors, and attacked the seventh legion that had gone out to forage, but to which Cæsar sent timely help. Some days afterwards, in an attempt upon the Roman camp, they were repulsed with loss, though, for want of cavalry, not pursued. On the same day they sent messengers to sue for peace, from whom Cæsar demanded a number of hostages, the double of that which he had previously required, and the equinox being at hand, hastened to avoid a dangerous contest with the elements by a speedy return to Gaul. The Romans at home were, however, elated at his account of their new acquisition, and in celebration of it decreed a festival of twenty days' continuance[1]. Thus terminating what—save for the gratification of his own vanity—may be considered a bootless adventure.

But this light prelude was soon to be followed by a sterner contest. The following summer Cæsar again trod the British shores with a greater power[2]—five legions, two thousand cavalry, and all their military engines, to which was attached an elephant armed with scales of iron, and bearing a tower containing archers and slingers[3],—and met with no resistance, the inhabitants of the coast, who had at first appeared in arms on the level shore, terrified at the magnitude of the approaching fleet, having retired to the higher points of land. An internal dissension, fostered by Mandubratius[4], the son of Imanuentius, the powerful prince of the Trinobantes, who had been slain by Cassivellaunus (Caswallon), devastated the country. Small was the benefit which the barricades, erected in the forests against domestic foes, afforded against the Romans, in comparison with the detriment they suffered, through their want of union, in allowing a foreign enemy to land unassailed, to repair his fleet, and, after victories easily achieved, to march

---

[1] Cæsar, B. G. iv. 20–38. Dio Cass. xxxix. 51–53. Luc. ii. v. 572.
[2] A.C. 54.   [3] Polyæn. Strat. viii. 23.
[4] Cæsar, B. G. v. 20. Orosius (vi. 9.) calls him Androgorius.

forward to the heart of the country. The Britons at length
sacrificing their petty quarrels to the pressing necessity of
struggling for independence, intrusted the chief military command to the brave prince of the Cassi, Caswallon, who had
hitherto been engaged in constant warfare with the neighbouring states. In their incursions and attacks great valour
was displayed by the Britons, yet was lack of discipline the
cause of much disorder after a mischance, and a preventive
to their engaging in a general battle. The enemy had advanced as far as the Thames, which at a shallow ford they
passed, unhindered by the strong piles that had been driven
into the bed of the river by order of Caswallon, remains of
which existed in the time of Beda[1], after an interval of seven
hundred years. The treachery of the Trinobantes and other
tribes, who had submitted to the invaders, disheartened the
British leader, whose fame has been preserved to us only in
the honourable testimony of Cæsar. His well-planned forest-
fastness was, with great difficulty, at length taken, and even
then he attempted an attack upon the Roman camp on the
coast of Kent, with the design, by destroying their fleet, of
turning the land they had conquered into a prison. No
other resource being left him, Commius negotiated for his
submission, by which the Romans obtained what alone they
could seek in this to them inhospitable land—the glory of
victory; while Caswallon gained that which, even with the
disgrace of apparent humiliation, was not too dearly bought
—the evacuation of his native country by hostile armies.
This time hostages were actually led home by the Romans,
grain was delivered to them, and Rome was dazzled[2] by

---

[1] " Quarum vestigia sudium ibidem usque hodie visuntur, et videtur in-
spectantibus quod singulæ earum ad modum humani femoris grossæ, et
circumfusæ plumbo immobiliter erant in profundum fluminis infixæ." H. E.
i. 2. The exact point at which Cæsar crossed is not known with certainty :
Camden supposes it to have been at Coway Stakes, near Laleham. See
Archæol. vol. i. p. 184 ; ii. 134, 168.—T.

[2] Not so the better informed. Cicero, in a letter to Atticus (iv. 16.),

Cæsar's account of the riches of this new portion of the world, and by a corselet adorned with British pearls which he dedicated to Venus[1]: yet the promised yearly contributions were not paid, and, with the exception of the hostages, the Britons were as free as they had been the year before, ere a passing cloud had for a moment darkened the sunshine of their independence, though to the steady yet powerful influence of the plastic rays of the Roman star the Britons could not continue insensible, and the coins of their prince Cynobellin, the Cymbeline ennobled in tradition and by Shakspere's muse, prove that the Roman alphabet was intelligible to the natives, that Roman art was cultivated in Britain[2].

A century had nearly elapsed, and the Britons had seen on their soil no other Romans than peaceful merchants. The duties levied in Gaul on their trifling exports and imports were moderate[3]. On the rumour of an intended invasion, envoys were sent by them to the emperor Augustus[4]; yet Rome heard of no homage from Britain, except the offerings said to have been made by some petty princes to the Capitol[5], and in the empty compositions of poets and panegyrists; and it is probable that the Britons would never have yielded to Roman sway—for the strength of the latter was already in its wane, their power near to the summit from which it must soon descend—had not pernicious discord prevailed among the British princely races, and reduced their country under a subjection of four hundred years' duration.

---

writes, " Britannici belli exitus exspectatur. Constat enim aditus insulæ esse munitos mirificis molibus. Etiam illud jam cognitum est, neque argenti scripulum esse ullum in illa insula, neque ullam spem prædæ, nisi ex mancipiis." Cæsar, v. 8–23.

[1] Plin. H. N. ix. 57.   Sol. Polyh. c. liii.

[2] See Pegge's Essay on the Coins of Cunobeline : London, 1766.   In Whitaker's History of Manchester representations of these coins are given. See also Henry's History of Great Britain, vol. ii.

[3] Strabo, iv.   [4] Dio Cass. liii. 22.

[5] Strabo, iv.

Adminius[1], the son of Cynobellin, a successor of Caswallon, having been banished by his father, had, with a few followers, placed himself under the power of Caligula, who, as if the whole island had been surrendered to him, immediately sent despatches to Rome announcing the glorious intelligence. The forces raised for the German war were hereupon ordered to the coast, where being arrayed, with their military engines in readiness, and while in suspense as to what was to follow, the emperor went on board a trireme, in which having proceeded a short distance from the shore, he placed himself at his return on a lofty throne, from whence he gave a signal as if for battle, and to the sound of trumpets ordered the soldiers to gather, and fill their helmets and bosoms with, shells, calling them 'the spoils of the ocean'; and, as a monument of victory, caused a lofty tower to be built, which at the same time should serve as a beacon. Considerable rewards were then given to the soldiers, and the shells borne in triumph to Rome[2].

This treachery, however, proved hurtful only through the example which it soon after afforded to an exile named Beric, at whose instigation the emperor Claudius resolved on sending an army to Britain[3]. The warlike reputation of the natives was so universally acknowledged, that the four legions destined to contend with them, under the command of Aulus Plautius, could scarcely be induced to break up their quarters. Surprised, however, by the landing of the enemy, the Britons were not in a condition to oppose it, and proved their valour only in a warfare of skirmishes. The Gaulish allies of the

---

[1] Orosius (vii. 5.) calls him Minocynobellinus.—T.

[2] Suet. de Calig. c. xlvi. Dio Cass. lix. 21. A.D. 40.

[3] A.D. 43. Dio Cass. lx.19. Suet. de Claud. c. xvii. Orosius says (vii. 6.), "Expeditionem in Britanniam movit, quæ excitata in tumultum propter non redhibitos transfugas videbatur." The fugitives were probably Beric and his associates, and the disturbance, caused by the emperor's refusal to deliver them up, seems to have served him as a pretext for invading the island.—T.

imperial forces, even if at the outset they spared the lives of
their kindred, and only slew their chariot-horses, must in the
end cause great injury to them.   The glory of the first important victory in Britain, and the honour of a triumph at
home, belong to Cn. Osidius Geta[1].   This country was the
palæstra of the Roman emperors.   Vespasian, at the head of
the second legion, accompanied by Titus, fought here thirty
battles, subdued the Isle of Wight, overcame two nations,
and took twenty places[2].   The war now assuming a more serious
character, Plautius, as he had been previously instructed, resolved on sending for the emperor.   Claudius was accompanied by Galba, the administration of the state being conducted
by Vitellius during the absence of the emperor.   Cynobellin
was now dead; of his sons, Togodumnus and Caractacus, or
Caradoc, the former had fallen in battle, the latter was driven
across the Thames, and Claudius, honoured with the surname
of the Britannic, entered their chief city, Camulodunum[3].
From this place, by means of negotiations and arms, he
began to mould the south-eastern parts of Britain into a
Roman province, the administration of which was committed
to Plautius, and afterwards to P. Ostorius Scapula[4].   A
prince named Cogidubnus obtained some territories in or
about Sussex, which he was proud to govern under the title
of an imperial legate, and devoted the rest of his life to the
establishment of the Roman power in his native country[5].

---

[1] Dio Cass. lx. 20.
[2] Dio Cass. lx. 20.   Eutrop. lib. vii. c. 19.   Suet. de Vespas. c. iv.; de
Tito, c. iv; de Galba, c. vii.   Tac. Agric. c. xiv.
[3] Dio Cass. lx. 21.   Suet. de Claud. xvii.   Camulodunum is usually
supposed to be the town of Maldon, but the cogent reasons assigned by
Mannert and others induce us rather to identify it with Colchester.   See
'Geogr. der Griechen und Römer,' p. 157.   [Roy, Milit. Antiq. p. 187.
Archæol. iii. p. 165.—T.]
[4] A.D. 50.   Tac. Agric. c. xiv.   Camden (edit. Gibson, p. 300) supposes
the Oyster hills near Hereford to have been one of his camps.   Ostorius
came in the year 47.
[5] Tac. Agric. c. xiv.   The hypothesis of several commentators on this

The majority of the inhabitants who had attached themselves
to the conqueror had, however, soon cause to repent that step,
on perceiving that while the duty of subjects was exacted from
them, they were at the same time deprived of the right of
bearing arms. While the west was submitting to the Roman
camps on the Avon and the Severn, the Iceni in the east
were the first to declare themselves against the new tyranny;
and history, when relating their defeat, celebrates at the same
time their many and brilliant achievements. Their misfortune disheartened the similarly disposed neighbouring states;
but the Cangi and the Silures, under the national hero,
Caradoc, continued a war of annihilation and despair. The
Brigantes also, in the yet unconquered northern parts, now
rose for the protection of the common liberty; but before the
league among them had become general, and they could appear prepared for the contest, they were, for the time, reduced
by Ostorius, who with his army marching rapidly against
them, caused the few who had taken up arms to be slain; the
others were pardoned[1].

With the design of securing the subjection of the vanquished,
and of those who were honoured with the name of allies, as
well as of establishing a stronghold in the country for Roman
interests and civilization, a colony of hardy veterans was placed
at Camulodunum[2]. The Roman eagles were already displayed
over the plains of Britain, when the Silures, Ordovices, and

passage of Tacitus, which Lingard also adopts, that Togodumnus and
Cogidubnus were the same person, appears, on comparison with Dio, untenable. The writers of the 'Universal History' (vol. xlvii. p. 32) make him
the son of Cartismandua, and to fall, instead of Togodumnus, in battle
against the Romans.   At Chichester, in 1723, an inscription was dug up
with the words, "Ex auctoritate Tiberii Claudii Cogidubni regis legati
Augusti in Britannia."   See Gale in Philos. Trans. 1723, Oct. 31.   Horsley, Brit. Rom. No. 76. pp. 192, 333; also Henry, History of Great
Britain, i. p. 336.   The fac-simile, with a somewhat different explanation,
is given in Hearne's Preface to Adam de Domerham.

[1] Tac. Ann. xii. 32.   [2] Ibid.

other mountaineers, who had flocked around Caradoc, begun
a new struggle, which for some time seemed ruinous to the
enemy; yet were their love of freedom, their reverence for the
gods of their country, their craft and valour forced to give way
before regular warfare.   Caradoc's town (Caer Caradoc[1]) was
taken ; his wife, daughter, and brother fell into the hands of
the conqueror.   Himself sought shelter and help among the
Brigantes, whom he had formerly befriended ; but their queen,
Cartismandua, expecting to obtain less by a noble struggle for
the independence of her people than through the favour of the
Romans, sought to purchase the latter by the treacherous sur-
render of her guest to his enemies, whom he had stoutly re-
sisted during a space of nine years[2].   But though with his
family compelled to appear as a glorious spectacle to proud
triumphant Rome, who looked on this fruit of treachery as
equal to the most brilliant victories of Publius Scipio and
Lucius Paullus, yet were the brave mountaineers whom
Caradoc had led still unsubdued.   The Silures attacked the
Roman legions appointed to erect fortresses among them, and
although they often gave ground, the enemy could boast of
no victory : his forces—which could hope only with the last
of the Silures to quell the spirit of British independence—
were daily diminishing, while the allies of the Britons daily
increased.   Ostorius died of grief[3].   His death was celebrated
as a victory by the Britons, for his successor Aulus Didius
Gallus was, by reason of his advanced age, far from formidable.   Some years had passed when Venusius, the husband
of Cartismandua, from whom he had parted, and who had
married Vellocatus, one of his shield-bearers, placed himself
at the head of his people, in opposition to the Romans, whose

---

[1] A lofty hill on the river Ony, near the junction of the Clun and the
Teme, in the south-eastern part of Shropshire, still bears the name of Caer
Caradoc, and exhibits traces of ancient fortifications.

[2] A.D. 51.   [3] A.D. 55.

arms, however, under the skilful guidance of Cæsius Nasica, succeeded in producing a momentary tranquillity. Didius was succeeded by Veranius[1].

The Britons of the present England were now, to all appearance, nearly subjected to the Romans; and the prefect or legate, Suetonius Paullinus, the successor of Veranius, after two years of tranquil administration, resolved on the reduction of the Isle of Mona (Anglesey)[2], the chief seat of druidism, and a receptacle for fugitives. To this end he ordered the construction of shallow vessels for the transport of the foot-soldiers, while the cavalry should either swim or wade across the strait. On arriving at the opposite shore they found a dense band of armed men, between whose ranks women like furies were seen passing, clad in mourning, with disheveled locks, and bearing torches; while the female druids with upraised hands poured forth maledictions on the invaders. Appalled and, as it were, petrified at this spectacle, the soldiers stood aghast and exposed to the missiles of the enemy, till, on the exhortation of their general, not to fear a band of fanatics and women, they rushed to the onset, overthrowing and destroying in their own fire all who had courage to resist. A garrison was then left on the isle, and the groves, stained with the blood of human victims, fell under the axe of the legionaries. But while the general was thus engaged[3], the Britons were near proving successful in extirpating the Romans from the country. These, as well as the other provincials, were bitterly exasperated by the heavy taxes, in the levying of which they were exposed not only to the rapacity of Roman usurers—among whom was Lucius Annæus Seneca[4], in whom the love of wisdom and of base lucre existed in a rare, though not unexampled combination—but also by the most intolerable oppression of the procurator Catus, and of other Roman officials.

[1] Tac. Ann. xii. 40, xiv. 29. Hist. iii. 45.   [2] A.D. 61.
[3] Tac. Ann. xiv. 29.   [4] Dio ap. Xiph. lxii. 2.

No tribe endured the incorporation of their country as a
province more impatiently than the Iceni. Their king, the
wealthy Prasutagus, in the view of securing both his kingdom and family from the officers and farmers of the revenue,
and, according to a practice then prevalent, seeking in degradation a safeguard against insult, had made the emperor
his joint heir with his two daughters. The atrocities perpetrated by the insolent and profligate officials of the provinces
(whom vice instigated more than the desire of possession, and
whose inordinate lusts had been excited by wantonness to a
recklessness of all the rights of humanity, as well as of their
own well-understood interest,) were at length the cause that,
under the conduct of Boudicea, the magnanimous widow of
Prasutagus, who had been scourged as a slave, and the chastity
of whose daughters had been violated, a multitude of a hundred and twenty thousand Britons[1] surprised the Romans, destroyed Camulodunum, the important emporium London[2], and
Verulam, and slaughtered seventy thousand Romans (including
the ninth legion under the legate Petilius Cerealis), and their
traitorous British allies, with all the fury of vengeance to
which the violation of their temples, their honour, and their
domestic hearths could impel them[3]. Suetonius Paullinus,
in a contest of despair, gained, through his wedge-shaped
array, a bloody victory, which, after the fall of eighty thousand Britons, Boudicea would not survive[4]: she ended her
days by poison[5]. Yet neither the want of regular discipline,

[1] Dio ap. Xiph. lxii. 1 sq.

[2] " Londinium, cognomento quidem coloniæ non insigne, sed copia nego-
tiatorum et commeatuum maxime celebre." Tac. Ann. xiv. 33.

[3] Dio ap. Xiph. lxii. The grove of Andraste or Andate, the British goddess of victory, is mentioned as the chief place where these atrocities were
perpetrated.—T.   [4] A.D. 62.

[5] Tac. Ann. xiv. 31–37. Boudicea is described by Dio (ap. Xiph.) as of the
largest size, most terrible of aspect, most savage of countenance, and harsh
of voice; having a profusion of yellow hair which fell down to her hips,
and wearing a large golden collar; she had on a party-coloured flowing
vest drawn close about her bosom, and over this she wore a thick mantle

nor the reinforcements of the Romans, but only a scarcity of
corn in the following winter compelled the Britons again to
submit to the dominion of the Cæsars. One point, however,
was gained: the necessity of a mild administration became
understood at Rome. The procurator Catus was succeeded
by Julius Classicianus; the general by Petronius Turpilianus;
his followers were the contemptible Trebellius Maximus, and
the inactive Vettius Bolanus, under whose inefficient command
the Roman soldiery became more licentious, the Britons more
bold[1]. Among the Brigantes, Venusius had fostered enmity
to Rome and her ally Cartismandua; and they might have
hoped to overpower the Romans, had not Vespasian, at that
time emperor, appointed Petilius Cerealis to the dignity of
consular legate, who, after an entire year of contest, succeeded
in subduing them: yet did these mountaineers ever rise again
with renewed strength[2]. The Silures could only be withheld
from further strife by his successor Julius Frontinus[3], who
was followed in the administration of the province by Cneius
Julius Agricola[4], a leader whose glorious memory will for ever
live in the noble monument raised to his father-in-law by the
great historian of the empire.

The first campaign of Agricola, after his arrival, was against
the Ordovices, who had attacked and nearly annihilated a
body of Roman cavalry stationed on their border. Having
destroyed the greater part of this people, he directed his attention to the reconquest of Mona, which had recovered its
liberty on the sudden departure of Paullinus to quell the insurrection under Boudicea. Though without vessels for the
transport of his soldiers, the energy of Agricola was not to
be subdued. He caused such of his auxiliaries as were most

fastened by a clasp. Such was her usual dress, but at this time she also
bore a spear. By the same authority we are informed that she died of
disease.—T.

[1] Tac. Ann. xiv. 38. Agric. c. xvi.; Hist. i. 60.   [2] A.D. 70–75.
[3] A.D. 75–78.   [4] Josephus de Bell. Jud. vii. 4. Tac. Agric. c. vii.

expert in swimming, and who were acquainted with the locality, to cross the strait, on whose unlooked-for approach the surprised inhabitants sued for peace, and again yielded to the Romans.

But Agricola had not to learn that tranquillity could be best maintained by removing the causes of discontent, and, acting on this conviction, he undertook the work of reform, wisely beginning with his own household. He checked the abuses connected with the levying of the taxes, which were even more intolerable than the taxes themselves. The summer immediately following[1] was employed in improving the state of the army, in the formation of camps, and other measures for the security of the province; and the winter was passed in introducing among the rugged natives the luxuries and refinements of the capital.

To this end neither exhortations nor aid were wanting on the part of Agricola. Temples, baths and other structures, both public and private, were erected; the British youth were instructed in the language and learning of Rome; elegant and costly entertainments became fashionable, and with the toga were adopted the vices of the imperial city. Among the inexperienced this passed under the name of politeness, while it was a part of their servitude.

In the third year of his government Agricola conducted his forces as far as the Tay, where he established strong garrisons. In his fourth year, for the security of his conquests, he caused a line of forts to be erected between the Firths of Forth and Clyde[2]. With a view to the future subjugation of Ireland, to which he had been excited by the representations of an exiled chief, Agricola, in the year following, extended his conquests

---

[1] A.D. 79.

[2] On the subject of the Roman walls in Britain, the reader will find a very able digest in a work entitled ' Eburacum, or York under the Romans, by C. Wellbeloved,' 8vo, 1842 : which contains also much valuable matter connected with the latest discoveries in Yorkshire and the North, as well as with the state of Roman Britain in general.—T.

to the western shores of Britain, where he stationed numerous forces, to be in readiness for ulterior operations.

In the summer of his sixth year he proceeded with an army to the country beyond the Forth, while a fleet coasting along the eastern shore seconded his designs. At the sight of the ships the Britons were struck with amazement, while the Romans were equally alarmed by accounts of the valour and activity of the Caledonians. These in the night attacked the ninth legion, and, having slain the sentinels, were already engaged in a sanguinary contest within the camp, when Agricola, informed of their movements by his scouts, commanded the fleetest of his horse and foot to follow in their track. The Caledonians having now an enemy to contend against in front and rear, were compelled to seek for safety in the shelter of their marshes and forests.

In the last year of his administration Agricola resolved on another expedition into Caledonia. For this purpose he assembled his sea and land forces, having added to the latter a corps of tried British auxiliaries. With these he advanced to the Grampian hills, where he found the Britons, under their general Calgacus, to the number of thirty thousand, drawn up in battle array, their foot being posted in lines on the declivity, while the chariots and horse occupied the level plain. In the centre of his battle Agricola placed eight thousand auxiliary foot; his legions were posted in front of the camp; three thousand horse were in the wings. As long as they fought with missiles, the advantage appears to have been on the side of the natives; but on the attack of three Batavian and two Tungrian cohorts with their pointed swords, the Britons, whose long ponderous swords without points and small targets were but ill fitted for close action, were compelled to give ground. On the advance of other cohorts their horse were put to flight, and the chariots driven in disorder among the infantry. Those of the Britons who had occupied the summit of the hills now descended, with the de-

sign of attacking the rear of the Romans, but were repulsed
by a body of cavalry which had been held in reserve by the
foresight of Agricola.   The following day exhibited to the
victors the spectacle of a vast solitude, at a distance the smoke
of burning dwellings, but not a vestige of a living being. The
loss of the Britons in this conflict is estimated at ten thousand, that of the Romans at three hundred and sixty.   The
army then retired into winter quarters, and the fleet, having
made the circuit of the island, returned to Sandwich (Portus
Trutulensis), from whence it had sailed. Triumphal ornaments
and the honour of a statue were decreed to Agricola, who
shortly after delivered up his province to a successor, returned
to Rome, which, according to order, he entered by night,
and, after a cold reception by Domitian, sank into obscurity
amid the servile crowd[1].

The quiet of the latter years in the greater part of South
Britain, not less than the power of arms in other districts of
the country, had now (when the Celtic tribes of the continent,
notwithstanding the fruitless endeavours of Cl. Civilis in
Belgic Gaul[2], had also submitted to the Romans) greatly
promoted the union of Britain with the Roman empire. The
politic and wise administration of Agricola completed the
Romanizing of the British Celts, and gave to the larger portion of Britain the form under which for several centuries it
was governed, and at the same time caused the political division of the country into the parts which from later settlers
have obtained the names of England and Scotland.   The
form of government under which the country was acknowledged as a part of Europe, while it destroyed the national
unity of the Britons, must in its connexion with the whole
administration of the empire be here briefly delineated.

The division into Britannia Inferior and Superior[3] is nearly
identical with the present one into England and Scotland.

---

[1] Tac. Agric. c. vii.—xl.   [2] Tac. Hist. iv. 15.   [3] Dio Cass. lv. 23.

The provinces were: Britannia Prima, or the district to the south of the Thames and the Bristol Channel; Britannia Secunda, the present principality of Wales; Flavia Cæsariensis, so called from the master of Agricola, which extended from the Thames to the Mersey and the Humber. Beyond the Humber, to the distance of twenty-five miles north of the Picts' wall, was the province of Maxima Cæsariensis, bordering on the fifth province Valentia, which extended to the firths, to the country beyond which the name of Vespasiana had, it is said, been given; but of which, as the memorial of a fruitless occupation, mention is made only in the work of Richard of Cirencester, discovered (if not fabricated) in the middle of the last century.

The supreme civil and military power in Britain was at first vested in a governor, who bore the high title of Legatus, or Consularis[1]. The Procurator or Quæstor administered the concerns of the imperial treasury, levied the land-tax, the poll-tax, and those laid on certain natural productions. Severus divided the government into two portions[2]. When Constantine parted the empire into four governments, Britannia fell to that which was placed under the Præfectus Prætorio Galliarum, who at first resided at Treves and subsequently at Arles. Under a vicar of the prefect, two consulars were appointed to the provinces of Maxima Cæsariensis and Valentia, and three presidents over those of Britannia Prima, Britannia Secunda, and Flavia Cæsariensis[3]. For the revenues of the country, a Rationalis Summarum Britanniarum, a Præpositus Thesaurorum Augustensium in Britanniis, and a Procurator Cynegii in Britannia Biennensis[4] were subordinate to the Comes Largitionum of the West.

[1] The title of Præfectus or Proprætor of Britain occurs only in later writers.

[2] Herodian. iii. 24.   [3] Zosim. ii. 33.   Not. Imp. Occid. c. lxviii.

[4] Not. Imp. c. xxxiv.   For *Biennensis* Pancirol. (p. 68) reads *Dremtensis*, but without adding any explanation.   Grævius (Thes. tom. vii.) has *Bentensis*, and *cynegii* instead of the *gynecii* of the earlier editors.

Under the Comes Largitionum Privatarum there was a special Rationalis Rei Privatæ per Britannias[1]. We can here give only an imperfect outline of the administration; the details, such as the amount of revenue, its increase or diminution, are totally unknown to us. It was not, however, till after the time of Appian[2] that the receipts of the state begun to cover the expenses of the government. The military force in Britain under the Magister Militum Præsentalis, which was intrusted to the Comes Militum Britanniarum, consisted of 2200 infantry and 200 cavalry; to the Comes Tractus Maritimi (at a later period, Litoris Saxonici per Britannias) 3000 infantry and 600 horse; and a still larger force to the Dux Limitum Britanniarum, of 14,000 infantry and 900 cavalry, forming together an army of 19,200 infantry and 1700 cavalry. The British Count had thirty-seven castella to defend; the Count of the Saxon shore, nine fortresses situated on the coast of South Britain, from the straits of Dover to Brancaster in Norfolk and Pevensey in Sussex[3]. The frontier fortresses were numerous and required strong garrisons.

The number of these officials and—when compared with the others of the empire—the narrow limits of the British province lead us to infer the existence of a sufficient object both for the activity and cupidity of those employed in the administration and their subalterns; an inference, indeed, which seems incompatible with the current opinion of the want of all civilization in the country. More important, however, for the Britons than those forms in which the am-

---

[1] Not. Imp. c. xli. [2] See his preface.

[3] Not. Imp. cc. xix., lxxii., and Pancirol. ibid. p. 157. The title of Comes Litoris Saxonici first occurs in the Notitia Imperii Occident. composed in the time of Arcadius and Honorius. The conservation of peace on the British coast on the Atlantic fell much more naturally to the Gaulish coast troops under the command of the Dux tractus Armoricani (Not. Imp. Occid. i. 86); though the chief command over the marine in those parts may, as in the instance of Carausius, have sometimes been held by one individual.

bition of a few Romans found a step to higher objects, or the rapacity of others sought the means of gratification, must have been the economy of the civic constitution; and here we behold those advantages, which even an enemy always brings to a previously isolated country. When the Romans abandoned Britain it contained twenty-eight cities, besides a considerable number of castella, ports, and small communities. Among the first, we know of two municipia, York and Verulam; nine colonies, Camulodunum (Maldon or Colchester), Rhutupiæ (Richborough), Londinium Augusta (London), Glevum Claudia (Gloucester), Thermæ Aquæ Solis (Bath), Isca Silurum (Carleon in Monmouthshire), Camboricum (Chesterford near Cambridge), Lindum (Lincoln), and Deva Colonia (Chester); also ten cities which had obtained the right of Latium: Pterotone (Inverness), Victoria (Perth), Durnomagus (Caister in Lincolnshire), Lugubalia (Carlisle), Cattaractone (Catterick), Cambodunum (Slack in Longwood), Coccium (Blackrode in Lancashire?), Theodosia (Dunbarton), Corinum (Cirencester), and Sorbiodunum (Old Sarum), the last colony to the south-west in the country of the free Damnonii. Volantium (Ellenborough in Cumberland), so rich in Roman remains, preserves an inscription, from which we learn that it had Decurions who assembled in a public building destined for the purpose[1]. These cities, therefore, possessed a council (Decuriones, Curiales, Municipes), with magistrates of their own choosing (Duumviri and Principales), and the right of contentious as well as of voluntary jurisdiction. To them was committed the levying of taxes in their districts, and it is known how the joint security of the civic decurions became both a burthen to themselves and brought the greatest obloquy on their order. That these abuses had also found their way into Britain, we learn from

---

[1] Petrie, C. H. p. cxiii. No. 123.   Horsl. B. R. 68.

an ordinance of Constantine for the remedying of the same
in this country[1]. Subsequently to the time of that emperor,
the Defensor elected by the whole city, more especially
against the oppressions of the governor, had become of consideration. The establishment of corporations at Rome, into
which certain artizans and handicraftsmen were united, was
extremely advantageous to them when they were removed
into foreign provinces. We find much information concerning these colleges in ancient inscriptions; and it is very probable that, together with the trades of Rome, this form of
social unions, as well as the hereditary obligation under
which the former were conducted, was propagated in Britain,
and was the original germ of those guilds, which became so
influential in Europe some centuries after the cessation of
the Roman dominion[2].

Great caution is necessary in endeavouring to show what
ancient British elements were preserved under the Romans.
From the Latin authors we can extract very little upon the
subject, and the old British accounts have reached us in a form
comparatively modern and demonstrably much corrupted.
In the larger eastern portion of the country, it is chiefly in
the names of rivers and mountains that the old British denominations have been preserved[3]; those of tribes and of
places being either wholly lost, or in their Roman disguise
scarcely to be recognised; while in Gaul the old names may
easily be traced. As rare exceptions may be mentioned a
few places known through commerce prior to the Roman
conquests in the north of Europe, viz. Vecta (the Isle of
Wight), Dubris (Dover), the county of Kent, and that universal mart on the Thames, which, though dignified by the

[1] Cod. Theod. xi. tit. 7, 2.

[2] 'Collegium lignatorum,' inscrip. at Middleby in Scotland : ' fabrorum,'
inscrip. at Chichester.   Horsley, B. R. pp. 337, 342.   Petrie, C. H. pp.
cxii, cxiii.   Cf. also Wilda, ' Das Gildenwesen im Mittelalter.'

[3] For a copious enumeration of these with illustrations, see Chalmers's
Caledonia, vol. i. p. 33–36.

Romans with the name of Augusta, has still preserved its ancient appellation of London[1].

It was otherwise beyond the mountains, the British Apennines, which separate the country into two portions, where, in the later territory of the Cymry, comprising Cumberland, the south-east of Scotland, Westmoreland and Lancashire; in Wales, Cornwall, Devonshire, Man and Anglesey, every philological deduction justifies the inference of a purer preservation of the British stock. Of the dialects and literature of Wales we shall have occasion to speak hereafter; it may, however, be here observed, that Cornwall, so late as the twelfth century, was by the Norwegians called Bretland[2], and until the middle of the sixteenth century only the primitive British or Lloegrian tongue was there spoken; since which time, through the reformation of the church and the spread of English printed books, it rapidly declined, till, about half a century ago, on the death of its last preserver, a very aged woman, it was entirely blotted from the list of living dialects[3]. Still longer has the old Celtic tongue been preserved in the Isle of Man[4]. With the old British terri-

[1] " Lundinium vetus oppidum, quod Augustam posteritas adpellavit." Amm. Marcell. xxvii. 8.

[2] See Theodoric the monk of Trondhjem, in Hist. et Antiq. Regum Norwegiæ, apud Langebek, Scriptores Rerum Danicarum, t. v. p. 315.

[3] From 1560 to 1602 the Cornish dialect greatly declined, and became limited to the western part of the county, where it was preserved till the beginning of the last century. Lhuyd (Archæologia Britannica, p. 225–253) gives a grammar of the Cornish. The printed books in this dialect are few, and only three or four in manuscript. Latterly, however, we are indebted to the late Davies Gilbert, Esq., for ' Mount Calvary,' and ' The Creation of the World,' 8vo. The first is in old Cornish with a slight mixture of Saxon or Norse. The other is in more modern Cornish, written in 1611. To both are added translations made by J. Knigwin in 1682, together with several small Cornish pieces. Cf. Borlase's ' Antiquities of Cornwall.' Oxf. 1758, folio. W. Price, ' Archæologia Cornu-Britannica, containing a Cornish Grammar and Vocabulary.' Sherborne, 1790, 4to. Daines Barrington on the expiration of the Cornish language, in Archæol. vol. iii. p. 279, vol. v. p. 81; also the treatises in Grose's ' Antiquarian Repertory,' vol. ii.

[4] See Henry Rowland's ' Mona Antiqua restaurata, with an Appendix

tories may perhaps be reckoned the tract of country extending from the Humber to the Firth of Forth, which after the
departure of the Romans was formed into two states, the
names of which, Deifyr and Bryneich, are undoubtedly British.   Here are also several British names of places that have
undergone but little corruption.

That British princes of the old reigning native families
were acknowledged by the Romans after the death of Cogidubnus, is by no means improbable, as, according to their
wise policy, it was thought useful, in the other provinces of
the empire, to preserve such mediators, as it were, between
themselves and nations wholly differing from them in speech,
habits, and notions of right ; yet as no mention of their names
is to be found even in the accounts of the several insurrec-
tions in Britain, nor on coins or other monuments, they must
have acted a part little beyond that of rich private individuals,
who were regarded by their oppressed countrymen with the
respect due to their lineage, as well as with lively sympathy,
and, sometimes, with secret hope. British tradition speaks of
princes of Colchester, of Cornwall, and among the ' Gewissi '
in Warwickshire and Worcestershire, during the sway of the
Romans, on which, however, a probable hypothesis may rest
in favour of the existence of certain princely families, from
whom many of the ancient, noble and wealthy races derived
their origin[1].

In no part of England are there fewer Roman remains than
among the Damnonii and in Wales.   To explain this slight
influence of the Romans by the supposition of greater pliancy

containing a comparative table of primitive and derivative words.' Lond.
1722 and 1766, 4to.   Also ' A Practical Grammar of the Ancient Gaelic,
or Language of the Isle of Man, usually called Manks,' by John Kelly,
Lond. 1808.   Some translations of the Scriptures exist in this dialect.

[1] The continuation of such princes in Britain with a subordinate authority is adopted by Whitaker (History of Manchester, i. p. 247).   By Gibbon (c. xxxi. note 184) the hypothesis is rejected, while Palgrave (Rise and
Progress, i. p. 324) favours it.   What is here stated may perhaps suggest
new grounds for the supposition.

and weakness in the natives of those parts is not justifiable, when we call to remembrance the noble struggles of the Silures : on the contrary, we may, both from the above circumstance and from the fact that the western coasts of England continued free from attacks from the opposite shore of Ireland, conclude that those people who were able to preserve the most striking sign of distinct nationality in their native tongue, continued in reality as respected allies of the Romans; the Roman chancery too might, in such a case, find it easy to forget, that to the unity of their power in Britannia Prima and Secunda some districts were wanting, and the treasury not unwillingly forgo the contributions and taxes of the coasts on the Atlantic.

This view of the limits of the real dominion of Rome, and of the condition of the western tribes, is in many respects important for later history : it explains and supports the British traditions, the accounts of the first introduction of Christianity, the state of the country after the departure of the Romans, and, in a degree, marks out the limits of the Anglo-Saxon conquests, which may frequently be traced by those of Roman Britain.

A fact worthy of notice in this place, is the existence down to recent times of the old British law of succession in Wales, Kent, and some parts of Northumberland, called Gavelkind. As far as we are enabled to understand it in its mixture with Anglo-Saxon law, all the sons of the same father inherited, but the youngest possessed the homestead ; the eldest, or the next following capable of bearing arms, had the heriot, that is, the arms offensive and defensive of his father, and his horse.   Even the son of an outlaw could not be deprived of the entire succession, but of the half only [1].

Of events in Britain under the Romans there is but little

---

[1] 'Ancient Laws and Institutes of Wales,' p. 266, and on the subject of Gavelkind in Kent see ' Statutes of the Realm,' vol. i.   The greater part of the usages there recorded are pure Germanic.

to relate.   A province has no individual existence ; its vege-
tative dreamlike being no history.   Most of the occurrences
of which it may have been the theatre, even the changes and
modifications in the machine of its government, belong to the
history of the empire or of its metropolis.   The laurels won
by British legions in distant lands seldom came to the knowledge, and still more seldom touched the hearts of their countrymen.   This last acquisition of a fragile state colossus was
particularly unfortunate : the culture of the Romans, grafted
with violence on the wild stock, not being that of the higher
intellectual life and exalted moral feeling, but of an age in
which talent and mental powers, deaf to the inward voice,
under, and in harmony with which they ought to be cultivated, were subservient only to sensuality, to all the failings
of humanity, and to the then prevailing disregard of the social
union.   Roman customs, Roman garb, and Roman extrava-
gance found entrance among the barbarians, with the temples,
language, and law of the metropolis of the world ; and every
benign as well as every hurtful influence of victory combined
to destroy the nationality of a conquered people amalgamated
with its conquerors.

From Scotland came the movement which, in the time of
the emperor Hadrian, awakened the spirit of British freedom
to new life, and to an apparently well-founded hope of totally
casting off the imperial yoke[1].   Though the Roman armies
maintained themselves in the elder province, the emperor,
nevertheless, deemed it advisable to retire from the boundary
line drawn and fortified by Agricola in Scotland[2], and, between
the Tyne and Solway Firth, to cast up a rampart with a ditch
—the Picts' wall still existing to the height of six feet—which

[1] Æl. Spart. Had. c. v.   Britanni teneri sub Romana ditione non po-
terant.   Fronto de Bello Parthico, § 4.   Hadriano imperium obtinente,
quantum militum a Britannis cæsum !   Orosius, vii. 17.   Severus victor in
Britannias defectu pene omnium sociorum trahitur.   Ubi magnis gravibus-
que præliis sæpe gestis, etc.   Cf. also Cassiodorus.
[2] Tac. Agric. c. xxiii.

should defend what was more strictly the Roman province[1]. An irruption of the Mæatæ, dwelling in the south of Scotland, was attended with the support and junction of many of the Brigantes, and probably of other Britons, seeing that they were able to penetrate to the Ordovices. They were, however, driven back by the proprætor Lollius Urbicus, who erected the rampart of earth bearing the name of his master, the emperor Antoninus Pius, between Caerriden on the Forth and Alcluid (Whiterne) on the Clyde[2]. Of a war in Britain during the reign of Marcus Antoninus[3], we know little more than the name of the Roman general, Calpurnius Agricola[4]. The emperor who, in the tranquillity of his palace, meditated on lessons of recondite wisdom, was satisfied if his name was bestowed on the northernmost monument of Roman sway; and the orator flattered both him and his people with the conceit that, in the delightful enjoyment of science and learning, he directed the helm of the mighty vessel of the state, as well as this remote warfare[5]. Under Commodus[6] the boundary wall was broken through by the Britons, to repel whom proved an arduous undertaking to the Roman general, Ulpius Marcellus[7]. He was succeeded by Clodius Albinus, who accepted the title of Cæsar, which had been offered to him by Commodus, from Severus[8], whose sole motive in conferring that honour seems to have been to lull suspicion in the mind of a

---

[1] A.D. 120. Æl. Spart. Had. c. xi.

[2] Jul. Capitol. de M. Anton. c. v. Horsley, B. R. p. 160. Petrie, C. H. p. cvii sqq. The account given in the text is the one generally followed, and in Graham's dyke traces of the rampart seem to be preserved : the inscriptions there found also refer to Antoninus ; still Pausanias (viii. 43. § 3.), under this supposition, remains to be explained, but whose account, nevertheless, agrees with the passage cited of Capitolinus, and is compatible with the hypothesis, that the vallum of Antoninus may have been raised near that of Hadrian, which had been destroyed by the Britons.

[3] A.D. 161–180.   [4] J. Capit. de M. Anton. c. viii.

[5] Fronto, cited by Eumenius (Panegyr. Const. Cæs. c. xiv.).

[6] A.D. 190–197.   [7] Dio ap. Xiph. lxxii. s. 8.

[8] Herod. ii. 48, iii. 16–23. Dio ap. Xiph. lxxiii. 14. J. Capit. cc. xiii., xiv. Aur. Vict. c. xx. Oros. vii. 17.

vain but potent officer, of whom he was jealous, and whose destruction he had resolved. On the intelligence that Severus was advancing with a hostile army, Albinus crossed with his forces over to Gaul: the armies met on the plain of Trevoux, near Lyons. For some time victory seemed to incline to the side of Albinus, Severus being unhorsed and disappearing from the field; but the arrival of fresh troops to his aid changed the face of things; the army of Albinus was routed, himself seized and beheaded in Lyons, where he had shut himself up from the commencement of the conflict. Having settled the affairs of Britain, Severus, as has already been observed, divided the government into two provinces[1].

At this time the power of the northern tribes had become so formidable, that the proprætor, Virius Lupus, was compelled not only to purchase with a considerable sum a short respite from the inroads of the Mæatæ, but to solicit either an additional force or the presence of the emperor himself. Though advanced in years and afflicted with gout, Severus obeyed the summons with alacrity. Attended by his sons, Antoninus Caracalla and Septimius Geta, he soon arrived in Britain, where he lost no time in making the most efficient preparations for the subjugation of the barbarians. To his younger son, Geta, he committed the civil administration of the province: Caracalla accompanied his father. On the arrival of the Romans beyond the limits of the province, the natives, though unfitted for regular warfare through the want of discipline and of defensive armour, harassed the Romans on their march, who, nevertheless, continued to advance, felling woods, levelling hills, rendering marshes passable, and constructing bridges. At length, after a loss of fifty thousand men, they reached nearly to the extremity of the island, where, having entered into a treaty with the natives, according to which a considerable portion of territory was to be yielded to the Romans, the emperor, who during the whole expedition

[1] Herodian. iii. 24.

had been borne in a covered litter, returned to York. On the intelligence of a fresh insurrection, Severus, whom age and sickness compelled to remain inactive, resolved on sending an army under Caracalla to extirpate the barbarians. That prince, however, who was far less intent on prosecuting the war than on corrupting the soldiery, in the view of excluding his brother from all share in the empire, on the death of his father, which shortly after took place at York[1], entered into a truce with the natives and returned to Rome[2].

Whether, after his expedition against the northern tribes, Severus enlarged and strengthened by a wall the rampart of Hadrian or that of Antoninus[3], is to the antiquary a question not devoid of interest; but in either case it is manifest that the south of the present Scotland was always a very insecure possession to the Romans, and in the hands of extremely doubtful allies, and that it was only in the modern England that Rome held any considerable influence.

The tranquillity which Britain enjoyed, with the exception of the northern border districts, began in this century to be disturbed by an event which, new in its kind and consequences in the history of the world, had on this country an incalculable influence. That element which had set a salutary limit to the hostile desolating wanderings of the savage, which is, as it were, appointed to be the securest medium and freest path for civilization and varied intercourse, was, in the north of Europe, in a state ill adapted to the purpose either of separation or communication. It was at that time infested with swarms of those daring pirates, to whom for many ages after

---

[1] A.D. 211.

[2] Dio ap. Xiph. lxxv. 5, lxxvi. 11–16, lxxvii. 1.   Herodian. iii. 46–51.

[3] The latter opinion has been started by Mannert; but would Dio (ap. Xiph. lxxvi. 12.) have said of the wall of Severus, if it were in Scotland, without thinking of that of Hadrian, that *it divides the island into two parts ?* He must also (l. 15.) have spoken in other terms of the new hostilities of the Mæatæ and Caledonians, if both people had, by the wall, been placed in a totally different position with regard to the Romans. Cf. also Smith's Beda, App. No. V.

it served as a home, and who, in their frail barks, exposing themselves to all the perils of the stormy ocean, evinced in every conflict the most desperate valour, with an endurance and skill in warfare, which, if applied to higher purposes, would have renewed in history the dazzling glory of Sparta and of ancient Rome.

In the historical records that have been handed down to us, the name of the Saxons does not occur before the end of the second century, when they are noticed as the possessors of the islands at the mouth of the Elbe, and probably also of the opposite districts of Holstein and Hadeln[1]. In the following century they became so troublesome to the Roman empire, through their piracies, that, for the purpose of warring against them and for the protection of the northern coasts, a commander was appointed by the emperors Diocletian and Maximian, in the person of Carausius, a Menapian[2], whose successor bore the title of Count of the Saxon shore[3]. But of such importance was this appointment, in consequence of the formidable power of the adversary, that Carausius, probably availing himself of the distraction caused by the Gaulish Bagaudæ, ventured, after entering into a compact and alliance with the Saxon pirates, to withdraw himself from subjection

---

[1] Ptol. Geogr. ii. 2.

[2] A.D. 287–296. ' Pirata.' Claud. Mam. ' Menapiæ civis.' Aur. Vict. de Viris Illust. c. xxxix. ' Bataviæ alumnus.' Eumen. ' Genere infimus.' Oros. vii. 25. ' Vilissime natus.' Eutrop. ix. 21. ' Juvenis in Britannia ex infima gente creatus.' Galf. Monum. v. 3. Richard of Cirencester, i. viii. 14, in speaking of the two Menapias (the Irish, and the present St. David's), says, "Harum unam, quam nam vero incertum, patriam habebat Carausius."

[3] This title first occurs in the ' Notitia Dignitatum Imperii,' compiled under Arcadius and Honorius. Earlier writers name him ' comes maritimi tractus ; ' a circumstance not to be overlooked, on account of the importance of the ' litus Saxonicum ' for the history of the Saxons. Of Carausius, Eutropius, (ix. 21) says, " Cum apud Bononiam, per tractum Belgicæ et Armoricæ, pacandum mare accepisset, quod Franci et Saxones infestabant, etc." Eumenius also in Constantio (c. xii.) says of the fleet of Carausius, " Quæ olim Gallias tuebatur."

to the Roman sceptre, to fortify Boulogne, and to assume the imperial title in Britain. The emperor Maximian found himself compelled to acknowledge him as a joint ruler, but without seeing an end put to the piracies, by which the coasts of the German ocean, of the Atlantic, and even of the Mediterranean were held in constant dread. Carausius had governed in this country for seven years, even after the loss of Boulogne, victorious against the Caledonians, and powerful in his internal administration, when· he fell by the hand of an assassin, his companion Allectus [1], who occupied his place for three years, when Asclepiodotus, the prefect of the emperor Constantius, having destroyed him and his forces, stormed London, and soon restored their most northern province to the dominion of the Cæsars [2].

The deeds of Augustus Carausius are of great moment for the later history of the country. Through him Britain first learned that it could maintain itself independent of Roman supremacy, and in security against its northern enemies; and the slumbering national spirit became, through this consciousness of self-dependence, powerfully excited [3]. He reigned chiefly by the help of Frankish warriors, under Roman forms

[1] Orosius, vii. 25. Aur. Vict. c. xxxix. Eutrop. ix. 22. Cf. Genebrier, Geschichte des Carausius aus Münzen (from the French, in the appendices to the 'Allegemeine Welthistorie,' Th. vi.). Stukeley's 'Medallic History of Carausius.' Some coins of Carausius and Allectus are given in Havercamp's 'Orosius,' p. 527. See also 'Eumenii Oratio pro restaurandis Scholis,' cc. xviii., xxi.

[2] Eumenius (Paneg. Const. cc. xv.–xvii.) is the only one of the ancients extant who gives the circumstances of the destruction of Allectus, with whose account Jeffrey of Monmouth agrees so closely, that we must suppose this extraordinary writer to have used ancient works no longer in existence. Even the name given by him of the defender of London, 'Livius Gallus,' is probably, like his other Roman names, genuine.

[3] A few years earlier a prefect of Britain, under the emperor Probus, having raised a rebellion, had by some artifice (περινοίᾳ οὐκ ἄφρονι) been circumvented and put to death by a minister of the emperor sent over for the purpose. Zosimus, i. 66.

of government, which, from their connexion with his memory, may have been held in a higher degree of veneration in the minds of later races[1].

But not less has Carausius influenced the later Germanizing of Britain by the Saxons. Himself a German by extraction, a Menapian by birth, if he did not cause the settling of the Saxons along the Saxon shore, in Gaul as well as in Britain, he at least promoted it by his alliance with them[2]. The prevailing opinion, that the ' Litus Saxonicum ' borrowed its name from the enemy to whose attacks it was exposed, appears as contrary to the principles of sound philology as it is unhistorical[3]. By the probably contemporaneous settlements of the Saxons on the Litus Saxonicum near Bayeux (to which, perhaps, the circumstance may partly be ascribed, that the manners and language of the French found slower admission into that place than into the other parts of Normandy[4]), the weakness of the Romans, even on the coasts of Gaul and elsewhere across the channel, is authentically shown, as well

[1] That the coins of Carausius, bearing the impress of the wolf and twins, were copied by the Bretwalda Æthelberht of Kent, can hardly be placed to the account of mere caprice. The circular temple, that remarkable and venerable relic which, till destroyed by the hand of modern barbarism, stood on the banks of the Carron, though in later times attributed to Julius Cæsar and to Arthur, was at a remoter period considered to be the work of Carausius. See Stukeley ; also Palgrave, vol. i. pp. 376, 377. Nennius, c. xix. Camden, and ' De Mirabilibus Britanniæ ' at the end of Hearne's Robert of Gloucester, p. 576.

[2] Eutropius, ix. 21, speaks only of the Belgian and Armorican coasts. Beda (H. E. i. 6.) here copies Orosius, who takes his account from Eutropius.

[3] See Palgrave, vol. i. p. 384, who takes the same view.—T.

[4] Grannona in litore Saxonico. Not. Imp. Occid. c. lxxxvi. Du Chesne, Hist. tom. i. p. 3. In the capitularies of Charles the Bald this district is called ' Otlingua Saxonica.' Bouquet, vii. p. 616. ' Saxones Bajocassini.' Greg. Turon. v. c. 27. a. 578. x. c. 9. Fortunati Carm. iii. 8, says, at the end of the sixth century, speaking of Felix, bishop of Nantes,

" Aspera gens Saxo, vivens quasi more ferino,
　　Te mediante, sacer, bellua reddit ovem."

as the proneness of the Saxons to similar settlements, of which also the ' Litus Saxonicum in Belgica Secunda' (Flanders)[1], not less than the just application of language, affords a further proof.

During the reign of Constantius Chlorus, the position of Britain in the Roman state must have been very prominent. Swayed both by inclination and probably by matrimonial connexions—his wife Helena being, it is said, the daughter, or at least the relative of a British prince[2]—and perhaps by the wish also to preserve this country to Rome, Constantius passed the greater part of his life in Britain. He died at York, where his son Constantine was proclaimed emperor. A German prince supported his nomination, a circumstance from which we may infer the presence of German warriors[3].

The name of Constantine the Great immediately reminds us of the rapid diffusion of Christianity during his time, and through him.

The Christian faith found at an early period, among both the Celtic and the German races, ready admission into Britain, and, even when persecuted, had, in solitary retirement, borne promising fruits for the future. It is, down to the latest times, so closely interwoven with the social constitution and, consequently, with the leading events of this country, that a glance at the history of religion is often indispensable for the illustration of political events. The ac-

[1] See Warnkönig, Flandrische Staats- und Rechtsgeschichte, vol. i. p. 95.

[2] Panegyr. Vet. pp. 192, 207. Henry of Huntingdon (lib. i., we know not on what authority) and Jeffrey of Monmouth (v. 6, 11.) give to this prince the name of Coel (of Colchester). On the other hand, in the ' Gesta Treberorum,' c. xxix., it is said, "Helena Treberorum nobilissima." Huntingdon relates, that the walls of London, existing in his time, were built by Helena. [It seems almost superfluous to remark, that Colchester derives its name, not from Coel, but rather from its ancient appellation, Colonia (Camulodunum).—T.]

[3] "Præcipue Eroco, Alamannorum rege, auxilii gratia Constantium comitato, imperium capit." Aur. Vict. Epit. c. xli. May not the name Erocus be a corruption of Ertocus, a Latinization of the Old-Saxon Heritogo (A.-S. Heretoga, Ger. Herzog), dux?

count that, less than thirty years after the death of the
Redeemer, a lady of distinction—Pomponia Græcina, the wife
of that Plautius whose victories in Britain had gained him the
honour of an ovation—adopted Christianity, stands probably
on no better foundation than other tales of a similar nature,
it being improbable that this lady ever set foot in Britain ;
yet as early as the close of the following century, Christianity
had advanced even into parts of Britain not subject to the
Romans, by which Cornwall and Wales are particularly to be
understood.　The agreement of the British with the Eastern
churches respecting the celebration of Easter[1], shows a conformity most satisfactorily, perhaps, to be accounted for by
the supposition of an historic basis for the several legends respecting the preaching of the doctrines of Christ by oriental
apostles.　It is even probable that the first tidings of the new
faith did not come from Rome, where it was still under oppression, but rather from one of those congregations of Asia
Minor, which the Mediterranean had long held in connexion
with Gaul, and from whence, by the great public roads, the
spirit of conversion easily found its way to Britain[2].

Less objectionable seems the tradition of the adoption of
Christianity by the British prince Lever Maur (the Great
Light), or Lucius, on comparing it with the testimony of
Tertullian[3].　Lucius is reported to have sent Fagan and
Dervan to Rome, for the sake of receiving from the bishop
Eleutherius more accurate instruction in the doctrines of
Christianity; whereupon Roman missions passed over to Bri-

---

[1] It appears that in the beginning of the fourth century the Britons and
Romans kept Easter on the same day. Euseb. Pamph. de Vita Constant,
iii. 19. κοινῇ πάντων ἤρεσε κρίσει, τὴν ἁγιωτάτην τῦ Πάσχα ἑορτὴν μιᾷ καὶ
τῇ αὐτῇ ἡμέρᾳ συντελεῖσθαι.　Cf. also Socrat. Hist. v. 22.　Conc. Arelat.
(Spelman, pp. 40, 42) and Lingard, H. E. vol. i. p. 45 *note*, edit.1837.—T.

[2] For the traditions respecting Glastonbury, see Will. Malmesb. 'De
Antiquitatibus Glastoniensis Ecclesiæ, apud Gale,' t. i.　Also Warner's
' History of the Abbey of Glastonbury,' 1826, 4to, who, by the way, gives
credit to the tradition of St. Paul's preaching in Britain.

[3] Adv. Jud. c. vii.

tain, and there founded three archbishoprics and twenty-eight bishoprics[1]—denominations which are of course to be understood in the sense of the time. The supposition seems by no means unreasonable, that the Anglo-Saxon Romanists, in their disputes with the British followers of the eastern church, would, in such tales, provide themselves with a weapon of controversy; yet how is it that we find them in a complete form precisely in those authors who have translated the old British authorities[2]?

Gaul, in the time of the predecessors of Eleutherius, had very numerous Christian congregations, which have been ennobled by the persecutions they underwent at Lyons and Vienne, in the year 177; fleeing from which, many of their members may have increased the number of believers among the kindred Britons. The controversy between the Jewish and the heathen Christians upon several external matters, and especially the celebration of Easter, had already at that time

[1] This number is, no doubt, connected with the catalogue of the twenty-eight cities of Britain mentioned in Nennius, c. ii.

[2] Beda (H. E. i. 4.) places Lucius (who, according to Jeffrey of Monmouth, died in 156) in the time of Marcus Aurelius, to the beginning of whose reign he assigns the date 156, instead of 161. In lib. v. c. 24, he places Eleutherius in the years 167–182. Nennius gives 167 as the year of the conversion of Lucius. In his 'Chronicon' Beda places this event in 180, which agrees better with the regnal years of pope Eleutherius, 167–182, or, according to 'Anastasii Vitæ Pontificum,' 179–194, where mention is made of Lucius in the words used by Beda in his history, " Hic accepit epistolam a Lucio, Britanniæ rege, ut Christianus efficeretur per ejus mandatum," of which passage the last three words are wanting in Beda's 'Chronicon.' On the other hand, Anastasius agrees with the 'Chronicon' in mentioning, under Victor, the successor of Eleutherius, the document (libelli) of the latter relative to the celebrating of Easter. If Beda had had the 'Vitæ Pontificum' before him, the account of Lucius must gain considerably in point of historic credibility; at the same time the confusion in the chronology is quite inexplicable. Not less hazardous does it appear to assume that the author of the 'Vitæ Pontificum' had both of Beda's works at hand. A thorough examination of the 'Gesta' or 'Vitæ Pontificum' would probably lead to the discovery of a common source to both authors. With regard to the accounts of Jeffrey of Monmouth, it may not be amiss to notice that he appeals (iv. 20.) to a work of Gildas, 'De Victoria Aurelii Ambrosii.' See Pref. to Stevenson's edit. of 'Gildas,' p. xi.

engaged the minds of men, and, among the new converts, who belonged to neither party, but had at once sprung from druid-ism, occasioned new scruples. Without, therefore, attaching much importance to later embellishments of the account of a mission from a distinguished British chieftain to Eleutherius, we may, perhaps, assume, that the former might have applied to the head of the Western church, with the view of effecting an arrangement of the contradictory opinions prevailing among the Christians under his dominion.

The gradual spread of Christianity in Britain drew upon it the unpropitious eye of the pagan emperors, and the perse-cution of the Christians under Diocletian has left behind it a terrific remembrance also in this country. The martyrdom of St. Alban at Verulam, and of the two citizens of Caerleon upon Usk, Aaron and Julius, could not be obscured, even in the following times of relapse into paganism[1]. The Christian faith and the measures adopted for its preservation were, however, not yet entirely suppressed. Under Constantius, the mild successor of Diocletian, Christianity again ventured to show itself, and under Constantine we meet with the names and dioceses of three British bishops, who were present at the first Council of Arles: Eborius of York, Restitutus of London, and Adelfius of Lincoln[2], and at the same time learn the dissidence of their tenets from those of the Romish church. This account supports a tradition, which has been too much called in doubt, that, besides the above-mentioned, Wales also (Britannia Secunda) had a bishop at Caerleon, and the most northern province one at St. Andrews (anciently Albin), and that each of these bishoprics was divided into twelve districts[3]. However erroneous this tradition may be

---

[1] Gildas, c. viii. Beda, i. 7.

[2] A.D. 314. Spelman, Conc. t. i. p. 42. The see of Adelfius is there called " Colonia Londinensium," for which, with Henry, I prefer reading ' Col. Lindum,' than to render it by ' Richborough.'

[3] Girald. Cambr. (' De Jure et Statu Menev. Eccl.,' ap. Wharton, 'Anglia Sacra,' t. i. p. 542) appeals to " tomum Anacleti papæ, sicut in pontifi-calibus Romanorum gestis et imperialibus, directum Galliarum episcopis."

in naming five archbishoprics and sixty bishoprics, it may, nevertheless, essentially not be void of foundation.

The first half of the fourth century is chiefly remarkable as regards Britain, on account of the harmony with which the natives and Romans, as well as other settlers—brought together in no small number by their common faith—united in the arts of peace[1]. The cultivation of grain had been carried to such a height, that Britain became the granary of the northern provinces of the empire, and by yearly exports supplied other countries with food, while it enriched itself[2]. Civic establishments were so flourishing, that builders and other artificers were demanded from Britain for the restoration of the desolated provinces[3].

The country was crossed by high-roads in various directions, many of which have served the later settlers in their marches, as well as their commercial operations. It is probable that the Romans themselves found some of these great highways already in existence, which were afterwards known by the names of Watling Street, leading from the southern shore of Kent, by Rhutupiæ and London, through St. Alban's and Stony Stratford to Caernarvon[4] (Segontium). Ikenild, or Rikenild Street, from Tynemouth, through York, Derby, and Birmingham to St. David's. The Irmin (Ermin) Street led from the latter place to Southampton ; the Foss from Cornwall to Caithness, or, perhaps, more correctly, only to Lincoln[5].

---

[1] "Britannia......terra tanto frugum ubere, tanto læta munere pastionum, tot metallorum fluens rivis, tot vectigalibus quæstuosa, tot accincta portubus." Eumen. Paneg. Const. Cæs. c. xi. Cf. ejusdem Paneg. Const. Aug. c. ix.

[2] Amm. Marcell. xviii. 2. Libanii Orat. x. t. ii. p. 281. Zosimus, iii. 5. Julian. Imp. ad S. P. Q. Athen. Epist. Eunapii Legat.

[3] Eumen. Paneg. Const. Cæs. c. xxi.—T.

[4] To Cardigan. Higd. Polychron.

[5] H. Hunt. lib. i., followed by Robert of Gloucester, ' Ric. Corinæus de Situ Britanniæ,' lib. i. c. 7, and ' Commentary on the Itinerary,' p. 110 sq. edit. 1809. R. Higden, Polychron, lib. i. cap. ' De Plateis Regalibus.' Whitaker's Hist. of Manchester, vol. i. p. 102 sq.

These roads, which, if not formed, were at least greatly improved by Roman labour, prove by their direction a lively internal traffic, as well as a commercial connexion with the countries lying east and west of Britain[1].

We are accustomed to regard Roman influence and Roman civilization in Britain as considerably less than in the southern provinces of the empire, chiefly because the language of modern England is not immediately based on that of Rome, and but few ancient monuments have been preserved in the country. Of these the number has been greatly diminished by frequent and early devastations, more especially in the richest provinces, and those first possessed by the Romans; yet, even in our days, many have been discovered, which sufficiently prove to us the importance of Roman Britain[2]. Many remains of Roman buildings, on sites long since traversed by the ploughshare, or from which, as from seed, modern towns have sprung up, were visible as late as the twelfth and thirteenth centuries[3]. Besides the two municipal towns, the remote Caerleon (the City of the Legion, Isca Silurum) also had its theatres, temples, and palaces, of which Giraldus speaks in terms of high admiration[4], and for which like Bath (Aquæ Solis), it may have partly been indebted to its hot springs. At a later period we have an account of various subterranean antiquities in the city of Chester (Deva)[5]. To the excavated remains of a temple of Neptune and Minerva at Chichester we are indebted for some highly important disclosures relative to the history of Britain under the Romans; but the most complete idea of Roman building is presented to us in a villa discovered at Bignor in Sussex; also in the

---

[1] The course of these roads is very uncertain. Compare Ric. Corin. with Higden.—T.

[2] See Horsley, 'Britannia Romana.'

[3] Will. Malmesb. de Gestis Regum, lib. i. c. 1. Id. de Gestis Pontificum, lib. iii. Prooem.

[4] Girald. Cambren. Itin. Camb. lib. i. c. 1. ap. Camden.

[5] R. Higden, Polychr. ap. Gale, i. 200.

antiquities at Woodchester in Gloucestershire[1]. Beda likewise mentions the Roman towns, lighthouses, roads, and bridges existing in his time[2]. Many a sacred spot of antiquity offers itself to our knowledge through the holier consecration it has received from Christianity, always ready to apply and hallow every legacy of the past. St. Peter's church and abbey at Westminster, St. Paul's cathedral at London, will appear to us only the more venerable, if we call to mind that at the former, in times remote, the worship of Apollo contributed to the culture of a rugged race, and at the latter, that a temple of Diana was mediate to the faith of so many people. Thus the Angles and the Saxons, when they had established themselves in Britain, dwelt within Roman walls, and walked amid spacious structures and beautiful works of Roman art. Ought it then to surprise us, if, when first made sensible, on their conversion to Christianity, of the necessity of new and ample edifices, they strove to restore the architecture of the Romans in their country, and that structures in imitation of the same were afterwards erected, which have erroneously been regarded as original productions of Saxon art. Of Roman vestiges, those of ramparts and fortresses are oftenest to be met with, though it is not to be denied that these, through their equivocal character, have but too often given rise to misconceptions and inveterate errors. As undoubted Roman remains may be cited those at Richborough (Rhutupiæ), Lincoln (Lindum), Burgh Castle in Suffolk (Gariannonum), Chester (Deva). At Dorchester vestiges of an amphitheatre are still visible.

From the great number of Roman towns and garrisons in Britain, it may be inferred that an intimate connexion sub-

[1] See Sam. Lysons's splendid work on this subject, London, 1797, 1815 : also his ' Reliquiæ Britannico-Romanæ,' 3 vol. fol. Lond. For Roman temples and other buildings at Bath, see Lysons, also Carter's ' Ancient Architecture of England.'

[2] H. E. i. 11. Vita S. Cuth. xxvii. Malmesb. de Gestis Pontif. ap. Savile, p. 258.

sisted between the Romans and the natives.   Hence the Roman language also had found general admission among the
provincials, as is evident from the number of Latin words occurring in the Welsh tongue; and in the British historical
traditions, as they have been preserved by Nennius, Jeffrey
of Monmouth, and others, we meet with too many points of
resemblance with Roman history and tradition, to allow the
supposition of a total abolition of the Roman tongue, with
the cessation of Roman sway, and the temporary extinction
of Christianity.

For their superiority as shipmen it has been thought that
the Britons were indebted to the Romans, though we know that
the Roman troops stationed in the island were by no means
a match by sea even for their usual enemy, the Saxons[1], and
that they were not practised in sea-fights.   The dwellers
along the shores of the Mediterranean may, perhaps, have
taught the rovers of the North an improved style of ship-
building, but confidence on the rocking element, the direct
dartlike course over and through the wild towering billows,
the placid gaze which spies the wind, ere its approach, on the
far distant curling surge, the unquenchable delight in the
amphibious life of a seaman—these have been brought to
Britain only by Saxons and Northmen; and not only does
the English language, but even those of southern Europe declare, who are the people called by nature to be master of the
vessel and the wave.

We must now turn from the subject of Roman civilization
in Britain, and cast a glance on those nations which chiefly
contributed to its extirpation[2]—to the Picts and Scots, who
are first mentioned as making their appearance in the present
Scotland in the fourth century.   Both these tribes were

---

[1] The passage of Eumenius (Paneg. Const. c. xii.) which has been cited
in proof of the maritime proficiency of the Romans, rather says that Carausius employed many foreigners—"exercitibus nostris in re maritima
novis."   [2] A.D. 364.

nearly related to the Caledonians and Mæatæ, though they
appear to have been more barbarous. It is certain that the
Scots, and probably the Picts likewise, passed over from Ireland and reduced the earlier inhabitants to subjection. Their
name, Picti, is by no means an appellation bestowed on enemies with painted bodies, but is a Roman corruption of
Peght[1]. They dwelt in the eastern part of Scotland, on both
sides of the Grampian hills, from Inverness and Elgin to
Dunbarton, or from the Firth of Murray to those of Forth
and Clyde, but, at a later period, in the south-west of Scotland, as far as the Picts' wall, where, on the river Nith in
Dumfriesshire, we meet with a particular tribe of them, the
Nithwaras[2]. In the south of Scotland the rustic still points
to many a memorial of the Picts, consisting of old walls and
excavations. The Scottish kings in the ninth century included their name among their titles. Pictland was attacked
by the Norwegians, and in the famous battle of the Standard,
in the year 1138, also in that of Clithero, the Peghts of Galloway[3] fought with their native savage valour. As no remains exist of a particular tongue spoken by this people, nor
even any accounts of its existence or decay, British antiquaries have indefatigably contended, some for a Gothic, and
others for a Celtic origin of the Pictish language—a dispute
certainly about less than words, for one or two very ancient
names of mountains, which at the present day we are unable
to explain by our insufficient knowledge of the old Gaelic,
can afford no proof of a distinct Pictish tongue, which probably differed from that of other British and Irish tribes only
in being a more barbarous dialect.

[1] Even Wittekind gives them their right name. Eumenius (Paneg.
Const. c. vii.) is the first who mentions them, " Caledonum aliorumque
Pictorum silvas et paludes." Amm. Mar. xxvii. 11. " Britanni Pictis mo-
do et Hibernis assueti hostibus."

[2] Bedæ Vitæ S. Cuthb. c. xi.   Cf. ejd. H. E. i. 1; iii. 4; v. 21. and
Chron. a. 452.

[3] See the Rev. R. Garnett's communication to the Philological Society,
June 9, 1843, p. 123.—T.

Together with the Scots, mention is also made of the At-tacotti[1]. A tribe of these, the Dalreudini, in the southern part of Argyleshire and the neighbouring isles preserved the name of their original home in Ulster. Historeth, son of Istorin, was the name of their leader, a name which has pro-bably no more historic truth in it, than that of Reuda as-signed to him by other traditions[2]. These were followed by their countrymen from Irin (Ierne, Hibernia) in multitudes, and it is probable, that under the name of Scots, against whom the Romans fought, we must frequently understand their kinsmen also, who left Ireland solely for the purpose of joining them. From West Wales, or the territory of the Dimetæ, as far as which they had endeavoured to extend their conquests, it is related that they were for ever driven by Cunedda Wledig, afterwards Prince of Gwynedd, who with his sons came from Manau Guotodin, before the Romans had yet left the other parts of the island[3].

The consideration of the old British princely families be-gan to revive when the pressure of the Roman government was lightened. The princes of Strathclyde and North Wales traced their descent from Cunedda Wledig, or the Glorious (a title answering to that of Cæsar Augustus), and to his an-cestor Coel, as did the Cornish dynasty to Bran ap Llyr[4], the ancestor of Arthur, and of those other heroes whose valour enabled them to avert the total subjection of their mountain followers by the Romans, and afterwards by the Saxons and the Danes[5].

Under Constantius, the son of Constantine, the condition

---

[1] Amm. Mar. xxvi. 4 ; xxvii. 8.   Hieron. Epist. lxxxii. ad Oceanum. Nennius, c. viii.

[2] Nennius, c. viii.   Bedæ H. E. i. 1.

[3] Nennius, c. viii. lxvi. Appen.   As Cunedda is said to have come to Gwynedd 146 years before the reign of Mailcun, who died A.D. 547, the date 370–380 is here given.   Guotodin is supposed to have been on the eastern coast of the south of Scotland.

[4] So called in Jeffrey of Monmouth.

[5] See Gunn in ' Historia Brittonum,' p. 119.

of Britain was rendered particularly deplorable by the tyranny
of the notary Paulus, a Spaniard by birth, who had been sent
by the emperor for the purpose of prosecuting certain individuals of the army accused of participation in the conspiracy
of Magnentius. This man, availing himself of the opportunities afforded him by his station, hesitated not, by means of
false accusations, to sacrifice the liberty and life of those individuals whose fortunes offered a temptation to his rapacity.
Martinus the pro-prefect, who had long lamented the sufferings of the innocent, finding his intercession vain, threatened
to resign his charge. Alarmed hereupon for the permanency
of his own power, Paulus took measures to involve him in the
common ruin, when, urged by the feelings of the moment,
Martinus attacked the notary with his sword, but failing to
strike a mortal blow, he plunged the blade into his own side,
a victim to his hatred of oppression and cruelty. Paulus
now freed from restraint set no bounds to his barbarity ;
many, loaded with chains, were led to torture, while many
were proscribed and driven into exile, or perished by the
sword of the executioner. Though applauded for his services by Constantius, by Julian, the succeeding emperor,
Paulus was condemned to be burnt alive[1].

In the century after the death of Constantine the Great,
during which Britain still continued a part of the Roman
empire, we know little more of the country than that it was
the theatre of devastation, caused by the Celtic and Germanic
tribes. It had indeed long been a school of war by land and
sea for the Romans, out of which many a conspicuous character arose, as well as the germ of new rebellions. The
anti-emperor Bonosus, who vainly strove to wrest from the
emperor Probus the island of Britain—which usually fell to
those tyrants who had made themselves masters of Gaul—
was the son of a rhetorician or pædagogue of British origin[2].

[1] Amm. Mar. xiv. 5, xx. 2.
[2] A.D. 280. Vopiscus de Probo, c. xviii. [Domo Hispaniensis fuit, origine

The Pannonian Valentinus, when banished to Britain, found there both friends and aid in his rebellion against the emperor Valentinian, the suppression of which, even after the capture and death of the chiefs, required all the prudence of the general Theodosius[1]. This success, but yet more his glorious triumph over the Picts and Scots[2], who had advanced as far as London and slain the general, Fullofaudes, and the count of the marine district, Nectaridus, the re-establishment of the province of Valentia, the restoration of the towns and garrisons, the security of the camps and frontiers, and the amelioration of the civil government, obtained for the British leader that renown and influence which raised himself to the rank of magister equitum, and contributed to the elevation of his yet more fortunate son to the imperial purple, by whom that dignity was once more, and for the last time, ennobled. Britain possessed also an upright, though severe governor in Civilis, and in Dulcitius, a general distinguished for his knowledge of the art of war[3].

But the spirit of independence had already stricken too deep a root for the example of Carausius ever to be without imitators. Maximus, of a distinguished British family[4], had gained the highest reputation in the wars against the Picts and Scots[5]. He was, against his will, proclaimed emperor by the army[6]; and in the treason of the warrior posterity would have seen only the strong national feeling of the noble Briton, had he not left his island realm, and, seduced by early success, been desirous of founding at Treves a Western Roman empire, which was at first acknowledged by Theo-

Britannus : Galla tamen matre ; ut ipse dicebat, rhetoris filius ; ut ab aliis comperi, pædagogi litterarii.   Id. de Bonoso, c. xiv.—T.]

[1] Amm. Mar. xxviii. 3.   [2] A.D. 368.
[3] Amm. Mar. xxviii. 3; xxvii. 8.   Claud. de Consul. Honorii.
[4] See the authorities in Palgrave, vol. i. pp. 381, 383.
[5] Prosp. Tyro, a. 382.
[6] Prosp. Tyro, a. 381.   Prosp. Aquitan. a. 384.   Sulp. Sev. Vita S. Martini, c. xx.   Orosius, vii. 34. and from him, Bedæ H. E. i. 9.   Paulus Diac. lib. xi.   Greg. Turon. i. 38.

dosius. He was taken prisoner at Aquileia and put to death[1]. His young son Victor, whom he had declared emperor and left behind in Gaul, shared the same fate[2]. Hence, though we must look with great mistrust on the Welsh pedigrees[3], which derive the independent princes of Gwent and Powys, as well as the more powerful ones of Cumberland and Strathclyde, from Constantine, who is described as the eldest son of this emperor, yet the impression must be acknowledged to have been extremely deep made on the Britons by the deeds of Maximus.

An event connected with the history of this prince may not be passed without notice; namely, the settlement of a Roman military colony (milites limitanei, læti), consisting of British warriors, in Armorica, which has given name, as well as a distinct character and history to the province of Bretagne[4]. Though that country had from the earliest times, by descent, language, and druidism, been related to Britain, yet the new colonists, who were followed by many others, both male and female[5], served unquestionably to bind more closely and to preserve the connexion between Bretagne and the Britons of Wales and Cornwall; and but for this event, the heroic poetry of France and Germany had probably been without the charm cast over it by the traditions of the Sangraal, of Tristan and Isolde, of Arthur and of Merlin. But Britain was thereby deprived of her bravest warriors, and

---

[1] A.D. 388.

[2] Prosp. Aquitan. a. 388. Orosius, vii. 35. Paul. Diac. lib. xii. Nennius, c. xxvi.

[3] See Gunn in Hist. Britt. p. 141.

[4] Gildas, c. x. Nennius, c. xxiii. Beda (H. E. i. 12) copies the words of Gildas. It is not apparent why Gibbon (c. xxxviii. note 136), who else frequently follows these authors, here wholly rejects them. See also Palgrave, vol. i. p. 382.

[5] The tradition of St. Ursula and the eleven thousand virgins who followed the colony of warriors, is recorded by Jeffrey of Monmouth, lib. v., according to whom the arrival of many of them in the Rhenish districts is not unfounded. See also my little work on Helgoland, note 17.

thence the more easily became an early prey to foreign invaders.

Scots, Picts, and Saxons continued to trouble Britain, and even the excellent administration of the vicar Chrysanthus[1] came too late to restore the state of things. Stilicho indeed felt himself at first powerful enough to send a body of Roman troops to the aid of the afflicted province, who both fulfilled the object of their mission, and, as tradition informs us, exhorted the natives to construct a wall across the island from sea to sea, as a barrier against the northern barbarians[2]. But the Roman general himself soon stood in need of all his united forces for the defence of Italy against the hordes of Alaric. The troops, a few years after, returned to Britain, but the country had in the meanwhile suffered new devastations from the Celtic invaders.

The Roman legions were soon afterwards, on the occupation of Gaul by the Alani, the Suevi, and the Vandals[3], withdrawn from the island by the emperor Honorius, who was compelled to leave it to its fate. An emperor of Britain was elected in the person of Marcus[4], who, being slain, found a successor to his dignity and his fate in Gratian, a burgher of a British municipal town[5]. The memory of Constantine

---

[1] Socratis H. E. vii. 12.

[2] [Or rather to restore the one already constructed.—T.] See Gildas, c. xii. This tradition is remarkable for the confusion it has caused : having been adopted by Beda (H. E. i. 12. and Chron. a. 426) it has frequently been copied. Nennius (Rubric to c. xxiv.) mixes the story with the older accounts of the wall of Severus, by the interpolation of a new emperor, Severus II., who built a wall from Boggenes (Bowness) to Tynemouth ; consequently, where Hadrian had caused the first wall of earth to be raised. Rich. Corinæus (De Situ Brit. ii. i. 37.) also considers the wall as the work of Stilicho, and appeals to the passage of Claudian (In Prim. Cons. Stilichonis, ii. 247) :—

" Me (Britanniam) quoque vicinis pereuntem gentibus, inquit,
Munivit Stilichon," etc.

[3] Oros. vii. 40, and from him Paul. Diac. Beda, i. 11.

[4] A.D. 406.

[5] Oros. vii. 40. Olymp. ap. Photium. Zosim. vi. 2. Sozom. ix. 11.

the Great was, after the lapse of a century, so highly revered in his real or adopted country, that the possession of that illustrious name, which at the time was borne by a humble soldier, procured for him the vacant British throne; though the vigour which also gained him the dominion of Gaul and Spain[1], might well justify the supposition, that a descent from the emperor Constantine and consanguinity to British princes raised him to that eminence[2]. He probably yielded to the hope of rendering his dignity and power hereditary; his son Constans having, it is said, exchanged the cowl for the diadem[3]. Honorius saw himself compelled to acknowledge Constantine as emperor[4]; but the count Constantius having proceeded to Gaul with an army, shut him up in Arles, took him prisoner and put him to death[5]. Constans his son was slain at Vienne by his count Gerontius[6]. Britain, however, never returned to Roman subjection, but continued under rebellious tyrants or pseudo-emperors[7].

A new inroad of the Picts and Scots appears to have occasioned a mission from Britain to Rome, which, in mourning weeds, had to deprecate the murder of the Roman generals in the last rebellion, and to implore forgiveness and protection[8]. Roman troops came over once more, to defend a province which contained not a little Roman property and interest; perhaps also, under the pretext of punishing the rebels, to get possession of the remaining treasures of the inhabitants[9]: but having repelled the invaders, the Roman cohorts were obliged to hasten away to warfare in distant regions, after

---

[1] A.D. 409. Oros. vii. 40, who adds, "sine merito virtutis." Olymp. ap. Phot. Zosim. vi. 3. Sozom. ix. 11. Procop. i. 2. Prosp. Aquit. a. 407.

[2] Procop. (i. 2) calls him οὐκ ἀφανῆ ἄνδρα.—T.

[3] Oros. vii. 40. Galf. Mon. vi. 5, who says that he had been a monk at Winchester.

[4] Olymp. ap. Phot. Zosim. v. 43.

[5] A.D. 412.

[6] Oros. vii. 42. Procop. i. 2.

[7] Procop. i. 2.

[8] Gildas, c. xii. Nennius, c. xxvii.

[9] " Hac tempestate præ valitudine Romanorum vires funditus attenuatæ Britanniæ." Prosp. Tyro, a. 409. Cf. also Sax. Chron. a. 418. Nennius, c. xxvii.

having repaired the forts along the wall, and the watch-towers on the sea-coasts, and left behind them arms for models, with instructions how to use them[1].

This gift availed but little—the Britons being not only strangers to the use of arms, but, in a still greater degree, to concord—for the re-establishment of the common good in the forsaken land, in which every town and every petty chieftain aspired to perfect independence. The Roman officials who had been left behind were driven from the island, and the emperor Honorius, conscious of his weakness, renouncing for the present all hopes of replacing them, authorized the British states to undertake their own defence: but liberty proved as useless to the Britons as the cunning did to the court of Ravenna, with which it appeared to grant what it had not the power to hinder[2]. The enemies from the north of the island soon returned, and the feeble inhabitants were unable either to defend their towns, or to escape from the murderous weapons of their foes. To this state of helplessness were added famine, and the pestilence which at that time raged throughout Europe[3].

Of one victory only, which for a short time checked the progress of the piratical Saxons and the Picts, has any tradition been preserved: this, from the cry of onset, bears the name of the Hallelujah victory[4]. The Gaulish bishop, St. Germain of Auxerre, during his stay in the island, in the year 429, is said to have led the orthodox Britons on this occasion, strengthening them by the penetrating virtue of his ghostly promises[5].

---

[1] Gildas, c. xiv. Nennius, c. xxvii.

[2] Zos. vi. 5, 10. aa. 409 and 410. The Saxon Chronicle (which places the landing of Cæsar in the year 60 a.c.) agrees remarkably herewith: it says (a. 409) that "they (the Romans) altogether ruled in Britain 470 years since Caius Julius first sought the land." So likewise Beda, H. E. i. 11, and v. 24. a. 409, "Roma a Gothis fracta; ex quo tempore Romani in Brittania regnare cessarunt."

[3] Gildas, cc. 19, 22.

[4] "Alleluiam tertio repetitam sacerdotes exclamant." Beda, i. 20.—T.

[5] Gildas, c. xviii., seems to allude to this victory. Cf. Beda, i. 17 ; Chron.

Yet once again a supplicating embassy was sent to the
Roman general Ætius, during his third consulship, in the
year 446. "The barbarians," said the ambassadors, "drive
us to the sea, the sea to the barbarians, we are massacred or
must be drowned[1]." Ætius was unable to help them. The

a. 459. Nennius. Prosp. Aquit. a. 429. Constan. Vita S. Ger. c. l. 28, also
Beda, i. 20, where the reading ' Saxones,' sanctioned by the best MSS., and
by the life of Germanus by Constantius, written within forty years of his
death, ought not to be questioned. To this expedition of the Saxons the
accounts refer which place the first landing of the Saxons in Britain in the
year 428 or 429 ; in the Appendix too of Nennius (Petrie, C. H. p. 77),
where "Felice et Tauro consulibus" indicates the year 428. Nennius,
c. xi., reckons, that till the fourth (twenty-fourth) year of King Mervin,
in which he wrote, viz. A.D. 858, 429 years had passed since the Saxons
first landed in Britain ; for which event, therefore, the half of 858, or the
year 429 is to be assigned. At a later period also this date is given.
Osbern, Precentor of Canterbury in the eleventh century, in his ' Life of
Dunstan,' speaking (cap. i.) of the year of Dunstan's birth, says, "Regnante Anglorum rege Ethelstano, anno quidem imperii ejus primo, adventus
vero Anglorum in Britanniam quadringentesimo nonagesimo septimo." The
editors (' Acta Sanctorum ' ed. Papebrock, Maii 19, t. iv. 359. Wharton,
' Anglia Sacra,' ii. 90 and 94) have been desirous of altering this number
into 479, and, supposing the year 449 as that of the coming of the Saxons,
have placed the birth of Dunstan in the year 928, which is the fourth of
the reign of Æthelstan, thereby making Dunstan so young, that Wharton
(p. 94) accuses Osbern of falsehood. But Osbern was not thinking of the
year 449, but of 428, according to which Dunstan would be born in 925, with
which the Saxon Chronicle agrees, which year is also the first of the reign
of Æthelstan. In the edition also of Nennius by Mark the Hermit, the
landings of the Saxons are confused between the years 429 and 447. In the
beginning of his work (p. 45) Mark gives the date of its composition very
accurately, viz. "Quintus annus Eadmundi, regis Anglorum," or A.D. 946,
according to our reckoning, or 976 according to the reckoning of the Welsh,
if, from Mark, c. i., and Nennius, cc. xi. xxix., we may conclude on this
point, who take the year in which we place the birth of Christ for that of
his passion, and consequently reckon thirty years more than we since the
birth of Christ. Mark, p. 62, is sufficiently explicit, " Saxones a Guther-
girno suscepti sunt anno 447 post passionem Christi. A tempore quo ad-
venerunt primo ad Bryttanniam Saxones (viz. 429.) usque ad primum imperii regis Eadmundi 542, ad hunc in quo nos scribimus annos, traditione
seniorum 547 didicimus." A chronology dating from the death of Christ
rarely occurs (Cf. Ideler, ' Handbuch der Chronologie,' ii. p. 411), and never
without adding the usually adopted year of the nativity.

[1] Gildas, c. xvii. Nennius, c. xxvii. Beda, i. 13, and from Beda's
Chron. Paulus, Diac. xiv. Ric. Corin. lib. ii. i. 39. Sax. Chron. a. 443.

clergy entertained a better hope, and showed greater courage. The state of the church in Britain during this early period, is indeed too remarkable not to claim a short notice in this place.

The ordinances of the Christian communities were observed in Britain, though many districts of a country exposed to the rapacity of the Roman officials were unable to satisfy the modest claims of the clergy. Three Britons, therefore, were the only bishops at the Council of Ariminum, in the year 359, who accepted the offer of the emperor Constantius, to receive their subsistence at the expense of the state[1]. That not only Romans in this country, but others also of British race were devoted to Christianity, is proved by the existence of British versions of the Bible[2]. Of the state of Christianity in Britain some idea may also be formed from the early opposition there manifested to the doctrines of Arius, and the subsequent strong tendency to that heresy. The holy places of Palestine, which the British Helena and her imperial son had adorned, were soon visited by their countrymen, to whom even to pray at the pillar of Symeon Stylites[3] seemed a sufficient motive for a perilous journey by sea and land, and the best pretension to the reward of everlasting life. The pilgrims returned with intelligence of the cloisters that were forming in the East; and the monastery of Bangor[4], near Chester, was a foundation as ancient as memorable of a society of brethren in this country (probably grafted on druidism) devoting themselves to pious contemplation and traditional wisdom, but who, however beneficial to individuals, contributed little to the spread and inculcation of Christianity, and were even unable to hinder its extinction and oblivion.

We are enabled to form some judgement of the acuteness

[1] Sulp. Sev. lib. ii. c. 55.—T.

[2] Chrysost. Opp. P. viii. p. 111. edit. Savile.

[3] Theodoreti Relig. Hist. c. xxxvi.—T.

[4] Ban gor, the great circle, is an universal denomination for a congregation or monastery. See Gunn in Hist. Britt. Pref. p. xxi.

and capacity of the British ecclesiastics by the celebrated
heresy of the Briton Morgan, better known under his Latinized name of Pelagius[1], as also of the Scot Cælestius, by which
Christendom was long agitated, and which, having been
propagated in their native country by the Pelagian Agricola,
found such favour, that the orthodox, through the intervention
of Palladius, who afterwards became the first Scottish bishop,
prevailed on the pope Cælestinus to send hither Germanus,
bishop of Auxerre, and Lupus, bishop of Troyes[2], to confute
their opponents in a public disputation. Their first attempt
proved that the majority were not incorrigibly devoted to the
new doctrine. Scriptural passages, relics, together with the
address with which Germanus came to the assistance of the
Britons, in the conflict before mentioned with the Picts and
Saxons, fought all at once against Pelagius[3]. In a second
journey, in the year 446, which probably preceded the above-

---

[1] Bishop Stillingfleet has the following notices of Pelagius, who appears
to have followed the doctrines of the Greek fathers and the Eastern churches,
and was approved by the council of Diospolis ; and, as the bishop observes,
was condemned by men who did not understand his meaning. " St. Augustine," he adds, " saith of Pelagius, ' he had the esteem of a very pious
man, and of being a Christian of no mean rank.' And of his learning and
eloquence St. Augustine gives sufficient testimony in his epistle to Juliana,
to whom Pelagius wrote an epistle highly magnified for the wit and elegance of it. And he saith, ' He lived very long in Rome, and kept the
best company there.' Pelagius wrote letters to clear himself, first to Pope
Innocentius, and then to Zosimus, who was so well satisfied, that he
wrote to the African bishops in his vindication, although he afterwards
complied in condemning him : "—"so that Pelagius and Cœlestius, by their
own natural wit, had in all probability been too hard for a whole succession of popes, Innocentius, Zosimus, and Xystus, had not the African
fathers interposed, and told them what the true doctrine of the Church
was." Orig. Brit. p. 114, where also honourable mention is made of two
British bishops charged with Pelagianism, Fastidius and Faustus, as men
of piety, learning and eloquence.—R. T.

[2] Prosp. Aquit. aa. 429, 431. Constant. Vita S. Germani. Vita S. Lupi.

[3] For the miracles said to be performed by Germanus, see Usher, Annal.
Hector Boetius relates that he caused the Pelagians to be burnt, by the
care and order of the magistrates. See Jortin, Six Dissertations : the
Second contains an historical account of this controversy, so much con-
nected with the early history of Britain, abridged from Le Clerc, Bibl.
Chois. viii. 308.—R. T.

mentioned mission of the Britons, but certainly stood in close connexion with it, Severus, bishop of Treves, accompanied Germanus to Britain, where, in the expulsion of the Pelagians[1], they performed one of the last acts of Roman power in this country; a measure indicating the weakness of that religious conviction which was so soon to be totally annihilated, and which allows us to attribute the earliest occupation of a Roman province by the pagans to the same contentious sectarian spirit, through which, a thousand years after, the last fragment of the unwieldy political conglomeration fell, in like manner, a prey to infidels.

The spectacle which Britain now presented is one of the saddest, but, at the same time, most memorable in the history of the world. It was relieved from the rapacity of the Roman procurator ; it was freed from the insolence of the Cæsarian cohorts ; but for this liberty the people were not indebted to their courage and higher impulses : for them, therefore, liberty was helplessness, independence anarchy: and however the historian may strive to show that corruption had long been gaining ground in the country, that the government had become gradually perverted, and that of the events and views of later times types are to be found in the earlier ; that many fundamental principles were constantly preserved, while the outer shell alone was changed ; yet it cannot be denied, that no country ever so quickly cast aside a polished language, which had for many generations been the mother-tongue, not only of the settlers but of the natives ; that the Christian religion had never so rapidly been exchanged, leaving not a trace behind, for paganism and infidelity: such a political and moral degradation as took place in the greater part of Roman Britain, after so many a mournful lesson, appears indeed an inexplicable enigma.

This was the deplorable state of the country whose nationality had been destroyed by Roman lust of conquest, after the annihilation of which it possessed not powers of resistance against its most barbarous enemies.

[1] Beda, i. 21. Vita S. Germani.

PART I.

FROM THE LANDING OF HENGEST AND HORSA TO THE ACCESSION OF ECGBERHT.

AFTER the extinction of the Roman power in Britain, the country had for many years been a prey to internal discord and foreign assailants, when, to subdue his northern foes, Vortigern[1], a powerful prince in Kent and the southern parts of Britain, with the concurrence of his counsellors and in the true spirit of Roman policy, formed the resolve to avail himself of the help of those German warriors who for many years had been known to the country only as formidable enemies. This resolve was executed; but these mercenaries took advantage of the weakness of the land and, with the aid of succeeding cognate tribes and kinsmen, subjected it to their dominion; a drama which, in the following century, was in a similar manner enacted in the north of Italy by the Lombards, who had been called in by Narses.

That the employment of the Jutish 'heretogas' or leaders, Hengest and Horsa, who, banished[2] from their native home, had been driven to gain for themselves a new country, was no very striking event, and that the number of their followers

---

[1] Vortigern was the son of Guortheneu, or Guortheu, the great-grandson of Gloui, who, according to the British tradition, built Cair-Gloui (Gloucester). Such is the account given by Nennius, c. liv. A later tradition ascribes the building of that city to the emperor Claudius, whom it states to have been the father of Gloui by a British girl named Geuissa. See Galfr. Mon. iv. 15. Malmesb. de Gestis Pontif. iv. p. 283.

[2] The banishment is mentioned not only by Jeffrey, but also by Nennius, c. xxviii. "Interea venerunt tres chiulæ a Germania in exilio pulsæ, in quibus erant Hors et Hengist, qui et ipsi fratres erant." Beda (i. 15) speaks only of the invitation, but Wittekind gives a circumstantial account of a mission of the Britons to the Saxons, and recites their speech, referring, for further information, to an 'Historia Anglo-Saxonum.'

was not considerable, is evident from the obscurity which
shrouds the history of England during the years immediately
following their arrival, and from their being contained in
three vessels (ceolas[1]), as well as from the fabulous traditions
(though unknown to Gildas and Beda) with which these
years were filled up by the later Welsh writers, as soon as
the growing preponderance of the Saxons in the British
islands had contributed rather to excite the imagination than
to cherish and freshen the memory.

Hengest, when, according to the British tradition, his band,
after Dido's example, had measured with a hide, or, with
greater probability, had, according to Roman usage, received
as a reward, the fertile and, from its position commanding
the Thames, important isle Ruoihin, by the Saxons called
Thanet[2], sent for new allies from his native country, together
with his son Ochta, Abisa[3] the son of Horsa, and for her
beauty his highly prized daughter Rowena. The British prince,
Vortigern, at a feast given by the Saxons,—who, in the accounts of the time, are represented as addicted to gluttony
and drunkenness,—received from Rowena a full golden cup,
with the old German salutation, "Wes hal," and learned the
answer, "Drinc hal[4]." Vortigern now forgot all regard for
the Christianity which he outwardly professed, and, excited
by love and wine, declared the fair Jute his consort, whom
her father granted to him in return for the cession of Kent,
at that time suffering under the mal-administration of a cer-

[1] "Tribus cyulis, nostra lingua, 'longis navibus.'" Gildæ Hist. c. xxiii.

[2] "Felix Thanet sua fecunditate—insula arridens bona rerum copia, regni
flos et thalamus, amenitate, gratia, in qua tanquam quodam elysio, etc."
Cf. Jocelinum de Vita Milburgæ. eund. de Vita S. Augustini, ap. Leland
Collect. t. iii. p. 170, t. iv. p. 8. The British name of this isle, of which
we have documentary evidence as late as the year 692 (Thorne, p. 2234),
shows, together with other proofs, that the British tongue had not been
driven out of Kent by the Latin.

[3] Later traditions relative to these individuals will be noticed, when we
come to the founding of the kingdoms of Northumbria.

[4] See von Arx, in 'Monum. Germ. Hist.' t. ii.

tain Gnoirangon[1]. His subjects saw with indignation the partiality for the strangers with which their king was inspired, in consequence of this connexion, and placed his son Vortemir on the throne. Hengest, who, according to Jeffrey of Monmouth, had called over three hundred thousand of his countrymen to Britain, under the pretext of defending the Picts' Wall against the Scots, with whom he afterwards entered into an alliance, had by the victorious arms of Vortemir been beaten in three battles, on the Darent, at Episford[2], in which Horsa and Categirn, a son of Vortigern, were slain, and at Folkestone[3], and for some years driven out of the country, but had been recalled by his son-in-law, after the latter (whose son had been poisoned by Rowena) had re-ascended the British throne. On the refusal of the Britons to restore to the Saxons their previous possessions, a conference was appointed of three hundred of each nation, during which, on the exclamation of Hengest to his followers, " Nimath eowere seaxas," they, with their long knives, which they had held concealed, fell on and murdered their opponents[4]. The ransom of Vortigern was three provinces, distinguished by their later denominations of Essex, Sussex, and Middlesex, over which Hengest, and after him his son Ochta, reigned[5].

In the perusal of this narrative, drawn from the writings

[1] Nenn. c. xxxvii. Gorongus. Will. Malmesb. lib. i. c. 1. [Some suppose this name to signify a title, as viceroy, governor, but from the words of Nennius it would rather seem to be a proper name : " Gnoirangono rege regnante in Cantia," though some MSS. omit the word ' rege.'—T.]

[2] Nenn. c. xlvii. *Br.* Saissenaeg-haibail, so called, says Camden, because the Saxons were conquered there. The Saxon Chron. a. 455. reads Æglesthrep and Æglesford.

[3] This reading is founded on a conjecture of Somner and Stillingfleet, that for Lapis Tituli (Nenn. c. xlvii.) we should read Lapis Populi ; while others suppose that Stonar, in the Isle of Thanet, is the place intended.

[4] Davies (in his ' Mythology and Rites of the British Druids ') would perceive in the ' Gododin' of Aneurin, a bard of the sixth century, an allusion to this event. Turner's refutation (b. iii. c. 4.) is very satisfactory, though his own interpretation seems no less arbitrary.

[5] Nenn. c. xlix.

of those who have recorded the British traditions, we feel at
no loss with regard to the several elements of which it is
composed. The Triad of the druidic religion and of British
fiction furnishes the groundwork and the standard, according
to which all events, without any chronological data, are shaped:
British and Roman traditions are mingled and embellished,
and the Old-Saxon saga of the craft and valour with which
the Saxons landed in Hadeln, gained possession of Thuringia,
bought land, and murdered the inhabitants with their knives[1],
is here again placed in account against them by the Britons.
The principal assertion in this narrative is, moreover, the
least true,—that Hengest received the above-mentioned three
provinces, which never fell to his share, but to that of other
German chieftains, and a part of them in much later years.

The evident worthlessness of these traditions renders the
more necessary a strict examination of the accounts of their
conquests in Britain given by the immigrants themselves.
We find these in Beda,—who, however, records but very few
circumstances relative to that event from his own sources,
but, for the most part, transcribing Gildas, mingles both traditions[2],—and in the earliest English chroniclers, among
whom Henry of Huntingdon, from his greater detail, is particularly valuable and interesting. As these narratives are
accompanied by dates, the first point to be ascertained by the
historic inquirer is, the system, according to which these dates
were calculated, before the Christian writers, through whom
only they are transmitted to us, reduced them to the Julian
calendar and the Christian era. Britain, in the latter half of
the fifth century, could no longer have reckoned its years by
Roman consuls and emperors; the epoch of the birth of

---

[1] For the earlier traditions of the Saxons see hereafter.

[2] Beda, i. 15, 16, 22, from Gildas, cc. xxiii. xxiv. xxv., while Henry of
Huntingdon copies Beda, adding, however, the accounts which are sub-
stantially given in the Saxon Chronicle. The passages copied from Beda
should be carefully detached from the rest, in order to form a correct idea
of the view here taken.

Christ, first introduced by Dionysius Exiguus in the sixth century, could not in any case have been adopted before its close, and before the conversion of an Anglo-Saxon prince, and probably not before the Christian religion had gained a considerable footing in the country[1]. Of the chronology brought by the Saxons into Britain we know little more than that they reckoned by lunar years, and increased their year (which, like that once in use among the Romans, consisted of ten months only[2]) by the addition of two new months, and of an intercalary month, on the adoption of the Christian Roman calendar[3]. Hence, in assaying, as it were, such chronological data, and whatever is dependent on them, we must have the greater regard to their intrinsic credibility, seeing that, for a period of nearly a hundred and fifty years, we are unable to adduce a single trustworthy authority for the history of the pagan Anglo-Saxons.

The Anglo-Saxon narratives are given to us by the chroniclers in the following words:—

In the year 449, on application made by Vortigern, king of the Britons, to the ' æthelings ' or chiefs of the Angles, or Saxons[4], for aid against the Picts and Scots, the leaders Hengest and Horsa, the sons of Wihtgils, a great-grandson of Woden, who, in the sixth generation, descended from God, landed with their followers from three ships at Ypwines-fleet[5] (Ebbsfleet) in Kent. The Picts and Scots had already ad-

---

[1] On the dates of the Anglo-Saxons subsequent to the introduction of Christianity, Kemble's Introduction to the ' Codex Diplomaticus Ævi Saxonici ' may be consulted with advantage.—T.

[2] See Ideler's ' Chronologie ' and Niebuhr's Roman History.

[3] Beda de Ratione Temp.

[4] Beda, i. 15. Sax. Chron. a. 443, which probably follows some other narrative in assigning the year 443, or the following year, to the invitation of the Angles.

[5] Sax. Chron. (which in other particulars of this event merely copies Beda). Ethelwerd, lib. i. It is remarkable that the Goths migrated in three ships ; see Jornandes, p. 98 : the Winili or Longobards in three divisions ; see P. Warnefrid, i. 3 : the Waräger under three leaders ; see Nestor.

vanced to Stamford in Lincolnshire. While on the one side they fight with darts and spears, on the other with battle-axes and long swords, the Picts, unable to withstand such force, seek for safety in flight[1]. The victorious Saxons triumph over the enemy whithersoever they advance, and gain vast booty. The strangers inform their countrymen in Saxony of the fertility of the island, and the sloth of its inhabitants; whereupon a fleet of sixteen sail immediately brings over a larger body of warriors, which, added to the former band, form an irresistible army. A fixed habitation is assigned them by the Britons, as reward and pay for the further defence of Britain, according to the difference of the three races: to the Jutes in Kent, to the Saxons in Wessex and Essex, to the Angles northwards. The story of Rowena is here mentioned merely as a British tradition[2]. Beda further relates, that Horsa fell in a battle against the Britons, and that his monument was yet to be seen in the eastern part of Kent[3]. The Saxons afterwards come in greater numbers, and form an alliance with the Picts[4]. He then gives some words from Gildas on the battles of Ambrosius Aurelianus with the Saxons, and immediately, through one of those singular hallucinations under which he occasionally labours, passes on to the battle of Bath, which he places in the year 492, or in the forty-fourth year after the arrival of the Saxons. On a later occasion he calls the son of Hengest, Oeric (Eric), surnamed Oisc[5] (Æsc), from whom the royal race of Kent derived its

[1] H. Hunt. lib. ii.

[2] H. Hunt. "dicitur a quibusdam." Cf. Nenn. cc. xxxvii. xlix.

[3] At Horsted. Archæol. vol. ii. p. 107; Hasted's Kent, vol. ii. p. 177. —T.

[4] This account of Beda, i. 15, is not to be found either in Gildas or Nennius, who would hardly have omitted it, had it been founded. It may possibly have arisen from a misunderstanding by Beda of the passage in Gildas, c. xxiii. "testantur se cuncta insulæ rupto fœdere (sc. cum Vortigerno inito) depopulaturos."

[5] It may be well to observe that, in the orthography of personal proper names, Beda uses the Northumbrian dialect, writing oi for æ and e, œ and

patronymic appellation of Oiscings[1] (Æscings). The other traditions which we are about to relate, were therefore unknown to, or regarded by Beda as unworthy of notice.

In a battle where Ambrosius Aurelianus, a chief of Roman lineage, with two sons of Vortigern, Gortimer and Catigern, lead each a separate body, Hengest and Horsa, though with an inferior number, each with his band, march boldly to the encounter[2]. This battle may be identical with that of the Derwent, recorded without particular details by the British traditionists. In the sixth or seventh year after the coming of the Germans, was fought the battle at Æglesthrep, supposed to be the present Aylesford, where tradition declares the British structure known by the name of Kits Coty house to be the sepulchral monument of Catigern. At the outset Horsa attacked the band led by Catigern with such impetuosity that, like dust, it was scattered in all directions, and the son of the king was struck by him to the earth. His brother Gortimer, however, a very valiant man, burst from the flank into the array of Horsa, and slew that hero. The remnant of Horsa's band fled to Hengest, who still fought unconquered with the wedge-formed array of Ambrosius. The whole weight of the conflict having now fallen on Hengest, who was also pressed by the brave Gortimer, after a long resistance, and a great loss on the side of the Britons, he who had never fled was now compelled to flee. This battle, though, from its name, regarded as the second mentioned by Nennius, agrees in its consequences more with the third and last recorded by him[3].

---

i for e, a and æ for ea, u for w, c and ch for h, d for th (ð). Examples of all these changes occur in the following, Oidilualch, Coinualch, Cœnred, Alcfrid, Ædwine, Sæberct; for Æthelwealh, Cenwealh, Cenred, Ealhfrið, Eadwine, Sæberht.—T.

[1] H. E. ii. 5.

[2] H. Hunt. lib. ii. The battle between Aurelianus and Hengest is also mentioned by Gildas, c. xxv., though without details.

[3] Sax. Chron. H. Hunt. a. 455.

In the eighth year after the coming of the Germans, the Britons led four large bodies under as many valiant chieftains to Crecganford (Crayford) in Kent, against Hengest and his son Æsc: though when the Britons had begun the game of war, they ill withstood the Saxons, who, strengthened by a body of newly-arrived chosen men, with their battle-axes and swords, fearfully hewed the bodies of the Britons, nor ceased they from the conflict until they beheld the slaughter of four thousand of their adversaries, who in dismay fled towards London, and never again ventured to enter Kent with a hostile purpose[1]. Hengest and his son Æsc[2] now assumed kingly power in Kent.

Eight years later, in 465, Hengest and Æsc assembled an invincible army, against which all Britain went forth in twelve noble warlike hosts. They fought long and bravely, until Hengest slew the twelve British chieftains, took their standards, and put the panic-struck bands to flight: but, together with other noted leaders and kinsmen, Hengest lost his valiant thane Wipped, after whom the battle-field, which, from the preceding narrative, we ought not to look for in Kent, received the name of Wippedes-fleot. This battle was followed by so many tears and so much sorrow, that neither people for a considerable time ventured beyond their own boundaries[3].

Again, after a term of eight years, in 473, Hengest and Æsc gained another victory over the Britons: the name of

[1] Sax. Chron. Ethelwerd. Flor. Wigorn. H. Hunt. a. 457.

[2] Sax. Chron. Flor. Wigorn. a. 455. Huntingdon places the assumption of the kingly power by Hengest and his son in 457, where the mention of Æsc seems a later addition to the text, the verb being left in the singular: "Exinde *regnavit* Hengist et Esc filius suus." Ethelwerd also (rightly I suspect) omits all mention of Æsc, saying merely, that Horsa being slain, Hengest "cepit regnum." Whether Hengest's assumption of the royal dignity was a consequence of Horsa's death or of the complete expulsion of the Britons from Kent, is doubtful, though the latter seems the more probable cause.—T.

[3] Sax. Chron. Ethelw. Flor. Wigorn. H. Hunt. a. 465.

the field is forgotten. They made vast booty, and the Britons fled before them as from fire[1].

In the fortieth year after his arrival[2], or twice eight years after the last battle, Hengest died, and after him Eric, surnamed Æsc, the patriarch of the dynasty of the Æscings, reigned twenty-four years, increasing his territory at the expense of the Britons, until the end of the eighth cycle of eight years after the coming of the Germans into England. From this time for the following eighty years, the history of the kingdom of Kent affords no chronological data, and records little beyond the names of the first Æscings, namely Octa or Ocha, the son of Eric or Æsc, and Eormenric, the son or brother of Octa. Under the year 568 Æthelberht is named, who reigned forty-eight years, whose successor Eadbald was followed by Earconberht, each of whom reigned twenty-four years.

The great importance in the history of England of the conquests of Hengest must justify us for occupying some space in an attempt more accurately to determine the value of the foregoing narratives. The first point for consideration is the year of the landing, which, according to the later Anglo-Saxon chronicles, is 449. The more ancient Beda, in three different places[3], merely says, that the first landing of the Saxons took place during the seven years' reign of Marcianus and Valentinianus, the beginning of which in his History he places in the year 449, but in his Chronicon in 459: the right year is known to be 450. The English accounts being thus evidently incorrect, the hitherto apparently neglected statement of the older and nearly contemporaneous Prosper

[1] Sax. Chron. a. 473.

[2] H. Hunt. a. 488. "Mortuus est Hengist xl. anno post adventum suum in Britanniam." The Sax. Chron. Ethelw. and Flor. Wigorn. make no mention of the fortieth year, which is, moreover, undoubtedly incorrect, and added apparently through prepossession for the number eight and its multiples.—T.

[3] H. E. i. 15, v. 24, "quorum tempore Angli a Brittonibus accersiti Brittaniam adierunt." Chron. a. 459.

Tyro becomes important, namely, that Britain, as early as in
the year 441, fell under the dominion of the Saxons[1].   With
this year the mission of the Britons to Ætius, at that time
resident in Gaul, might possibly be brought into connexion :
yet Beda himself, in other parts of his work, where he gives
the dates with greater exactitude, fixes 446, that of the third
consulship of Ætius[2], for the year of the landing of the Angles
and Saxons.   It would seem that Beda, whose glaring deficiency in historic criticism has never been duly attended to,
followed in the one account the Kentish narratives, in the
other, the North-Anglian authorities, both of whom may be
correct for their respective localities.   On the first-mentioned
account of Beda later chroniclers have founded the beginning
of their Saxon era.

The oldest Anglo-Saxon chronologists reckoning their years
from the arrival of the Saxons, we have, in the adoption sometimes of the year 445 and sometimes 449, an explanation why
the dates of the earliest annals so frequently differ from each
other by exactly four years[3].   The year 428, to be found in

[1] " Britanniæ usque ad hoc tempus variis cladibus eventibusque latæ
(laceratæ) in ditionem Saxonum rediguntur."   Pr. Tyro, a. 441, ap. Canisium, and Petrie, C. H. p. lxxxii. 2.

[2] H. E. v. 23, " anno adventus Anglorum in Britanniam, circiter ducen-
tesimo octogesimo quinto, Dominicæ autem incarnationis anno septingen-
tesimo tricesimo primo."   Id. i. 23, " anno decimo quarto ejusdem principis
(Mauricii, hoc est anno 696) adventus vero Anglorum in Brittaniam circiter
centesimo quinquagesimo."   The ' Northumbrian Chronology ' (Wanley,
p. 288 ; Petrie, C. H. p. 290) places the arrival of the Angles 292 years
before 737, consequently in 445.   See also Petrie, p. 120, note ᵃ.   Nennius
(c. xxviii.) assigns a period of forty years from the extinction of the Roman
power in Britain till the landing of the Germans, where it is evident that,
as well as in other parts of his history, he mixes up Anglo-Saxon with
British traditions.

[3] See also the ' Annales Juvavienses Majores,' where the death of Æthelberht of Kent is mentioned under the year 620, but which is usually assigned to 616, while, according to a contrary calculation, the year of the
death of Finnan bishop of Lindisfarne is placed in 658, instead of 662.   A
similar confusion occurs in the year of the death of Penda of Mercia,
which is usually given in 654, but in the Northumbrian chronology already
cited, in 658.

writers of no very late times, as that of the landing of the Saxons in England, having been already considered[1], need be merely mentioned in this place.

We have in our detail endeavoured to draw attention to a circumstance hitherto entirely overlooked,—that the events in the saga of the Æscings, or founders of the kingdom of Kent, take place in an eight times repeated cycle of eight years. If so many traces of fiction did not betray a poetic source from which these meagre chroniclers derived their narrative, yet must those numbers awaken the suspicion, that of a people, who have preserved no more ancient chronological notices, whose genealogies, ascending in the tenth or twelfth generation to the first Creator of the world, betray a very short historic memory, we possess a fragment only, arbitrarily taken by the Scalds, of a myth founded on some historic sagas.

Though so little of the Old-Saxon traditions has been transmitted to us through the literature of the Christian Anglo-Saxons, we possess, however, two poetic pieces in which Hengest appears as a conspicuous character: the one a fragment only, "The Battle of Finnesburh[2]," the other an episode in Beowulf[3], the oldest national epic extant of Germanic Europe. We should therefore not be startled at the supposition of poems, founded on his most memorable deed, sung by heathen Anglo-Saxons in the first century after it took place[4]; nor if in the history of the later founded Anglo-Saxon

[1] See p. 62, note[5].

[2] See Hickes, Thes. t. i. p. 192 ; Conybeare's 'Illustrations,' p. 173, and Beowulf by Kemble, vol. i. p. 238.

[3] [First published by Thorkelin at Copenhagen in 1815, 4to, whose text abounds in the grossest errors, but from which his original transcript, now at Copenhagen, is, singularly enough, in great measure exempt. His "versio Latina" is worthy of the text. An edition of a different character appeared in 1833, and again, with considerable improvements, in 1835, by J. M. Kemble, Esq. M.A., which was in 1837 followed by a prose translation of the poem, a valuable glossary and body of notes by the same able hand.—T.] The name of Hengest [as well as that of Hnæf], though occurring several times in the poem, has at each time been misunderstood by Thorkelin !

[4] This is perhaps not exactly the place to remark, that in Büsching's

kingdoms, we detect many traces of poetic conception in the fragments preserved by the chroniclers.

Whether the number eight was merely the division given by the probably historic numbers forty and sixty-four, or whether it had an astronomic allusion, or was founded on some myth, we are unable to discover. That the Saxons were not strangers to astronomic traditions, appears probable from their primitive saga, in which 354, the number of the ships with which their forefathers migrated from the land of sunrise[1], corresponds with that of the days of the lunar year. We find the number eight in the division of the twenty-four hours, from one morning to another, usual among the Anglo-Saxons and Icelanders. A similar division exists in the eight watches among mariners. As at Rome the period of eight days was superseded only by the Jewish-Christian week of seven days, so both German and Scandinavian colloquial terms point to a similar division of time in the heathen North. This number reminds us, moreover, of the ὀκταετηρὶς of the Greeks, so frequently occurring in their games and other institutions.

If, in considering the cyclic chronology of the dominion of the Æscings, we recollect how many centuries of history are a later work of men, we shall be unable wholly to suppress our doubts regarding the existence in Kent of the first founder of that race. Among the reasons against the historic truth of the traditions of Hengest and Horsa, the first that presents itself is the extraordinary, and, except in poetical tradition, almost unheard of circumstance, of two leaders, at the same time, at the head of a band of followers. Beda gives the story of the two brothers as a tradition only[2].

'Volkslieder' there is a child's song in which allusion is made to the Saxon invasion of Britain. The mention therein of the Old-Saxon weapon, the long knife (seax), is remarkable.

[1] See i. a. Sachsenspiegel, lib. iii. c. 44.

[2] H. E. i. 15. [The circumstance of two brothers being joint kings or leaders, and bearing alliterative names, is far from unheard of in the annals of the North: as instances may be cited the sons of Ragnar, Ingvar and Ubba, of whom hereafter; also two kings in Rumedal (Snorre, t. i. p. 81), Herlaug and Hrollaug. See also the early Danish chronicles.—T.]

Their synonymous names are yet more striking, which have been considered as bearing allusion to the horse held sacred by the Germans[1], to their military banner[2], and to the white horse, the arms of the county of Kent. The poems of the founding of the kingdom of Kent are unfortunately, through the early decay of that power, irretrievably lost, and there is as little hope of illustrating the traditions from historic narratives as from the heroic compositions of the bard or gleeman[3].

The inquiry into the chronology of the Anglo-Saxons naturally leads to the question, what were the means employed by them to aid the memory, and preserve to posterity the remembrance of past generations? That the art of writing was not very general among them we must conclude from their numerous symbolical legal usages; nevertheless the

[1] Tac. Ger. c. x.   [2] Ibid. c. vii.   Ejd. Hist. iv. 22.

[3] According to a tradition of Ocka Scharlensis, a Frisian historian of the tenth century (printed at Amsterdam in 1507), Hengist and Horsa were the sons of Udolph Haro, the seventh and last duke of the Frisians, and of Svana, a daughter of the noble Witgistus (Wihtgils?), dwelling near Hamburg, and sister of two earlier individuals deceased, named also Hengist and Horsa. I am acquainted with this story (which is justly rejected by Verstegan and later English writers) only through the work of Suffridus Petri, ʻ De Frisionum Antiquitate et Origine,ʼ Colon. Agrip. 1590.

Having, since the foregoing was written, received the original work of Ocka, revised and enlarged by John Vlitarp and Andreas Cornelisz (Leeuwaarden, 1597, fol.), I find that, in speaking of Hengist, born in 361, and Horsus, who had already served in the army of Valentinian, and landed in Britain in 385, the author generally follows Jeffrey of Monmouth. According to the Frisian historian this Hengist was hanged in the year 389 by Eldol (Cf. Galfr. Monum. vi. 6), and the conquest of Britain was achieved by the followers of the sons of the second Frisian king Odilbalt, who were born in 441, and likewise called Hengist and Horsa, and had been taught the art of war under the Northern kings, but were at last slain by Gormund and his Irishmen. In Ocka's work no mention is made of Svana nor of her father ʻ Wæthgist ʼ (Wihtgisl, Wihtgils). [From the tale of the scop or gleeman in Beowulf, Hengest certainly appears as (what he has always till of late been considered) a Jutish leader. The whole episode will be found at the end of the volume, accompanied by what I believe to be a literal translation, with a few conjectural readings of the text, which do not, however, affect the parts relating to the country of Hengest.—T.]

Anglo-Saxon, and in part English expressions for writing and alphabetic signs, viz. writan, *to write*, and stæf, *letter*, and the many Anglo-Saxon derivatives from these roots, as stæf-cræft, *art of letters, grammar*; stæfen-row, *alphabet*; stæf-gewrit, stæflic, stæf-plega, etc., justify the conclusion, that if the Anglo-Saxons had appropriate names for writing and objects connected with it, the art itself could not have been unknown to them. Of runes, the use of which among the Germans seems to have been known to Tacitus[1], many traces still exist in England, where the word *rune*, however, rather signified *a mystery*, than, as among the Scandinavian nations, *an alphabetic character*. That the Germans brought alphabetic writing with them to Britain appears partly from the circumstance that they were acquainted only with the old runic alphabet of sixteen letters, and that their characters closely resembled those of the northern Germans[2], but particularly from the adoption of some of the Saxon characters into the Roman alphabet introduced by the Christian priests, which was found inadequate to express all the Anglo-Saxon sounds. These are the runes ƿ, afterwards expressed by V or W, and þ, þ (for which the later Ð, ð was also used), now expressed by Th. During the early culture of the Anglo-Saxons by the missionaries, the other runic characters the sooner fell into disuse from being unknown to the Britons, who at a later period exercised over them considerable influence. Although we have to regret the loss of all the alpha-

---

[1] Ger. c. iii. "Aram Ulixi consecratam, monumentaque et tumulos quosdam Græcis literis inscriptos in confinio Germaniæ Rætiæque adhuc extare." Ib. c. x. "Virgam frugiferæ arbori decisam in surculos amputant, eosque notis quibusdam discretos super candidam vestem......spargunt." Were these twigs, used for casting lots, marked with runes ? [See a passage connected with this subject in 'The Legend of St. Andrew,' edited by Mr. Kemble for the Ælfric Society, or in Archæol. vol. xxviii. p. 332.—T.]

[2] Cf. W. C. Grimm, 'Ueber Deutsche Runen,' Göttingen 1821, and his supplement to that work in the 'Wiener Jahrbücher,' 1828, Bd. 43. Geijer, 'Svea Rikes Häfder,' T. i. 134–185, with whom I agree in the result, though not in particular points.

betic writings of the Anglo-Saxons from the time of paganism, which, on perishable wood, recorded the genealogies of their kings, legal documents and poems,—yet are lasting though somewhat later monuments inscribed with them not wanting, from which we may conclude that here, as in the North, they were in use as the writing of the people for some centuries; hence we meet with them on boundary stones, fonts, and similar public monuments.

The use of runes as a peculiar kind of writing may be traced in England till the fourteenth century[1]; and, if we err not, they continued in use both there and in Germany for inscriptions and seals to even a later period, in consequence of the superior facility which their right-lined forms afforded to the engraver over those of the usual round monkish characters. That we have failed in discovering their numerals is much to be regretted, by an acquaintance with which many an enigmatic myth of the North might be found susceptible of an historic interpretation. From the undoubted connexion of the runic characters with the Phœnician and, consequently, with the ancient Greek alphabet, we may perhaps conclude that the runic numerals were those characters in their ancient order, which we know from some manuscripts; a supposition which as far as the number 19 finds confirmation in the notation used on the old runic calendar, in reference to the cycle of nineteen years[2]. If we further consider how long these characters continued in use among the common people and perhaps in commerce, the question, however repugnant to received opinion, may be asked, whether, notwithstanding the influence of the Arabian or Indian numeral

---

[1] See Cod. Sangallens. 270 and 878 ; it. Cod. Isidor. Paris. in Grimm, tab. ii., and ibid. tab. iii.; from later A.-S. manuscripts in Hickes, t. i. pp. 135, 136, and t. iii. tab. 6 ; Duncan and Repp's account of the monument in Ruthwell Garden, Edinb. 1833 [and Kemble's paper on Anglo-Saxon Runes, in Archæologia, vol. xxviii.—T.].

[2] Hickes, t. i. p. 34.

system on our own, the present so-called Arabian first eight numerals are not eight runes, to which, as they appear in ancient manuscripts, they bear a closer resemblance than to the real Arabian ciphers? That this supposed similarity is less striking in the Northern than in the later wide-spread Anglo-Saxon runes, seems in favour of the hypothesis. Planudes indeed says, that the numerals used by him are of Indian origin[1]; but how different from our ciphers are those figures as we find them in his time and, some centuries earlier, in Roger Bacon, as well as in other manuscripts! It would be rash to pretend to decide on a point regarding which our materials for judging are so scanty and so uncertain; yet the doubt may be forgiven on calling to remembrance that science and art have often been found nearer to their home than short-sighted learning imagined.

Of greater importance for historical investigation would be the knowledge of the numeral system in use among the Saxons. I am inclined to the belief that the octonary, on account of its facility of division, was the one followed, and that herein may be found a further reason for the frequent use of the number eight in the Anglo-Saxon narratives. From this system it appears also probable that the name of the eighth rune, 'hûn,' is nearly connected with *hundred*; also, that both Scandinavians and Germans had a small and a great hundred and thousand, by the latter of which the numbers 120 and 1200 were denoted[2], and hence perhaps the frequent occurrence of the number 12 (3 × 4). The greatest weight usual in the North, which emphatically bore the name of ' vætt,' contained eighty pounds, and was increased to a hun-

---

[1] See Montucla, Histoire des Mathématiques, i. p. 375 sq. The second rune Ur resembles in all the alphabets the cipher for two as it appears in manuscripts of the fourteenth century.

[2] Rask, Anvisning til Isländskan, p. 130. Mone, Gesch. des Heidenthums, ii. 79, p. 89. For traces of a reckoning by a great hundred see Diss. on Domesday Book, p. xlvii. Ellis, Introd. to Domesday, vol. i. p. 148.

dred[1] in later times only. The Anglo-Saxons placed the word
'hund' before the numbers 70 to 120, a practice evidently derived from a time when that syllable had not acquired its later
signification of number, but indicated only a certain multipli-
cation; which notation might perhaps have connexion with the
number of the sixteen ancient runes, the eleventh of which
might denote 20, and so on, the fifteenth 60, and the last
100; in like manner, at a later period, after six new runes
had been added, the twenty-first might have been employed
for the great hundred, and the last rune for its multiple,
the great thousand. As an idiom now lost in the English
tongue, but as showing the close relationship subsisting
between the Anglo-Saxon method of reckoning and that of
the Scandinavian and other Germanic people, may be cited
the use of the word 'healf,' *half*, which they subtract from
the preceding whole number, while in other tongues the half
is added to the same; an idiom which receives illustration
from the custom adopted, in writing the numerals during the
middle age, of drawing a stroke through the whole number,
thereby signifying that a half is to be subtracted from it[2].

Before we resume the subject of the settlements of the
Germans in Britain, the manifest deficiency of the historic
picture,—which in this instance has very little claim to be
regarded as a faithful mirror,—renders it necessary to give a
more detailed account of the descent of these people; a subject
the more important, as with greater rapidity and more lasting consequences, they converted the newly acquired land, in
language, laws and customs, into a native country for their
posterity.

It is a remarkable circumstance attending the invasion of
Britain by the Germanic races, that people whose language
was sufficiently formed to supplant both the old mother-

---

[1] Grágás II. in Gloss., though Biörn Haldorsen, voc. Vætt, explains it
by 'octoginta pondo, nonnunquam *olim* centum pondo.'

[2] This practice is not yet entirely obsolete in Scotland.—T.

tongue, and the language of business, of education, and of
the church,—while in every other province of the Roman empire, with the exception of border districts, the language of
the barbarians expired,—should have preserved only meagre
genealogic memorials, but no ancestral tradition, historic records, or even any distinct allusions to the country which
they had previously occupied. But this want of native history will appear the less singular, when we call to mind that
the immigration did not take place in great bodies, but gradually, frequently by very small settlements, which spread
themselves over the greater part of England and the south
of Scotland, during the course of one or two centuries. In
the English language, particularly in the rural districts,
where the Norman French has exercised less influence, we
still possess living witnesses of the identity of the invaders
with the inhabitants of the banks of the Lower Elbe and of
the neighbouring countries, to the north and south, from
Jutland to the mouths of the Rhine. The existing monuments of the old Lower Saxon dialect, especially the 'Harmony of the Four Gospels,' of the ninth century, known by
the name of the Heliand[1], agree much more closely with
the Anglo-Saxon in the formation of words, in inflexion, and
the whole vocabulary, than the Upper German writings of
the same period. Widely as the modern English tongue
deviates from the present German, there, nevertheless, yet
lives in the various dialects of England, and particularly of
Scotland, a rich store of Old-Saxon, and the speech and the
song of the Scottish ploughman not unfrequently receive their
best illustration by a comparison with the expressions of the
Holsteiner, Hadeler, or Frisic husbandman or mariner.

An insight into the very close, immediate connexion between the Anglo-Saxon and Low German dialects is not

---

[1] Heliand. Poema Saxonicum seculi noni, edidit J. A. Schmeller.
Monachii, Stutgartiæ et Tubingæ. 1830, 4to. Also, Glossarium Saxonicum e Poemate Heliand, ib. 1840.—T.

without important results for many centuries of English history, and a firm footing for the illustration of the civil institutes in both these neighbouring countries is thereby obtained. The Scandinavian dialects are far more remote from the Anglo-Saxon, and we are fully justified in regarding the traces yet to be found in English of the old Norse tongue as the echo of the invasion of the Jutes, and yet more of the later ones by the Danes or Northmen, and are enabled to fix with confidence the period of the introduction of certain Northern elements, which, as legal antiquities, sometimes at the present day present themselves as still living.

To the proofs derived from language regarding the native land of the Saxons who passed over to Britain, belongs the resemblance both of the personal names of the Anglo-Saxons, and of local names in the western parts of England to those of Lower Saxony; though with respect to the former, the comparison is rendered very difficult by the want of old Lower Saxon documents, few of which reach beyond, or even so far as the twelfth century, besides being exposed to much uncertainty, through the early spread of originally national proper names by wanderings and intermarriages. But the resemblance of local names, exclusive even of those that preserve historical and mythological recollections, is too striking not to have been long ago called into notice[1]; yet the lists may be greatly increased, and gain in value by the aid of more ancient records. The most important names to us must be those which, occurring in Old-Saxony only, lead to the inference of similar political institutions there, where it is worthy of notice that the name of the Anglo-Saxon noble, ' æthel,' is to be found in Ethelingstede[2], and that the local termination in *Wick, wich,* so frequent in England, with its compounds

---

[1] See Ch. U. Grupens, Abh. ' De Lingua Hengisti ' in Observat. Rer. et Antiquit. Germanic. et Romanar.; and, with particular reference to districts on the Elbe, Wedekinds noten zu deutschen Geschichtschreibern, Bd. i.

[2] Now Tellingstädt in Dithmarschen.

Wykgraf, wykvogt, *Wykscheffel* (wispel), are not common to all Germany, but exist only in Old-Saxony and Friesland.

Of greater and more immediate interest for the history of England is the agreement between the public and private legal institutions of the Germans and those of the English Saxons, which abundantly manifests itself as well in their general characteristics as in incidental notices and detached fragments, the further consideration of which we defer for the present, as an opportunity will hereafter be given for the discussion of them in connexion with the history of the Anglo-Saxon constitution.

But if, on every close comparative consideration of the copious language, numerous settlements, and civil institutes of both nations, new proofs of identity shall be found, a more favourable and more faithful picture will present itself of the state of civilization of the continental and of the insular Saxons than the meagre narratives of the older historians have been able to supply. Even though it were the petulant, rugged youth who first forsook their home, and took possession of a foreign land, yet these emigrants, unconsciously to themselves, had their share in the transmission to England of the most valuable possession of their country, in language and customs, which succeeding multitudes of their elder and more peaceful kinsmen afterwards fully effected. But let the modern world not forget, that the existing notions of property, of inheritance, and the institutions founded thereon, are the slow and artificial production of many centuries, and that states of society sometimes present themselves to the geographer and the historian exhibiting no inconsiderable degree of mental culture, yet with no consciousness of the necessity of those fundamental principles of present social order. The system of an annual changing, or at least changeable possession of land, and the custom necessarily attending it, of migrating, prejudicial as they were to the solid interests of nations, nevertheless required activity and strength of mind:

the individual too, whose home afforded him no permanent settlement, would not respect that of a stranger ; while piracy, ennobled by stratagem and valour, is indebted only to an established system of social order for its disgrace and punishment. Even in later times the prince of the Hebrides bore without scruple the title of ‘archpirate’: the Barbary States also afford examples of odious but not wholly savage communities, professing piracy as a trade; and the letters of marque of the Europeans prove how easy, even to ourselves at the present day, is the suspension of the fundamental principles of our whole legal system, and the return to lawful private robbery.

The ancestral traditions of the Saxons belong scarcely to the province of history. The tradition that they sprung from the Danes and Northmen, though questioned by Wittekind, was probably founded on the transient dominion of the Danes over the northern Saxons[1], and receives some countenance in the intermediate position of these people between Germany and the North. As neighbours of the Danes, on the confines of the Cimbric Chersonesus, the Saxons were known to Ptolemy. We find them soon afterwards in the South, extending themselves along the sea-shore towards the Rhine[2]. With both these traditions, a third, to which the monks of Corvey gave full credit, is not incompatible, viz. that the Saxons having come to their neighbourhood in ships, and first landing in Hadeln, drove the Thuringians thence by craft and violence. If this event took place, it cannot have been later than at the time stated, that of the emperor Vespasian,

---

[1] “ Confinalis Daniæ est patria quæ nominatur Saxonia, quæ antiquitus et ipsa ex Dania pertinere dicebatur.” Geog. Raven. iv. c. 17.

[2] “ Saxones, gentem oceani in litoribus et paludibus inviis sitam.” Orosius, vii. 32, whose words here as elsewhere are copied by Paulus Diac. de Gest. Roman. lib. xi. In geographical notices the unaltered confirmations of a copyist are sometimes of value. The ‘ Insulæ Saxonum ’ of Ptolemy are probably to be sought for in the present North Friesland : Eiderstedt, Nordstrand, Wieking-Harde and Böking-Harde. See Falck, Schleswig-Holsteinsches Privat-recht, Th. ii. p. 10.

as we soon afterwards find the Saxons in league with the Franks. Wittekind does not inform us whence these Saxons came who landed in Hadeln, and there is no ground for controverting, but, in accordance with other narratives and with the ordinary march of nations from north to south, for supposing that they were from the north shore of the Elbe, or Nordalbingian Saxons, who took possession of the southern shore of that river, and soon spread themselves over those tracts, as far as the Weser and the Rhine[1], until, in the time of Charlemagne, they were in possession of the territory forming the eight bishoprics founded by him, or of the ' gaus,' or districts, of the later Upper and Lower Saxony and Westphalia. In the account which makes the Saxons to have passed from Britain to Hadeln[2], a later inversion of the tradition is to be recognised, originating, perhaps, in the return of some bodies, of Saxons from England[3].

That a considerable portion of the German invaders of Britain were strictly Saxons[4] is the more probable, as the names of the territories occupied by them, Essex, Sussex, Middlesex and Wessex, prove their Saxon origin ; and even at the present day, after all the immigrations of other races,

[1] This is the country which Beda, Ælfred and other English writers call Old-Saxony in contradistinction to the newer Saxon realm in England. Herewith also agrees the account of Adam of Bremen, i. 3, that the Saxons first had their habitation on the Rhine, and thence passed over to Britain. To seek for Old-Saxony in Holstein, with Camden and others after him, is not admissible, as in the oldest accounts we always find the latter country written Holsatia. Adam. Brem. ii. 8. " Holsati dicti a sylvis quas accolunt." And from him, Annalista Saxo a. 983. " Holcetæ dicti a sylvis quas incolunt." Cf. also Albert. Stad. a. 917. The Sachsenspiegel (b. iii. art. 64. § 3.) has ' Holtseten.'

[2] Meginhard, Transl. S. Alexandri, and Adam. Brem. i. 4, from Einhard.

[3] Gildas, Hist. c. xxv. Beda, i. 16. Galf. Mon. vi. 13.

[4] The oldest continental writers for the most part mention only the Saxons as immigrants. Prosp. Aquit. a. 441. " Britanniæ..............in ditionem Saxonum rediguntur." Geog. Raven. v. § 31. " In oceano occidentale est insula quæ dicitur Britannia, ubi olim gens Saxonum, veniens ab antiqua Saxonia, cum principe suo, nomine Anschis, modo habitare videtur ;" also Wittekind, lib. i. [The territories occupied by the Saxons were small in comparison with those of the Angles. See note [2], p. 89.—T.]

their Celtic neighbours, the Highland Scots, the Welsh, the Irish, and the Bretons, speak of the English only under the denomination of Saxons, though other hordes either accompanied or followed them, among which the Angles are chiefly conspicuous, but whose origin—though they were undoubtedly more numerous than even the Saxons, and sufficiently powerful to impart their name, as a national denomination, to the whole new Germanic land, to the exclusion of that of the Saxons[1], until, for the sake of convenience, historians introduced that of ANGLO-SAXONS, — is, nevertheless, involved in very considerable obscurity. Both Beda and Ælfred distinctly mention the district of Angeln as the original seat of this people[2], a name now confined to the country between the Slie, or Schley, and Flensburg, but which anciently must have comprised a much larger territory[3]. The testimony of Beda, who lived in one of the states founded by the Angles, and scarcely a century from the time of its foundation, is here particularly valuable. The old British tradition makes Hengest and his companions embark for Britain from the Isle of Angul[4], although they are else confidently spoken of as Sax-

[1] Already in a letter of Gregory I., a. 596, the inhabitants of ' Saxonia transmarina,' as they are denominated in the superscription, are in the text called 'gens Anglorum.' Hardt. iii. p. 509. Du Chesne, t. i. p. 897. So also in all the letters of the same pope in Smith's Beda, Appendix vi., and in Bedæ Opera Historica Minora, Appendix, ed. Stevenson.

[2] Beda, i. 15. " Porro de Anglis, hoc est, de illa patria quæ Angulus dicitur, et ab eo tempore usque hodie manere desertus inter provincias Jutarum et Saxonum perhibetur, Orientales Angli, Mediterranei Angli, Merci, tota Nordanhymbrorum progenies, id est, illarum gentium quæ ad boream Humbri fluminis inhabitant, ceterique Anglorum populi sunt orti." Ælfred's Account, § 3. Ohther's Voyage, § 10. Dahlmann's Forschungen, Th. i. p. 418 sq. Nestor also, the Russian chronicler, makes mention of the Angles.

[3] See Ethelwerd, lib. i., who mentions Sleswic, by the Danes called Haithaby, as the capital of that country.

[4] Nennius, c. xxxvii. " Hengistus......cum suis senioribus, qui secum venerant de insula Angul." [Some MSS. read Oghgul.—T.] Gerv. Tilb. ed. Maderus, p. 41. "Ab illis Saxonibus ab Engla insula venientibus seminarium ortum est Anglorum."

ons, and the peopling of the kingdom of Kent, founded by them, was ascribed to Jutes[1].

The Angles[2] possessed in Britain those parts which afterwards formed the kingdoms of East Anglia, Mercia, and Northumbria (in the ancient and literal acceptation of that name, comprising the country to the north of the Humber, viz. the county of York and the present Northumberland, the latter, if it were already included under that appellation, forming but a small, and the most remote portion of it), or, in other words, the country to the north of the counties of Hertford, Northampton, and Warwick. This northern portion of England is distinguished from the south by two denominations, which can be ascribed only to the Angles : while the parts inhabited by the Saxons were divided into hundreds, the like division in all the Anglian territories bore the name of *wapentake*[3], which is still retained in the county of York, and partially in those of Derby and Lincoln. It will hardly be objected that this appellation was introduced at a later period by the Danes, since, of all the Anglian states, East Anglia, which first fell under a regular Danish government, is the only one where it does not occur. In the present counties of Northumberland and Durham, which had early

---

[1] Beda, i. 15. Procopius, lib. iv., says, Βριττίαν δὲ τὴν νῆσον ἔθνη τρία πολυανθρωπότατα ἔχουσι............Ἄγγιλοι τε καὶ Φρίσσονες καὶ οἱ τῇ νήσῳ ὁμώνυμοι Βρίττωνες, without mentioning the Saxons.

[2] Of the Old Angles we possess two remarkable monuments : the poem of Beowulf (see p. 77 and note), in which the old Anglian saga is ennobled by an Anglo-Saxon of the eighth century, and the laws of the Angles of Haithaby, generally known under the probably corrupt title of ' Leges Angliorum et Werinorum,' for which Dahlmann acutely proposes to read ' Angliorum Etverinorum,' or ' Hetverinorum.' See Kraut on the Lex Angl. et Werin. in Falk's Eranien, iii. [The reading ' Werinorum ' is, however, as old as Cnut's Forest Laws : see p. 93, note[4].—T.]

[3] Leges Edw. Conf. xxx. " Everwichescire, Nicholescire, Notingehamscire, Leicestrescire, Norhamtunescire, et usque ad Watlingestrete, et VII. milliaria ultra Watlingestrete, sub lege Anglorum. Et quod alii (' Angli,' some MSS.) vocant hundredum, supradicti comitatus vocant wapentagium." Ancient Laws and Institutes of England, folio edit. p. 196.

and long been Danish, as well as in Cumberland and West-moreland, the division called *a ward* is met with, which may, however, date only from the Norman times. Another national denomination of the Angles accords precisely with the pre-ceding, viz. that of the civic establishment, the 'by.' Fre-quently as local names with this termination occur to the north of Warwick, we shall vainly seek for them southwards of that town[1]. To the distinction between Angles and Saxons it may, perhaps, also be ascribed, that beyond the Watling Street, many of the local names end or begin with 'kirk' (church), while to the south we find 'minster' (monastery). These remarks on isolated differences of expression between Angles and Saxons, here confined to local instances, may be extended to the important and well-ascertained variations in dialect prevailing between the inhabitants of Mercia and those of Wessex.

The testimony of manuscripts of the same work in the dia-lects of Wessex and Mercia[2], and of a period when the Danes, having scarcely obtained their first peaceful settlement in England, could exercise no influence over the language and culture of their territory, seems to place the age of both dia-lects, and, consequently, the difference of both races, beyond a doubt; and will, when the investigation is rendered more easy, probably remove all uncertainty regarding the descent of the Angles.

Another hypothesis must not, however, be entirely over-looked, according to which the Angles were either the Anglii of Tacitus, or the Angrivarii, the inhabitants of the later duchy of Engern. Ptolemy relates that a nation, bearing the name

[1] The correctness of this observation, with reference to the earliest times, cannot indeed be proved, in consequence of the want of documents. Derby, in which I have first met with this termination, owed its name of Deoraby to the Danes, having been originally called Northweorthig. Ethelwerd, iv. 2.

[2] In that of Mercia is the Cambridge MS. of the Chronicle (C. C. S. 11, Wanley, p. 130), and a MS. of Ælfred's Boethius used by Rawlinson in his edition. [I believe the genuine Anglian dialect to be that which is usually denominated the Northumbrian.—T.]

of Angles, dwelt to the south of the Elbe, in a territory which, perhaps, may be sought for in the old North Thuringia[1]. No account of, not even the slightest allusion to, any connexion between these southern Angles and those of Sleswig is extant; yet, if the supposition be not groundless, that the Saxons moved southwards from the northern bank of the Elbe, it is not improbable that hordes also of their Anglian neighbours in the north might have accompanied them.

Nor may we seek for the Anglian settlers in the midst of the German continent, seeing that the grounds alleged in favour of that opinion rest on a manifest misunderstanding[2]. At an early period the servility of genealogists had declared Hengest and Horsa for sons of the duke of Engern, with the view of bestowing on those individuals an origin that should be welcome both to the Saxons and English[3]; but of an argument, however specious, founded merely on blazonry, we ought to be extremely distrustful. The duchy of Engern bore, it is said, a white horse in its banner, whence that charge came into the shield of the dukes of Lüneburg and the present Guelphs[4]; the same is also borne by the county of Kent,

[1] Von Wersebe, Beschreibung der Gauen zwischen Elbe und Werra, p. 69. Von Ledebur, Land und Volk der Bructerer, p. 274, but who, in what he says about the Old-Saxons, is far from satisfactory; and, in what he states concerning the Angli and Warni, misunderstands in an extraordinary manner the passage of Procopius, lib. iv., who does not consider the Angli and Warni as allies in England, but speaks of the Angli who from Britain overcame the Warni encamped on the opposite coast of Belgium.

[2] In Adam. Brem. i. 4, where he speaks of the Saxons who had gone over to Britain, the words " et vocati sunt Angli," after " Saxones circa Rhenum sedes habebant," are wanting in the Vienna MS.

[3] Gobelini Personæ Cosmodrom. ætate vi. " Duces exercitus illius, qui de Saxonia in Britanniam profectus est, filii ducis Angariæ sive de Engere fuerunt,........et inde forte est quod arma ducis Saxoniæ sunt equus albus." See also Verstegan, p. 131.

[4] Not the device of the Saxons, who, according to Wittekind, bore an eagle hovering over a lion and a dragon. The golden dragon was the royal standard of Wessex. H. Hunt., lib. iv, " Edelhun præcedens Westsexenses, regis insigne, draconem scilicet aureum gerens," etc. The horse in the arms of Brunswick-Lüneburg was not added till the year 1362. See Müller in Neue vaterländische Archiv. 1832, p. 176; Scheidt vom deutschen Adel, p. 228.

where Hengest and Horsa, according to tradition, first landed and ruled. But here all dates are wanting, and Kent, as we have already seen, was not occupied by a race of Angles.

Of the laws of the Angles there is no collection extant; the loss of them, more especially those of Offa, is matter of deep regret, as they would, no doubt, have afforded us some important data whereby to judge of the identity of the British Angles with one of the continental races. We know, however, from detached sources, that the laws of the southern and northern English, or of the Saxons and Angles, even in their later form, differed in many points from each other[1]; but the law of Mercia is usually cited as agreeing with that of East Anglia[2]; hence an accordance of the law of Mercia with that of the continental Anglians ought not to be overlooked—in the latter of which, among all the written German laws, the denomination ' adaling' (ætheling) is alone to be found—viz. that both fix the wergild of the free at two hundred shillings[3]. The disproportion in the wergild of the noble among the Anglians may perhaps be accounted for by the circumstance, that a new nobility, the ' sixhyndesmen,' formed out of the military retainers that had passed into Britain, had stept into the place of the old nobles, while the wergild of the old nobility by birth was doubled, and their rank raised in proportion. We possess, however, a very remarkable testimony of the origin of the wergild of the free from the law of the Anglians, and of its validity in England, in the Forest Laws of Cnut, which seems to place even the later application of that law in England beyond a doubt[4].

---

[1] See Laws of Æthelred, vii. 9, 13, and the title ' Wergilds,' in the Ancient Laws and Institutes of England.

[2] Cnut's Sec. Laws, lxxii.

[3] See tit. ' Mercian Law,' in Anc. Laws and Instt. Lex Angl. et Wer. tit. i.

[4] Const. de Foresta, xxxiii..........." emendet secundum pretium hominis mediocris, quod secundum legem Werinorum, i. Thuringorum, est ducentorum solidorum." [The reading ' Churingorum,' for 'Thuringorum,' given

But the accordance of the laws of the Anglians with those
of the Anglo-Saxons is in general, and even in many individual points, very remarkable. Particularly important in
the former is the precept regarding the succession to inheritances in the male line[1] (*lancea*, the *spear-side* of the Anglo-
Saxons[2]) ; the Saxons also acknowledging only heirs male,
to which, as far as the fifth generation, they give the preference over descendants in the female line. Important also is
the title 'De Postestate Testandi,' or, Of freedom in testa-
mentary bequests[3]. The higher fine imposed for injury done
to the hand of the harper, the goldsmith, and the embroider-
ess[4], of which no mention occurs in the other German laws,
calls to mind the harp of the North, of Denmark and of England, at the same time that the several female ornaments[5]
imply the existence of cities, such as from the foregoing we
may suppose Haithaby to have been. A striking characteristic of the Anglians was the sanctity of domestic security,
which manifests itself in the heavy penalty affixed to its violation, implying both civilization and notions of property, the
later advancement of which appears in the great respect shown
by the laws for the house of the English burgher[6].

In the laws of the Anglians and of the Anglo-Saxons is
found also the common principle, that those who first forcibly

---

in Spelman's Glossarium, is apparently a mere clerical or typographical
error : Canciani has, " hoc est Thuringorum."—T.]

[1] Lex Angl. et Wer. tit. vi.   Leges Henrici I. lxx. § 20, where, though
the passage is copied from the Leges Ripuariorum, c. lvi., yet it in principle
agrees with the Anglian law, and can have been adopted only in consequence of its conformity with the Anglo-Saxon.

[2] See Testamentum Ælfredi Regis.   Hence is also the proverb to be explained, "Bicge spere of side oðer bere :" "lanceam eme de latere, aut
fer eam," which in Leges Edw. Conf. xii. is thus cited in the law of
' Manbote,' " Emendationem faciat parentibus, aut guerram paciatur."

[3] Lex Angl. et Wer. tit. xiii.   That the Anglo-Saxons were acquainted
with this appears from Cnut's Sec. Laws, lxxi.   LL. Hen. I. lxxv. § 11.
See also Anc. Laws and Instt. p. 185.

[4] Lex Angl. tit. v. 20.   [5] Lex Angl. tit. vii. 3.

[6] See title ' Hamsocn,' in Anc. Laws and Instt. of England.—T.

enter another's property shall pay a heavier fine than those who
follow[1].   According to both laws a thief might be slain, if his
crime was affirmed by oath[2].   Whether the enactments of the
Anglians regarding duels, among whom they were allowed in
all cases of two shillings and upwards, show any connexion
between their laws and those of the Anglo-Saxons, will be
doubted by those who deny the existence of that mode of
judicial proof among the latter, on the ground that the word
for single combat, ' eornest,'—though certainly Germanic,—
is not of Anglo-Saxon[3] origin : yet William the Conqueror
speaks of the judicial combat as a known English custom ;
and that the Anglians themselves lacked an appropriate term
is evident from the language of their law, which says, " let
the field (campus) decide[4]." The omission of all mention in
the Anglo-Saxon laws of this undeniably existing custom
may, perhaps, justify the inference, that the laws of East
Anglia contained circumstantial provisions regarding judicial
combats.   The existence, however, in England of another
means of proof in judicial proceedings, similar in form and
application to what is enacted in that old Germanic law, is
undoubted—the fire, or iron proof, for accused females, consisting in walking over nine red-hot ploughshares[5].

Thus may the assertion appear justified, that the laws of
the Anglians agree, not only in general characteristics common to all Germanic laws, with those of the Anglo-Saxons,
and may be regarded as a chief source of them, but also, that
no other Germanic laws coincide with them so closely in single

[1] Lex Angl. tit. x. c. 9.   Laws of Æthelberht, xvii.

[2] Lex Angl. tit. vii. 4.   Laws of Ine, xvi. xxxv.   Laws of Wihtræd, xxv.

[3] Palgrave, vol. i. p. 223.

[4] " Campus judicat ; " hence, Kampe, *champion, campio* ; Kamp, Low
Saxon for *field*.

[5] Lex Angl. tit. xiv.   Annal. Winton. ap. Du Cange, voce ' Vomeres ' ;
Wharton, Anglia Sacra, t. i.   Cf. Theodor. Monach. Hist. Reg. Norv.
c. xxxiv. ap. Langebek, t. v. p. 340.   Capit. ad Leg. Salic. c. ix.   Capit. l. iv.
App. ii. c. 3.   LL. Longob. l. i. c. 10. § 3, and even LL. Hen. I. lxxxix.
§ 1.   Other laws enjoin twelve ploughshares.

points; so that if all other historic grounds were wanting, we must, nevertheless, place the laws of the Anglians in the nearest relationship to those of the Anglo-Saxons.

The third race which increased the new population of Britain was that of the Jutes, apparently less numerous than either of the before-mentioned, as they possessed only Kent, the Isle of Wight, and a part of Wessex, where for some centuries the Jutish race was distinguished from the Saxon[1]. Kent has certain customs of its own, among which the law of inheritance called Gavelkind[2] is well known, and also a peculiar dialect[3]. Even on a slight glance over the history of England, we must be repeatedly reminded of the distinguishing nationality of the men of Kent. More accurate inquiries, however, into the history of nations than have hitherto taken place, and especially into the history of England, will alone enable us to ascertain whether the oldest Jutish law resembles the custumal of Kent, and whether the Jutish forefather may yet be traced in the Kentish man of the present day. One circumstance is, however, too striking not to have drawn to it the attention of others—while the other English shires are parted into hundreds or wapentakes, the county of Kent alone is divided into six *lathes*[4] of regular form, and of nearly equal magnitude. These divisions, which have in later times become mere districts for judicial purposes, served at an earlier period for the quartering and muster of the military and of the general levy. But in the Jutish law[5] a military expedition is still called a 'lething' (in modern Danish, 'leding');

---

[1] Beda, i. 15, iv. 16. Sax. Chron. a. 449. Juti Vectiani, and Cantiani Juti, about the year 900 are mentioned by Wallingford, ap. Gale, i. p. 538.

[2] See page 39.

[3] A remarkable and valuable specimen of the Kentish dialect exists in the 'Ayenbyte of Inwyt' (MS. Arundel. 57.), which, though written in 1340, may still be regarded as Anglo-Saxon. See Cædmon, Pref. p. xii. Mr. T. Wright, to whom all lovers of early English lore are greatly beholden, has announced an edition of this interesting relic.—T.

[4] LL. Edw. Conf. xxxi. var. lect. 13.

[5] Lib. iii. c. 2. 12.

whence the district summoned together for such expedition may have borne that name. In like manner the word ' fyrd,' the military levy of the Anglo-Saxons,—the old signification of which does not appear to have been preserved in any other monuments of the German tongue,—is still used in Holstein, where it signifies the assembly of the States, originally for military purposes, at Bornhöved. The earliest record known to us of any of the customary laws of Kent[1] refers chiefly to circumstances arising out of the feudal system; while the Jutish Law of King Waldemar the Second, in the thirteenth century, has adopted many Saxon and other foreign principles; both, however, contain the enactment, that the son, in reference to the property of the deceased husband, shall be considered of age in his fifteenth year[2]; a principle which, though on the one side in accordance with the Danish laws, and, on the other, valid among the socmen[3] in other parts of England, is probably not derived from the Saxon laws, but rather to be referred to the immigration of the Jutes.

It is hardly probable that, in those days of national migrations and military services, so splendid an enterprise as the conquest of Britain should not have allured many bands from the kindred tribes of Germany; these, however, were not, it seems, sufficiently numerous to claim notice in the most authentic narratives. Frisians, on account of their proximity, their skill in seamanship, their language so nearly resembling the Anglo-Saxon, and the traditions already mentioned, we might expect to meet with before all others[4]; but from affinity

[1] Statutes of the Realm, vol. i. p. 223–225. Many of the usages there mentioned will, however, be recognised as common Anglo-Saxon law.

[2] Jüt. Lov, lib. i. c. 7.

[3] Glanvile, lib. vii. c. 9. § 2.

[4] Fin filius Folcwald, who was a Frisian chief, appears as an ancestor of Hengest in the genealogies as given by Nennius and those following him; but the Saxon authorities, viz. the Chronicle, Asser, Ethelwerd, the Textus Roffensis, also Florence and Snorre, concur in naming Godwulf as the father of this Fin; while in ' Beowulf,' ' The Scôp's Tale ' (Traveller's Song), and ' The Battle of Finnesburh,' Fin son of Folcwalda appears, not

of language, however, no inference is to be drawn, as it would
tend to the exclusion of the remoter German races; nor
should too much importance be attached to such words as
' seax,' the long knife of the Saxons, from which they are supposed to have derived their name, and which was common
also to the Frisians[1], and is still to be met with in that country;
as on the same ground the Icelanders must also be considered
as Saxons[2]. Even the striking similitude between the old
Frisic and the Anglo-Saxon public and private law, although
affording the most decisive testimony as to the relationship
of the two nations, does not allow us to make any further inference with regard to Britain; more especially as our oldest
accounts of the Frisians are too defective to enable us to ascertain what influence the connexion with the Anglo-Saxons,
and the migration of the latter may have had on the tribes
of Friesland. The assertion of Procopius[3], that Angles and
Frisians dwelt on the isle of ' Brittia,' notwithstanding the
fables in the rest of the narrative, appears credible on account
of its antiquity and other circumstances to be discussed hereafter. Later testimonies show with greater certainty the existence of the descendants of Frisic forefathers in England,

as an ancestor, but as an adversary of Hengest, by whom he is attacked
and slain in his dwelling, Finnesburh or Finnesham, in Friesland. I find
it therefore much more reasonable to prefer in this case the Saxon authorities, and to suppose that there were two Fins, living at very distant times,
than to seek to reconcile them with an apparent error of Nennius, by the
aid of hypotheses hardly in accordance with our notions of a more than
semi-barbarous people. In these meagre traditions exist, I firmly believe,
faint traces of persons that once had being, and actions that once took
place; but that they generally require a mythic interpretation is to me
more than questionable.—T.

[1] Asega-Buch, tit. iii. § 13, tit. v. § 17. [J. Grimm considers the de-
rivation from *sax* (sahs, *a stone or stone weapon, saxum*) as undeniable. D.
M. p. 204, and Massmann's ' Abschwörungsformeln,' p. 18. At all events,
the coincidence of the words, seax, franca and angul, signifying weapons,
with the names of three warlike nations, is, if accidental, not a little remarkable.—T.]

[2] Sax, *machæra*. B. Haldorsen.—T.

[3] De Bello Goth. lib. iv. c. 20.

but do not prove the establishment of any state or considerable settlement of that people in the country[1].

Of the participation of the Franks there exists some, though not sufficiently specific accounts : the same may be observed with respect to the Longobards. Little doubt can, however, be entertained regarding either the one or the other, as we elsewhere, in similar undertakings, find Saxons united with Franks and Longobards; the latter especially, when the complete occupation of the British southern or eastern coasts made a new field for conquests desirable[2].

But little attention has hitherto been paid to the national diversity of the Germanic races which established themselves in Britain, and the collective appellation of Angles, which became common at an early period, as well as the subsequent political unity, have caused us to overlook the variety of elements of which the population of Great Britain is composed; although, at the present day, after a lapse of nearly fifteen centuries, even in the instance of the Celtic tribes, striking varieties in laws and dialect, as well as peculiarities of figure, hair, and eyes, are still discernible, and prove their indelible

---

[1] Vita S. Swiberti : " Egbertus sitiens salutem Frisonum et Saxonum, eo quod Angli ab eis propagati sunt." The Sax. Chron., a. 897, mentions, that the ships constructed by Ælfred were shaped neither like the Frisian nor the Danish ; and also gives us the names of three Frisians of distinction slain in a sea-fight with the Danes, together with seventy-two men, Frisians and English. The circumstance, however, that they are mentioned separately leads us to regard these Frisians rather as allies than inhabitants. In Vita S. Liudgeri, c. xi., Frisian merchants are spoken of as strangers. Beda also (iv. 22) has a story of a slave bought by a Frisian in London.

[2] See Paul. Diacon. De Gestis Longob. lib. ii. c. 6, and lib. iii. c. 6. Of the connexion between the Anglo-Saxons and Longobards we shall again have occasion to speak ; but will here observe, that Sceaf, one of the ancestors of Woden in the genealogy of the West Saxon kings, is called a king of the Longobards, and that the old Longobardic kings, Agelmund, Lethus, Audoin, and his son Alboin, are celebrated in Anglo-Saxon song. See ' The Song of the Traveller ' in Conybeare's Illustrations, p. 9. [Also Cod. Exon. p. 318 ; Beowulf, edit. Kemble ; and Ettmüller's ' Scôpes Vidsidh,' accompanied by a valuable commentary, illustrative of the persons mentioned in the poem and its ethnography.—T.]

natural affinity with those of the ancient country. Must not these characteristics have displayed themselves in early times much more manifestly than at present? The answer is obvious ; and to this cause, no doubt, may be ascribed the great weakness of the Anglo-Saxon power, when, fleeing before the invading Northmen, the sons yielded the dominion of the land which their valiant forefathers had conquered. The slow introduction of Christianity, the disputes of the clergy in the north and south of England by which it was followed, the disunion which prevailed during the invasions of foreign foes, the treaties with them,—in short, the most important events of the Anglo-Saxon sovereignty, find their true and natural illustration in an attentive consideration of the diversities of race.

These original, though not strongly marked differences among the invaders, lead us to the obvious, though neglected remark, that a considerable part of what we are accustomed to regard as the religion, law, customs, and language of the Anglo-Saxons, arose only in the course of some centuries, from the blending of the several elements. As any attempt at detail of what the immigrants brought with them from their home is not admissible in this place, we shall defer till a future opportunity the discussion of that which may be more strictly regarded as Anglo-Saxon, occasionally adverting to what appears originally to belong to the Saxons, to the Angles, or to the Jutes.

Such were the races which, in the course of a century and a half, succeeded in gaining possession of the greater eastern portion of Britain. The more Roman the several districts had been, the sooner did the forsaken cities and towns become the prey of the barbarians. Of the resistance made by the Lloegrians, or Britons of the present England, at the outset of the struggle, few accounts are preserved. The discord among the British princes, by which the progress of the enemy was greatly facilitated, seems to have caused in the

53825

British traditionists themselves an indifference towards the fallen or lost states. Contemporary, though apparently not in alliance with Vortigern was Ambrosius Aurelianus, a chieftain of Roman descent, perhaps one of the British provincial emperors, who, though involved in a war with the British prince Guitolin, or Wetheling, withstood the advances of the Saxons with Roman tactics. It is probable that there were yet both Roman and Romanized warriors in detached fastnesses, who, however, would seem only to have increased the general disorder[1]. A defeat sustained by the Saxons, which compelled them to return home for the purpose of seeking reinforcements, was wisely turned to account by Ambrosius, in exciting the Lloegrians, and strengthening them against a further advance of the enemy. In many successive battles and skirmishes, the Lloegrians were alternately conquerors and conquered. The last considerable defeat sustained by the Saxons was at the siege of Bath[2]: other though inconsiderable contests took place, but which are known to us only through the accounts of the establishing of the several Anglo-Saxon kingdoms.

The contemporary who records the victory at Bath, gained by his countrymen in the first year of his life, and who bears witness of its consequences after a lapse of forty-four years[3], Gildas, surnamed the Wise, considers it superfluous to mention the name of the far-famed victor; but his wide-spread work, and the yet more wide-spread extracts from it in Beda, have reached no region in which the fame of king Arthur had not outstript them,—the noble champion who defended the liberty, usages and language of the ancient country from

[1] Gildas, c. xxv., and from him Beda, i. 16.   Nenn. c. xxviii. " Dum ipse (Gorthigernus) regnabat, urgebatur......et a Romanico impetu, necnon et a timore Ambrosii." id. c. i., and Gale, ibid.

[2] Gildas, c. xxvi.   Annal. Camb. a. 516.

[3] Beda, i. 16, has misunderstood this passage, and placed the battle in the forty-fourth year after the coming of the Saxons, i. e. in 492.   The ' Annales Cambriæ ' give 516 for the year.   Matt. Westmon. 520.

destruction by savage enemies; who protected the cross
against the pagans, and gained security to the churches most
distinguished for their antiquity and various knowledge, to
which a considerable portion of Europe owes both its Christianity and some of its most celebrated monasteries. Called
to such high-famed deeds, he needed not the historian to live
through all ages more brilliantly than the heroes of the chronicles, among whom he is counted from the time of Jeffrey of
Monmouth : but—not to mention the works which, about the
year 720, Eremita Britannus is said to have composed on the
Holy Graal, and on the deeds of king Arthur[1],—the rapid
spread of Jeffrey's work over the greater part of Europe
proves that the belief in the hero of it was deeply rooted. In
the twelfth century a Greek poem, recently restored to light,
was composed, in celebration of Arthur and the heroes of the
round table[2]. Still more manifestly, however, do the numerous local memorials which, throughout the whole of the then
Christian part of Europe, from the Scottish hills to Mount
Etna[3], bear allusion to the name of Arthur ; while on the
other hand, the more measured veneration of the Welsh poets
for that prince, who esteem his general, Geraint, more highly
than the king himself, and even relate that the latter, far from
being always victorious, surrendered Hampshire and Somersetshire to the Saxons, may be adduced as no worthless testimony for the historic existence of king Arthur[4]. Even those

[1] See Warton, H. E. P. vol. i. p. x. note b, edit. 1840.—T.

[2] This fragment of 306 verses was first published by Von der Hagen in
his 'Denkmale des Mittelalters,' Berlin, 1824, 8vo. Godfrey of Viterbo
also proves how rapidly the story became spread over Europe through Jeffrey of Monmouth. Part xviii. of his Chronicle contains some stories, in
hexameters and pentameters, of Voltiger, Orsus, Engist, Corinna (Rowena),
Uterpendragon, Merlin, Hierna (Hibernia), etc.

[3] Gervas. Tilbur. ap. Leibnitz, i. p. 921.

[4] Turner, Hist. of the A.-S. b. iii. c. 3.   He regards Llywarch Hên
and other poets as contemporary with Arthur. Similar accounts are also
to be found in the ' Historia Angliæ ad primordia Regis Stephani,' ascribed
by Bale and Pits to Richard of Devizes (see Stevenson's Preface to Chron.

traditions concerning him, which, at the first glance, seem composed in determined defiance of all historic truth,—those which recount the expedition against the Romans, on their demand of subjection from him, appear not totally void of foundation, when we call to mind that a similar expedition actually took place in Gaul; and are, moreover, informed, on the most unquestionable authority, of another undertaken in the year 468, on the demand of Anthemius, by the British general Riothamus,—who led twelve thousand Britons across the ocean against the Visigoths in Gaul,—and of his battles on the Loire[1]. This very valuable narrative gives us some insight into the connexions and resources of those parts of Britain which had not yet been afflicted with the Saxon pirates.

Arthur fell in a conflict on the river Camel in Cornwall, against his nephew Medrawd[2]: his death was, however, long kept secret, and his countrymen waited many years for his return and his protection against the Saxons. The discovery of his long-concealed grave in the abbey of Glastonbury is mentioned by credible contemporaries[3], and excited at the time no suspicion of any religious or political deception. Had the

---

Ric. Div, p. vii.), and in Chron. Radulfi Nigri, composed about 1161, both existing only in manuscript.

[1] Jornandes de Rebus Geticis, c. 45.   Sidonius Apollin. iii. ep. 9.

[2] So Annal. Cambr. a. 537.   According to Jeffrey, lib. xi. c. 2, Arthur in the year 542 resigned his crown.

[3] Girald. Cambrens. de Inst. Principis. [Bromton, coll. 1152, places the exhumation in the time of Henry II., Wendover in that of Richard I. His words are, "Eodem anno (1191) inventa sunt apud Glasconiam ossa famosissimi regis Britanniæ Arthuri, in quodam vetustissimo recondita sarcophago, circa quod duæ antiquissimæ pyramides stabant erectæ, in quibus literæ erant exaratæ, sed ob nimiam barbariem et deformitatem legi minime potuerunt......cui (sarcophago) crux plumbea superposita fuerat, in qua exaratum erat, ‘ Hic jacet inclytus Britonum rex Arthurus, in insula Avalonis sepultus.'" Roger de Wendover Chronica, t. iii. p. 48.   The veracity of the story seems extremely questionable.   Malmesbury (lib. iii.) says, "Arturis sepulchrum nusquam visitur, unde antiquitas næniarum adhuc eum venturum fabulatur."--T.]

king of England, Henry the Second, who caused the exhumation of the coffin in the year 1189, wished merely, through an artifice, to convince the Welsh of the death of their national hero, he would hardly himself have acted so conspicuous a part on the occasion. Poem and tradition bear witness to the spirit, and his ashes and the gravestone to the life and name of Arthur. Faith in the existence of this Christian, Celtic Hector cannot be shaken by short-sighted doubt, though much must yet be done for British story, to render the sense latent in the poems of inspired bards, which have in many cases reached us only in spiritless paraphrases, into the sober language of historic criticism.

While the British nation was more obstinately than successfully defending itself against the power of the Saxons[1], as it had done of old against the Romans, the greater part of the island was becoming the prey and the home of strangers. The British narratives of this period are extremely deficient, and the Anglo-Saxon accounts, particularly their chronology, seem deeply tinged with the fabulous.

Hengest was yet living when, in the year 477, Ælle (Ælli)[2] and his three sons, Cymen, ·Wlencing, and Cissa, landed from three ships at the place afterwards called Cymenes-ora[3], on the coast of Sussex. On the landing of the Saxons the Britons raised a loud cry, numerous bodies of them hastened from the neighbouring country, and war instantly commenced. The Saxons, who excelled in stature and bodily strength, re-

---

[1] Many of the natives fled to the ancient seats of the Veneti and Coriosolytani, where it is said that their successors, both in manners and language, still evince their affinity to the Welsh. Einh. Annal. a. 786.

[2] Beda (ii. 5) merely mentions his name as the first Bretwalda. The remaining account is from Henry of Huntingdon, the accuracy of whose excerpts from sources with which we are acquainted is a voucher for the same quality in those from lost or unknown authorities. See also Sax. Chron. Of the two forms (Ælle, Ælli) that in ' i ' is the more ancient.

[3] Keynor on Selsea. The locality of Cymenes-ora appears from a charter a. 673 in Monast. Angl. t. vi. p. 1163.

ceived their enemies with undaunted valour, while the latter imprudently hurrying forwards, were, as they approached disorderly and in separate bodies, slaughtered by the compact phalanx of Saxons, each successive band arriving only to witness and share the fate of its predecessor. The Britons were driven into the neighbouring forest of Andredes-leah, while the Saxons established themselves on the coast, and gradually extended their settlements, until, in the eighth year after their landing in Sussex, the princes and chieftains of the Britons, having united their forces, engaged with them in a great battle at Mearcredes-burne, the issue of which is doubtful. The armies much injured and weakened, each exercrating its conflict with the other, returned to their habitations: but Ælle sent to his German countrymen to demand reinforcements, which, arriving six years after, proceeded with that chieftain to the siege of the strong old Roman city of Andredes-ceaster, or Anderida. The Britons now gathered like swarms of bees, and warred on the besiegers by day with stratagems, by night with attacks. No day nor night passed in which new tidings of disaster did not embitter the minds of the Saxons, who with redoubled ardour continued their assaults on the city ; but the Britons were constantly at hand, with their arrows and other missiles, in the rear of the assailants; and when the Saxons, turning from the walls, directed their steps and arms against them, the Britons, who excelled in speed, hastened to the forests, issuing from whence, on the return of the Saxons to the works, they were again ready to assail them from behind. The Saxons being thus wearied, many too having fallen, divided their army into two bodies, of which while one attacked the city, the other might be armed against the assaults of the British. The citizens, now worn out by hunger, and no longer in a condition to withstand the ardour of the besiegers, found, with their wives and children, their death by the sword. Not one escaped, and Anderida was razed to the ground by the exasperated

victors.   Henry of Huntingdon knew merely the site of the
once noble city; in our days even this is become an object of
fruitless research.   Ælle, who had assumed the royal dignity
in Sussex, was now regarded as the supreme head of all England, as the first Bretwalda of the Anglo-Saxons: so at least
we are informed by Beda; though if we take into consideration the narrow compass of the Germanic possessions in
Britain at that time, if we call to mind that for almost a century no mention is made of a second Bretwalda, we may perhaps safely ascribe the Bretwaldaship of Ælle to the liberal
pen of the poet who has left us so circumstantial an account
of those early conflicts[1].

Ælle's death is said to have taken place between the years
514 and 519: it appears, therefore, that to him, as to Hengest,
was assigned a term of fifty years in England.   He was succeeded by his son Cissa[2], after whom we have a period of a
hundred and thirty years, during which neither chronicler nor
poet has transmitted to us one line concerning the kingdom
of Sussex, which, enclosed between two of the new Germanic
states, could not extend its limits by conquests in the British
territories.   Even the name which it bore before the rise of
other Saxon states gave occasion to the distinctive appellation
of South Saxons, has not been preserved.   We are, however,
informed that its thick forest and barriers of rock preserved
Sussex, the last hold of paganism, against the arms of the
other states; also that Cissa's posterity maintained the royal
dignity in Sussex, although their influence, through the rising
greatness of the other Germanic kingdoms, was necessarily
much diminished[3].

---

[1] It is remarkable that the genealogy of Ælle, the first Bretwalda, is the
only one not given among those of the founders of the several kingdoms of
the Octarchy.

[2] His memory is preserved in the name of Cissan-ceaster, now Chichester.

[3] H. Hunt. lib. ii. " Regnavit post eum Cissa, filius ejus, progeniesque
eorum post eos; at in processu temporum valde minorati sunt." Æddii

To its first German population belongs apparently the singular division of Sussex into six 'rapes[1],' each of which is
again divided into hundreds. These districts were probably
intended for military purposes.

The establishment of the third German kingdom in the
south of Britain is, through the supremacy afterwards acquired by Wessex, a subject of paramount interest. Cerdic,
a descendant in the ninth generation from Woden, who in
conflicts at home had already proved the energy of his soul,
in the view of adding to his military renown, landed nine
years after the death of Hengest[2], attended by his enterprising
and emulous son Cynric, from five ships at a spot afterwards
called Cerdices-ora[3], the locality of which is no longer known.
He posted his Saxons in close order of battle before his ships,
where they obstinately maintained their ground against the
repeated bold attacks of the islanders, until the approach of
night. Cerdic and his son proved their valour also in another
battle with the Britons, and extended themselves along the
sea-shore. The progress of the Saxons, however, was not
great until six years later, when Port with his two sons, Bieda
and Mægla, landed from two large ships[4]. The error committed on the earlier landings of the Germans, as well as on
Cæsar's, and at a later period on that of William the Norman, was here repeated—the disembarkation was not prevented; the country was called together with great clamour;
uncombined attacks, boldly commenced and by great numbers, were repulsed by the firmness of the enemy; the im-
prudent Britons fled in amazement, and Port remained victor
on the spot, which from him, as it is said, derives the name

Vita S. Wilfridi, c. xl. (South sex) "provincia gentilis, quæ præ rupium
multitudine et silvarum densitate aliis provinciis inexpugnabilis extitit."
Ædde was contemporary with Beda. The assertion of Matthew of Westminster, that, after Cissa's death, Sussex became a province of Wessex, is
of little weight against the foregoing.

[1] The Old Norse 'hreppr' denotes a nearly similar territorial division.
[2] A.D. 495.   [3] Sax. Chron. Fl. Wigorn. a. 495.   [4] A.D. 501.

of Portsmouth.   Mention is made of the death of a noble
young Briton in one of these conflicts, probably Geraint ab
Erbin, prince of Dyvnaint, whose fall in the battle of Llong-
borth is lamented in the elegies of his friend Llywarch Hên[1].
With extraordinary pomp of diction[2] the war is announced
of the greatest king of the Britons, Nazaleod or Natanleod,
but who is described elsewhere only as a general of the British
king Uther.   All Britain united against the foreign intruders ;
Cerdic on his side formed an alliance with Æsc king of Kent,
with Ælle the great king of the South Saxons, also with Port
and his sons.   Cerdic and Cynric led the two orders of battle.
Of these Natanleod attacked the most powerful, the right
wing commanded by Cerdic; the Saxon banners were beaten
down, their ranks broken; Cerdic fled, and vast slaughter
was instantly made among his forces: his son, however, at
the head of the left wing, pressed on the rear of the pursuers :
a new and bloody fight began; Natanleod fell, and with him
five thousand Britons; the rest found safety in their speed.

A few years only had passed in the tranquillity of secure
possession, when new auxiliaries arrived for new exploits.   In
the year 514 Stuf and Wihtgar, nephews of Cerdic, came with
three ships and landed at Cerdices-ora.   On the following
morning the British leaders arrayed their forces according to
the rules of war.   As one division advanced over the hills,
and another was proceeding cautiously through the valley,
the beams of the rising sun, which just shone out, gleamed
on their golden shields : the hills around were illumined with
their brilliancy, and the air seemed brighter.   The Saxons,
dreading with great dread, marched to the encounter; but
when these two great armies met in conflict, the energy of

[1] So Turner, who does not, however, notice an inconsistency in the
chronology of 29 years.   Palgrave too, vol. ii. p. ccxxxiv, says that Geraint
was slain in the year 501, and at p. cclxiii, in 530.

[2] H. Hunt. "Bellum scripturus sum quod Nazaleod, rex maximus Brittannorum," etc. Cf. Sax. Chron. a. 508, and ibidem Gibson. Fl. Wigorn.

the Britons was extinguished. Stuf and Wihtgar conquered many districts, and Cerdic's power through them became formidable: he now marched through the land confident in his strength. After twice eight years, Stuf and Wihtgar with their uncle gained a great victory in the Isle of Wight, at a place which afterwards bore the name of Wihtgares-burh (Carisbrook). This victory put Cerdic in possession of that isle, which he bestowed on his two nephews[1].

Cerdic also fought a great battle against the Britons at a place afterwards named Cerdices-ford (Charford in Hampshire), in which the latter displayed great valour, until, on the approach of evening, the Saxons gained the victory. Though great the loss sustained on this occasion by the inhabitants of Albion, it would have been yet greater had not the setting sun put an end to the conflict[2].

Having now passed thrice eight years in Britain, in the midst of battles, Cerdic and Cynric assumed the kingly title. The original kingdom of the Gewissas[3], or West Saxons, was, as is evident from the site of the last-mentioned battle, hardly more extensive than the other Germanic states in Britain, and barely reached beyond the borders of Hampshire and the territory of the Sumersætas. These provinces are stated to have been surrendered to the Saxons by King Arthur, after

---

[1] A.D. 530.

[2] A.D. 519.   H. Hunt. lib. ii.

[3] Beda, iii. 7, and Smith's note. " Occidentales Saxones, qui antiquitus Gevissæ vocabantur."—So called either from their western locality, analogously with Visigothi, or from Gewis, the great-grandfather of Cerdic. Asser, Vita Ælfr. *init.*, says, " Gewis, a quo Britones totam illam gentem Gegwis nominant." The British historians also, who never distinguish the other tribes, know the Giuoys. See Annal. Camb. a. 900. Galf. Mon. iv. 15, v. 8, viii. 10, xii. 14, [who speaks of Gewissi in Warwickshire and Worcestershire during the time of the Romans. (See p. 38.) The denomination, as applied to a British tribe, was probably derived by the traditionists of that nation from Gevissa, the mother of Glovi, from whom, according to them, the city of Gloucester was named. See p. 67, note [1].—T.]

he had given a check to their further advances near Bath[1]:
the possession of them, however, implies also that of a portion of the land of the Dorsætas and the Wiltsætas.   Eight
years afterwards the Gewissas gained another great battle
over the Britons at Cerdices-leah[2].   Cerdic's death is recorded in the sixteenth year of his reign over the West Saxons,
and like that of Hengest and Ælle, in the fortieth after his
arrival in Britain[3], a number, as already observed, used merely
to denote a long reign, the precise duration of which is not
known.   A similar custom of using this number for any un-
determined large number prevailed also among the Persians,
even when the real number was known to be larger.   Cynric
succeeded his father in Wessex : the Isle of Wight was given,
as a kingdom dependent on Wessex, to his cousins, of whom
Wihtgar, it is said, was a son of Cerdic's sister[4].   The Isle
of Wight was peopled by Jutes; hence it is probable that
Cerdic's sister was married to a powerful Jute, whose sons
led their victorious followers from Jutland, if not from Kent,
which had been long inhabited by that people.

Cynric gradually extended the boundaries of his kingdom,
the capital of which was Winchester (Wintan-ceaster), the
old Venta Belgarum.   A vast army of Britons being assembled to attack him, he, in conjunction with the forces of his
friends, hastened to encounter them, and near Searobyrig
(Old Sarum[5]) totally defeated and put their numerous host

---

[1] Gildas, c. xxvi., where see Stevenson's pref. p. viii.   Radulphus in R.
Higdeni Polychron. p. 224.   Ric. Divisiensis MS. ap. Langhorne, Chron.
Regum Angliæ, p. 70.   See p. 102.

[2] A.D. 527.

[3] So W. Malm.   According to the Sax. Chron., which places his death
in 534, he died in the thirty-ninth year after his arrival, according to the
calculation of the lunar year before noticed with regard to Hengest.   [Ac-
cording to five MSS., Malmesbury assigns a reign of only fifteen years to
Cerdic; only two MSS. have sixteen.—T.]

[4] Asseri Vita Ælfredi, init.   W. Malm. lib. i.   According to H. Hunt.
lib. ii. this donation took place in 534, shortly before the death of Cerdic.

[5] A.D. 552.

to flight. Less favourable to Cynric and his son Ceawlin
was a great battle fought some years later against the united
forces of the Britons, in which the latter were indebted to
their order of battle, according to the rules of Roman tactics[1],
for their preservation from the defeat with which they were
threatened from the strength and valour of the Saxons. The
chronicles assign to Cynric a reign of twenty-six years, yet
state his death to have taken place in the sixty-fifth year after
his landing in Britain; but an account seems to have existed,
according to which he, like the son of Hengest, died in the
sixty-fourth year after his arrival, and consequently in the
twenty-fourth year after the death of Cerdic[2]. Contradic-
tions between historic traditions and the verses of the poet
were difficult to reconcile, and they are much more so now :
all that is incumbent on us is to point out the great uncertainty of the several accounts, though the facts which are recorded may in their general outlines be acknowledged as authentic.

Although it may excite in us no surprise that, in a time of
universal dissolution, the occupation of isolated tracts of coast
by an enemy attracted at first but little notice, and that at a
later period the reward of historic glory was bestowed only
on the new and powerful lords of the soil, it might, nevertheless, have been expected that circumstantial and trustworthy accounts would have communicated to us the events

[1] A.D. 556. H. Hunt. lib. ii. " Novem acies......tribus scilicet in fronte
locatis, et tribus in medio, et tribus in fine, ducibusque in ipsis aciebus
convenienter institutis, virisque sagittariis et telorum jaculatoribus equiti-
busque jure Romanorum dispositis." A similar passage occurs shortly
after, "Cum autem Brittones more Romanorum acies distincte admo-
verent."

[2] Sax. Chron. Fl. Wigorn. a. 560. H. Hunt. " Regnum Westsexe
incipit anno adventus Anglorum lxxi., anno ab incarnatione Domini 519."
" Cerdic regnavit xvii. annis in Westsexe." According to this account
Cynric succeeded his father in 536, or twenty-four years before his death ;
though the same chronicler says, " Kinric cum regnasset xxvi. annis mortuus est."

connected with the city of London, a place of prominent interest in every age, through its commerce and the arts in-
separable therefrom.   But the pen of the genius of trade is,
like the net of the fisher, devoted only to the contemplated
gain.   No territory ever passed so obscurely into the possession of an enemy as the north bank of the Thames, where
the kingdom of the East Saxons comprised the counties of
Essex and Middlesex, of which the latter continued probably
for some time in a state of independence.   The year 527 is
mentioned as that of the first landing of the Saxons there;
and Æscwine, or Ercenwine[1], as its first prince, a son of
Offa, a descendant of Seaxneat (Saxnôt), the abjuration of
whose worship, together with that of Thor (Thunaer) and
Woden, was, after a lapse of ages, exacted from the Saxon
converts of the continent[2].   Æscwine is said to have reigned
during a patriarchal period of sixty years : his name reminds
us of Æsc, the prince of the Jutes, on the southern shore of
the Thames, and of the race of the Æscings, though that of
his father would indicate a relationship to the Offings, the
royal race of Mercia ; while his descent from the Saxon gods,
as well as the name of his kingdom, speak for his pure Saxon
lineage.   The geographical position of this state may, however, be rather in favour of the supposition of a mixture of
several races, to which the account of a more critical chronicler, who gives Sleda, in the year 587, as the first king of
Essex, seems no contradiction[3]; though it is far from improbable, that the earliest settlements of the Germans on this
coast reach up to a much remoter period, and have connexion
with the appellation of ' Litus Saxonicum.'

Northwards of the East Saxons was established the king-

---

[1] H. Hunt.   Geneal. ap. Fl. Wigorn.

[2] See Grimm, D. M. p. 203.   Massmann's 'Abschwörungsformeln,'
pp. 14, 67.   Pertz, Monum. Hist. Germ. t. iii. p. 19.—T.

[3] W. Malm. lib. i.   He makes no mention of his father, but says merely
that he was the tenth in descent from Woden, which involves no inconsistency with the other accounts.

dom of the East Angles, in which a northern and a southern people (Northfolc and Suthfolc) were distinguished. It is probable that, even during the last period of the Roman sway, Germans were settled in this part of Britain; a supposition that gains in probability from several old Saxon sagas, which have reference to East Anglia at a period anterior to the coming of Hengest and Horsa. The land of the Gyrwas, containing twelve hundred hides, which was also accurately divided into a southern and a northern portion, comprised the neighbouring marsh districts of Ely and Huntingdonshire, almost as far as Lincoln. Of the East Angles Wehha or Wewa[1], or more commonly his son, Uffa or Wuffa, from whom his race derived their patronymic of Uffings or Wuffings, is recorded as the first king[2].

The neighbouring states of Mercia originated in the marsh districts of the Lindisware, or inhabitants of Lindsey (Lindesig), the northern part of Lincolnshire. With these were united the Middle Angles[3]. This kingdom, divided by the Trent into a southern and a northern portion, gradually extended itself to the borders of Wales. Among the states which it comprised was the little kingdom of the Hwiccas, conterminous with the later diocese of Worcester, or the counties of Gloucester, Worcester, and a part of Warwick. This state, together with that of the Hecanas, comprising the ancient bishopric of Hereford, bore the common Germanic appellation of the land of the Magesætas[4].

Henry of Huntingdon, though a writer abounding in traditions, and, at the same time, a native or inhabitant of those parts, gives us no legends relative to the establishment of the two last-mentioned states. After the victory at Cerdicesford, and probably at an earlier period, many chieftains

---

[1] Fl. Wigorn. Geneal. ap. Petrie. Nennii App.

[2] Beda, ii. 15. H. Hunt. a. 571.

[3] Beda, i. 15, iii. 21. Malmesb. de Antiq. Glaston. Eccles. ap. Gale, i. p. 295.   [4] Fl. Wigorn. Appen.

passed over from Germany to those territories, and, in emulation of each other, possessed themselves of several tracts.
Their number has caused their names to be forgotten : their
territories towards the end of the century were united with
the two last-mentioned kingdoms[1]. Creoda, or Cridda, the
son of Cynewald, and tenth in descent from Woden[2], appears
as the first king of Mercia.

In addition to the doubts attending the descent, and even
the name of the Angles, the genealogies of their kings demand
and merit discussion. In that of the kings of Mercia we
find three names in succession, which accord with a similar
unbroken series in the Danish traditions, viz. the descendants
of Woden, Wihtlæg, Wærmund, and Offa[3], who stand in the
Danish chronicles as Wiglet, Wermund, and Uffo, descendants of Odin, and ancestors of the conquerors of Britain[4].
Even the resemblance of the names of Offa's posterity, Angeltheow and Eomer, to the Danish Ingeld and Iaomer is very
remarkable ; and that the progenitors of Woden, both in the
Anglo-Saxon and Scandinavian genealogies, have many names
in common, and that among these Sceaf is regarded in the
latter as a king of Sleswig, or the country of Angeln, may,
after what has already been stated, seem the more worthy of
notice. An inquiry into the value of these resemblances in
an historic point of view would here, perhaps, be out of place ;
but attention should be directed to the evidence furnished by
this accordance of the traditions, in favour of deriving the

[1] H. Hunt. p. 313. "Ea tempestate venerunt multi et sæpe de Germania, et occupaverunt Eastangle et Merce." Matt. Westmon. a. 527.
Radulphus ap. Higden Polychron. lib. v. p. 224, has the year 492. Florence
says of Mercia merely, "Post initium regni Cantuariorum, principium extitit regni Merciorum." But of East Anglia, "Regno *posterius* Cantuariorum, et *prius* regno Occidentalium Saxonum exortum est ;" consequently
before the year 495.   [2] Sax. Chron. a. 626.

[3] Sax. Chron. In Nennius, Guithleg, Guerdmund, and Offa.

[4] See Erici Chron. Sax. Grammat. Sv. Aggonis Hist. Reg. Dan. c. i.
has only the two last. The Icelandic Langfedgatal also omits the first, and
calls Uffo, Olaf.

origin of the Angles and Mercians from the country north of the Eider.

The history of the Angles receives some light from a Byzantine historian. Procopius, who died in 562, before Uffa reigned in East Anglia, mentions a king of the Angles in Brittia or Britain, in the years 534–547, whose sister was betrothed to Radiger, king of the Warni, but who, on the death of his father, in violation of his engagement, married his stepmother, a sister of the Frankish king Theudebert. To revenge the slight, the Anglian lady, after a fruitless expostulation by embassy, sailed, with an army, and attended by one of her brothers, to an outlet of the Rhine. In a battle which followed their landing, the Warni were defeated, and their prince, being captured in his flight, was brought bound into the presence of the Angle, who, to his glad surprise, after reproaching him for his want of faith, and on his promise to atone for it by renouncing his stepmother and fulfilling his prior engagement, restored him to liberty and treated him honourably. Their marriage followed as a matter of course[1]. However fabulous other accounts communicated by that writer may be, concerning some Angles sent to the emperor Justinian at Constantinople, the fact is, nevertheless, worthy of notice, that Angles and Frisians are mentioned by him as inhabitants of the island; also a king of the Angles at that period, and (as in the before-mentioned laws[2]) a connexion between the Angles and the Warni. What the same author states, that the powerful king of the Franks, Theudebert, took advantage of the emigration of some Angles to his country, and of the distracted condition of Britain, for the purpose of arrogating to himself the appearance of a supremacy over it, was a natural consequence of the pretensions of the Frankish monarchs to the dignity of Emperor of the West, which must also find additional grounds in the ancient provincial administration, under which Britain was considered a diocese subordinate to Gaul.

[1] De Bello Gothico, iv. 20.   [2] See pp. 93–96.

Political relations between the Anglo-Saxons and the court of Byzantium, of a tendency hostile to the Franks, were in the following century apprehended by the latter[1], a suspicion which at least implies other close connexions between them. Pope Gregory the Great also, in a letter to the Frankish kings, Theuderic and Theudebert, relative to his design of converting the Angles, appears to speak of them as subjects of those princes; from which, however, nothing is perhaps to be inferred beyond pretensions, which he deemed it advisable to treat with delicacy and favour in his intercourse with his royal Christian allies[2].

The history and the poetry of those remote and unlettered ages have long lain reconciled in the same grave, and we cannot awaken the ashes of the one without—and often unconsciously—bringing the other back to light. As connected with this remark, we must not omit to mention that East Anglia contains a rich store, little known and still less investigated, of old traditions: among others the saga of King Atla of Northfolk, the founder of Attlebury; of Roud, king of Thetford[3]; also the yet more wide-spread one of Havelok, or Cuharan (Cwiran), king of Northfolk, and son of Ethelbert the Dane, who dwelt in that country before the time of

---

[1] Beda, iv. 1.

[2] Gregorii Epist. lib. vi. c. 58.   Bedæ Opera Minora ed. Stevenson, p. 234. .... "magnam de vobis materiam præsumendi concepimus, quod subjectos vestros ad eam converti fidem per omnia capiatis, in qua eorum nempe reges estis et domini.   Atque ideo pervenit ad nos Anglorum gentem ad fidem Christianam, Deo miserante, desideranter velle converti."

[3] This poem, consisting of about 12,000 verses, was originally either in Anglo-Saxon or Semi-Saxon, and was translated into French verse at the desire of a certain countess, *when the original could not be understood* (i. e. by the Anglo-Norman nobility), probably in the thirteenth century; which version was translated into Latin by John Brame or Brome, who informs us that the French differed considerably from the English original.   The original name of the king appears to have been Waldeus, not Atla.   The Latin elaboration of the poem is in the library of C.C.C. Camb.   A manuscript of the French Romance of King Atla, once Mr. Heber's, is now in the possession of Sir T. Phillipps, Bart.   See Sir F. Madden's note in Warton, H. E. P. vol. i. p. 41, edit. 1840.—T.

Hengest and Horsa[1],—traditions which seem to confirm what history, from the days of Carausius, renders far from improbable.

The country to the north of the Humber had suffered the most severely from the inroads of the Picts and Scots. It became at an early period separated into two British states, the names of which were retained for some centuries, viz. Deifyr (Deora rice), afterwards Latinized into Deira, extending from the Humber to the Tyne, and Berneich (Beorna rice), afterwards Bernicia, from the Tyne to the Clyde. Here also the settlements of the German races appear anterior to the date given in the common accounts of the first Anglian kings of those territories, in the middle of the sixth century. The traditions respecting Hengest relate that he founded for his son Octa, and for Ebusa the son of Horsa[2], Germanic states in the north of Northumbria, or, according to the older traditions, beyond the Firth of Forth, whither they sailed with forty ships, but which seem inconsistent with the account, that Hengest himself, when driving before him the Picts and Scots, did not advance further than Lincolnshire. According to a much neglected account, Deira had already been sepa-

---

[1] A limited edition of 'The Ancient English Romance of Havelok the Dane,' 4to, accompanied by the French text and a valuable glossary, was published in 1828 by Sir F. Madden, of which the French text has been reprinted at Paris. The tale of Havelok is also given in 'L'Estorie des Engles, solum la Translation Maistre Geffrei Gaimar,' ap. Petrie, C. H. p. 764. Later English chroniclers likewise (as Knyghton, lib. i. c. 5, who cites a Historia de Grimesby) make mention of the story. See also, in 'Literary Introduction,' remarks on Robert de Brunne.

[2] Nennius, c. xxxviii. W. Malm. lib. i., who calls Octa the brother of Hengest and Ebusa the son. A confirmation of these accounts may be found in Galfr. Monum. lib. i. c. i., where Modrawd promises to Childeric the country between the Humber and Scotland, and that which in Vortigern's time Horsa and Hengest possessed in Kent. According to Jeffrey, who is here very prolix, Octa son of Hengest received York, and his cousin Eosa, Alcluyd with the remaining country bordering on Scotland. See lib. viii. c. 6, 8, 18, 21, 23. Abisa, Ebusa, Eowis, Eosa denote the same individual.

rated from Bernicia by Soemil the son of Zegulf (Sæfugl), whose grandson Guilglis (Wihtgils) was the father of Hengest, and grandfather of Yffe (Yffi), of whom we are about to speak[1]; and we know also, from other accounts, that both Hengest and Yffe descended from the same son of Woden, Wecta or Wægdæg[2]. This tradition is important from the information it contains that the Saxon settlements in the North of Britain were older than those in the South. Attention must also here again be drawn to the circumstance already noticed, that while the South-English chronicles fix the landing of Hengest and Horsa in, or rather after, the year 449, the oldest North-English authorities place the arrival of the Angles in 445 or 446, not to mention the earlier invasion of these people. Nennius fixes 447 for the year of Hengest's landing, from which it would seem that the Saxon chieftains of the North threw off the supremacy of the Kentish kings after a lapse of a full century, instead of founding, according to the received tradition, a new kingdom in the year 547. Fifty years later, or about the year 500, the city of Eboracum is said to have been taken by the Saxons, and the archbishop to have fled to Armorica, where he founded the bishopric of Dol. Nor perhaps to be totally rejected is the story that Colgrim and his brother Baldwulph conquered these countries, but were beaten by Arthur in the year 516, on the river Duglas[3].

Ida, the son of Eoppa, a descendant of Woden (to whom in this genealogy five forefathers are assigned), is, according to the Anglo-Saxon traditions, regarded as the founder of the Anglian kingdom of Bernicia, in the year 547; or rather as the first who freed the land, hitherto governed by nine sub-

---

[1] Nenn. App. Soemil and his son Swearta (Swerthing) are wanting in the genealogy given in the Sax. Chron. Swerthing, a prince of the Saxons, was the slayer of Frothi IV. See Saxo. pp. 273, 282, edit. Müller.

[2] Sax. Chron. a. 560, etc.

[3] Nenn. c. lxiv. Galf. Monum. lib. ix. c. 1, and from the latter, Matt. Westm. a. 516.

ordinate rulers, from the supremacy of the kings of Kent[1]. He arrived with forty or sixty ships of the Angles[2], and, after having reigned twelve years, is said to have fallen in a battle against Urien of Cumberland and Reged, leaving twelve sons. Bebbanburh, now Bamborough, perpetuates the name of his consort Bebbe[3]. His immediate successor seems to have been Glappa, who was followed by Adda, Æthelric, and Theodric, sons of Ida. About the same time Ælle son of Yffe (Yffi), of descent equally illustrious, conquered the greater part of the kingdom of Deira[4].

So trivial, and yet more uncertain, are the accounts left us of the conquest of a great kingdom by the barbarous dwellers on the shores of the German Ocean, and of the spoliation perpetrated among structures and other property, the fruits of Roman civilization, on a people accustomed to servitude, who knew but little how to use them and still less to defend them.

The Britons were soon restricted to the western parts of the island, where they maintained themselves in several small states, of which those lying to the east yielded more and more to Germanic influence; the others, protected by their mountains, preserved for a considerable time a gradually decreasing independence. As opportunities for touching on the history

---

[1] Scala Chron. Cf. Gale ad Nennium, c. lxv. W. Malm. lib. i.

[2] Chronol. ap. Wanley and Petrie. Fl. Wig. Sim. Dunelm. Wallingford.

[3] Sax. Chron. a. 547. According to Nenn. App. Bebbe was the consort of Æthelfrith, the grandson of Ida. " Eqdfered Flesaurs reguavit xii. annis in Berneich, et alios xii. in Deur,......et dedit uxori suæ Dinguo Aroy, quæ vocatur Bebbbab, et de nomine suæ uxoris suscepit nomen, id est, Bebbanburch." The passage in Beda (iii. 6) does not decide who was the husband of Bebbe.

[4] Sax. Chron. a. 560. In stating the perplexed genealogy of the kings of Bernicia to the year 592, the authority has been followed of the chronicle in Wanley and Petrie, and of Simeon, who in matters connected with Northumbria is particularly trustworthy. These two authorities, though slightly differing in the regnal years, agree in the order of succession, while the lists in Florence and Nennius are irreconcileable both with the above authorities and with each other.—T.

of these small British states will hereafter be but rarely afforded, a short notice of them is the more desirable : though
some separate states occasionally occur as united into one,
while others may have arisen from comparatively later par-
titions.

In the south-west we meet with the powerful territory of
Damnonia, the kingdom of Arthur, which bore also the name
of West Wales. Damnonia, at a later period, was limited to
Dyvnaint, or Devonshire, by the separation of Cernau, or
Cornwall. The districts called by the Saxons those of the
Sumorsætas, of the Thornsætas (Dorsetshire), and the Wiltsætas were lost to the kings of Dyvnaint at an early period ;
though for centuries afterwards a large British population
maintained itself in those parts among the Saxon settlers, as
well as among the Defnsætas, long after the Saxon conquest
of Dyvnaint, who for a considerable time preserved to the
natives of that shire the appellation of the ' Welsh kind.'

Cambria (Cymru), the country which at the present day
we call Wales, was divided into several states, the chief of
which were—Venedotia (Gwynedd), consisting of the greater
part of North Wales. The king of Gwynedd was supreme
over the other states ; his residence was at Aberfraw[1];—Dimetia (Dyved), or West Wales[2], comprising the district bounded
by the Tywi on the south-east, and the Tewi on the north-
west, or, in a wider sense, the country over which the ecclesiastical supremacy of the see of Mynyw or Menevia (St.

---

[1] Now a village on the west coast of Anglesey. Its name (aber Fraw,
the efflux of the Fraw,) is derived from being situated where the brook Fraw
flows into the sea. Glossary to Anc. LL. and Instt. of Wales.—T.

[2] Or South Wales ; but as Cornwall is sometimes called South Wales,
in like manner the name of West Wales is applied to Dimetia. Much
valuable information respecting the old geography and inhabitants of Wales
is to be found in the ' Itinerarium,' ' Cambriæ Descriptio,' and ' De Illaudabilibus Walliæ ' of Giraldus. [See also Ancient Laws and Institutes of
Wales, from which, and from Mr. Owen's notes, the account of the ancient territorial division of Wales given in this translation has been chiefly
compiled.—T.]

David's) extended. The residence of the Dimetian princes was at Dinevwr[1]. To the east of Gwynedd and the mountains, of which Snowdon forms the highest point, was Powys, the princes of which resided at Mathraval[2]. In Deheubarth, or South Wales, were several small states, the southernmost of which, Gwent (Monmouthshire), or South-east Wales, the country of the Silures, forming the present diocese of Llandaff (Landav), the royal seat of which was at Caerleon upon Usk, and Morganwg (Glamorganshire) lay on the northern bank of the Severn. Near, if not comprised within this state, between the rivers Usk and Taff, was the small principality of Gleguising. Along the Irish Channel lay Ceredigion and Brecheiniog, whose names are easily recognised in those of the present counties, and which appear to have been under separate rulers.

The chief tribes of the Britons, or, as they call themselves, Cymry, are distinguished by the various dialects of their common mother-tongue, among which the Venedotian, the Dimetian, and that of Glamorgan, are the principal. The Cymrian tongue was polished by illustrious poets,—Aneurin and Taliesin in the sixth, Llywarch Hên and others in the next following centuries, whose works in a state of tolerable purity have been preserved to the present time[3].

The usages and laws of the Cambrians were in all these states essentially the same. An invaluable and venerable monument of them, although of an age in which the Welsh had long been subject to the Anglo-Saxons, and had adopted many of their institutions and customs, are the laws of the

[1] Near Llandilo vawr, in the Vale of Tywi. Some remains of the castle are visible. Gloss. ut sup.—T.

[2] Situated in the upper part of the Vale of Meivod, near the junction of the two streams which form the river Evyrnwy. Gloss. ut sup.—T.

[3] See Turner's Vindication of the genuineness of the ancient British poems, at the end of the last volume of the third and following editions of his History of the Anglo-Saxons.

king Howel Dda[1], who reigned in the early part of the tenth century, which, with some local modifications, were acknowledged as valid in the other states of Wales.

The partition of Cambria into several small states is not, as it has often been supposed, the consequence of a division made by king Rodri Mawr, or Roderic the Great, among his sons; but which, supposing it to have taken place, could have reference only to the sovereignty over territories which many centuries before occur as separate states. Of Dyfed, during the first centuries after the coming of the Saxons, we know very little; but with regard to Gwynedd, which was in constant warfare with Northumbria and Mercia, our information is less scanty: of Gwent also, as the bulwark of Dimetia, frequent mention occurs. On the whole we are less in want of a mass of information respecting the Welsh, than of accuracy and precision in that which we possess. While the Welsh, in their historic narratives, as remarkable for singularity of expression as for their poetic garb, give either no dates whatever, or dates on which no reliance can be placed, the several states and their rulers are seldom spoken of in the Anglo-Saxon chronicles otherwise than under the universal appellation of the Britons, and their kings: hence a comparison of their respective accounts is frequently impracticable, each nation usually speaking only of its victories, very rarely of its reverses.

An obscurity still more dense than that over Wales involves the district lying to the north of that country, comprised under the name of Cumbria. This territory, sometimes united under a supreme chief, or Pendragon, called also Tyern (Tyrannus), who, like the other British princes, considered themselves not only as the successors, but also as the descendants of Constantine, or of Maximus, consisted of three

---

[1] In the Venedotian and Dimetian Codes, Howel styles himself 'king' or 'prince of all Cymru;' in the Gwentian Code, 'king of Cymru, when Cymru was in his possession in its bounds.'—T.

principal parts. The southern, or Cumberland, properly so called, comprised, besides the present county of that name, also Lancashire and Westmoreland, which latter appears likewise as a petty kingdom—Westmere. It extended into the later kingdom of Northumbria; and as the little state of Elmet seems also to have belonged to it, the town of Leeds must have been on its border. The old Roman Lugubalia, or Carleol, was its largest city, in which Arthur, Rhyddrich Hael, or the Liberal, and other princes celebrated in ancient song, are said to have held their Round Table or court[1]. The two northernmost kingdoms of the Britons, Reged and Strathcluyd, belong to the history of Scotland; yet as England extended as far as Edinburgh, they must not be passed without mention. Reged, a territory in the south of Scotland, in or near Annandale, is rendered worthy of notice on account of the protection offered to the bard Taliesin by its prince Urien, celebrated by Llywarch Hên, who was himself a prince of Argoed in Cumberland. The kingdom of Strathcluyd, comprising Clydesdale or Dunbartonshire—where its chief city, Alcluyd, was situated—the counties of Renfrew and Dumfries, and probably those of Peebles, Selkirk, and Lanark, in the east, continued to a much later period; and, although in constant warfare with the Anglo-Saxons, as well as with the Picts and Scots, its chiefs extended their power over all Cumberland, from which they were not expelled till the early part of the tenth century, when Cumberland, under Anglo-Saxon suzerainty, became a principality held by the heir of Scotland.

With respect to the first institutions adopted by the German chieftains in the conquered country, how the relations of service and tribute were fixed; how the Germans gradually united themselves into considerable kingdoms; how far the remains of Roman civilization, when they afforded no apparent or palpable advantage, were respected,—with regard to all

[1] A.D. 561.

this we have little beyond supposition; though the result, the Saxonizing of Britain by the Germanic heretogas, or ealdormen, and their followers, is as manifest as the Romanizing of Spanish America by Columbus and Pizarro. Of the history of these kingdoms from their foundation till their gradual conversion to Christianity, there exist scarcely any written accounts besides the series of their kings, which, in detached traditions, form but a very insignificant component of the national history.

While Anglo-Saxon sources are wanting, the British ones also either fail us, or must undergo a stricter critical ordeal than they have hitherto passed through, before any reliance can be placed on them. The Anglo-Saxon laws, even the earliest, are too recent and too exclusively restricted to the Germanic scale of penalties and atonements to aid us in drawing a picture of the condition of the country immediately after the Saxon conquest. Their silence on many points leads us, perhaps, on comparing them with the laws of other Germanic conquerors, to divine more than their scanty diction expresses.

The public affairs had, in consequence of the departure of the Romans and the inroads of enemies, fallen into the utmost disorder. What had formerly been public or private property of the Romans became, either by purchase or usurpation, a new unsettled possession in the hands of a people who had long forgotten how to govern. The inhabitants of the island were at that time, as their language sufficiently shows, scarcely to be called Romanized : on the contrary, the posterity of the Romans among them had rather assimilated themselves to the original Britons. In this state of dissolution it must have been an easier task to the conquerors of Britain than that which their warlike brethren found it in the better organized states of Europe, to obtain possession of the object of their efforts, without causing the rights of the stronger to be felt in the most oppressive manner. The former Roman property, which in the south, and especially on the coasts, must have been considerable, would satisfy the small number of strangers. That a certain portion of landed property, or of rents, or of produce, was regularly set apart for the conquerors, as was the custom in other Germanic states, is not probable, as in the accounts of the later conquests of the Anglo-Saxons in Britain, we meet with nothing leading to such a conclusion. Indeed the very gradual progress made in the occupation of many parts of Britain by detached hordes, independent of each other, and of various races, almost induces us to regard it less as a conquest than as a progressive usurpation of the British territory. From the circumstance that the Anglo-Saxons had to pass over in ships to the country destined for their future home, it follows that they brought with them but few women and children; and as Vortigern had no repugnance to an union with the daughter of Hengest, it is probable that the German warriors, with the exception, perhaps, of a few of noble race, would not disdain to unite themselves with the British women. If thereby the natives soon became intermingled with the strangers, still the latter, in virtue of the almost exclusive advantage of the male line with respect to inheritances, would not find such marriages prejudicial to their political independence. Many Britons fled before the pagan Germans, but the facility of flight weakened the power of resistance, and accelerated the advances of the enemy. Those Britons who, not being prisoners of war, peaceably remained, appear to have preserved their previous rights; since we find no considerable difference with regard to the wergild, the capability of bearing witness, and other rights, between the Britons and the Saxons[1].

A most important subject for consideration, observable from an early period, is the dignity of Bretwalda, borne by one of the most influential of the Anglo-Saxon princes during the period of his life, and which is said to have contained within

[1] Laws of Ine, xxiii., xxiv., xxxii.

one common bond all the inhabitants of Britain. The desire
to detect the continuation of Roman institutions has also in
this dignity been anxious to recognise an imitation of the
Roman emperors of the West, acknowledged at the same time
both by Saxons and Britons[1]. The acknowledgment of the
Britons, who were still united under a sovereignty of their
own, may be most confidently denied; the passion for imitation in the Saxon warriors, which could prompt them to
favour one of their fellows, who aspired to the authority of
their most formidable and hated enemy, may be very strongly
doubted. The pretensions of the most powerful Anglo-Saxon
king scarcely extended over the Germanic provinces of the
southern part of Britain : to other portions of the Roman
dominion they never reached. Imitation, both in the uncivilized and the weak, begins with the tinsel of unsubstantial
show, with the assumption of an empty name, of neither of
which any trace appears among the Anglo-Saxons till after
the lapse of some centuries. With the inquiry into the origin
of the office of Bretwalda, which in its later form exhibited
perhaps some traces of Roman imperial influence, may, in the
absence of more satisfactory accounts respecting the duties
and rights ascribed to that dignity, be joined the questions,
What notions the Germans brought from their native country,
and what occasion they found in Britain for the appointment
of that relative supremacy ?

To the North-Germanic and Danish nations kings ruling
over the whole race were unknown ; they were divided under
several chieftains[2], and we know that among these, although
the consideration of birth prevailed, their leaders in war were
chosen from the most valiant. To them nothing could be
more foreign than to found the dominion of a whole race on
the common language or on kinship.

Of the Jutes and Danes especially, we know that they for

[1] Palgrave, vol. i. p. 563.
[2] Cf. Dahlmann's Forschungen, Bd. i. p. 431 sq.

several centuries lived under a great number of kings, but
that they acknowledged the supremacy of the kings of Leire:
in like manner as the Swedish kings were subordinate to those
of Upsala; but that monarchy (einvalld) was a later institution among them[1]. The Frisian chiefs also acknowledged
a superior. In Britain a connexion between the southern
and northern Saxons was, as we have already seen, established
as early as the first conquests of Hengest: though the necessity of a common chief over all the Germanic provinces arose
in Britain partly from the great number of independent kings,
ealdormen and other potentates, whose states only in the
course of time lapsed into the kingdoms of the ' Heptarchy ';
and partly from the necessity of opposing a united resistance
to the Britons, combined against the divided power of the
foreign intruders, as well as to the Picts and Scots. For this
purpose—nor of any other is a trace to be discovered, and
for no other does such an union seem necessary, or even con-
ceivable—the Germans in Britain must have soon found an
alliance among their tribes indispensable. A common warfare
of several states without a dictator was not to be conceived;
and the call to that post was on the most powerful, or on him
whose territory was most exposed to hostile inroads. The
latter case we find the most frequent. Sussex is said to have
first enjoyed that supremacy when it had to defend Kent.
Kent laid claim to it while it yet possessed rights of suzerainty in the north, and subsequently obtained it; possibly as
an indemnity for its renunciation of such rights.

Wessex next formed the bulwark; but this state having
strengthened itself, and the struggle being carried on more
northwards, the chief military command passed to East Anglia, and lastly to Northumbria; neither of whose Anglian
states acknowledged the authority of the Bretwalda[2] until

---

[1] Snorre, Ynglinga Saga, c. xlv.
[2] Beda, i. 25. "Rex Ædilberctus in Cantia potentissimus, qui ad con-
finium usque Humbræ fluminis maximi, quo meridiani et septentrionales

the state of things had become changed. That those states
used the transient power for the aggrandizement of their territory was in the nature of things, and, at the same time, not
inconsistent with the object of the institution. The elective
emperor of the Germans, whose dignity was not attached to
hereditary states, nor to descent, but to the importance of the
individual, represents what the Bretwalda might have been, if
the general interest could have been conceived by the bar-
barian conquerors in a higher point of view. It is probable
that not only the choice of the other kings, but also of the
collective nobility and ealdormen, determined the nomination
of the Bretwalda ; for as, according to the words of an old
writer, he possessed sovereign power over all these[1], it is to
be inferred that, in the spirit of Germanic forms of government, the appointment was the result of a preceding free
election.

Notwithstanding the high estimation in which this dignity
was held from a very early period, yet Beda is unable to inform us who was invested with it after Ælle[2], until Ceawlin,
the grandson of Cerdic, became its possessor. A noble
Æscing, the young Æthelberht of Kent, would dispute it
with him, and invaded with his arms the territory of Wessex.
A defeat at Wibbandun (Wimbledon in Surrey[3]) humbled
the bold aspiring youth, whose disgrace was not effaced till
twenty years afterwards, when he attained the object of his
ambition. To his brother Cuthwulf, whom he unfortunately
lost in the same year, Ceawlin was indebted for a most important victory over the Britons, which brought the towns of
Lenbury, Aylesbury, Bensington and Eynsham under his

Anglorum populi dirimuntur, fines imperii tetenderat." Lib. ii. 5. "Ædil-
berct......tertius quidem in regibus gentis Anglorum, cunctis australibus
eorum provinciis quæ Humbræ fluvio et contiguis ei terminis sequestrantur
a borealibus, imperavit." See also lib. ii. 3.

[1] " Omnia jura regni Anglorum, reges scilicet et proceres et tribunos in
ditione sua tenebat." H. Hunt. lib. ii.   [2] Beda, ii. 5.

[3] Sax. Chron. a. 568. W. Malm. lib. i. H. Hunt. lib. ii.

dominion[1]. Not less fortunate was Ceawlin some time afterwards, when, with the aid of his brother Cutha, or Cuthwine,
after a battle at Derham in Gloucestershire, in which three
British kings were slain—Conmail, Farinmail (probably of
Gwent), and Condidan or Cyndillom (of Pengwern or Shrewsbury)—he won three cities, Bath, Gloucester, and Cirencester[2]. The last-mentioned places did not, however, continue under his dominion; probably because he did not fight
with his West Saxons only, but with the Angles also, in his
character of Bretwalda, since we find the territory of the
Hwiccas, in which those cities lie, subsequently attached to
Mercia. The Britons were now confined to their mountains
and forests. A great victory at Fethanleah (Frithern) on the
Severn, which gained him many towns, much treasure, and
vast booty, was yet granted to Ceawlin, though purchased
with the life of his valiant brother Cutha, and probably also
with that of his own son, of whom the former fell in the
beginning of the contest[3]; of the other no further mention
occurs in the chronicles. With those friends Ceawlin lost
much; the star of his prosperity was set. Great guilt must
have accumulated on the head of him[4], against whom, after
thirty years of prosperous sway and successful warfare, his
kindred, even though instigated by the ambition of Æthelberht of Kent, could be induced to enter into a disgraceful
league with the Britons and Scots[5]. He was defeated in
a great battle fought in his own territory at Wodnesbeorh in
Berkshire, not far from the frontier of Mercia, and compelled to abdicate the throne, which Ceolric, the son of his

---

[1] Sax. Chron. a. 571. [2] Sax. Chron. a. 577.

[3] Sax. Chron. aa. 568, 597. Fl. Wigorn. W. Malm.

[4] Malmesbury says of him, " Diebus ultimis regno extorris, miserandum
sui spectaculum hostibus exhibuit. Quia enim in odium sui quasi classicum
utrobique cecinerat, conspirantibus tam Anglis quam Britonibus apud
Wodnesdic, cæso exercitu, anno xxxi. regno nudatus in exilium concessit,
et continuo decessit.

[5] Forduni Scotichron. lib. iii. Cf. also Langhorne ut sup.

brother Cutha, ascended[1], and Æthelberht was now acknowledged as Bretwalda.   Ceawlin, for many years to come the
mightiest monarch of the Anglo-Saxons, died two years afterwards in all the misery of exile[2].   His successor, Ceolric,
survived him only five years[3].

The strife and discord which tore and threatened destruction to the Anglo-Saxons was, however, soon to be met by
the kindliest palliative.   The grandsons of the Saxon conquerors had been so far civilized by peaceable possession and
gradual acquaintance with the arts of peace, that they could
lend their ear to the preaching of Christianity.   Of all the
people of unmixed Germanic race the first converted to the
faith of Christ, the Anglo-Saxons were called to impart its
sanctity, and all the highest moral feeling attached to it, to
the rest of Germanic and Northern Europe.   The Roman
civilization which they found in England had expanded the
narrow boundary of their habits, their energies, and perhaps
of their activity, without, at the same time, destroying the
nationality of their institutions, their laws, or their language.
Their mental cultivation, which must have been much promoted in their intercourse with the Britons, had no doubt
greatly refined even their pagan notions.   Hence we see that
Christianity was received by the Anglo-Saxon states in the
order according to which they had been favoured over others,
by greater extent of settlements and length of peaceable possession.

An important event, through which the Anglo-Saxons first
approached the pale of the Christian commonwealth of Europe,
was the marriage of king Æthelberht with Berhta, daughter
of Charibert, king of the Franks,—a connexion between the
princes which admits the supposition of an intercourse between
their subjects, and which, at a somewhat later period, does in

---

[1] Sax. Chron.   Fl. Wigorn. a. 591.
[2] Sax. Chron.   Fl. Wigorn. a. 593.   W. Malm. lib. i.
[3] Sax. Chron.   Fl. Wigorn. a. 591.

fact appear to have subsisted at the great commercial fair of St. Denis, which was visited by Anglo-Saxons[1].

The ordinances of the Christian church, simple and humble as they were, could not maintain themselves in the new pagan Anglo-Saxon kingdoms, where royalty and the sacerdotal office were in close connexion. We find them longest in the North, where the Angles established themselves but slowly as independent states. Samson was nominated bishop of York about the year 500, in which well-fortified city a Christian Roman school may probably have continued till the occupation of the place by the Angles. The Anglo-Saxons could not be otherwise than ill-disposed to the worship of Rome and of their enemies in Britain, as well as to other Roman institutions, which might threaten to be prejudicial to their independence: the teachers of Christianity, therefore, found among their most barbarous Celtic neighbours earlier admission than among the German invaders. The pupil of Germanus, who is said to have accompanied him on his visit to Britain, St. Patric, the son of a deacon on the southern shore of the Clyde, who died in 493, continued in Ireland, as Palladius (since the year 430) among the Scots, successfully to spread the faith of Christ during the time when the Saxons were establishing themselves in Britain. Among the southern Picts, Christianity is said to have maintained itself from the period of their conversion by the Briton Nynias in the year 394, and Christian Anglo-Saxons, in later times, celebrated their worship in the stone church of St. Martin, founded by him at Hwitern (Candida Casa) in Galloway, when that territory had been annexed to the kingdom of Bernicia[2]. In the year 563 St. Columba passed over from Ireland to the

---

[1] Charter of Dagobert of the year 629, ap. Bouquet, t. iv. p. 629, and more correct in Marini, ' Papiri Diplomatici,' p. 97, in which those Saxons only who came from beyond sea to Rouen and Quentavic to fetch honey and wood are to be held as Anglo-Saxons. See also under Offa K. of Mercia.

[2] Beda, iii. 4.

northern Picts, with whom, employed in the propagation of his faith, he continued thirty-two years[1], and formed excellent disciples, through whom a pleasing image of pious zeal, deep learning, and varied acquirement attaches itself to the memory of the Scottish monks. St. Columba received from the Pictish prince the island of Hii, now Iona or I-Colm-Kill, (the isle of the church, or cell of Columba,) which his name has consecrated, and which, in honour of him, continued for ages to be the real or fabled burial-place of many Northern princes,—of Scotland, Ireland, Norway, and even of Northumbria[2].

In the Cambrian or Welsh states, as also in Cumbria, no apostasy from the Christian faith had taken place, though no conformity with the church of Rome existed; and the later accounts, which ascribe to Rome the sending of the before-mentioned missionaries, appear for the most part very unworthy of credit[3]. Contrast, and their contests with the pagans must have strengthened a faith among them which reserves its noblest crown for the martyr. Many churches in Wales trace their foundation back to those British saints, who, in the time of Cerdic and his immediate successors, sought protection for their faith and tranquillity for self-contemplation behind the rocks and in the sylvan solitudes of that country[4]. The connexion into which the church had already entered with the state, as well as that very peculiar one, which almost identified the form of the Western empire with the existence of the clergy, became known also in this country, and preserved its ecclesiastical institutions. Of

---

[1] Adamni Vita S. Columbæ ap. Canisii Lectt. Antiquæ. His biographer was one of his successors in the abbey at Iona, and is known also by his work, ' De Locis Sanctis.'

[2] According to Simeon (De Eccles. Dunelm., c. ix.), Ecgfrith king of Northumberland was buried at Iona.

[3] As regards Patricius, cf. Neander's Geschichte der christlichen Religion, Bd. ii. 259.

[4] See the genealogies of the Saints in Lhuyd's Archæologia Britannica.

these we may mention the distribution into seven bishoprics, also the monasteries of Bangor, and Avallon or Glastonbury. We find bishops at the election of kings: Dubritius, at first bishop of Llandaff, subsequently of Caerleon, where there were two ecclesiastical seminaries, crowned king Arthur in the year 516[1]. St. David, who transferred the see from Caerleon to the ancient Menevia, exerted himself at a British synod, held in 519, to eradicate the traces of the Pelagian heresy[2]. Mention also occurs of three provincial synods of the bishopric of Llandaff[3], which, although they testify to a knowledge of existing vices and to a desire to remedy them, at the same time justify the mournful picture which the monk of Bangor has with black lineaments and chastening zeal drawn of his contemporaries in the British church. Gildas may unquestionably be numbered among the most distinguished men of his age, as of all writings of a similar description, it has transmitted his alone to posterity and to the present time. Though his style be bombastic, his conception bordering on the absurd, his historic delineations undefined, without chronology, he is, nevertheless, a very instructive voucher at a period, the other relics of which would, without his labours, be much more obscure and questionable than they are at present. We believe we err not, if in him we recognise the speaking representative of the more serious and pious Britons of the time, and a model of Christian Bri-

---

[1] This report, as far as the bishop's name is concerned, seems doubtful, as he may have been mistaken for Dibric, who died in 612. See Annal. Camb. and Monast. Angl. t. vi. p. 1220.

[2] This synod is not to be placed, as it is generally, in the year 519. The Annales Cambriæ record it, with the death of bishop David, under 601, and (according to a later MS.) the synod of Victoria, perhaps too early, in 569. The historians who place David, Daniel of Bangor (ob. 584. see Annal. Camb.), and Dubritius, in the beginning of the sixth century, have not considered that Giraldus, their chief authority, here only follows Jeffrey of Monmouth.

[3] Spelm. Concilia, t. i. p. 62 sq. Wilkins, Conc. t. i. p. 17. Usser. Primord. Eccles. Angl.

tish Roman refinement. What pious, modest, apt sentiments, what rare learning, what pure endeavour prevailed in the British church, we know from the favourable testimony of an opponent, the Venerable Beda, who praises and exalts no catholic Anglo-Saxon ecclesiastics so highly as he does those, held out to them as patterns, of the Britons and Scots. The struggle between both churches in Britain is not less interesting from the sympathy which we cannot refuse to the fathers of the national church, than from the incalculable political importance of its suppression.

The points of difference between the catholic and the British churches had reference to the time of celebrating Easter, the form of the tonsure, the administration of baptism, the ecclesiastical benediction of matrimony, the marriage of priests[1], the manner of the ordination of the British bishops (of which almost every church possessed one), and other trifling differences; but, above all things, to the refusal to acknowledge the supremacy of the pope and the councils. Of these points, however, those only regarding the computation of Easter and the administration of baptism were insisted on by Augustine, with the condition that the British priests should unite with the missionaries in preaching to the Angles.

The British church, established probably on the oldest direct traditions from Judea, in closest connexion with conversions of the highest importance in the history of mankind, appeared no less by its geographical position than by its exalted spiritual endowments, fitted to become the foundation of a Northern patriarchate, which by its counterpoise to Rome and the rest of the South, its guardianship over a Celtic and Germanic population, sanctified by the doctrine of Christ, might have been the instrument to impart to those within its pale that which both meditative and ambitious

---

[1] See Giesler, Kirchengeschichte, Bd. i.

men, in the middle age, sometimes ventured to think on, but which, in comparatively modern times, Martin Luther first strove to extort for Romanized Europe [1].

The struggles between the Britons and the Anglo-Saxons were carried on for centuries with so much rancour, that it ought to excite no astonishment, and still less call for blame, that the former did not attempt the conversion of their barbarous enemies and oppressors. Most worthy therefore of admiration appears pope Gregory the Great, who first conceived the idea of gaining the Anglo-Saxon states for Christendom and the catholic church, and applied to the holy work with a perseverance and caution worthy of the happy result by which it was followed. The obstacles, amid which the introduction of Christianity among the Anglo-Saxons was effected, were, nevertheless, very great, and it required almost a century for the completion of the task. The language of the Roman missionaries proved the first check to the convincing powers of their eloquence. Though the prince, by family connexion, remonstrances, preaching, by papal briefs, which flattered his vanity, and presents, as they are given in modern times and for a similar purpose to the savages of remote regions,—though he by such inducements felt favourably disposed, and acknowledged himself a Christian, yet were his

[1] On the old British church see bishop Münter's treatise in Ullmann's u. A. 'Theologischen Studien und Kritiken,' 1833. Doellinger (Kirchengeschichte, t. i. sect. 2), proceeding on catholic principles, explains several points by much research, but is too zealous in endeavouring to obliterate all traces of views and discipline, in which the ancient British church differed from that of Rome, ascribing to the former an acknowledgment of the Roman supremacy. The passage he quotes from the epistle of Gildas does not prove that the British procured for themselves at Rome dignities in the church of their own country, but merely that some of them had surreptitiously obtained ordination in transmarine parts, perhaps Ireland or Bretagne. The mention made of the bishop of Caerleon, in the letter of the abbot of Bangor to Augustine, in which the supremacy of the Roman pontiff is not recognised, will no longer, after what has been before said of bishop David, raise critical doubts, but may be reckoned among the tests of its authenticity.

court and the rest of his people still unconverted. If he died, the history of all the large Anglo-Saxon states testifies, that his successor, attached to its adherents, would most probably raise again the banner of paganism. Nor in attempting the spiritual conquest of any of the other small states was there a prospect of any great result, since, from their slender connexion with each other, and the inconsiderable influence of the Bretwalda, which, in this case especially, proved wholly ineffectual, the conversion of his kingdom was for the neighbouring ones an occasion of a more vigilant opposition. At the same time, however, it must be noticed, as a favourable circumstance, that, notwithstanding repeated relapses into paganism, Christianity in one or other of the states always preserved an altar and a sanctuary.

The wish and the plan to draw the Anglo-Saxons within the pale of the Roman catholic church must have been long entertained at Rome, though the external impulse, which is necessary to the production of the greatest events, was wanting, and which at the first glance is wont to appear so capricious, so insignificant, and so incredible, that an attentive consideration of human affairs might pronounce it much too wonderful for accident, but rather the leading clew of hidden wisdom made perceptible only to those directed by it. Some young Angles were standing in the Forum at Rome, there to be sold as slaves. By whom they had been conveyed thither is wholly unknown; they possibly formed a portion of the booty taken in the wars of the Bretwalda with the Northumbrians, and had been brought from the public market at London. These foreign boys, distinguished by their beautiful countenance, fair skin, and—that which was the sign of good descent—their comely locks, attracted the notice of Gregory, who some years afterwards was elected pope, and was famed for his attention to the education of youth, who for more than a thousand years after his death were accustomed to celebrate the day dedicated to his name.

On learning that they were from Britain and heathens, he loudly lamented that they with such bright countenances must become the prey of the prince of darkness; and that such grace of aspect was not accompanied with the grace of inward light. On being told that they were called Angles (Angli), he exclaimed, "And rightly so, for they have an angelic mien, and should be the co-heirs of angels in heaven." On inquiring the name of the province from whence they came, he was answered, that the people to which they belonged were called Deiri. "It is well," said he, "de ira eruti, snatched from wrath and called to the mercy of Christ." On being informed that their king was named Ælle, "Alleluiah," said he, in allusion to the name, "the praise of God the Creator ought to be sung in that country." Whereupon he hastened to the pope, for the purpose of beseeching him to send some ministers of the Word to Britain, who might convert the inhabitants to Christ, offering to accompany them himself; and though the pope was willing to grant his request, the people would not admit of his absence from the city for so long a period: but Gregory, immediately after his elevation to the papacy, executed his serious purpose by sending missionaries to the land of the slaves who had been the objects of his commiseration[1]. These, under the guidance of Augustine, had performed but an inconsiderable part of their journey, when they were so terrified at the description given them of the barbarity of the savage pagans, of whose speech even they were entirely ignorant, that, on their arrival in Provence, they sent home Augustine[2],—who was destined to be bishop of the Angles, and who on all occasions appears rather as a faithful instrument subservient to general opinion and higher command, than as an inspired preacher of the Word which brings life,—for the purpose of supplicating the pope to release them from so dangerous, laborious, and doubt-

[1] Beda, ii. 1.   [2] Id. i. 23.

ful a mission. But Gregory exhorted them to continue their journey, recommended them to the protection of the Frankish kings, Theuderic and Theudebert, to their powerful grandmother, Brunhild, also to the several bishops, and caused Frankish interpreters to accompany them. On the isle of Thanet, the earliest Anglo-Saxon acquisition, Augustine likewise made his landing, with a number of monks, which Anglo-Saxon tradition fixes at about forty. To the king of Kent, Augustine announced his coming from Rome, with a message that promised to the obedient eternal joy in heaven, and kingdom without end with the true and living God. Though Æthelberht might not have paid attention to the faith professed by the great number of his subjects forming the oppressed British population, he must, nevertheless, have had some knowledge of the religion of his consort Berhta, who, by the terms of her marriage contract, enjoyed the free exercise of her worship, the duties attending which were fulfilled by Liudhard, a Frankish bishop, who had accompanied her to England, in the church of St. Martin near Canterbury, which had been preserved from the time of the Christian Romans.

The king, soon after their landing, proceeded to the isle for the purpose of meeting the strangers, where, apprehending the influence of their sorcery under a roof, he received them in the open air. The missionaries approached, bearing, in place of a banner, a silver cross, also a representation of the Saviour painted on a board, singing litanies, supplicating for the eternal salvation of themselves and of those for whom and to whom they were come. The words and promises of the sermon preached before the king seemed to him beautiful, yet being new and uncertain, he would not renounce the faith of the whole nation: at the same time he gave the foreigners an hospitable reception in his chief city, Canterbury, and allowed them, by their preaching and example, to propagate their faith among his people, to baptize, and to solemnize their worship in the church of his queen. The conversion and baptism of Æthelberht himself[1], which soon followed, was attended with the restoration of the old British church of the Holy Saviour in the royal city, the acknowledgment of the archiepiscopal authority of Augustine, who had made a journey to Arles, where, by command of Gregory, he had received consecration at the hands of the archbishop Virgilius[2], and who on his return sent Laurentius and Petrus, two of his companions, to announce to Gregory the progress of his mission. These brought back with them several coadjutors, among whom were Mellitus, Justus, Paulinus and Rufinianus, together with gifts for the new church, consisting of holy vessels and vestments, books and relics, also letters from the pope to Augustine, granting him the use of the pall. Gregory now saw the general conversion of the nation assume a form[3], and the active head of the church, in the leisure and tranquillity which his great mind was able to command for the purpose of recording the fruits of his profound and learned contemplations, could thank the Almighty, that the inhabitants of Britain, whose language had erst been employed only for heathenish and barbarous purposes, now chanted forth the Hebrew Hallelujah to the praise of God[4]. Who does not here call to mind his early wish? Well might he rejoice in the progress of the great work of which he had laid the foundation!

The failure of an important step contemplated by Augus-

---

[1] Beda, i. 26. A.D. 597, on the feast of Pentecost, or June 2. See Smith's note, also Stevenson's.—T.

[2] A.D. 597. Beda, i. 24 (where see Smith's note) and id. i. 27.

[3] Beda, i. 27, 29. We learn from a letter of Gregory to Eulogius, bishop of Alexandria, that before the following Christmas more than ten thousand of the English had been baptized by Augustine and his followers. By Thorne it is stated that Æthelberht resigned Canterbury and the surrounding country to Augustine, and retired to Reculver: "Ipse Ædilberctus Regulbium demigravit, ibique novum sibi palatium condidit." See Smith's and Stevenson's notes.—T.

[4] Expositio Jobi ap. Bedæ H. E. ii. 1.

tine proved a check to the more rapid spread of Christianity. In Wales the Christian faith as well as much Roman civilization had been preserved and transmitted, especially through the schools of Bangor and Llancarvan; and Augustine was not slow to perceive how desirable for the propagation of Christianity an union would be between the Roman and the British clergy. Through the influence of Æthelberht a meeting between the missionaries and the heads of the British church was effected, at a spot afterwards known by the name of Augustine's Oak[1], on the confines of Wessex and the territory of the Hwiccas; when, after a long and fruitless discussion of the points on which the two churches were at variance, the chief of which, it appears, was the time of celebrating Easter, Augustine, as we are told by Beda, having, in proof of his authority, miraculously restored a blind man to sight[2], the meeting was adjourned to a future day.

Previous to the second conference, which was attended by seven British bishops, by the abbot Dinoot, or Dunawd, and several learned divines from Bangor, the Britons consulted a certain hermit, who was held by them in high veneration, as to whether, in compliance with the preaching of Augustine, they should renounce their own traditions? He answered, " If the man is of God, follow him." To their inquiry, " How are we to prove this?" he replied, " The Lord says, Take my yoke upon you, and learn of me, for I am meek and humble of heart. If, therefore, Augustine is meek and humble of heart, it is to be believed that he himself bears the yoke of Christ, and offers it to be borne by you; but if he is arrogant

---

[1] The conference was, without doubt, literally held in the open air, under the spreading branches of an oak. On this interesting subject see Palgrave, vol. i. p. 238 sq.—T.

[2] From an extract of a letter from Gregory to Augustine, it appears that the great work of the latter was promoted by the intervention of other miracles besides the one here recorded. In this letter the pontiff exhorts the missionary not to be presumptuous on account of such miracles. See Beda, i. 31; and, for the remainder of the letter, ejd. Opera Minora, ed. Stevenson, p. 248.—T.

and proud, it is manifest that he is not of God, and that we need not heed his words." To their further question, "But how shall we ascertain this?" "Order it so," said he, "that he and his followers be the first at the conference, and if he rise up to meet you, do you, knowing him to be the servant of Christ, hear him obediently; but if he contemn you, and will not rise up to you, you being in number the greater, be he contemned of you."

On their arrival at the place of conference, finding Augustine seated, they, according to the instructions of the hermit, as well perhaps as from predisposition, met all his proposals with a refusal. Whereupon he said, " Though in many points you act contrary to us and to the universal church, yet, if you will agree with me in these three,—to celebrate Easter at the proper season; to perform baptism, whereby we are born again to God, after the manner of the holy Roman and apostolic church; and, together with us, to preach the word of God to the Anglian nation,—we will kindly bear with you." They answered, that they would do none of those things, nor acknowledge him for their archbishop. In reply, Augustine, in a threatening tone, is said to have predicted to them, that, if they would not accept peace with their brothers, they should have war with their enemies: and if they would not preach the way of life to the Angles, they should suffer vengeance at their hands. The fulfilling of the prophecy, or what was regarded as its fulfilling, will be seen hereafter[1].

From the above it will, perhaps, appear obvious to the unprejudiced reader, that the arrogance of the foreign missionary on the one side, and, on the other, the stubbornness of the British ecclesiastics, called into activity by that arrogance, were the chief causes why a conference, held for so holy a purpose, ended in the evocation of feelings the reverse of those of peace and good-will to men.

With more satisfaction we, at the present day, regard the

[1] This important narrative is wholly taken from Beda, ii. 2.—T.

wisdom and liberality with which Gregory answers the question of Augustine, as to the course he was to follow with regard to the diversity prevailing in the customs of the Roman
and Gallican churches. " It is my wish," writes Gregory,
" that you sedulously select what you may think most accept-
able to Almighty God, be it in the Roman, or in the Gallican,
or in any other church ; and introduce into the church of the
Angles that which you shall have so collected ; for things are
not to be loved for the sake of places, but places for the sake
of good things. Choose, therefore, from the several churches
whatever is pious, and religious, and right, and these, gathered
as it were into one whole, instil, as observances, into the
minds of the Angles[1]."

A connexion similar to that which had caused the introduction of Christianity into Kent facilitated its entrance into
Essex. Ricole, a sister of Æthelberht, was the mother of
Sæberht (Sæbriht), king of that small but, on account of the
cities it contained, important state[2]. The king soon attached
himself to the new faith of his uncle and Bretwalda, and his
people, following the example of their prince, yielded to the
preaching of Mellitus, to whom, through the influence of
Æthelberht, a church in London, dedicated to St. Paul, was
assigned as an episcopal see, where had formerly stood a
temple of Diana ; while Justus was by Augustine consecrated
to the see of Rochester, in which city a church, dedicated to
St. Andrew the apostle, was founded by Æthelberht, and, as
at Canterbury, endowed with lands and other possessions[3].

It was the happy lot of Augustine to pass to the higher
reward of his deeds with untroubled looks on his great acquisition for the church, which gathered strength under the
powerful sceptre of Æthelberht. He had made a very praiseworthy choice of a successor in his associate Laurentius, who,
in conjunction with Justus, renewed the attempt to unite the

[1] Beda, i. 27.   [2] Beda, ii. 3.   Sax. Chron. a. 604.
[3] A.D. 604.   Beda, ii. 3.

Britons with his church, and even took similar steps among the Scots of Ireland[1].

Mellitus was in the meanwhile gone to Rome on business of the church : it happened, therefore, that Boniface IV. counted in the Synod then sitting[2] one Anglo-Saxon bishop. In Kent the wholesome influence of the Roman ecclesiastics was manifested also in the circumstance, that Æthelberht caused to be recorded, in the language of his country, the first written collection among the Anglo-Saxons—perhaps among all the Germanic nations—of the ancient laws of his people, comprising those newly introduced by the Christian priests. But the welfare of the church was not to rest on the written letter. On the death of Æthelberht[3], which was soon followed by that of Sæberht, the faith had been established among the Anglo-Saxons about twenty-one years, when it was suddenly brought near to its suppression ; Eadbald, the son of Æthelberht, having not only refused to listen to its doctrines, but, yielding to the frenzy of the most passionate excitement, had not hesitated to espouse his father's widow. The sons of Sæberht had in like manner refused to receive baptism, had granted to their subjects permission to return to the worship of idols, and driven Mellitus from the kingdom, for having refused to give them the bread of the eucharist. Mellitus and Justus fled to Gaul, whither Laurentius was preparing to follow them, when a sudden change in the mind of Eadbald, occasioned by the last representations of the archbishop, was followed by the suppression of idolatry in his dominions, the dismissal of his step-mother, and the restoration of Christianity[4].

[1] A.D. 605. Beda, ii. 3, 4, where see the letter of Laurentius to the Scottish bishops and abbots.—T.

[2] A.D. 610, Feb. 27.   [3] Sax. Chron. a. 616.

[4] The device by which these desirable events were brought to pass, though unfit to be recorded on the pages of history at the present day, affords, nevertheless, too striking an example of the means, it is to be feared, but too frequently employed in propagating the new faith among

Not so soon did the East Saxons become sensible of their error, though the three sons of Sæberht had fallen in a battle. Mellitus succeeded Laurentius in the archiepiscopal dignity, but his former diocese still persisted in their idolatry[1]. It was a new generation only that followed king Sigeberht the Good and the majority of the Anglo-Saxons, who now generally professed the doctrines of Christianity: yet even then the appearance of an unusually destructive pestilence, called the yellow plague, prompted the East Saxons to look for aid in the restoration of the heathen temples, and Sigehere (Sige-heri), one of their two kings, had relapsed into paganism; but the example given by the pious king Sebbe (Sebbi), together with the spiritual exertions of bishop Jaruman, led to the final destruction of the old national idolatry with its temples, and to the permanent establishment of the new faith[2].

While on a visit to Æthelberht of Kent, Rædwald, king of the East Angles, had also declared himself a convert to Christianity, a step the more important, as, after the death of Æthelberht, the dignity of Bretwalda had passed over to the Uffings. Induced, however, by the importunity of his wife and friends, Rædwald soon rejected the newly acquired con-

---

our simple forefathers, to be wholly unnoticed. We are told by Beda (ii. 6), that Laurentius, on the eve of his departure, had directed that his bed should be placed in the church of St. Peter and St. Paul. In the dead of the night St. Peter appeared to him, and scourging him asked, why he abandoned the flock entrusted to his care? In the morning he presented himself before the king, and showed him his body lacerated with the scourging, who, on his inquiry, who had dared to inflict such stripes on such a man, received for answer, that he had been so wounded and tormented by the apostle of Christ, for the sake of his (Eadbald's) salvation; who thereupon, anathematizing his old idolatry, dismissed his stepmother, adopted the Christian faith, and received baptism. See also Sax. Chron. a. 616.—T.   [1] Beda, ii. 6.

[2] Beda, iii. 22, 30. Fl. Wigorn. a. 653. From the date given in the margin of the latter of these chapters of Beda, it might seem that the reign of Sighere and Sebbe commenced in 665; but in Wulfhere's charter of endowment to Peterborough abbey, dated 664, their names as kings appear among the signatures. See Sax. Chron. a. 657.

viction, but, in the view of satisfying both parties, caused to be erected in the same temple an altar to Christ by the side of that devoted to the rites of paganism[1].

His neighbour beyond the Humber, Æthelfrith (Æthelferth), the son of Æthelric and grandson of Ida, who had forcibly united Deira, the kingdom of Ælle his deceased father-in-law, with his own paternal state, Bernicia, was a foe to Christianity. He had acquired a reputation for great valour in the glorious victory, purchased with the loss of his brother Theodbald, at Dægsanstan, or Degsastan[2], over Aidan, the son of Gabran, king of the Dalreods or Albanians, the remembrance of which long deterred the latter from further contests with the Angles of Northumbria. His wars had hitherto been chiefly with the Britons, vast numbers of whom he had exterminated, or rendered tributary to his sceptre; and the fear which those conquests spread among his neighbours occasioned an alliance, till then unheard of, between Anglo-Saxon and British princes. Eadwine (Eadwini), the son of Ælle, a child of three years, had it appears, on the seizure of his inheritance by Æthelfrith, been committed for safety to the care of Cadvan, king of Gwynedd[3], and there educated under the British clergy, till he had attained the age of manhood. Cadvan, for the sake of his ward, having formed an alliance with Brocmail, king of Powis, the patron of the poet Taliesin, hazarded a war with the persecutor of Eadwine, which ended in a battle fought near Chester (Caer-

---

[1] Beda, ii. 15.

[2] Beda, i. 34. Sax. Chron. a. 603. Dalston near Carlisle, according to Gibson, whose supposition is favoured by the various reading, Deglastan. Dawstane in Liddesdale has also been conjectured as the spot. Tigernach makes no mention of this battle, unless he alludes to it a. 600, " Prælium Saxonum contra Ædanum, ubi cecidit Eanfrac (Eanfrith) frater Etalfraich, occisus a Maeluma, filio Baodani, in quo victor erat." Annal. Ulton. a. 599, " Bellum Saxonum, in quo victus est Aeda."

[3] Vaughan, Diss. on Brit. Chronol. Langhorne, Chron. Angl., though in other respects confuting Jeffrey of Monmouth, considers this tradition as probable.

legion, Lægacester) and the destruction of the celebrated
monastery of Bangor, the seat of Celtic Christian learning[1].
Previous to the battle Æthelfrith espied an unarmed body,
standing apart in a place of apparent security. On being informed that they belonged for the most part to the monastery
of Bangor, and had with others assembled on that spot to
pray, under the protection of Brocmail, he exclaimed, " If
they cry to their God against us, and load us with impreca-
tions, though unarmed, they fight against us :" whereupon
he ordered them to be attacked and put to the sword. Eadwine fled before his brother-in-law and persecutor to Mercia,
whence, finding no security there, he took refuge with Rædwald of East Anglia ; and thus, a homeless wanderer, established, through the protection which he there sought and
obtained, a connexion which was followed by a result far more
important than that attending his previous alliance with the
Britons.

   To the first and second application of Æthelfrith, for the
death or delivery of the fugitive, though accompanied by
tempting pecuniary offers, the Bretwalda gave no ear; but
on the third solicitation, and the proffer of a larger sum, and
threatening war in case of refusal, the faith of Rædwald gave
way, and he promised compliance with the wishes of the
Northumbrian. It was night, and Eadwine was preparing
for rest, when a faithful friend, calling him from his chamber,
informed him of Rædwald's promise, and engaged to convey
him to an asylum, where neither the one nor the other should
be able to discover him. " Thanks for your good will," said
Eadwine, " but I cannot yield to your proposal, and be the
first to break my compact with a king who has done me no
injury, nor shown any ill-will towards me. If I am to die,

---

[1] In 607 according to the Sax. Chron. Fl. Wigorn. a. 603. says, "longo
post tempore (Æthelfrido) collecto exercitu," etc. Annal. Camb. and Tigern.
613. Beda, ii. 2, does not give the year of this event. The British kings, Seysil
son of Conan, Jacobus son of Beli, and Cetul are named among the slain.

let him rather than a less noble hand deliver me to death. Whither can I flee, who, in striving to escape from the snares of my enemies, have so long been a wanderer through all the provinces of Britain?" His friend departed, and Eadwine was left alone sitting on a stone before the palace, sad and at a loss what to do, or whither to bend his steps.

While thus sitting, wrapt in agonizing thoughts, he was startled by the approach of a stranger, who, after greeting, asked him, why, when others were at rest, he was there so sad and lonely? "Yet think not," continued he, "that the cause of your affliction and your vigil is unknown to me: I know who you are, and why you are depressed, and the impending evils which you dread. But say, what reward would you give to any one, if such there be, who should free you from these cares, and prevail on Rædwald neither to do you aught of harm himself, nor to deliver you to your enemies?" On his answering, that for such a benefit he would be grateful to the utmost of his power—"But what, if he should promise that you shall destroy your adversaries, and be a king more powerful not only than any of your forefathers, but than any who has ever reigned over the Angles?" On Eadwine repeating his assurances of gratitude, the stranger, a third time, asked, "If he, who shall have truly promised such great benefits, should impart to you doctrines of life and salvation, better and more efficacious than any one of your relatives has ever heard, would you obey him, and listen to his admonitions?" On receiving the promise of Eadwine, the stranger laid his right hand on the prince's head, saying, "When this sign shall be repeated, remember this hour and this discourse, and delay not to fulfil that which you now promise." Having uttered these words, it is said, he suddenly disappeared, that he might be known to be no man, but a spirit.

The royal youth remained: his mind, though gladdened by the consolation he had received, was yet not free from

anxiety, when his before-mentioned friend returned to him
with a joyful countenance, and informed him that he might
safely retire to rest, and that Rædwald had resolved to keep
his faith; for that on communicating to the queen the promise he had made to Æthelfrith, she had made manifest to
him how ill it became so great a king to sell his best friend
in his distress for gold, and to break his faith, more precious
than all ornaments, through love of money [1].

The Bretwalda having thus resolved on the juster course,
marched with a powerful well-appointed army against the
Northumbrian, who met him with inferior forces in a battle
fought on the eastern bank of the river Idle in Nottingham-
shire, on the border of Mercia. Rædwald remained master
of the field, which was covered with the bodies of the slain,
among whom was Æthelfrith himself, who, in an impetuous
onset, having destroyed one of the three divisions into which
the adverse army was divided, together with its valiant leader
Ræginhere (Ræginheri), the son of Rædwald, being overpowered by numbers, was found far from his followers amid
the slain heaps of the enemy [2]. After this victory, which was
attended with most important results for Britain, Eadwine
took possession of his paternal kingdom as well as of the vacant throne of Bernicia. One of his earliest deeds seems to
have been the conquest of the little British territory of Elmet [3],
which had existed as an independent state under its king
Cerdic—a name susceptible both of a British and a Saxon in-

---

[1] Beda, ii. 12. Regarding this legend of the child of Ælle as too beautiful and graphic, as well as too intimately connected with the account of
his conversion, to be omitted or even abridged, I have, at the risk of cen-
sure from the severer class of readers, not hesitated to give it entire and
almost literally from the work of the 'Venerable' father of English history,
who, for his love of the legendary and fascinating descriptive powers, may
be not inaptly called the Walter Scott of the eighth century.—T.

[2] Beda, ii. 12. Sax. Chron. a. 617. Fl. Wigorn. H. Hunt. a. 616.

[3] A district in Yorkshire about Leeds. Camden conjectures that the
ruins visible at Barwick in Elmet indicate the site of the palace of the
Northumbrian kings.

terpretation—whom he expelled, for having, under the guise
of hospitality, received and afterwards poisoned Hereric, the
nephew of Eadwine, who, like his uncle, had been persecuted
by Æthelfrith[1].

The states of kindred origin now attached themselves to
the North Angles, and the first Bretwaldaship over all the
Anglo-Saxons, with the exception of Kent, devolved on their
mighty and widely allied king. The British states, and even
the Isle of Man, were subject to him; also the island of Mona,
which, though from the colonists brought thither it had received the name of Anglesey[2], afterwards resumed its Celtic
character. Eadwine, after the death of his consort Cwenburh,
a daughter of the Mercian king Ceorl, obtained the hand of
a Christian princess of the family of the Æscings, the former
suzerains of his country, Æthelburh or Tate, a daughter of
Æthelberht of Kent. This marriage had been permitted
under conditions and expectations similar to those attending
that of the Frankish princess Berhta with Æthelberht himself. The bishop Paulinus accompanied the young queen, to
preserve her in the Christian faith and attend to the duties
of divine worship. Shortly after letters, accompanied by precious gifts, arrived from pope Boniface[3] " to Eadwine, king

[1] Nennii App. " Eaguin, filius Alli,......occupavit Elmet et expulit Cer-
tic, regem illius regionis." Beda, iv. 23. " Cum Hereric exularet sub rege
Brittonum Cerdice, ubi et veneno periit." The above passages will, it is
hoped, justify the view I have taken of this event, which receives confirmation from the respect shown by Eadwine to Hild, the daughter of Hereric, with whom, it appears, she received the rites of baptism : " Cum quo
(Æduino)," says Beda, ibid., " ad prædicationem beatæ memoriæ Paulini,
primi Nordanhymbrorum episcopi, fidem et sacramenta Christi suscepit."
Hereric, the son of the elder deceased son of Ælle, was therefore dead before the death of Æthelfrith ; whereby it appears how Eadwine, Ælle's
second son, succeeded Æthelfrith without opposition. Cf. also Annal.
Camb. a. 616, and Fl. Wigorn. Geneal.

[2] Beda, ii. 5, 9.

[3] As Boniface V. died Oct. 22, a. 625, his letters must have been written
in that year, though probably not received till the spring following; a supposition which may account for their being placed by Beda after events of
626.

of the Angles, and Æthelburh, his consort," for the purpose
of effecting the conversion of the former. Eadwine was probably neither unprepared nor unwilling to receive baptism,
to which he must have often been invited in his earlier years :
he, nevertheless, weighed the difficulties and the danger of
such a step with regard to his subjects. Two events, which
occurred almost at the same moment, appear to have accelerated his conversion. Cwichelm, king of the West Saxons,
anxious to free himself from the supremacy of Northumbria,
had recourse to the arm of an assassin. His emissary,
Eomer, reached the royal residence on the first day of Easter,
and, while delivering a feigned message from Cwichelm, suddenly started up, and drawing from under his garment an
envenomed two-edged dagger, rushed on the king, when an
affectionate thane named Lilla threw himself between them,
and at the price of his own life saved that of his master. So
violent was the stroke that Eadwine was wounded through the
body of his follower, nor did the assassin fall beneath the
swords of those present until he had slain Forthhere (Forth-
heri), another thane of Eadwine's. On the same night Æthelburh was delivered of a daughter, named Eanflæd; when
Eadwine, in the presence of Paulinus, returning thanks to
his gods for the gift, the bishop returned thanks to Christ,
assuring the king that it was to his prayers that the queen
owed her safe and happy delivery. Moved by these words,
Eadwine promised to renounce his idols and serve Christ, if
he would grant him the victory over that king who had employed an assassin to destroy him, and, in pledge of his promise, intrusted his daughter to Paulinus, by whom she was
baptized with eleven others of his household. Being cured
of his wound, he collected an army and marched against the
West Saxons, who were defeated with great loss, five kings
being mentioned among the slain[1].

[1] Sax. Chron. a. 626.   Beda, ii. 9.

On his return, though he abstained from the worship of his gods, he was yet unwilling, without due reflection, to partake of the sacraments of the Christian faith; but, listening to the discourses of Paulinus on the one hand, and of his priests on the other, meditated in private on their respective arguments, when a means of hastening his resolve presented itself to Paulinus, such as spiritual superiority has seldom scrupled to apply for the attainment of an adequate object.

The predictions of the vision were now realized, but the sign had not been repeated, when Paulinus, as Beda conjectures, already apprized in spirit of what had taken place[1], approaching the solitary king, while wrapt in deep meditation, laid his right hand on his head, and asked him whether he acknowledged that sign? Eadwine, trembling, was about to cast himself at the feet of Paulinus, but the latter, raising him up, addressed him thus : " By the grace of God you have escaped from the hands of your enemies; by his bounty, you have obtained the kingdom which you desired: be mindful not to delay the promise you made, to receive his faith and keep his commandments, and, by promoting his will, as announced by me, to free yourself from everlasting punishment, and become a partaker of the heavenly kingdom[2]."

The king promised to receive the faith, and, with the view of effecting the universal adoption of Christianity, called a meeting of his friends and witan. On Eadwine's inquiring of each one separately his opinion of the new doctrines, Cæfi, the high priest[3], immediately answered, " Judge you, O king, of that which is now announced to us ; but I must truly confess to you, that the religion which we have hitherto followed has neither power nor utility. For not one of your subjects

---

[1] Beda, ii. 12. See p. 140 for a miracle performed by Augustine : and for one performed on Laurentius, see p. 143, note [4].—T.

[2] A.D. 626. Beda. ii. 12.

[3] " Primus pontificum " (regis). Beda, ii. 13, who in his Anglian or Northumbrian dialect, writes the name ' Coifi ': one MS. of Ælfred's version reads ' Cæfi,' and ' Cefi,' another has ' Cyfi.' See p. 72, note [5].—T.

has more diligently attended to the worship of the gods than I; and, nevertheless, there are many who have received from you greater benefits and greater honours, and prosper more in all their undertakings: whereas, if the gods were worth anything, they would rather favour me, who have so zealously served them. If therefore, on examination, the new doctrine shall appear to you better and more efficacious, let us, without further delay, hasten to adopt it."

One of the ealdormen approving these words, added, " Such seems to me, O king, the present life of man, in comparison of the time which is hidden from us, as when you are sitting in your hall at your repast, with your thanes and attendants, in the winter season, with a fire lighted in the middle, the apartment warm, but the chilling storms of rain and snow raging everywhere without, a sparrow rapidly flies through, entering at one door, and instantly escaping by another. While it is within it is not touched by the winter's storm, but, after having passed through a very short space of serenity, it goes forthwith from storm to storm, and vanishes from your sight. So also seems the short life of man : what follows or what precedes we know not : if, therefore, this new doctrine brings us something more certain, it is also my opinion that it should be adopted." In accordance with this were the sentiments of the other ealdormen and witan. Cæfi now expressed his wish to hear Paulinus discourse concerning God : his conversion was the result, and Eadwine himself, convinced by the preaching of the bishop, renouncing idolatry, professed himself also a believer in the doctrines of Christianity[1]. To the inquiry of Paulinus : Who would be the first to profane the altars and temples of the idols, with their enclosures[2]? Cæfi answered, " I ; for who is fitter than

---

[1] Beda, ii. 14.   Sax. Chron. a. 627.

[2] The 'septum' around a temple was the 'frithgeard,' or asylum.   See Law of the Northumbrian Priests, liv. in Anc. LL. and Instt., and Gloss. *v.* Friðgeard.—T.

I am to destroy, through the wisdom given me by God, and
as an example to all, that which I have worshiped in my
folly?" Whereupon he prayed of the king that arms and a
horse might be given to him—it being forbidden to the sacrificing priests both to bear arms and to ride except on a mare
—and, girded with a sword, and with lance in hand, having
mounted the horse, he proceeded to execute his design. The
people thought him mad, but he, hastening to the temple,
instantly profaned it by casting his lance against it, and in
his exultation commanded his associates to set it on fire with
all its enclosures. This event took place at Godmundinga-
ham, now Godmundham, in the East Riding of Yorkshire.
Eadwine was baptized at York on the following Easter-day,
in a church built of wood, and dedicated to St. Peter the
Apostle, which he had there caused to be erected, but which
was shortly after succeeded by a larger one of stone on the
same spot. York was assigned as an archiepiscopal see to
Paulinus, who received the pall from pope Honorius[1].

Paulinus preached also on the other side of the Humber,
and converted the inhabitants of Lindisse, a territory the
name of which is preserved in that of Lindsey. Its chief,
Blecca, a descendant of Woden, and his household, were his
first converts[2].

The peace and tranquillity which the power of the Bretwalda procured for his kingdom must have been very favourable to the spread of the new doctrine, such security being
said to have prevailed that, according to the Anglo-Saxon
proverb, a woman with her new-born babe might have travelled from sea to sea without sustaining injury. By the con-
duits which he had caused to be constructed on the high roads,
he directed brazen cups to be suspended, which no hand
touched save that of the parched wanderer. Eadwine loved
the display of authority: not only were ensigns borne before

---

[1] A.D. 627. Beda, ii. 13, 14.
[2] Beda, ii. 16. Sax. Chron. a. 627. Geneal. ap. Florentium.

him in battle, but even in the public ways he was constantly
preceded by the Roman *tufa,* or tûf as it was called by the
Anglo-Saxons[1].

Eadwine zealously exerted himself for the propagation of
the new faith, and though it appears that he raised no altar in
Bernicia[2], he succeeded in the thorough conversion of Eorpwald, the son of Rædwald, king of the East Angles; and
though the murder of Eorpwald by a pagan[3] plunged East
Anglia into darkness and strife, yet Eadwine lived to see the
return and establishment of Christianity in that country after
a lapse of three years.   Sigeberht, who had received the doctrines of Christianity while in Gaul, whither he had fled from
the hostility of his brother Rædwald, now conjointly with his
brother Ecgric took possession of the throne, chiefly, it would
seem, for the sake of propagating his newly adopted faith.
In the work of conversion he was aided by Felix, a Burgun-
dian bishop, sent to him from Kent by Honorius, archbishop
of Canterbury, under whose wise guidance it prospered
admirably.   Desirous of improving the minds of his people,
Sigeberht founded a Latin school on the plan of those he had
seen in Gaul, in which laudable undertaking he availed himself of the counsel of Felix, who supplied fitting persons as
teachers, according to the Kentish practice[4].   On the foundation of the see of Domuc (Dunwich), Felix was appointed
its first bishop[5].

---

[1] Beda, ii. 16.

[2] This is manifest from Beda, iii. 2, a. 635, where, speaking of Oswald's
cross, he says, " Nullum, ut comperimus, fidei Christianæ signum, nulla
ecclesia, nullum altare in tota Berniciorum gente erectum est, priusquam
hoc sacræ crucis vexillum," etc.   [3] A.D. 627. Beda, ii. 15.

[4] Beda, iii. 18. " Juxta morem Cantuariorum." Malmes. de Gestis Pont.
lib. ii. " Scholas opportunis locis instituens, barbariem gentis sensim
comitate Latina informabat."   The above passage of Beda has been adduced in the dispute between Oxford and Cambridge, to prove the higher
antiquity of the latter.   See Smith, Append. xiv. ad Bedam.   The proof
is, however, wanting that Cambridge, formerly Grantabrycge, belonged to
East Anglia, and not, as is generally understood, to Mercia.

[5] Beda, ii. 15.

Scarcely had these events taken place when we find the king of the East Angles resigning his crown, and, following the old Frankish example, giving the earliest instance of an Anglo-Saxon royal monk. The sceptre now devolved on Ecgric, who was already a sharer in the government of this small state. So deep-rooted was the conviction which led the East Anglian to a renunciation of earthly sway, that not even the danger of his native land, at that time suffering under the cruel ravages of Penda, king of Mercia, could induce him to forsake the quiet of his cloister. When forcibly brought forth by his subjects, in the hope that the sight of a leader, once honoured for his valour, might cheer and stimulate his warriors, he stood still amid the raging battle, with a staff in his hand, until he was slain together with his brother Ecgric. Christianity was not, however, again driven from East Anglia, Anna, the successor of the slain prince, being not only devoted to its doctrines, but, at the instance of Fursæus, a pious man of Scottish race, from Ireland, the founder of several monasteries[1].

But a season of calamity was now at hand for Northumbria. Penda, the son of Wibba, and successor of Ceorl, had rendered Southumbria, or Mercia, independent of Eadwine[2], and, in alliance with the powerful British prince Cædwalla of Gwynedd, the son of Cadvan, made war on Eadwine, who, together with his son Osfrith, was slain in a great battle fought at Hæthfeld[3]. Another of his sons, Eadfrith, who had

---

[1] A.D. 635. Beda, iii. 18, 19, Vita Ethelredæ. According to the Chronicle and Florence, Eorpwald's conversion took place in 632, the preaching of Felix in 636. I follow Beda.

[2] According to the Chronicle, Penda had been king of Mercia from 626; but Beda, ii. 22, says expressly, that he was of royal race (de regio genere Merciorum), and reigned twenty-two years. Therefore, as the accounts concur in placing his death in 655, he must have been king from 633 only, the year of his victory over Eadwine.

[3] Beda, ii. 20. Sax. Chron. Oct. 14, a. 633. Fl. Wigorn. Oct. 12. Annal. Ult. and Tigernach, a. 631. Camden supposes Hatfield, in the West Riding of Yorkshire, to have been the spot.—T.

fled to his relation Penda as a suppliant, was by him treacherously murdered. Eadwine's queen, Æthelburh, and the
archbishop Paulinus fled to Kent, where they met with an
honourable reception from her brother Eadbald and the archbishop Honorius, who appointed Paulinus to the see of
Rochester. Wuscfrea, another son of Eadwine, and Yffe
(Yffi), son of Osfrith, were subsequently, from fear of her
own brother Eadbald, and Oswald of Northumbria, sent by
the queen to the Frankish king Dagobert, through the mediation of the archbishop Paulinus. The early death of these
children, the heirs of the founder of Edinburgh (Eadwines
burh), prevented probably an early example of the Frankish
influence so often exercised in after-ages on the fate of North
Britain; but a sepulchre within the church, not unusual at
that time, long bore witness both to the antiquity of this connexion, and to the asylum afforded by the monarch[1].

The respect paid to the royal races of the Anglo-Saxons is
strikingly proved by the circumstance, that neither Penda,
who retained only his paternal kingdom of Mercia, nor the
king of Gwynedd took possession of the conquered state, the
northern part of which, Bernicia, the land of Æthelfrith, devolved on his son Eanfrith, who, after the death of his father,
had with several friends wandered to the Scots or Picts, and
adopted Christianity, according to the doctrines followed
among those people. The southern portion, Deira, was held
by Osric, the nearest kinsman of Eadwine, who had been
baptized by Paulinus. Both relapsed into the errors of paganism. Osric was slain at York, in an attempt to surprise
Cædwalla, who had shut himself up in that city; Eanfrith
fell by the same hand, being treacherously murdered by him
when, accompanied by twelve followers only, he came to sue
for peace. Their countries were ravaged by the Britons in
the most cruel manner. The names of these apostate princes
were erased from the catalogue of Christian kings, and the

[1] Beda, ii. 14, 20.

unhappy year of their reign assigned to Oswald, their pious successor[1].

But the apostasy of these princes and the sufferings of the Northumbrians may be said to have constituted the revolving point, as it were, not only of the immediate fortunes of the North Angles, but of the successful struggle of Christianity against paganism. Oswald, a younger son of Æthelfrith, bred like his elder brother among the Scots, placed himself at the head of a small force, and at Hefenfeld, not far from the Roman wall, near Denisburn, in the neighbourhood of Hexham, having erected a cross, the first sign of Christian devotion in Bernicia, assembled his followers before it, commanded them to kneel, and having sent forth a fervent prayer to the God of armies, attacked the numerous warriors of Cædwalla, who lost their leader, and—what in those days was the usual consequence of such a loss—betook themselves to flight[2]. In Cædwalla expired the last renowned hero of old British race: in fourteen pitched battles and sixty encounters he had revived and confirmed the military fame of his country, and acquired dominion over a considerable part of Lloegria (Lloegyr). No wonder then if his life and death, though claiming a far higher degree of credibility than Arthur's, were soon surrounded by the glittering imagery of tradition[3], and that we are now unable to ascertain the truth, either in the apotheosis of his adoring countrymen, or in the vindictive narrative of the Anglo-Saxons.

History informs us that Oswald's cross decided the fate of Britain for ever. Oswald obtained the sovereignty of Bernicia, and also of Deira, being entitled to the latter country

---

[1] Beda, iii. 2. Sax. Chron. Fl. Wigorn. a. 634. Eanfrith is the Anfraith, whose decapitation is mentioned by Tigernach a. 632.

[2] A.D. 635. Beda, iii. 2. Fl. Wigorn. a. 634. Nennius (Appen.) calls the battle, bellum Catscaul., Annal. Camb. a. 631, b. Cantscaul (Cædwealla).

[3] Galf. Monum. lib. xii. Llywarch Hên, Elegies. Cf. Turner, vol. i. p. 366.

by his maternal descent, his mother 'Acha,' the sister of
Eadwine, being descended from Ælle[1]. He was acknowledged as Bretwalda, the sixth who held that dignity, and is
said to have reigned over the four tongues of Britain,—of the
Angles, the Britons, the Picts, and the Scots. Oswald combined great vigour with much mildness and religious enthusiasm. By him Christianity was introduced anew into his
kingdom, but it was that of his teachers, the Scots, by whom
Aidan was sent to him from the isle of St. Columba (Hii or
Icolmkill), and to whom, as an episcopal seat, he granted the
isle of Lindisfarne, now Holy Island, the hallowed abode of
many heroes of the Christian faith[2]. Severity towards himself and the powerful, humility and benevolence towards the
poor and lowly, activity in the cause of religion, zeal for
learning, were the admirable qualities that were praised in
Aidan, and shed the purest lustre on the old Scottish church
to which he belonged; and few will feel disposed to doubt
that the general impression which the lives of such men made
on the minds of people disgusted with paganism, together
with the internal truth of the Christian doctrines, has ever,
and in a greater degree contributed to their first conversion
than even the most convincing and solid arguments. How
else could the so-often vainly attempted conversion of the
Northumbrians have been effected by Aidan, who, sprung from
a hostile race, sent from a hostile school, strove to propagate
the doctrines of the defeated Scots and Picts, the former oppressors of the Britons, in a tongue for which Oswald himself was compelled to act as the interpreter?

Of Aidan's fitness for the pious work committed to him, a
judgement may be formed from the following anecdote, related by Beda[3]. At the solicitation of Oswald, a priest had
been sent by the Scots to preach the word to the pagans of

---

[1] Beda, iii. 6.
[2] See Beda's prose and metrical Lives of S. Cuthberht.
[3] A.D. 634.   H. E., iii. 5.

Northumbria, who proving unqualified for the task, and unwelcome to the people, through the austerity of his character,
returned to his country, where, in an assembly of his brethren,
he declared his inability to effect any good among a people
so ungovernable and barbarous. On hearing this declaration,
Aidan, who was present at the meeting, said to him, "Brother,
it seems to me that you have been harsher than was fitting
towards such uninstructed hearers, and have not, in conformity with apostolic usage, first offered the milk of milder
instruction, until, gradually nourished by the divine word,
they might become capable both of receiving the more perfect, and of executing the higher precepts of God." A discussion, to which these words gave rise, terminated in the
unanimous declaration, that Aidan was worthy of the episcopal dignity, and that he ought to be sent to teach the ignorant unbelievers.

In such, and in every other manner possible, Oswald promoted the religion of the cross planted by him, not in his
own kingdom only, but in the states encircling his British
empire[1]. In this he followed the impressions of his youth
and the conviction which had steeled his arm to victory. He
might also have cherished the hope, that in a British Christian
church the surest spiritual support would be found to consist
in the union of all the tongues of Britain.

Since the days of the Bretwalda Ceawlin the kingdom of
Wessex had been engaged in constant warfare with its British
and Saxon neighbours. Though the result may not always
have been unfavourable, yet the state, split into many parts,
bore the semblance of a great camp. In the year 626 we
find mention of at least seven kings of the Gewissas[2]. Ceolwulf had succeeded his brother Ceolric[3], who fighting against

---

[1] "Oswald totius Britanniæ imperator." Cummini Vita Columbæ, c. 26.
[2] Beda, ii. 9. Sax. Chron. a. 626.
[3] Sax. Chron. a. 597, where and by Florence he is called Ceol.

all, proved against all the valour of the bravest[1], though of his deeds we know but little. Beda, in general a poor source for the history of Wessex, does not once mention his name. The record of an obstinate battle with the then still apparently independent people of Sussex, in which he had the advantage, has alone been preserved in the annals of his country[2]; though a memorial equally favourable to the warrior has been transmitted to us in the records of his enemies, the Britons. Tewdric or Theodric, the valiant king of Morganwg[3], had at the beginning of the century renounced the world, having left his crown to his son Mouric, and amid the sylvan scenes of Dindyrn (Tintern), on the pleasant winding shores of the Wye, resigned himself to the enjoyment of solitary reflection, purified from all earthly contamination. Ceolwulf, taking advantage of the reign of the son, marched across the Severn, the northern boundary of Wessex, as far as the Wye. The cry of his faithful people drew the aged hero from his ten years' solitude, and his forces under their old leader were again victorious against the pagan Saxons. The dragon of Wessex was banished to the southern bank of the Severn; but Tewdric received a wound which clove his skull, and was buried at the confluence of the Wye and the Severn[4]. Over his grave an oratory was raised, and at a later period a church, in honour of the royal martyr, on the spot afterwards called Mathern[5], where for many ages his memory was celebrated by the race of his enemies on the an-

[1] H. Hunt. W. Malm. lib. i. "quippe qui nulli unquam ignaviæ locum dederit."

[2] Sax. Chron. Fl. Wigorn. H. Hunt. a. 607.   [3] See p. 121.

[4] Calendar 3rd Jan. For the other particulars see Cod. MS. Eccl. Cath. Landav. in Monast. Angl. t. vi. p. 1222. The year of the battle, being in the time of bishop Oudoceus, the second successor of Dubritius (ob. 612), to whom the oratory was dedicated, must be subsequent to 610. See also Godwinus de Præsul. Angl. edit. 1616, p. 619. Usher, de Primord. p. 292. Langhorne, p. 148.

[5] From Merthyr Tewdric. He was accounted a martyr, having lost his life in fighting against pagans.

niversary of his martyrdom. His remains in a stone coffin, exhibiting the cloven skull, discovered in the sixteenth century, bore witness to the valiant heart once dwelling in the breast of the noble Tewdric of Morganwg.

Cynegils, a son of Ceolric, and his son or brother, Cwichelm, succeeded Ceolwulf on the throne of Wessex[1]. It was in the reign of these princes that bishop Birinus landed in that kingdom. By the advice of pope Honorius, this missionary had undertaken to penetrate to the innermost parts of the country, for the purpose of propagating the Christian faith; but finding himself on his landing surrounded by the darkest paganism, he deemed it more useful to remain in those parts than to prosecute his original design. Cynegils, convinced by his preaching, was baptized at Dorchester[2], being received from the font by Oswald of Northumbria, who had visited him for the purpose of marrying his daughter. In the following year Cwichelm also, a short time before his death, professed himself a convert to the new doctrine. To Birinus, who had also baptized Cuthred[3], the son of Cwichelm, Dorchester was assigned as an episcopal see; and though Cenwealh, the son of Cynegils, after his father's death not only refused baptism, but strove to effect in Wessex a relapse into paganism, similar to that which had taken place in other states, yet his expulsion, and conversion, which followed soon after, through converse with Anna, the pious king of the East Angles, and his steady adherence to the Christian faith after his restoration, prove that his conviction was sincerely shared by his people[4].

To the life of Oswald, not less distinguished for its activity than its spirit of fervent Christian beneficence, but a short duration was decreed. The restless foe of his country, Penda of Mercia, involved him in a war, in which he fell at a place

[1] A.D. 611.　　　[2] A.D. 635.　　　[3] A.D. 639.
[4] Beda, iii. 7. Sax. Chron. a. 643.

called Maserfeld [1]. His last words when, surrounded with arms and enemies, death appeared inevitable, were a prayer for the souls of his people.

The scornful treatment to which the corpse of Oswald was exposed, bears witness alike to the ferocity of the pagan conquerors and to the fear in which they had stood of the Christian Bretwalda. Penda ordered the head and arms to be severed from the trunk and fixed on poles: these were removed by Oswiu in the year following, who caused the head to be buried at Lindisfarne, the arms and hands at Bamborough, the royal residence. The body of Oswald was some time afterwards, by the care of his niece Osthryth, queen of Mercia, buried at Bardeney, where his banner of purple and gold was placed over his sepulchre.

His amiable character had obtained for Oswald, even among his hereditary foes, the Britons, the surname of ' Lamngwin,' *the fair or free of hand.* His Christian merits and his martyrdom made him a hero of the Christian world. He had attained only to the age of thirty-eight, and reigned eight years, exclusive of the unhappy year assigned by an innocent fiction to his reign, though belonging to that of his predecessors.

Penda withdrew from Northumbria and the coast to his inland kingdom, after having glutted his vengeance and thirst for destruction, but certainly from other motives than those assigned by the credulous monks of those times. He had penetrated to Bamborough, which, defended by its position

---

[1] Sax. Chron. a. 642. Beda, iii. 9, " in loco, qui lingua Anglorum nuncupatur Maserfelth." There is a place called Maserfield near Winwich in Lancashire, but the site of the battle seems with more probability to have been Oswestry in Shropshire. See Monast. Angl. and Camden Brit. By the Britons this battle is called ' bellum Cocboy ' (or Chochui). See Nennius and Annal. Camb. a. 644., where it is said that Eoba (Eowa), the brother of Penda, also fell. Tigernach places the battle in which Oswald fell in 639 ; and another battle, unknown to our chronicles, of Oswiu against the Britons, in 642. See Annal. Ulton. aa. 638, 641.

on a rock and by the waters of the ocean, defied his efforts to
capture it either by assault or siege : he, therefore, resolved
on its destruction by fire, to effect which he ordered a heap
to be raised against the city, formed of timbers, thatch and
other combustibles, brought from the ruins of the neighbouring hamlets, which he had commanded to be demolished for
the purpose. This, when the wind was blowing towards the
city, he caused to be set on fire; but at that instant the wind
suddenly, as we are told, at the prayer of Aidan, changed to
the opposite direction, driving the flames on the Mercians,
of whom some were injured and all terrified[1]. Possibly the
state constitution of the Anglo-Saxons, though without authority to prevent one kingdom from warring against another,
did not permit the arbitrary aggrandizement or incorporation
of the greater states, unless based on hereditary right ; as in
Germany, while under the emperors, we find the principle
valid, that two dukedoms might not be united in one hand.

On the death of Oswald, his dominions were again separated into their chief constituent parts. His brother Oswiu
succeeded to Bernicia and the Bretwaldaship; and two years
later, Oswine (Oswini), son of Osric, to Deira. Oswine was
distinguished by the comeliness of his person and the amiable
qualities of his mind; he was munificent, pious and humble :
attracted by his liberality, the noblest men from the provinces
dedicated themselves to his service : but the virtues of Oswine
availed him little as a shield against aggression on the part
of Oswiu. On the eve of a conflict between these princes,
Oswine, perceiving that the forces of his adversary were
greatly superior to his own, and despairing of success, dismissed his army and withdrew for concealment, accompanied
by one faithful follower named Tondhere, to the house of the
ealdorman Hunwald, near Gilling, by whom he was betrayed
to Oswiu, and, together with his attendant, murdered at that
king's command by his officer Æthelwine[2]. Twelve days after

---

[1] Beda, iii. 16.   [2] A.D. 651. Beda, iii. 14.

his death the venerable Aidan followed his royal friend to the grave. In atonement for his crime Oswiu founded a monastery at Ongetlingum, now Gilling, the spot where it had been perpetrated, near Richmond in Yorkshire.

Oswine was succeeded in a part of Deira by Æthelwald, a son of Oswald, who had just reached the age of majority[1].

The chief deed of Oswiu, which as a warrior covered him with glory, and had the greatest influence on the history of the Anglo-Saxons, is the overthrow of Penda. This prince, whose name is rendered memorable by many successful enterprises against the other Germanic states in Britain, and on whom the surname of the Strenuous[2] has justly been bestowed, presents a striking and almost inexplicable phenomenon. Ruler of a territory surrounded more than any of the other states by a numerous hostile British population; a state which—whatever sense may be given to a few obscure and doubtful traditions—was of all the youngest; a state formed in the middle of the country, of immigrants and aftercomers, who found the maritime parts already occupied; protected by marshes, rivers, mountains,—ruler of this state, the first of the race of Woden among the Teutonic warriors dwelling in this territory; succeeding to power at the age of fifty[3], yet displaying the energy of youth; the last unshaken and powerful adherent of paganism among the Anglo-Saxons, —this prince, in alliance with, if not in the pay of, a British Christian king, had, during his reign of thirty years, first

[1] St. Adelbert, a pupil of St. Willibrord, who preached at Kennemaren, and was buried at Hollum, afterwards called Egmond (Annal. Xanten. aa. 690, 694), is said to have been a son of Oswald, king of Deira.

[2] I do not hesitate restoring this surname to Penda, which has been overlooked by modern historians. By Hen. Hunt. he is repeatedly called ' Penda strenuus '; also Beda (ii. 20), in speaking of him, says, " auxilium præbente Penda viro strenuissimo."

[3] Sax. Chron. a. 626. W. Malm. lib. i. Beda, ii. 20 (who pronounces him "de genere regio Merciorum"), begins his reign in 633, after the death of Eadwine. It may, therefore, not be purely accidental that the Chronicle in aa. 628 and 633 does not dignify him with the title of king.

assailed the Bretwalda of Northumbria, and afterwards repeatedly the other states of his countrymen, with great success and still greater cruelty, yet, notwithstanding the destruction of five kings, without securing to himself any lasting result.   Cynegils of Wessex had alone met him with any
powerful resistance in the battle at Cirencester, where both
armies, having fought obstinately till separated by the darkness, were, when about to renew the contest on the following
morning, so disheartened by the mutual havoc, that terms of
reconciliation were easily agreed to[1].   After the above-mentioned wars, with the cause of which we are unacquainted, we
find Penda engaged in an expedition against Cenwealh, the
son of Cynegils, for the purpose of avenging his sister, whom
Cenwealh had married but afterwards repudiated[2].   With his
usual success, he defeated Cenwealh and drove him from his
kingdom.   The fugitive found an asylum and protection with
Anna, king of the East Angles, and, after an exile of three
years, was, with the aid of his nephew Cuthred, reinstated
in his dominions.

The protection afforded to Cenwealh was probably the pretext—if Penda needed a pretext—of a war between the Mercian and the king of East Anglia, in which the latter fell[3],
being the third Uffing who had lost his life in contest with
Penda.   Æthelhere (Æthelheri), the brother of Anna, succeeded to the throne, whom the conqueror compelled to accompany him in a campaign against the Bretwalda Oswiu.
The latter had striven to live on peaceable and even friendly
terms with the formidable Penda, the slayer of his brother
Oswald.   His son Ealhfrith was married to Cyneburh, a
daughter of Penda; his daughter, Ealhflæd, to Peada son of
Penda, ealdorman of the Middle Angles, who before this
union had, with all his thanes and followers, been baptized
by Finan bishop of Lindisfarne, the successor of Aidan, from

[1] Sax. Chron.   Fl. Wigorn.   H. Hunt. a. 628.
[2] Sax. Chron. a. 645.   Beda, iii. 7.   [3] Sax. Chron. a. 654.

the isle of Hii.　Oswiu had delivered to Penda Ecgfrith (Ecgferth), one of his sons, as a hostage, and, in the hope of checking the repeated and intolerable inroads of the Mercians, had
promised to their king innumerable royal ornaments and
other gifts: notwithstanding which Penda, with his allies,
Æthelhere of East Anglia, Æthelwald the son of Oswald,
and Catgabail king of Gwynedd, marched against him with
the avowed purpose of exterminating the entire nation.　His
thirty well-appointed legions under experienced leaders were
arrayed against the little band of Oswiu, who felt strengthened by their faith in Christ.　"If the heathen," cried Oswiu,
"will not accept our gifts, let us offer them to him who will,
to the Lord our God."　He vowed to give twelve estates in
land for the erection of cloisters, also to dedicate his daughter
Ælflæd, a child of twelve months, to perpetual virginity and
a monastic life, if he proved victorious.　On the banks of the
Winwæd Oswiu and his son Ealhfrith, with their enthusiastic
band, begun the conflict.　On their side fought the God of
battles, the remembrance of five slaughtered kings and count-
less victims of foul treachery; but treachery, which had
hitherto been on the part of Penda, now turned against him:
Æthelwald ventured not to fight against his uncle and his
country, but, withdrawing to a place of security before the
beginning of the conflict, awaited its result.　Penda fell: his
death was preceded by that of Æthelhere and nearly all the
thirty auxiliary chieftains; Catgabail fled under the veil of
night, many perished by the sword, but many more in their
flight were drowned in the Are, which, in consequence of the
heavy rains, had overflowed its banks[1].　Oswiu fulfilled his
vows; his victory over the pagans gave to the church six
monasteries in Deira and six in Bernicia, but her greatest
gain was in the undisturbed diffusion of Christianity.　In

---

[1] Nennius, c. 66, who names the battle in which Penda fell, ' campus
Gai.'　The Annal. Camb. place it in 656, and Penda's death in the year
following; the Annal. Ulton. in 649; Tigernach both events in 650.

Mercia the new faith was now firmly established; for, having budded under a pagan king who, at least in his latter years, did not persecute, but was content with despising the Christians, it soon surmounted the dangers of a violent political change. Peada, to whom Oswiu had ceded South Mercia, was in the Easter following murdered, it is said through the treachery of his wife. Two years later Oswiu, who at the time ruled over the whole of Mercia and the southern provinces, was expelled from Mercia by the revolt of three ealdormen, Immin, Eafha, and Eadberht, when Wulfhere (Wulfheri), a younger son of Penda, who had fled on the death of his father, and been long kept in concealment, ascended the throne of his ancestors [1].

Diuma, a Scot, consecrated by Finan, was the first bishop of the Middle Angles and Mercians; the paucity of ecclesiastics rendering it necessary to place the two people under the spiritual government of one individual [2]. Essex also, whose king Sigeberht had, with the advice of his counsellors, yielded to the earnest remonstrances of his friend Oswiu, whom he frequently visited, abjured idolatry and returned to the faith which had been suppressed in the country since the expulsion of Mellitus. Cedd, an Englishman, consecrated also by Finan, was appointed by Oswiu bishop of the East Saxons [3]. Not long before, Ithamar, on the death of Paulinus, had been nominated to the see of Rochester [4], being the first Anglo-Saxon raised to the episcopal dignity; and shortly after Thomas, from the province of the Gyrwas, received the bishopric of the East Angles: even the only archiepiscopal dignity was possessed by an Anglo-Saxon, Deusdedit of Wessex. Already under Honorius, the predecessor of Deusdedit, the pope had remitted to the archbishops of Canterbury and

---

[1] Beda, iii. 24.   [2] Beda, iii. 21.   [3] Beda, iii. 21, 22.
[4] Sax. Chron. Fl. Wigorn. a. 644. Beda, iii. 14. " Honorius archiepiscopus ordinavit Ithamar, oriundum quidem de gente Cantuariorum, sed vita et eruditione antecessoribus suis æquandum."

York the journey to Rome for the purpose of obtaining the pall, and transferred to the survivor of either the consecration of the newly chosen archbishop; thereby acknowledging the great independence of the Anglo-Saxon church : but as the archbishopric of York, since the flight of Paulinus, had not been repossessed, Deusdedit received his consecration at the hands of his countryman, the Kentish bishop Ithamar[1], who was himself succeeded by Damianus, a South Saxon[2].

The need of a bishop familiar with the language of the country was most openly declared in Wessex. Cenwealh had, after his restoration, elevated Agilbert, a Frank, educated in Ireland, to the bishopric of the West Saxons; but becoming at length weary of a foreign tongue, he established a new bishop at Winchester, in the person of Wine (Wini), an Anglo-Saxon[3], greatly to the displeasure of Agilbert, who returned to France, where he was raised to the see of Paris. A few years after the departure of Agilbert, the king expelled Wine from his see, so that the West Saxons were for a considerable time without a bishop. Wine betook himself to Wulfhere of Mercia, of whom he bought the bishopric of London, in which he continued till his death[4]. In Mercia also two Scots (the before-mentioned Diuma, and Ceollach, who soon returned to the quiet of his cloister at Hii) were succeeded by Trumhere (Trumheri), an Anglo-Saxon and relation of king Oswiu, but educated among the Scots[5]. Though a lack of foreign ecclesiastics may be assigned as the cause of these appointments, it was certainly owing to the frequent elevation of natives to the highest spiritual dignities that the English church so early became a national one, that liturgy, ritual, prayers, and sermons so soon resounded in the Ger-

[1] Fl. Wigorn. a. 653.   [2] A.D. 664. Beda, iii. 20.
[3] Beda, iii. 7. " Rex, qui Saxonum tantum linguam noverat, pertæsus barbaræ loquelæ, subintroduxit in provinciam alium suæ linguæ episcopum, vocabulo Uini, et ipse in Gallia ordinatum."
[4] Beda, iii. 7.   [5] Beda, iii. 21. Fl. Wigorn. a. 659.

manic dialect of the people and penetrated to their hearts.
The retention of German proper names, the peculiarity of the
Anglo-Saxon calendar and festivals, the slight influence of the
Roman ecclesiastical law, the cultivation of the native tongue
by the ecclesiastics, the weakened influence of Rome on the
princes, are the beneficial fruits accruing to the church, which
thus in reality became enriched by its early wants.

An important measure, both for the benefit of the church
and the closer union of the Anglo-Saxons, was reserved for
king Oswiu.   The Anglo-Saxons, according as they had
been converted by Augustine and his followers, or by those
of Columba, were attached to the Roman catholic, or to the
British church.   The majority of the ecclesiastics, at least of
the more distinguished, belonged to the latter; hence arose
a difference in religious views and worship not only in the
several kingdoms, but in the several provinces, which threatened to become extremely dangerous to the new faith.   We
see this religious disunion introduced through marriages even
among the royal families, and that Oswiu himself celebrated
the Easter festival, according to the Scottish practice, on a
different day from that observed by his queen Eanflæd, a
daughter of the king of Kent[1].   Ealhfrith also, the son and
co-regent with Oswiu, was, through the persuasion of his
friend Cenwealh, favourable to the Roman church[2].   Differences of this kind, though affecting externals only, greatly
endangered the Christian faith among a people scarcely

---

[1] The Easter festival was regulated by the commencement of the equi-
noctial lunation, which, according to the Roman calculation, might begin
as early as the fifth, while by the Alexandrian it could not begin before
the eighth of March.   Another point of controversy was the tonsure!
The Romans, in defence of their usage, pleaded the example of St. Peter,
charging their adversaries with bearing the mark of Simon Magus, against
which dire accusation their opponents could shield themselves only under
the virtues of those whose example they followed.   See Beda, ii. 4, iii. 3, 25,
v. 21, and Smith's App. ix.—T.

[2] Eddii Vita S. Wilfridi, c. vii.

weaned from the worship of their forefathers, and acquainted
with Christianity only in the closest connexion with the new
external observances.   Colman, a Scot, the third bishop of
Lindisfarne after the death of Finan, zealously strove to establish the principles of his sect.   A synod was called at
Streoneshealh (Whitby)[1], in which, under the presidency of
Oswiu, the most distinguished ecclesiastics of each church
defended their respective doctrines.   Among the partizans of
Rome were Agilbert, bishop of Wessex, and Wilfrith (Wil-
ferth), the future celebrated bishop of York.   The disputation was maintained on both sides with learning and acuteness, and the Scottish clergy might have succeeded in setting
for ever a strong barrier against the catholic pretensions of
the Roman church, if the king, wavering under the weight of
so many conflicting arguments, had not remarked, that the
Scots appealed to St. Columba, but the catholics to the
apostle Peter; for Wilfrith had not forgotten to adduce, in
support of the Roman tenets, that Peter was the rock on which
the Lord had founded his church, and that to him were committed the keys of heaven.   " Has Columba also received such
power?" demanded the king.   Colman could not answer in
the affirmative.   " Do you both agree that to Peter the Lord
has given the keys of heaven?"   Both affirmed it.   " Then,"
said the king, " I will not oppose the heavenly porter, but,
to my utmost ability, will follow all his commands and precepts, lest when I come to the gates of heaven, there be no
one to open to me, should he, who is shown to have the key
in his custody, turn his back upon me."   Those sitting in
the council as well as those standing around, noble and vul-
gar[2], alike anxious for their eternal salvation, approved of

---

[1] Beda, iii. 25.   Fl. Wigorn. a. 664.

[2] Beda, iii. 25.   " Hæc dicente rege, faverunt adsidentes quique sive ad-
stantes, majores una cum mediocribus ; et abdicata minus perfecta institu-
tione, ad ea quæ meliora cognoverant sese transferre festinabant."   This
synod is also mentioned by Liutprand, Chron. a. 664.

this determination, and were thus, in the usual spirit of large
assemblies, and without further investigation of the arguments adduced, impelled to a decision by the excited feelings
of the moment. The Scots either returned to their friends,
or yielded to the opinions of the majority[1], and thus, by the
learning of their school, became useful to the Anglo-Saxons;
but, together with these apparently trivial externals, the great
latent influence was sacrificed, which their church would probably have acquired in opposition to the then less firmly
established one of Rome.

Oswiu himself appears to have been impressed with the
necessity of the unity of the Anglo-Saxon church, and his
character of Bretwalda—for we occasionally find him influ-
encing, in a manner otherwise inexplicable, the concerns of
the church[2]—justified him in, and prompted him to, the execution of this important design. When the archiepiscopal
see of Canterbury became vacant by the death of the sixth
archbishop, Deusdedit[3], Oswiu consulted with Ecgberht,
king of Kent, who had in the same year succeeded his father,
Earconberht, concerning the interests of the national church,
and concurred with him in recommending the presbyter
Wigheard as primate to pope Vitalian, to the end that he
might consecrate catholic prelates throughout the whole country[4]. The answers of Vitalian and the presents sent to Oswiu
and his queen bear sufficient testimony to the gratitude of
the Roman bishop[5]. The death of Wigheard, who fell a victim to the pestilence then raging[6], soon after his arrival at

---

[1] Beda, iii. 26.

[2] Beda, iii. 7. Thus, conjointly with Cynegils, Oswald appears as
founder of the see of Dorchester. " Donaverunt ambo reges eidem episcopo
civitatem quæ vocatur Dorcic, ad faciendum inibi sedem episcopalem."
Wulfhere also sold, as we have just seen, the bishopric of London to
Wine.   [3] Sax. Chron. a. 664.

[4] Beda, iii. 29. Sax. Chron. a. 667.   [5] Beda, iii. 29, iv. 1.

[6] A.D. 664. This year there was a total eclipse of the sun, which was
followed by the yellow plague, which, from time to time, desolated Britain,
particularly Northumbria, during a period of twenty years. Among its

Rome, was taken advantage of by the pope to set over the
Anglo-Saxon bishops a primate devoted to his views, venerable by his age and experience, and distinguished by his
rare knowledge and learning. The dignity was, therefore,
offered to an African named Hadrian, a monk of Niridano,
near Monte Cassino in the kingdom of Naples, who, declining the honour for himself, recommended as worthier of
it the monk Theodore, born at Tarsus in Cilicia, a man eminently qualified by his attainments. The recommendation
was accepted by the pontiff, on condition that Hadrian should
accompany the new primate to Britain. From Rome the
travellers proceeded to Marseilles by sea, and from thence by
way of Arles to Paris, where they were kindly received by
Agilbert, with whom having staid some time, they prosecuted
their journey, and landed safely in Kent.

Immediately after his arrival, Theodore, accompanied by
Hadrian, visited all the Anglo-Saxon states, where, by incul-
cating the apparently indifferent doctrine regarding the time
of celebrating Easter, he effected an universal acknowledge-
ment of the Roman catholic church, and strove to obliterate
all further and even every existing trace of the earlier influence of the Scottish clergy on the choice and consecration
of bishops in his province. It was in his time that the Roman
or Gregorian chant, which, with the exception of the Northumbrian churches, had been used only in Kent[1], became

victims were Catgualet, king of Gwynedd, Earconberht of Kent, Æthelwealh of Sussex, Deusdedit, archbishop of Canterbury; the bishops Wine of
London and Tuda of Lindisfarne; Boisil, abbot of Mailros, and Æthelburh,
abbess of Barking. In Ireland, it is said that two thirds of the inhabitants
perished. The pestilence of which Wigheard died at Rome was probably
the same disease. Beda, iii. 27, iv. i. Usher, Antiq. pp. 948, 1164.—T.

[1] Beda, iv. 2. ["Sed et sonos cantandi in ecclesia, quos eatenus in
Cantia tantum noverant, ab hoc tempore per omnes Anglorum ecclesias
discere cœperunt; primusque, excepto Jacobo, de quo supra diximus, cantandi magister Nordanhymbrorum ecclesiis (Cf. H. E. ii. 20) Æddi cognomento Stephanus fuit, invitatus de Cantia a reverentissimo viro Uilfrido,
qui primus inter episcopos, qui de Anglorum gente essent, catholicum

general throughout the kingdom; and while he thus united
and strengthened the Anglo-Saxon church[1], and connected it
with that of the continent, he exerted himself, by the communication of his own higher acquirements, to place the
clergy of this country on a level with that of the rest of the
Christian world. We learn also from Beda that to Theodore
and Hadrian the country was indebted for the knowledge of
prosody, astronomy, ecclesiastical arithmetic, and also for
men who were as familiar with Greek and Latin as with their
mother-tongue[2].

Theodore found a most ardent and able adherent in that
devoted champion of the Roman church, Wilfrith, bishop of
York, a man eminently distinguished for Christian zeal, rare
knowledge and vigorous powers of mind, whose eventful life
attracts our attention even for its own sake, and imperatively
demands it through its connexion with important events in
the history of the country, at that time so closely interwoven
with that of the church.

Wilfrith, though not of noble birth[3], was endowed with all
those natural advantages, the influence of which over rugged
uncivilized people appears almost fabulous. In his thirteenth
year, the period at which an Anglo-Saxon youth was considered of age, he resolved to leave his parents and renounce
the world. Equipped suitably to his station, he was sent to
the court of Oswiu, and, through the influence of the queen

vivendi morem ecclesiis Anglorum tradere didicit." To this Æddi we owe
the valuable Vita Wilfridi, printed in Gale's collection, t. i., from whom,
from Beda, a metrical life by Fridegod, Eadmer (ap. Mabillon, Sæc. iii.
p. 1) and W. Malm. (De Gest. Pont. lib. iii.), Smith (App. ad Bed. xix.)
has compiled a very useful chronological view of the life of Wilfrith. [For
an account of the introduction of the Gregorian chant into England, see
Smith's Appendix, No. xii.—T.]

[1] Beda, iv. 2. " Isque primus erat in archiepiscopis, cui omnis Anglorum
ecclesia manus dare consentiret."   [2] H. E. iv. 2.

[2] Malmesb. de Gestis Pont. lib. iii. "Non infimis parentibus apud
Northanimbros natus, si quid natalibus defuit gratiæ, generositate morum
explevit."—T.

Eanflæd, was received into the monastery of Lindisfarne by
the chamberlain Cudda, who had exchanged earthly joys and
sorrows for the retirement and observances of a cloister.
Here he was as remarkable for humility as for mental endowments. Besides other books he had read the entire psalter,
according to the emendation of St. Jerome, as in use among
the Scots. His anxious desire to behold and pray in the
church of the apostle Peter must have been the more grateful
to the queen and her Roman catholic friends from the novelty
and singularity of such a wish among his countrymen. In
furtherance of his object she sent him to her brother Earconberht, king of Kent, where he made himself familiar with the
doctrines of the Roman church, including the psalms according to the fifth edition. He was attached, as travelling companion, to Benedict, surnamed Biscop[1], a distinguished man,
who at a later period exerted himself so beneficially in the
cause of the church, and in the civilization and instruction of
the Northumbrians. Benedict died abbot of the monastery
founded by him at Wearmouth, an establishment not less famed
for arts and scientific treasures, than ennobled through its celebrated priest, the Venerable Beda[2]. On Wilfrith's arrival at

[1] Eddius (c. iii.) calls him Biscop Baducing, no doubt from the name of
his father.

[2] It will be allowed in the history of the Anglo-Saxons, where allusions
so often occur indicative of a higher degree of culture among them than
has generally been supposed to exist, to call attention to the account,
hitherto unnoticed in our histories of art, of the pictures which Benedict,
in the year 678, brought from Rome to Wearmouth, which is, moreover,
exparticularly interesting as showing not only how much must have been
executed, or at least collected at Rome, but that the subjects chosen for
representation were the same as those on which artists have been chiefly
engaged from that time almost to the present. [The entire passages are
so curious that I cannot resist the temptation to give them at length.
"Picturas imaginum sanctarum, quas ad ornandum ecclesiam beati Petri
Apostoli, quam construxerat, detulit; imaginem, videlicet, beatæ Dei genetricis semperque virginis Mariæ, simul et duodecim apostolorum, quibus
mediam ejusdem ecclesiæ testudinem, ducto a pariete ad parietem tabulato,
præcingeret; imagines evangelicæ historiæ, quibus australem ecclesiæ parietem decoraret; imagines visionum Apocalypsis beati Johannis, quibus sep-

Lyons, Dalfinus, the archbishop, was so struck by his judicious discourse, comely countenance, and mature understanding, that he retained him long with him, offered to adopt him for his son, to give him the hand of his brother's daughter, and to procure for him the government of a part of Gaul.

But Wilfrith hastened to Rome, acquired there a thorough knowledge of the four gospels, also the Roman computation of Easter, which, as we have already seen, he afterwards so triumphantly employed; and at the same time made himself familiar with many rules of ecclesiastical discipline, and whatever else was proper for a minister of the Roman church. On his return he passed three years at Lyons with his friend Dalfinus, and extended his knowledge by attending the most learned teachers. He now declared himself wholly devoted to the church of Rome, and received from Dalfinus the tonsure of St. Peter, consisting of a circle of hair in imitation of the crown of thorns, while the Scots shaved the entire front, leaving the hair only on the hinder part of the head. Here he nearly shared the fate of his unfortunate friend, the archbishop, in the persecution raised against him by the queen Baldhild, the widow of Clovis the Second[1], and the mayor of

tentrionalem æque parietem ornaret, quatenus intrantes ecclesiam omnes, etiam literarum ignari, quaquaversum intenderent, vel semper amabilem Christi sanctorumque ejus, quamvis in imagine, contemplarentur aspectum ; vel Dominicæ incarnationis gratiam vigilantiore mente recolerent; vel extremi discrimen examinis, quasi coram oculis habentes, districtius se ipsi examinare meminissent.........Dominicæ historiæ picturas, quibus totam beatæ Dei genetricis, quam in monasterio majore fecerat, ecclesiam in gyro coronaret, adtulit ; imagines quoque ad ornandum monasterium ecclesiamque beati Pauli Apostoli, de concordia Veteris et Novi Testamenti, summa ratione compositas, exhibuit : verbi gratia, Isaac ligna, quibus immolaretur, portantem ; et Dominum crucem, in qua pateretur, æque portantem, proxima super invicem regione, pictura conjunxit. Item serpenti in eremo a Moyse exaltato, Filium hominis in cruce exaltatum comparavit."—T.] One of these pictures, though not specially mentioned, yet perhaps comprised among the ' imagines evangelicæ historiæ,' Beda seems to have had in his eye when describing the three holy kings. Cf. Bedæ Vita S. Bened.

[1] Baldhild is said to have been an Anglo-Saxon slave. Act. Sanc. Mabill. Sæc. ii. p. 777 sq. Script. Rer. Fr. t. ii. p. 449.

the palace, Ebruin ; but the comely young stranger, through
the extraordinary compassion of his persecutors, was saved
from the death of a martyr.   He now hastened back to his
country, where he was honourably received by king Ealhfrith[1],
consecrated abbot of the monastery of Ripon, and regarded as
a prophet by high and low. After the disputation with bishop
Colman at Whitby, Oswiu and his son with their witan chose
the abbot Wilfrith for bishop of York, who passed over to
Paris to be consecrated by Agilbert. On his return to Northumbria he was driven by a storm on the coast among the
pagan South Saxons, who proceeded vigorously to exercise
the right of wreck on the strangers.   The chief priest of the
idolaters stood on an eminence, for the purpose of depriving
them of power by his maledictions and magic, when one of
their number, with David's courage and luck, hurled a stone
at him from a sling which struck him to the brain.   At the
fall of their priest the fury of the people was excited against
the little band, who succeeded, however, after a conflict four
times renewed, in re-embarking with the return of the tide,
and reached Sandwich in safety.

So arbitrary at that time was the spirit in which affairs of
the highest moment were conducted, so wavering the mind
of Oswiu, of so little worth the royal word, that the king,
during Wilfrith's absence, influenced by the Scottish party,
had consented to the election of the presbyter Ceadda to the
see of York.   Wilfrith retired submissively to his cloister at
Ripon, where he introduced the Roman ritual and the rule of
St. Benedict, occasionally performing episcopal duties, at the
desire of the kings Wulfhere of Mercia and Ecgberht of
Kent.   Archbishop Theodore, however, during his visitation
of Bernicia and Deira, effected his restoration to his see,
while that of Lichfield was by Wulfhere, at the instance of
Wilfrith, bestowed on Ceadda.

With other arts and knowledge architecture also came in
the suite of the Roman church.   The Scottish clergy, from

[1] See p. 169.

the preference perhaps of the northern nations for that material, had built their churches of wood, thatching them with reeds, an example of which existed in the new cathedral at Lindisfarne. It was at a later period only that reeds were exchanged for sheets of lead, with which the walls also were sometimes covered. Wilfrith sent for masons from Kent, and the abbot Benedict for workmen from Gaul. The stone basilica erected by Paulinus at York, which had fallen into a disgraceful state of dilapidation, was restored by Wilfrith, the roof covered with lead, the windows filled with glass, till then unknown among his countrymen[1]. At Ripon he caused a new basilica of polished stone to be erected, supported by pillars, with a portico. The consecration—at which the kings Ecgfrith and Ælfwine were present—was concluded by a feasting reminding us of pagan times, which lasted during three days and nights[2]. The four gospels written with golden letters on purple vellum, adorned with paintings, in a case of pure gold set with precious stones, enables us to judge both of the wealth and munificence of the patrons of Wilfrith. An edifice still more remarkable was erected by the bishop at Hexham, which, it is said, had not its like on this side of the Alps[3]. Benedict's structure too at Wearmouth was the work of masters from Gaul, after the Roman model. Thus we perceive, in the instance of the most memorable buildings of which mention is found in the history of the Anglo-Saxons,

[1] Eddius, cc. xvi., xvii. Beda, Vita Benedicti. "Benedictus......Gallias petens cæmentarios, qui lapideam sibi ecclesiam juxta Romanorum morem facerent, postulavit, accepit, attulit. Misit legatarios Galliam, qui vitri factores, artifices videlicet Brittaniis eatenus incognitos, ad cancellandas ecclesiæ porticuumque et cœnaculorum ejus fenestras adducerent." [For much curious information on this subject, see Dissertation ' On the Introduction of Learning into England,' in Warton's H. E. P. vol. i.—T.]

[2] Eddius, c. xvii.

[3] Eddius, c. xxii. "Domus, cujus profunditatem in terra cum domibus mirifice politis lapidibus fundatam, et super terram multiplicem domum, columnis variis et porticibus multis suffultam, mirabilique longitudine et altitudine murorum ornatam, et variis linearum anfractibus viarum, aliquando sursum, aliquando deorsum, per cochleas circumductam."

how their architecture sprang from that of ancient Rome, however it may have been modified in England to suit a difference of circumstances and climate.

Oswiu had greatly enlarged his dominions by victories over the Picts, and held his state in obedience and tranquillity till his death[1]. His eldest son Ealhfrith had died before him, and his kingdom, composed of so many discordant parts, fell to his younger sons Ecgfrith and Ælfwine. Despising their youth, the Picts, under their king Birdei, lost no time in attempting to regain their independence; but the Northumbrian princes, under the direction of the valiant Bernhæth, were enabled for a considerable time to hold them in subjection. A more dangerous enemy threatened them in Mercia, whose king, Wulfhere, seems to have been regarded as Bretwalda. This prince strove to form an alliance with the southern states against Northumbria, and to render that kingdom tributary: so unsuccessful, however, was the plan, that Wulfhere, being himself overcome by the Northumbrians, saw his own state divided and made tributary, and the territory of Lindisse annexed to Northumbria[2]. Wulfhere did not long survive this reverse. He was the first prince who, after some struggles with Wessex, preserved Mercia in a long state of tranquillity and reputation among the Anglo-Saxon kingdoms: his exertions for the spread of Christianity, to which he had converted Æthelwealh[3], king of Sussex; his endeavour, in conjunction with Wilfrith, by the ministry of the priest Eoppa, to convert the inhabitants of the Isle of

---

[1] Beda, iv. 5.   Sax. Chron. a. 670.

[2] Palgrave, vol. ii. p. cccxi, places this event about the year 678, apparently because Beda, iv. 12, says, "quam (provinciam) *nuperrime* rex Ecgfrid......superato in bello et fugato Vulfhere, obtinuerat."   But Wulfhere died in 675 (see Sax. Chron.), and his successor Æthelred ravaged Kent in 676.   Beda, iv. 12.   Ædde also (c. xx. sq.) places this victory "in primis annis Ecgfridi regis," before Wulfhere's, and several years before Dagobert's death (678).   The Chronol. in Wanley and Petrie gives the date 674.

[3] The Sax. Chron. a. 661 erroneously calls this prince Æthelwald.

Wight[1]; his friendship for Wilfrith and other Christian
teachers, show that he was susceptible of higher instruction,
and understood the true policy of his time. Of his last act,
which reminds us strongly of his father Penda, we cannot
judge with confidence, our knowledge of it being derived
solely from Northumbrian sources.

With the increasing power of Northumbria the authority
of the bishop of York was in a like degree extended. Clerical
influence became exceedingly powerful over the Anglo-
Saxons, and among the newly converted people we soon
discover the same erroneous notions as those which in that
age were so prevalent on the continent. Æthelthryth, the
daughter of Anna king of the East Angles, had been first
married to Tunberht, prince or ealdorman of the South Gyrwas, after whose premature death she was demanded by
Oswiu for his son Ecgfrith, then a youth of fourteen years
only. This princess, desirous of imitating what in those
times was regarded as the acme of female perfection, had
made and kept a vow of perpetual virginity[2]. In the view
of turning her from her resolve, Ecgfrith demanded the mediation of Wilfrith, promising him lands and money in the
event of his success. That Wilfrith's influence was unavail-
ing, or exerted in a way contrary to the king's expectation,
may be concluded from the circumstance that, after being for
twelve years the wife of Ecgfrith, Æthelthryth became a nun
in the monastery of Coldingham. From this event the ill-
will of Ecgfrith towards Wilfrith is said to have taken its
origin.

After his separation from Æthelthryth, Ecgfrith espoused
Eormenburh, sister of the wife of Centwine, king of Wessex[3],

---

[1] Sax. Chron. a. 661. [Where it is at the same time stated that he had
previously laid it waste.—T.]

[2] Beda, iv. 19, ejd. Chron. a. 688. W. Malm. lib. iv. and her Life by
Thomas of Ely, ap. Mabillon, Sæc. ii. [Æthelthryth died abbess of Ely.—T.]

[3] Eddius, c. xxxix.

a princess whose violence of disposition seems to have widened the breach between her consort and the prelate, and hastened the outbreak of the dissensions among the higher clergy, and the incipient jealousy of the secular towards the ecclesiastical power. Though Wilfrith had not recovered for his see the old archiepiscopal title, yet the primate of Canterbury might hardly expect that the northern prelate would not seek to regain the ancient rights of his vast province ; he consequently delayed not to represent to the kings Ecgfrith and Ælfwine the danger to which the riches and authority of the bishop of York might expose him. The kings and the archbishop agreed therefore to divide the northern bishopric into two dioceses ; one at York for Deira, and one at Hexham or Lindisfarne for Bernicia. Though the violence of this proceeding may not meet with approval, the partition of the bishopric seems justified by the example afforded by Wilfrith himself, with whose co-operation the kingdom of Mercia, containing one bishopric of equal extent with itself, was shortly after separated between two, and afterwards among three prelates[2]. East Anglia was also in the time of Theodore divided into two bishoprics.

The personal consideration enjoyed by Wilfrith was powerless in effecting any change in this decision : on the contrary, his opponents were so exasperated, that, on his leaving England[3], attended by a company of ecclesiastics, the king of Neustria and his powerful mayor of the palace, Ebruin, were prevailed on to cause him to be waylaid on his journey towards Rome ; a request which implies a closer connexion between the two courts than the obscurity in which those times are shrouded enables us otherwise to recognise ; though the

---

[1] Beda, iv. 12.   [2] Malmesb. de Gestis Pontif. lib. iv. p. 288.

[3] Wilfrith's flight must, as by Fl. Wigorn., be placed in 677, as in the following spring he had an interview with Dagobert who was murdered in 678. The date 678 given in Beda, iv. 12, and in the Chronicle, may have reference to the consecration of his successors. [Some MSS. read septimo for octavo. See Stevenson's note, p. 275 of his edit.—T.]

readiness of the Neustrians to persecute the exile may have been a consequence of the circumstance, that Wilfrith, at the solicitation of the friends of the Austrasian king, Dagobert (Dægberht) the Second, who, after a long exile, had discovered that prince in Ireland, had, supported by the arms of his partizans, effected his return to his realm, and presented him with costly gifts. A storm, which drove his vessel to the coast of Friesland, saved Wilfrith; but a delusive similarity of name threw the bishop of Lichfield, Wulfrith, also an exile, into the hands of the waylayers. The landing of Wilfrith in Friesland was productive of the most important consequences, both for the inhabitants of that country, and afterwards for a great part of the north of Europe. Wilfrith found an hospitable reception with the king Aldgisl, as well as protection against the machinations of Ebruin, who even there ceased not to persecute him. Called on through a notion of the people, who ascribed to his presence the abundant fishing season and the rich harvest of that year, he preached to them the doctrine of Christ in the intelligible dialect of the Anglo-Saxons, and baptized nearly all the princes, with many thousands of the people [1].

It was thus decreed to Wilfrith to be the first of the numerous Anglo-Saxon missionaries and ecclesiastics to whom the countries on the Baltic and German Ocean, also many provinces to the south, are indebted for their conversion to Christianity and the elements of civilization intimately connected therewith. His immediate followers were his pupil Willebrord, afterwards, under the name of Clement, first bishop of the Frisians; Winfrith or Boniface, the apostle of the Thuringians, archbishop of Mentz; Leofwine, the successful converter of the Saxons; Willehad of Northumbria, the friend of Alcwine (Ealhwine) and first bishop of Bremen; Willebald, first bishop of Eichstädt, and his brother Wunibald. We also find in Germany many devout and zealous

[1] Eddius, c. xxvi.—xxviii.

Anglo-Saxon ladies, as Leobgyth, who had learned the art of poetry from the abbess Eadburh; Thecla, abbess of the cloister at Kitzingen, and others. In consequence of the connexion between Denmark and England, a considerable number of distinguished men followed in the same course, whose influence on the civilization of the North has been generally disregarded, and certainly never sufficiently appreciated. Those remaining behind were cheered and confirmed in the faith by the example and teaching of Aldhelm, first abbot of Malmesbury (Mældulfsburh), and afterwards bishop of Shireburn, who first among the Anglo-Saxons made the whole heritage of Roman learning his own, and gained the still greater glory of being one of the earliest and best poets in his own Germanic mother-tongue[1].

Let us not, however, exalt the merits of the Anglo-Saxons without acknowledging those of their teachers, the Scots, especially as both worked sometimes in common in the same field, and the former are often comprised under the name of the latter. As applicable to both, it may be remarked that their emigrations had not always the work of conversion for immediate object, but that, in consequence of the lack, during several centuries, of regular monastic orders, those desirous of devoting themselves to a severe and contemplative course of life, either alone or with a few kindred spirits, were induced to leave their home and betake themselves to some lonely cell, or hallowed spot[2], a practice long retained among the Scots. At a time when the Anglo-Saxons had scarcely begun to spread a new paganism in Britain,

---

[1] Of Aldhelm we have the following testimony: "Aldhelmus nativæ linguæ non negligebat carmina, adeo ut, teste libro Elfredi (manuali libro sive handboc) nulla ætate par ei fuerit quisquam poesim Anglicam posse facere." W. Malm. lib. v. ap. Savile and Gale; and Wharton, Angl. Sac. t. ii. p. 1. Aldhelm died May 25, a. 709. An edition of Cædmon's Scriptural Paraphrase with an English version, by the translator of the present work, was published in 1832, at the expense of the Society of Antiquaries. Cædmon died in 680.

[2] Osberni Vita S. Dunstani, lib. i. c. i.

Fridolin, a native of Ireland, had already founded a convent at Seckingen, an island in the Rhine[1], and dedicated a church to St. Hilarius, the possessions of which have given name to the canton of Glarus[2]. At the beginning of the seventh century, Columbanus, the friend of St. Columba, with his pupil Gallus, travelled to those parts, where the name of the latter is preserved in that of the canton of St. Gall, and where his monastery may be regarded as the choicest storehouse of the learning and poetry of the middle age. From Columbanus the cloister of Luxeuil, also that of Bobbio and others derive their origin. At a later period[3] Kilian a Scot, with his companions Coloman and Tottman, founded a monastery at Würzburg, the library of which preserves the proof of its descent in precious monuments in the Irish language. Virgilius, a Scot, contemporary with Boniface, was bishop of Salzburg. The convent at Peronne seems also to be among the oldest foundations of the Scots[4]. Gertrude, abbess of Nivelles, a daughter of Pepin, a daughter also of the mayor of the palace, Grimwald, caused many learned Scots to settle in France. Ultanus was the founder of the abbey of St. Quentin[5]. The convent of St. Martin at Cologne[6], of St. James at Ratisbon, of St. Mary at Vienna, are only some among the many Scottish foundations to which Germany, as well as other countries, is indebted for the establishment and spread of Christian doctrines, the preservation of learning, and the beneficent applications of worldly goods[7]. The possession

---

[1] A.D. 490.   [2] J. v. Müller's Geschichte der Schweizer, Bd. i. c. 9.
[3] A.D. 680.

[4] Annales Mettenses, a. 690. Beda, iii. 19, and Smith's note; also Gall. Christ. t. ix. 1035, and Mabill. Annal. Ord. S. Bened. xiv. 1, 2.

[5] See charter in SS. Rer. Francic. t. ix. p. 735.

[6] In the Monum. Hist. Germ. t. ii. p. 215. Pertz has, for the first time, printed a chronicle of this monastery, from a. 756 to 1021.

[7] Cf. Murray, Comment. 'De Britannia et Hibernia, sec. vi.–x.' 'Literarum Domicilio,' in Nov. Comment. Soc. Göttingens. t. ii. For Scots in Iceland and other parts of the North, cf. Diculius de Mensura Orbis, ap. Langebek, SS. Rer. Dan. t. ii. p. 31, and Adam. Bremen.

of rich benefices often excited the national jealousy against the Scots, who, however, were always able to recover their lost rights[1]. Of the ancient connexion between the Scottish cloisters and the mother country, which was never broken, and had often proved of mutual benefit, both in secular and ecclesiastical respects[2], traces exist even at the present day.

As Germany was especially indebted to British ecclesiastics, whether of kindred or of Celtic race, both for its Christianity and its early mental formation, it may reasonably be inferred that many historic traditions passed over from the old country to the new acquisition of the Saxons. We will here merely allude to the before-mentioned saga of the landing of the Saxons in Hadeln; though the old Danish history is also interwoven with traditions of England. With the writings of the Anglo-Saxons, the oldest written chronicles also passed over to Germany, and in the earliest annals of German cloisters are to be found some chronological notices of which all traces are lost in England. To these strangers may also be ascribed the circumstance, that in the oldest small chronicles, in which almost every word must shed some welcome light on dark antiquity, are often contained, instead of German names and narratives, the unintelligible and indifferent names of British ecclesiastics: still to these individuals is owing the introduction of Beda's chronology into Germany at that early stage of learning[3].

In the following year Wilfrith continued his journey towards Rome, after having declined the bishopric of Strasburg, offered to him by his royal friend Dagobert. Bertari, king

---

[1] As early as the year 846 the French bishops recommended to Charles the Bald that the Hospitalia Scotorum might be kept according to the intentions of their pious founders. Pertz, t. iii. p. 390. It is in later times only that we find them stigmatized and prosecuted as pseudo-bishops and vagabonds. Hludovici Imper. Capit. Addit. iii. 37.

[2] See hereafter, a. 929.

[3] See Literary Introduction.

of the Longobards[1], a friend and relative of the Anglo-Saxon rulers, received the exile with respect, rejecting with disdain the demand of his enemies to detain him. The protection of the pope had not yet been claimed by Anglo-Saxon churchmen; we may, therefore, considering the connexion still subsisting with the old British clergy, as well as the short time that Northumbria had belonged to the catholic church, regard it only as a very bold experiment, when pope Agatho, with the synod assembled at Rome, commanded, under threats of all spiritual punishments, the restoration of Wilfrith to his former Saxon bishopric[2]. But the thunders of the Vatican proved as powerless as had been for many centuries the decrees of the Capitol. Ecgfrith not only held in contempt the command of the pope, but caused its object on his return to linger nine months in prison, from which he was released only by bold artifice and the representations of his adherents. He was, however, compelled to leave the dominions of Ecgfrith, who, moreover, effected his expulsion from Mercia, whose king, Æthelred, had married Osthryth, a sister of the Northumbrian; as also from Wessex, where a sister of queen Eormenburh was, as we have seen, the consort of the king Centwine. As an asylum beyond the influence of Ecgfrith, the remote territory of the South Saxons alone presented itself to the fearless energetic man, to the shore of which he

[1] The passage of Eddius (c. xxviii.), "pervenerunt ad Berchterum regem Campaniæ," has been often misunderstood. The words which he attributes to that prince about his flight to the king of the Huns agree fully with what Paul Warnefrid relates concerning Bertari, who had himself been desirous of seeking aid in England, and whose son Cunibert was married to an Anglo-Saxon lady named Hermelind. See hereafter under Ceadwealla of Wessex, and Paul. Diac. v. 32, 37.

[2] Beda, v. 19. Fl. Wigorn. a. 679. In his petition to the pope, Wilfrith styles himself 'episcopus Saxoniæ.' See Eddius, c. xxix. In like manner Hwætberht, in his letter to Gregory,—" Hwætberchtus abbas cœnobii beatissimi apostolorum principis Petri in Saxonia." Beda, Vita Hwætberchti. How readily Rome received this appeal, from which a faint dawn of future authority over all the British islands seemed to arise, appears from the acts of this synod. Cf. Alberici Chron. a. 680.

had formerly been driven under such inauspicious circumstances, and where the people, notwithstanding the earlier
attempt to convert them, had either persisted in, or fallen
back to, paganism.

The king of Sussex, Æthelwealh, as well as his queen,
Eabe[1], of the family of the petty kings of the Hwiccas, had
been baptized. Thus to the homeless exile, whom the secular
power would not, and the highest spiritual power could not
protect, was the work committed, to bring within the pale of
Christendom the last heathen people of his native land. Here
too were the efforts of Wilfrith successful, and the establishment of a bishopric in Sussex was the early consequence.
Selsea was assigned to him as an episcopal see, together with
sufficient lands and revenues, which was subsequently transferred to Chichester.

Even here the most important events of Britain are gathered
round the person of Wilfrith. Ceadwealla, son of Cenbyrht[2],
of the race of Ceawlin of Wessex, had lived an exile in the
wilds of Chiltene and Andredesweald: he visited the bishop,
who received the noble youth with kindness; though yet
unconverted, treated him as his son, and was greatly helpful
to him in the acquisition of his kingdom[3]. Previously to this
event, Ceadwealla (under what pretext, or how Wilfrith's
conduct on the occasion is to be explained, we are ignorant)
had conquered Sussex,—in defence of which Æthelwealh
had fallen,—but had again lost it. Wilfrith now received the
bishopric of Wessex from Ceadwealla, who, though still unbaptized, was zealous for the advancement of Christian institutions. Having reconquered Sussex, the Isle of Wight,—
the conversion of which was also the work of Wilfrith,—and

---

[1] Eabe had already been baptized in her own country: "Eaba in sua,
id est, Huicciorum provincia, fuerit baptizata; erat autem filia Eanfridi,
fratris Eanheri, qui ambo cum suo populo Christiani fuere." Beda, iv. 13.
—T.

[2] Ob. a. 661.   [3] Eddius, c. xli.   H. Hunt. a. 686.

finally Kent, where an appalling event had taken place, to be detailed hereafter, and which probably accelerated the execution of his design, Ceadwealla resolved not only to adopt the faith professed by the majority of his subjects, but to give an example hardly occurring a second time in the whole course of history,—that of a youthful vigorous prince renouncing his sceptre, to sever himself from paganism by baptism at the hands of the sovereign pontiff, in the church of St. Peter, and in monastic solitude to await in serious meditation the day of admission to a better life.

Wilfrith had in the meanwhile become reconciled with the repentant archbishop Theodore, not long before the death of the latter in 690, and, through his mediation, also with Æthelred of Mercia, who bestowed on him the see of Lichfield[1], —the fourth that had fallen to him—in his kingdom, and, after the death of Ecgfrith, effected his reconciliation with Aldfrith[2], his successor.   Ecgfrith, after an unjust and cruel

---

[1] Malmesb. de Gest. Pontif. lib. iii.

[2] Aldfrith, who, according to Sim. Dunelm., in the year 685, May 20, succeeded Ecgfrith, has by most English historians (with the exception of Carte, Lingard and Palgrave) been regarded as the same son of Oswiu who ruled jointly, and thirty years previously commanded with his father in the decisive battle against Penda on the Winwæd; but it is to be remarked that Beda, whenever he mentions the eldest son, calls him Alchfrid (in Alfred's version, Ealhfrith), without the slightest allusion to illegitimacy. See H. E. iii. 14, 21, 24, etc. Vita S. Benedicti, p. 293.   The later king he always calls Aldfrid (in Alfred's version, Ealdfrith), H. E. iv. 26, v. 19, 21, 24. Vita S. Ceolfridi, Vita S. Cuthb. Ep. ad Ecgb. p. 309 ed. Smith, ed. Stev. p. 219.   Sax. Chron. aa. 685 and 705.   Alcuinus, de Pontif. Eccles. Ebor. a. 843.   Adamnani Vita S. Columbæ, ii. 46.   Even in the incorrect printed text of Ædde we find the distinction of the names, c. viii. 56.   But we nowhere find that the peaceful Irish student, the inexorable opponent of Wilfrith, of whom he had been the early friend and scholar, and the valiant conqueror of Penda, the rebellious son of Oswiu, were one and the same individual.   Malmesbury indeed informs us that Aldfrith was the elder brother ("Is quia nothus erat, factione optimatum, quamvis senior, regno indignus æstimatus, in Hiberniam, seu vi seu indignatione, secesserat; ibi et odio germani tutus, et magno otio literis imbutus, omni philosophia composuerat animum," lib. i.), a fact which, if well founded, proves nothing against Beda's testimony.   Alchfrid was in 653 married to

war on Ireland, the conduct of which he had committed to
Beorht[1], and after the conquest of Cumberland, where he had
bestowed Carlisle and the land of Cartmel on the church of
Lindisfarne, was slain in an invasion of the Pictish territory,
at Nechtansmere (Drumnechtan). Aldfrith was an illegitimate son of Oswiu, who having passed some time in Ireland[2], devoted to study, and being very eminent at the time
for his attainments, had by his brother been destined to a
bishopric.

But for Wilfrith there was no tranquillity. Though he had
declined the succession to the archiepiscopal see of Canterbury offered to him by Theodore, and had even aided Berhtwald in obtaining that dignity, the latter, nevertheless, five
years afterwards, during which time Wilfrith had recovered
possession of the see of York and his other benefices, placed
himself, with king Aldfrith, at the head of a synod, at which
most of the British bishops were present, who in that spirit
of independence of the papal chair which had been maintained for the last twenty-two years, demanded of Wilfrith,
in the first place, an acknowledgment of the statutes and ordinances of archbishop Theodore, and, on his refusal, resolved
to deprive him of his benefices, excepting only the monastery
of Ripon which he had founded[3].

a daughter of Penda. Beda, iii. 21. Aldfrid in 705 left a successor eight
years of age. The similitude of names needs excite no doubt. Aldfrid
(Ealdfrith) is well associated with Alchfrid (Ealhfrith) and Ecgfrid (Ecg-
frith) to suit the Anglo-Saxon usage. Thus Penda's son was named Peada ;
two brothers, Cedd and Ceadda. Oswiu's daughter, married in 653 to
Peada, was named Alchfled (Ealhflæd), and one born the year following,
Ælflæd. Beda, iii. 21, 24. Tigernach, a. 704, calls him Altfrith mac Ossu.
O'Connor (MSS. Stowens. t. i.) refers to a poem by him.

[1] Beda, iv. 26. Tigernach, a. 685. "Saxones campum (Bregrae) vastant,
et ecclesias plurimas in mense Junii."

[2] Beda, Vita S. Cuthb. c. xxiv. "In insulis Scottorum ob studium
literarum exulabat—in regionibus Scottorum lectioni operam dabat, ipse
ob amorem sapientiæ spontaneum passus exsilium." Also, Vita Cuthb.
Anon. § 28. "Qui (Alfridus) tunc erat in insula quam Hy nominant."—T.

[3] Eddius, c. xlv.

Wilfrith, far from tamely submitting to his disgrace and to the diminution of the papal authority, again undertook, though in his seventieth year, the perilous journey to Rome, where, however, the English clergy, in the character of accusers, strove to anticipate him. Though their efforts against Wilfrith were fruitless, yet the honourable exculpatory decision and mediation of the pope, John the Sixth, availed him little on his return to his native country. The archbishop received him with apparent kindness, but Aldfrith, on whom even Wilfrith's friend and biographer bestows the surname of 'the Wisest,' was too deeply imbued with the tenets of the old British church to allow the decrees made by his predecessors and himself, with the concurrence of the witan and clergy, to be annulled by a sheet of parchment from the chair at Rome[1]. The death of Aldfrith, and the declaration of his sister, the abbess Ælflæd and other adherents of Wilfrith, that the king in his last hours had desired the restoration of peace, but more effectually, perhaps, the death of Bosa, bishop of York, accomplished at length an accommodation, in the synod on the Nith[2], which, as far as Wilfrith's pretensions were concerned, can be looked on only as a disregard of the papal authority. He did not even recover the bishopric of York, which was given to John bishop of Hexham, a man highly venerated for his many virtues; while the vacant see of Hexham, together with the monastery of Ripon, was assigned to Wilfrith. After a few years passed in almsgiving and the improvement of church discipline, Wilfrith died in his seventy-sixth year, a man whose fortunes, and activity in the European relations of England, were long without a parallel[3].

Wilfrith by his own power accomplished what Augustine, animated by the spirit of Gregory the Great, had begun. The Anglo-Saxon states were converted not only to Christianity, but to catholicism. For secular learning they were

---

[1] Eddius, c. lvi. [2] A.D. 705.
[3] Eddius, c. lxii. Beda, v. 19. Sax. Chron. a. 709.

chiefly indebted to the Scots and Britons, for their accession
to the European system of faith to these two men; for however successful Augustine may appear in his first spiritual
acquisitions for the church of Rome, the course of Anglo-
Saxon history, nevertheless, shows that, although the Roman
ecclesiastical system was acknowledged, the influence of Rome
was exceedingly weak, and that the Anglo-Saxons, even after
they were no longer anti-catholic, continued always anti-pa-
pistical. Wilfrith's history itself proves indeed how little
even this zealous partizan of the popes could effect; hence it
is the more desirable to take a view of the internal relations
of religion in England.

We notice, in the first place, in every kingdom, a bishop,
who, travelling about with his coadjutors, propagated both
doctrine and discipline. This kind of church regimen was
well calculated to succeed that of the pagan priesthood. The
bishops, when chosen by the clergy, always required the confirmation of the prince, but, in most instances, they were nominated by him. In later times it is observable that the
royal chaplains always obtained the episcopal dignities. Over
these bishops, he who resided at Canterbury, the capital of
the Bretwalda Æthelberht, was set as archbishop, in like
manner as the bishop of Rome had originally assumed the
supremacy over the Roman provinces. The archbishopric of
York, established by Gregory the Great, which might act as
a check to a primacy of the Kentish archbishop dangerous to
the papal authority, ceased to exist after the flight of Paulinus,
and was not re-established till a century afterwards, when
Ecgberht, the brother of king Eadberht, after many representations to the papal chair, received the pall[1]. A third
archiepiscopal see was established for the country between

---

[1] Sax. Chron. a. 735. Appendix ad Bedæ H. E. Beda, Epist. ad Ecgberht. Malmesb. de Gestis Pont. lib. iii. Wilfrith never bore the archiepiscopal title. Neither Beda nor Ædde allege anything to justify the supposition, but the contrary.

the Thames and the Humber by the powerful Offa of Mercia, —who held the dignity necessary for the honour of his kingdom—with the consent of pope Hadrian, to whom this augmentation of his slight influence over the Anglo-Saxon clergy might have been welcome[1]. The old state of things was, however, shortly after restored.

Almost contemporaneously with the bishoprics, some monasteries were founded by the bounty of the kings and their relatives, which served as residences to numerous monks. Many of these cloisters in the north of England were destroyed by the Danes, the very sites of which are not now known with certainty. The superintendence over clergy and laity in the larger states soon required more than the single bishop of the territory, whose influence might, moreover, as we have seen in the case of Wilfrith, excite the jealousy of the king. In the choice of episcopal sees and monasteries, especial regard was had to the security of the new establishment; hence the fortified residence of the king, or a spot particularly defended by nature, like the isle of Lindisfarne, was selected. So completely had Christianity perished in Germanic Britain after the departure of the Romans, or so little was it acknowledged by the Saxons, that no religious foundation of Roman times was preserved or could be restored, and only some old Roman buildings and walls were used as churches. A small, probably old British, church was discovered in a wild thorny spot, which gave rise to the foundation of the abbey of Evesham[2]. If the abbey of Glastonbury or Ynisvitrain, which appealed to charters of donation from the ancient kings of Damnonia, seems to form an exception to the above statement, the circumstance must not be over-

---

[1] Sax. Chron. Fl. Wigorn. a. 785. W. Malm.

[2] Malmesb. de Gestis Pontif. lib. iv. ["constat eum (Ecgwinum) locum illum, quo nunc cœnobium visitur, peculiariter amasse, incultum antea et spinetis horridum, sed ecclesiolam ab antiquo habentem, ex opere forsitan Brittannorum." The spurious charters of Cœnræd and Ecgwine relating to this foundation are in Kemble's Codex Dipl. t. i. p. 68 sqq.—T.]

looked, that this cloister, in the isle of Avallon, where the corpse of Arthur rested, remained long in the hands of the Britons[1].

A glance at the Anglo-Saxon bishoprics, together with a brief notice of the most eminent monasteries, will render the geographical idea of the several kingdoms more familiar: this knowledge is, moreover, indispensable with reference even to the political history of a country in which bishops and prelates shared the privileges and duties of secular nobles.

The little kingdom of Kent contained, besides the archiepiscopal see, the bishopric of Rochester, founded by Augustine. In Essex the only bishop was at London, whose diocese comprised the present counties of Essex and Middlesex with the half of Hertfordshire[2].

In East Anglia dwelt the bishop of Domuc (Dunwich)[3], though, as early as the time of archbishop Theodore, advantage was taken of the death of bishop Bisi to erect a separate see for the North-folc at Elmham, which, in the time of William the Conqueror, was transferred to Thetford, and under William Rufus, to Norwich[4].

In Wessex the first episcopal see was at Dorcic (Dorchester), from which, as has been already mentioned, a bishopric at Winchester was afterwards detached. The former retained Hampshire and Surrey. A third at Shireburn—famed for its first possessor, Aldhelm, as also for a later one, Asser, the friend of Ælfred,—was, under the Conqueror, in conformity to the canonical prescript for the transfer of episcopal sees

---

[1] Malmesb. de Antiq. Eccl. Glaston. ap. Gale, t. i. p. 308. The Domnonian charter is, however, dated as late as 601, consequently after the arrival of Augustine, and his conference with the British bishops. [See also the charter of Henry II. printed by Hearne from the chartulary of Glastonbury, and Hemingi Cartularium, app. 603.] This is one of the few cloisters of which the charters granted by the early Anglo-Saxon kings have not entirely perished. See Cod. Diplom. t. i.

[2] A.D. 604. Beda, ii. 3. Fl. Wigorn. Malmesb. de Gestis Pontif. lib. iii. R. Higden, Polychron. ap. Gale, t. i. p. 204 sq.

[3] A.D. 631. Beda, ii. 15.   [4] Malmesb. de Gestis, ii.

from small places to large towns, removed to Old Sarum, and afterwards to Salisbury, though not till the following bishoprics had been taken from it, viz. Wells, afterwards Bath; Ramesbury, subsequently reunited to Sarum; Crediton, afterwards transferred to Exeter, with which that of St. Petroc or St. Germain's (Cornwall) was subsequently united. In Sussex was the bishopric of Selsea, afterwards transferred to Chichester.

In Mercia, from the original diocese of Lichfield (which comprised also the territory of the Lindisfaras) were detached by Theodore the sees of Worcester, Leicester, Lindesey (at Sidnacester) and Hereford. At the same time the see of Dorchester appears to have belonged to the state of Mercia[1].

The diocese of York comprised originally the whole of Northumbria, including the south of Scotland. Under Oswald, the see of Lindisfarne or Holy Island—the Iona of the Anglo-Saxons—was founded, containing within its jurisdiction the kingdom of Bernicia, until the establishment by Theodore of another see at Hexham[2]. On the ruin of Lindisfarne by the Danes, the see was transferred to Chester-le-Street, and finally to Durham. That portion of the diocese which was in the present Scotland, fell in the reign of Malcolm Canmore to the see of St. Andrew's.

The conquests of the Northumbrian princes were followed by an extension of the diocese of York. Hwitern (Candida Casa), now Whitherne in Galloway, where Nynias had formerly erected a church of bright white stone for the southern Picts, had, in Beda's time, its first Anglo-Saxon bishop, Pecthelm, supposing that the authority of Trumwine—who was sent from Northumbria to the Picts in the year 681, but expelled after the defeat of Ecgfrith,—was limited to the northern portion of the Pictish territory[3]. It appears that this bishopric was for some time dissolved, and that its inhabitants were

---

[1] Malmesb. de Gestis. Higden, Polychron. p. 206.
[2] Beda, iv. 12.   [3] Beda, iv. 12, v. 23.

under the charge of the bishop of Sodor and Man[1]; though, on the restoration of the see of Hwitern, the archbishops of York made good their authority over it. At a later period this district, as well as the whole of Strathclyde, belonged to the diocese of Glasgow.

The clergy of Wales refused subjection to Augustine; and although isolated instances may be cited to show the subjection of a Welsh bishop to the see of Canterbury, it is nevertheless certain that no acknowledgment of the English primate on the part of the Welsh took place, previously to the conquest of the country by the English under the Norman dynasty. Of the four dioceses, St. David's (Menevia), Llandaff, Bangor and St. Asaph (Llan Elwy), the first possessed the archiepiscopal title, which at a former period had been held by the church of Caerleon[2].

Cumberland, as an independent state, had without doubt its own bishop at an early period, though he probably did not reside at Carlisle, which city king Ecgfrith bestowed on St. Cuthberht as an endowment of the see of Lindisfarne. The foundation of the bishopric of Carlisle is the work of Henry the First.

The dioceses of the present England are, with the exception of a few changes made at the time of the Reformation under Henry the Eighth,—when Gloucester, Bristol, Oxford and Peterborough were erected into bishoprics,—identical with those of the Anglo-Saxons, as above described. The voice of the bishops in the Upper House is derived from the rights of their predecessors in the Witena-gemôt. The vast differences in their revenues may be immediately traced to the disproportion of the states founded by the Jutes, Angles,

---

[1] This see, which for a time had been transferred to Iona, was, during the sway of the Northmen, under the archbishop of Trondhjem. See documents in Thorkelin, 'Diplomata Arna-Magnæana.'

[2] Giraldi Camb. Itiner. lib. i. c. 4, lib. ii. c. 1, ejd. Descriptio Cambriæ, c. iv. Particularly his 'Distinctiones VII. de Jure et Statu Menevensis Ecclesiæ.'

and Saxons. Even the Bretwaldaship of Æthelberht, with the functions of which our acquaintance is so imperfect, is to be recognised in the several dioceses comprised in the province of the Metropolitan and Primate of all England. The province of the Primate of England, containing two dioceses only, preserves the memory of the conquests of Eadwine and Oswiu, as well as of the firmness and vigour of Wilfrith.

A cloister with a church was the first requisite of the newly introduced faith; a place of meeting and shelter for the missionaries, teachers and disciples, as well as others devoted to piety. The number of these increased rapidly in the larger states; and in their rich endowments, as well as in the numerous ecclesiastics of the noblest and even of royal families, we have a sufficient explanation of the great influence soon possessed by abbots and abbesses. Sigeberht of Essex has been already mentioned, as well as the holy queen Æthelthryth, whose sister Sexburh was her successor at Ely. Æbbe, a sister of Oswiu, was abbess of Coldingham (Coludesburh) on the coast of Berwickshire. Hild, a grandniece of Eadwine, enjoyed a similar dignity at Hartlepool (Heorutu) in Durham, and subsequently at Whitby (Streoneshealh) in Yorkshire; in the latter she was succeeded by her niece Ælflæd, a daughter of Oswiu. Previously to the foundation of these monasteries, the need of them among the Anglo-Saxons was so great, that they frequently sent their children to Frankish cloisters for education and consecration to a religious life. Small cloisters arose from the pious exertions of individuals, as in Northumbria, from an oratory which Wilgis, the father of Willebrord the apostle of Friesland, had founded and dedicated to St. Andrew, and subsequently enlarged, in the cells of which Alcwine, the celebrated biographer of Willebrord, passed his youth[1].

But abuses of almost every kind were not wanting. Wine,

---

[1] Alcuini Vita Willebrordi, lib. i. c. 1.

one of the first bishops of London, bought, as we have seen,
his see of Wulfhere, king of Mercia. Many ecclesiastics were
so ignorant of the language of the church, that Beda translated for their use the Creed and Paternoster from the Latin
into their mother-tongue. A vice peculiar to the time consisted in the facility with which laymen of rank, ealdormen,
and other officials of the king were permitted to found monasteries for themselves and wives. The land, free from all
secular service, was, under this pretext, obtained by money
from the kings, and secured to the purchasers and their heirs
by royal charter, confirmed by the bishops, abbots, and other
dignitaries. In these foundations, the layman assuming the
abbot's staff, devoted to worldly indulgences, free from all
burthens, surrounded by profligate monks, whose vices had
caused their expulsion from other monasteries, or by his own
former followers, shaven in the guise of monks, lived without rule or discipline, to the detriment and scandal of the
country[1].

The small number of parish churches was very favourable
to the erection of numerous monasteries. A knowledge of
their foundations and of the parochial divisions, when attain-
able, enables us to form some idea of the population and circumstances of the commonalty, and of its increase in times
when other sources of information are looked for in vain.
But even in England records of the origin of the earliest
parish churches are wanting. They seem to have been first
erected in the south under archbishop Theodore, and, about
half a century later, that is, before and during the time of
Ecgberht, archbishop of York, in the northern parts of England. St. Cuthberht, abbot of Melrose[2], wandered from
place to place, to confirm and animate believers by his preaching ; yet, when Beda subjoins to this narrative that such was
the custom of the clergy at that time[3], it would follow that

---

[1] Bedæ Epist. ad Ecgb. p. 310 sq. edit. Smith.   [2] Ob. a. 687.
[3] Beda, iv. 27. Epist. ad Ecgb. p. 306.

in his own days the case was otherwise in those northern countries; at the same time it cannot be doubted that the dioceses or districts there, as in other countries, were, at the beginning, too extensive. We find however in Holstein, very shortly after its conversion by the Anglo-Saxon Wille-had, the foundation of four churches for baptism, from the districts of which the later parochial division was established[1]. Similar churches those also appear to have been which, before the time of Theodore, were founded by Cedd, bishop of Essex, at Ythancester and Tilaburg (Tilbury)[2]. In the later Anglo-Saxon laws, provisions are not wanting for the regulation of the parochial system[3]. That the laity were soon aware of their rights in the administration of church property, may be inferred both from a similar state of things in the Christian North, and from the community of all Anglo-Saxon property: if proof from the earliest times is wanting for England, we may perhaps assume that the clergy at a later period did not concede ampler rights to the laity than those which they had formerly possessed[4].

The Anglo-Saxon clergy were, however, by no means so free and influential as their brethren in most of the continental states; for though ecclesiastics sometimes gained power over individual kings, such cases were of rare occurrence and without lasting consequences. That close connexion between the Anglo-Saxon states and Rome did not exist, whereby the latter could extend powerful aid to its servants. The archbishop of Mentz, Boniface, himself an Anglo-Saxon, declares, in his letter to Cuthberht, archbishop of Canterbury[5], that no cloisters were in such a state of slavery as those of

---

[1] Remberti Vita S. Anscharii, c. xix.

[2] Beda, iii. 22. " Cedd.........fecit per loca ecclesias, presbyteros et diaconos ordinavit, qui se in verbo fidei et ministerio baptizandi adjuvarent (circa a. 655)."

[3] Laws of Edgar I. i. 2. Eccles. Laws of Cnut, iii.

[4] For a later period see ' Conc. Exancest.' a. 1287.

[5] Wilkins, Conc. t. i. p. 93.

the Anglo-Saxons,—a declaration confirmed by the language
of their charters of donation, whereby they were bound to
pay not only the ' trinoda necessitâs,' the ' brycg-bôt,' ' burh-
bôt,' and 'fyrd,' or contribution for keeping in repair the
bridges and fortresses, and for the maintenance of the military
levy, but were sometimes also taxable like the rest of the community, and bound to harbour and entertain in their monasteries the king's huntsmen and followers[1].

Hence the more remarkable will appear, a celebrated donation made by Æthelwulf, king of Wessex, to the clergy of
his states, after his return from Rome, which some older English historians, as Ingulf, William of Malmesbury and other
monks, together with Selden, have been inclined to regard as
the origin of tithes ; an untenable interpretation, partly re-
futed by the very uncertain tenor of apparently fictitious
chartérs[2], and partly by the much earlier introduction of
tithes, by the assignment to the church of older imposts belonging to the king and other lords of the soil[3].

According to a recent interpretation, Æthelwulf bestowed
one tenth part of the land in his kingdom of Wessex and its
dependencies, Kent and Sussex, upon the servants of the
altar, or for the sustenance of the indigent, exonerated from
every territorial tax and duty[4]. But here two donations are
blended together ; by the one, sometimes called the Testament
of Æthelwulf, the obligation is imposed on every ten farmers
or farms in his hereditary states[5] to provide one poor person

---

[1] See Palgrave, vol. i. p. 156, and the documents there referred to. The
last-mentioned burthen was often imposed on the cloisters of the continent,
though they were relieved from it by the Carlovingian legislation.

[2] A.D. 854, 855. Wilkins, Conc. t. i. Cod. Diplom. t. ii. pp. 50 sq.
W. Malm. lib. ii.

[3] Excerptiones Ecgberti, iv., v., xxiv. See also Phillips, Angelsächsische
Rechtsgeschichte, § 70 ; with whom, however, we cannot agree in ascribing, on the weak authority of Bromton, either the introduction of tithes
to Offa of Mercia, or the confirmation of them to Æthelwulf.

[4] So Palgrave, vol. i. p. 158.

[5] Asser, a. 855, and ejd. Annales : " Per omnem hæreditariam terram

with meat, drink and clothing, and is remarkable as the beginning of secular provision for the poor. The other document, with which we are here more particularly concerned, directs, (according to the oldest copies of the Latin text, made probably from an Anglo-Saxon original, as well as according to the interpretation of the oldest and nearly contemporaneous author,) that king Æthelwulf, with the advice of his bishops and ealdormen, resolved to exonerate, for monks, nuns and laymen possessing hereditary land, every tenth mansus of their property, or, of smaller possessions, the tenth part, from the before-mentioned three obligations, usually considered as irredeemable, and from all other burthens ; for which grace certain masses and prayers were to be said for the souls of the king and of the consenting prelates and ealdormen[1].

suam............in decem manentibus." W. Malm. lib. ii. "in omni suæ hæreditatis decima hida pauperem vestiri et cibari præcepit." Sim. Dunelm. a. 855 : "in decem mansis." Matt. Westm. a. 857 : "in decem hydis vel mansionibus."

[1] Asser, the friend of Æthelwulf's son Ælfred, is the oldest testimony we have relative to this grant : " Eodem anno (855) Æthelwulfus decimam totius regni sui partem ab omni regali servitio et tributo liberavit." So Asseri Annal., Fl. Wigorn., Ingulph., W. Malm. ; though the last-mentioned has falsely interpreted it, he nevertheless gives the words so that no doubt can arise as to their essential meaning. " Affirmavi ut aliquam portionem terrarum hæreditariam antea possidentibus omnibus gradibus, sive famulis et famulabus Dei, Deo servientibus, sive laicis (miseris, addit *Ing.*), semper decimam mansionem ubi minimum sit, tamen (tum, *Ing.*) partem decimam (omnium bonorum, addit *Ing.*) in libertatem perpetuam perdonari (donari sanctæ ecclesiæ, *Ing.*) dijudicavi, ut sit tuta atque munita ab omnibus secularibus servitutibus, necnon regalibus tributis, etc.......quo eorum servitutem in aliqua parte levigamus." The last words seem fully to confirm my interpretation. Spelman, Conc. p. 348 (Wilk. t. i. p. 183) has the same text as Malmesbury. Turner is undecided, and misunderstands the word ' minimum,' which does not here signify *the least* or *the smallest*, but *very little, but a little, less than ten mansi.* The widely different text of the document in Matthew of Westminster might be passed without notice, had it not been the cause of the errors committed by the latest writers of history. Instead of " portionem.........servitutibus," he gives " portionem terræ meæ Deo, et B. Mariæ, et omnibus sanctis, jure perpetuo possidendam concedam, decimam scilicet partem terræ meæ, ut sit tuta muneribus, et libera ab omnibus servitiis," etc.

The Roman ecclesiastical canons took root but slowly, and never so deeply among the Germanic nations as among the Romanized people of the continent; the former not being, like the latter, familiar with the Roman law, the fountain of the canon law. We must not suffer ourselves to be misled by the letters of Gregory to Augustine, dictated, as it were, by a conqueror in the flush of victory, who expected to organize the whole country on the capture of the first fortress. Let it be remembered how Kent itself wavered in its new faith, how unfavourable to the papal authority the circumstances were under which the Christian religion was gradually propagated. A few priests only passed over from Rome to England; the majority were Anglo-Saxons, acquainted only with their mother-tongue and the law of their country. Even if not wanting in zeal for the interest of the church, still they were less attached than their continental brethren to the bishop of Rome, who soon became sensible that, at a great distance, even spiritual weapons lose their force. To bishop Wilfrith, neither his profound knowledge of the canon law [1], nor the sentence of the pope in his favour, proved of any use with the English synod. To the slight regard paid to the papal canons, the great number of Anglo-Saxon ecclesiastical laws, often issued by the king, seem to owe their existence: hence the church law of the Anglo-Saxons was, more than that of any other Christian state, a national law. It was only for matters of a purely spiritual nature that the synod was composed wholly of ecclesiastics [2]. The consent of the king appears to have preceded the appointing and summoning of a synod; and it was by his approbation, and by admission among his laws, that its decrees became binding on the laity. Whatever at the same time concerned the rights of the laity was treated in the general witena-gemôt with the participation of the clergy. Their own jurisdiction was con-

[1] Eddius, c. xlii. " In omni sapientia et in judiciis Romanorum eruditissimum."   [2] Cf. Palgrave, vol. i. p. 176.

ceded to the clergy in cases only affecting themselves; every extension of it was strictly guarded against. Mention has already been made of the tonsure and other points, in which the Anglo-Saxons did not follow the Roman practice until at a later period. The long narrow habit was first assumed by the Anglo-Saxons in Rome, when pope John the Seventh seized the occasion to introduce the use both of that and the mitre among the clergy in England, according to the custom of the Roman church[1]. The celibacy of the clergy was not so soon established among the Anglo-Saxons[2], and only the prohibition of a second marriage, and severe penalties for acts of immorality, were observed among them. The Germanic descent of the clergy manifested itself also in the prohibitions occasioned by their propensity to drunkenness[3]. To confine the marriages of the laity within the degrees prescribed by the church of Rome, among a people so impatient of restraint, was impossible; and the pope soon found it necessary to modify for the people of England the restrictions regarding marriage[4].

The knowledge of Roman law possessed by individual Anglo-Saxons is to be ascribed to the necessity they were under of learning the canon law, which is modified and defined by the Roman. Frequent appeals to the papal court stimulated also many ecclesiastics to a profounder study of the same in Rome itself, as England then possessed no schools appropriated to that object. What such men as Theodore of Tarsus and other foreign or Kentish ecclesiastics may have accomplished in this respect we are without the means of

---

[1] See the pope's letter in Baluzii Miscell. t. v. p. 478.

[2] Even a son of St. Wilfrith is mentioned. Edd. c. lvii. " Sanctus pontifex noster de exilio cum filio suo proprio veniens."

[3] Theod. Pœnitent. xxvi. 2, 4, 3, 13. Ecgb. Penitent. iv. 33, 34, 35. Edg. Can. lvii., lviii. in Ancient Laws and Institutes. Cf. also the systematic view of Anglo-Saxon ecclesiastical law in Phillips.

[4] See Boniface's letter to Æthelbald in W. Malm. lib. i., and excerpt from Gregorii Epist. ad Augustinum in Decret. p. ii. causa 35, qu. 2. c. 20.

ascertaining, though among the various branches of knowledge possessed by Beda himself, no trace is discernible of
his acquaintance with the Roman law; the more remarkable,
therefore, appears the knowledge of it manifested by Aldhelm,
not only in occasional expressions, but also in a special composition[1].

To the distance from Rome, and their slender dependence
on the papal chair, the people of England are apparently indebted for the advantage of having retained their mother-
tongue as the language of the church, which was never entirely banished by the priests from their most sacred services.
Their careless sensual course of life, and perhaps the preju-
dice which prevented them from learning even so much Latin
as was requisite to enable them to repeat the Paternoster and
Creed in that language[2], have proved more conducive to the
highest interests of the country than the dark subtilty of the
learned Romanized monk, pondering over authorities. Even
the mass itself was not read entirely in the Latin tongue.
The wedding form was, no doubt, in Anglo-Saxon; and its
hearty sound and simple sterling substance are preserved in
the English ritual to the present day[3]. The numerous versions[4] and paraphrases of the Old and New Testaments made
those books known to the laity and more familiar to the clergy.
That these were in general circulation in Beda's time, may
perhaps be inferred from his omission of all mention of them,
though the learned and celebrated Anglo-Saxon poet, Aldhelm,

[1] This fragment was to have been printed under the direction of C. P.
Cooper, Esq., among the publications of the late Record Commission.
Respecting Aldhelm see also Beda, v. 18. W. Malm. Gesta Reg. Angl.
lib. i., and De Gestis Pont. Angl. lib. v. ap. Gale: his letters are printed
in Wharton, Anglia Sacra, and his Latin poetry in Canisii Lectt. Antiq.

[2] Conc. Clovesh. a. 742, art. x. ap. Wilkins, t. i. p. 96.

[3] Palgrave, vol. ii. p. cxxxvi.

[4] The Anglo-Saxon Gospels were first printed under the auspices of
archbp. Parker in 1571. The second edition is that of Marshall in 1665.
The third and last (probably Ælfric's version) is by the translator of the
present volume, in small 8vo, 1842.—T.

had already translated the psalms, and Ecgberht, bishop of Lindisfarne, the four gospels. Beda is also said to have translated both the Old and the New Testament into his mother-tongue[1], an assertion which, like a similar one regarding king Ælfred, must be limited to the gospel of St. John[2], and, in the case of Ælfred, to some fragments of the psalms[3]. An abridged version of the Pentateuch, and of some other books of the Old Testament by Ælfric in the end of the tenth century, is still extant. The vast collection of Anglo-Saxon homilies, still preserved in manuscript, once enlarged and ennobled the language and the feelings of Christianity[4] ; and the ear which continued deaf to the mother-tongue was, in the Anglo-Saxon church, yet more sensibly addressed, and in a way to agitate or gently move the heart. Large organs are described and spoken of as donations to the church in the beginning of the eighth century[5]. The mention of this in-

---

[1] Aldred's Northumbrian gloss to the four gospels in the St. Cuthberht's book (MS. Cott. Nero D. IV.) seems not to be earlier than the middle of the tenth century. See Mr. Stevenson's paper in the ' Graphic Illustrator,' p. 355, and Sir F. Madden's letter to Sir H. Ellis in ' Letters of Eminent Literary Men,' printed for the Camden Society.—T.

[2] W. Malm. lib. i.   [3] Ib. lib. ii.

[4] These venerable monuments of our early church are now in course of publication by the Ælfric Society, with a modern English version by the translator of the present work. A MS. discovered at Vercelli by Professor Blume contains not only homilies, but the valuable metrical pieces, printed for the late Record Commission by the present translator, but not published, though now given to the world, with a translation by J. M. Kemble, Esq., for the Ælfric Society. The homilies contained in the Vercelli MS. are all to be found in the various public libraries of England. An Anglo-Saxon version of the Psalms, possibly Aldhelm's, transcribed by the present translator from a MS. in the Royal Library at Paris, has been published at the expense of the University of Oxford.—T.

[5] Áldhelmus de Laude Virgin. ap. Canisium, t. i. p. 715.

> " Maxima millenis auscultare organa flabris
>   Mulceat auditum ventosis follibus iste,
>   Quamlibet auratis fulgescant cætera capsis."—

W. Malm. De Gestis Pont. Angl. lib. v. ap. Gale : " Organa, ubi per æreas fistulas musicis mensuris elaboratas, dudum conceptas follis vomit strument at Malmesbury affords ground for the conjecture, that it might have been introduced by the musical Welsh. Church music was first brought into Kent by the Roman clergy, and from thence into the northern parts, where it underwent improvement. This was an object of such interest, that the arrival of a Roman singing-master [1] is mentioned by contemporary authors as a matter of almost equal importance with a new victory gained by the catholic faith over the pagans or the Scots [2].

A glance at the religious feelings of the people will suffice to show us a striking propensity among them to pilgrimages [3]; and we may discern under the pilgrim's gown not only a longing after the beams of a warmer sun, but also the hereditary craving for restless wandering. The testimonies relative to such wanderers, more especially the numerous females, are highly unfavourable [4]. The Anglo-Saxon kings established in many places hospitals for the entertainment of pilgrims, the most celebrated of which was in Rome, under the denomination of the ' Schola Saxonum,' called at a later period, ' Hospitale di S. Spirito in Vico di Sassia.' A writer of no

anxius auras." Of Dunstan also it is said that he played the organ ("modificans organa"). See Osbern, Vita S. Dunstani, ap. Wharton, Angl. Sac. t. ii. p. 93.

[1] Beda, H. E. ii. 20, iv. 2. Vita S. Bened. a. 678.

[2] With the exception of the Te Deum the Scots had none of the usual Ambrosian and Gregorian hymns, as appears from the antiphoner of Bangor composed in the seventh century, now in the Ambrosian library, but formerly belonging to the monastery of Bobbio. See Muratori Anect. t. iv. These Latin hymns of the fifth and sixth centuries have long lain unheard, and were forgotten, until again brought to light by the praiseworthy researches of modern literati. It is remarkable that some of the hymns of the Scot Sedulius have, in a German version, been preserved in the Protestant church. Cf. Rambach, Christl. Anthol. i. 85, 110.

[3] Beda, v. 7. " Peregrinari.........quod his temporibus plures de gente Anglorum, nobiles, ignobiles, laici, clerici, viri ac feminæ, certatim facere consuerunt."

[4] See Boniface's letter to Æthelbald. To bishop Cuthberht he writes: " Paucæ sunt civitates in Longobardia vel in Francia aut in Gallia, in qua non sit adultera vel meretrix generis Anglorum."

great authority ascribes the founding of this establishment to Ine, king of Wessex[1], who, after his abdication, ended his days at Rome[2]. The object of this foundation, which comprised a church dedicated to St. Mary, and a cemetery for the English, was not only to provide for needy West Saxons and other English at Rome, but for the instruction of young Anglo-Saxons in the catholic faith, who were exposed to the danger of so many heresies in their native country. For its support Ine is said to have laid, under the name of Rom-feoh or Rome-scot, a tax of a penny on every house in his kingdom, the amount of which was sent to the pope for that purpose. At a later period the St. Peter's penny was a subject of repeated complaints, after its original intention had been lost sight of. William of Malmesbury knew nothing certain relative to the foundation of this institution at Rome, and merely mentions, without any allusion to Rom-feoh, that tradition ascribed it to Offa, king of Mercia. A life of Offa, the fidelity of which has perhaps been too greatly underrated, reconciles both these accounts, by stating that Offa, about the year 790, richly endowed the Saxon school already existing at Rome, and for that purpose introduced the perpetual burthen of Peter's pence[3]. According to a probably

[1] Matt. Westmon. a. 727. His account is rendered rather incredible by his ascribing to the same prince (Ine abdicated in 726) the imposition of Rom-feoh or St. Peter's pence. Spelman (Conc. t. i. p. 290) endeavours, from a manuscript at Chichester, to prove that the Schola Saxonum was founded as early as 714, while the passage refers to Offa of Mercia, from the date of whose death, DCCXCIV., the last c seems to have been omitted. Cf. also J. Ross Antiquarii Warw. Hist. Reg. Angl. p. 72.

[2] Sax. Chron. a. 728. The year of Ine's death is unknown.

[3] This life is ascribed to Matt. Paris, and is to be found, with the Vitæ XXIII. S. Albani Abbatum, in Watts's edit. p. 29 : "Rex.........scholam Anglorum, quæ tunc Romæ floruit, ingressus, dedit ibi ex regali munificentia, ad sustentationem gentis regni sui illuc venientis, singulos argenteos de familiis singulis, omnibus in posterum diebus, singulis annis. Et tunc tali largitate obtinuit, ut de regno Angliæ nullus publice pœnitens, pro executione sibi injunctæ pœnitentiæ, subiret exilium.........p. 31, annuum reditum contulit ad sustentationem scholæ memoratæ, propter Anglorum

contemporaneous account, it appears that in the year 816 the school of the Angles at Rome was burnt[1]. Mention is made of its inmates at the commencement of that century as forming part of the procession which met pope Leo the Third on his return from his visit to Charles the Great[2]. It was again destroyed by fire in the beginning of the reign of Leo the Fourth[3], when it lay for some years in ruins, till king Æthelwulf, during his stay at Rome[4], caused it to be rebuilt. The rebuilding of this structure has given occasion to the ascribing to that king the introduction of Rome-scot, or rather the transfer of the same to the papal chair[5]. Pope Marinus relieved the school of the Angles from all taxes and burthens, at the request of king Ælfred[6], who showed his gratitude to that pontiff. Of this privilege king Cnut, during his stay at Rome, obtained a new confirmation from pope John[7], and in return caused Rome-scot for the pope to be collected with greater strictness[8].

However interesting the Saxon school may appear to us,

rudium et illuc peregrinantium eruditionem." This passage is extracted in Matt. Westmon. a. 794. Vitæ Abbat. S. Albani, c. i. " Offa......Romæ scholam peregrinorum pie constituit, ut ibidem peregrini, qui ad Romanam ecclesiam et curiam confluxerant, ex diversis mundi partibus barbari, vel votivæ orationis gratia vel expediendorum negotiorum necessitate, linguas, quas non noverant, addiscerent: quæ schola, propter peregrinorum confluxum ibidem solatia suscipientium, versa est in xenodochium, quod Sancti Spiritus dicitur."   [1] Sax. Chron. h. a.

[2] "Pastorem.........simul etiam cunctæ scholæ peregrinorum, videlicet Francorum, Frisonum, Saxonum, atque Longobardorum.........susceperunt." Anastasius, ap. Muratori Script. iii. p. 198.

[3] So Anastasius, lib. i. p. 233. " B. Pontificii sui exordio Saxonum vicum validus ignis invasit," etc.   [4] Sax. Chron. a. 855.

[5] W. Malm. lib. ii. " Æthelwulfus Romam abiit, ibique tributum, quod Anglia hodieque pensitat, sancto Petro obtulit.........scholam Anglorum, quæ, ut fertur, ab Offa, rege Merciorum, primitus instituta, proximo anno conflagraverat, reparavit egregie."

[6] Sax. Chron. aa. 885 and 890. Matt. Westmon. a. 889. Sim. Dunelm. a. 884, ap. Twysden, pp. 130, 148 and 355.

[7] Rad. Dicet. Abbrev. a. 1031.

[8] Eccl. Laws of Cnut, ix. Law of North. Priests, lvii. Also Laws of Æthelred *passim*.

especially with regard to the St. Peter's penny, we must nevertheless be careful not to ascribe to it an immediate influence in respect to the legal instruction of the Anglo-Saxon clergy. In its early time it could not have had such a predominant object, although it might occasionally have contributed to it; in later times it was transformed into the hospital nominally still in existence: yet how important would its old archives be, for the moral and ecclesiastical history of England, should some fortunate explorer one day discover them[4]!

Among the chief objects of attraction to the Anglo-Saxons, both at home and in their pilgrimages, were relics. In finding this superstition so extremely prevalent among them, we are almost led to the supposition that it did not originate in the catholic faith, but was rather, if not entirely produced, at least greatly promoted, by the belief of the Germanic nations, who solemnly buried the bones of the dead in barrows, threw up vast mounds over them, raised monuments of rude workmanship[2], and thought to conquer in battle with the aid of the corpses of their dead chieftains. The judicial superstition, brought to Britain by the Saxons, that the lifeless body of a murdered person would begin to bleed on the approach of the murderer, also supposes the presence of supernatural powers in the corpse[3].

No Germanic people preserved so many memorials of paganism as the Anglo-Saxons. Their days of the week have to the present time retained their heathen names; even that of Woden (Wednesday) is still unconsciously so called in both

---

[1] The conversion of the school into an hospital is ascribed to Innocent III. See also Spelmanni Vita Ælfredi, p. 7, note ª. Fea, Description de Rome, t. iii. Some documents relating to prebends, claimed by the hospital of S. Spiritus in Saxia de Urbe, from 1284 to 1291, are to be found in Rymer, t. i. pp. 648, 740, 752.

[2] So the Jutes for Horsa. Beda, i. 15.

[3] Edg. Can. lxv. Ælfr. Can. xxxv. For Germany see my tract, 'Ueber ältere Geschichte und Rechte des Landes Hadeln,' p. 59.

worlds, and by more tongues than when he was the chief object of religious veneration. In the north of England and the Germanic parts of Scotland the Yule feast (geohol, geol) has never been supplanted by the name of Christmas. That these denominations, throughout ages, were not a senseless echo of superannuated customs, is evident from the Anglo-Saxon laws of later times, which strictly forbid the worship of heathen gods, of the sun, the moon, fire, rivers, water-wells, stones, or forest-trees[1]. It is, however, probable that some of this heathenism may have been awakened by contact with the pagan Northmen. A part of the old theology lost its pernicious power when, reduced to history, it became subservient to the purposes of epic poetry, as instances of which may be cited the genealogies of the Anglo-Saxon kings and the poem of Beowulf. Of many superstitions, which long maintained their ground, relative to the power of magic, to amulets, magical medicaments, as well as to the innocent belief, so intimately connected with poetry, in elves and swarms of benevolent, or at least harmless unearthly, though sublunary spirits, it is often difficult to point out the historic elements from which they have sprung, as precisely in the northern parts of England, where they were longest preserved, the intermixture of the Britons with the Germans was the most intimate.

The adoption of Christianity does not appear to have been attended with any sudden and important consequences with regard to the political relations of the Anglo-Saxons, and is chiefly indebted to this circumstance for its final settlement. It also very soon promoted the general and literary instruction of the nation, brought it into connexion with Roman Europe,—operating thereby with increased power on the prospects of the country,—and, by strengthening the state by principles and spiritual means, prevented the threatened dismemberment of the land among military chieftains, striving

[1] Sec. Laws of Cnut, v.

for independence. These causes soon contributed to aug-
ment the power of the larger kingdoms; and the history of
the Anglo-Saxons, during a long period, is to be sought
chiefly in that of Northumbria, of Mercia, and of Wessex,
which subsequently comprised that of all England. These
three states were those which, inured to arms, had in earlier
times maintained themselves, and extended their dominions
by many victories over the Welsh, the kingdoms of Strathclyde and Cumbria, and those of the Picts and Scots.

After Ecgfrith's death, in the battle of Nechtansmere against
the Picts[1], the boundaries of Northumbria became much
contracted. His successor, Aldfrith, acquired the epithet of
'The wisest,' or 'The most learned.' He had been well
instructed in the theology and dialectics of the Irish school,
which was one day to send forth a Johannes Scotus, or Eri-
gena, the founder of the scholastic philosophy. But other
intellectual pursuits were not less welcome to Aldfrith, as is
proved by the friendly reception given by him to the Gallic
bishop Arculf, who had been driven by a storm on the western coast of Britain, on his return from his travels in the
East, to which we cannot allude without at the same time
mentioning the account of his journey recorded by Adamnan,
abbot of Iona, from the mouth of Arculf himself, as well as
an extract from it by Beda, which became the foundation of
the numerous guides to the Land of Promise, so characteristic of the knowledge and sentiments of the middle age.

But no one imparts to the age of the 'Wisest king' greater
brilliancy than the man just named, whom the epithet of
'The Venerable' adorns, whose knowledge was profound and
almost universal. Born in the neighbourhood of Wearmouth,
he enjoyed in that abbey the instructions of Benedict, its first
abbot, of whom we have already had occasion to make honourable mention, as well as those of his successor, Ceolfrith,

---

[1] See p. 188.

equally distinguished for his zeal in the promotion of learning. In the neighbouring cloister of Jarrow Beda passed his
life in exercises of piety and in varied study, and gave life and
form to almost all the knowledge which the age could offer
him. If, on a consideration of his works, it must appear
manifest that that age possessed more means of knowledge,
both in manuscripts and learned ecclesiastics, than we are
wont to ascribe to it ; and even if we must recognise in Beda
the high culture of the Roman church, rather than Anglo-
Saxon nationality, yet the acknowledgment which his merits
found in Rome during his life, and, shortly after his death,
wherever learning could penetrate, proves that in him we
justly venerate a wonder of the time. His numerous theo-
logical writings, his illustrations of the books of the Old and
New Testaments have throughout many ages, until the total
revolution in that branch of learning, found readers and
transcribers in every cloister of Europe. His knowledge of
Greek, of medicine, of astronomy, of prosody, he made subservient to the instruction of his contemporaries ; his work
' De sex hujus seculi ætatibus,' though less used than it deserves to be, is the basis of most of the universal chronicles
of the middle age. But his greatest merit, which will preserve his name through all future generations, consists in his
historic works, as far as they concern his own native land.
If a second man like himself had arisen in his days, who with
the same clear, circumspect glance, the same honest and pious
purpose, had recorded the secular transactions of his forefathers, as Beda has transmitted to us those chiefly of the
church, then would the history of England have been to
posterity almost like revelation for Germanic antiquity.

Among the learned contemporaries and countrymen of
king Aldfrith, the monk Ecgberht claims especial notice.
Like him instructed during a long abode in Ireland, he employed the facility and knowledge there acquired in the conversion of the monks of Iona; but he is more particularly in-

teresting to the Germans through his early wish to undertake personally their conversion, and, on renouncing his design for himself, for having sent Willebrord and his companions to the Frisians, thereby stimulating the two Ewalds, the White and the Black, so distinguished from the colour of their hair, to a like attempt among the Old-Saxons, but which was frustrated by their murder[1].

With the death of Aldfrith[2] the star of Northumbria began to set. Eadwulf, regarding whose pretensions we are not informed, although the general acknowledgment, and the readiness of Wilfrith to receive him amicably, allow us to suppose their existence, assumed the sovereignty, which he was unable to maintain longer than two months[3]. Through the influence of Berhtfrith, the most powerful ealdorman of the country, Osred, the son of Aldfrith, a child of eight years, was raised to the throne, and by him protected against disturbers within, and, by a brilliant victory, against the Picts and Scots from without[4]. While the will of the royal infant was apparently obeyed, and all legitimate forms were observed, the greatest licentiousness burst out among the nobles, to which the clergy would have shown no indulgence, but for the part taken in it by themselves[5]. The government, during the long minority of Osred, was conducted by his mother Cuthburh[6], sister of Ine king of Wessex, whose failings were for-

---

[1] Beda, v. 10. At Merseburg their memory is celebrated on Oct. 2 (Zeitschrift für Archivkunde, i. 123). According to Beda and the Calendar the day of their martyrdom is, "quinto nonarum Octobrium" (Oct. 3), a. 695.

[2] Sax. Chron. a. 705.   [3] Eddius, c. 57.

[4] This victory was gained between Hæfe and Cære (Caraw, Tindale hundred in Northumberland). Tigernach, a. 711, also mentions it: "Strages Pictorum in campo Manand a Saxonis, ubi Fingaine mac Deleroith immatura morte jacuit."

[5] Bedæ Epist. ad Ecgbertum.

[6] I assume this guardianship (although it seems at variance with the Chronicle which (a. 718) says, that Cuthburh was separated from Aldferth during his life) from the fragment No. 71 among the letters of Boni-

gotten in the subsequent foundation of the abbey of Winburne. Osred followed not in the footsteps of his father, but, sunk in debaucheries, which spared not even the sanctity of the cloister, he was slain in his nineteenth year, in an ambush laid for him by his kinsmen on the southern border by the sea[1].

The successors of Osred were—1. Cenred, descended from Occa, an illegitimate son of Ida; 2. Osric, the son of Ealhfrith; and 3. Ceolwulf, the brother of Cenred. The two years' reign of the first-mentioned prince, as well as that of the second of eleven years, are of no importance. The tranquillity of the country during the first years of Ceolwulf was disturbed by violent internal dissensions. The king himself was seized by his enemies, confined in a cloister, and had already received the tonsure, when his friends reseated him on the throne[2]. Though able to preserve peace on the frontiers of his kingdom, he could not stifle discord within : of his love for piety and learning, we have the most honourable testimony of the Venerable Beda, who dedicated to him his ecclesiastical history of the Angles. During the reign of Ceol-

---

face, where, speaking of a vision, it is said, "Aspexit.........in pœnalibus puteis Cuthbergam simulque Wialan quondam reginali potestate fruentes, demersas usque ad ascellas, i. e. Cuthbergam capite tenus humeroque præclaram, cæteris membris maculis conspersam; alteriusque, i. e. Wialan, supra caput flammam extendere, totamque animam simul cremari intuebatur." Queen Wiala is unknown to me. This purgatory must have been devised after the death of Boniface, not earlier, as it makes mention of "Æthilbealdus, quondam regalis tyrannus."

[1] Beda, v. 22. W. Malm. lib. i. Matt. Westmon., a. 717, says of him, "belli infortunio interemptus est." Boniface, in his letter to Æthelbald of Mercia (epist. xix.), of which Malmesbury gives only an extract, says, "Osredum spiritus luxuriæ fornicantem, et per monasteria nonnarum sacratas virgines stuprantem et furentem agitavit, usque quo ipse gloriosum regnum et inutilem vitam contemptibili et despecta morte perdidit." [R. Wendover, t. i. p. 211. Eodem anno (717) "Osredus.........juxta mare pugnans, belli infortunio interemptus est."—T.]

[2] Beda, v. 23, 24, ejd. App. aa. 731, 737. Sim. Dunelm. a. 731. Tigernach also mentions the imprisonment of Cuthwine's son, by which correct Annal. Ulton. a. 730.

wulf, the archiepiscopal dignity was restored to York, his kinsman Ecgberht being the first who received the pall formerly bestowed on Paulinus[1]. He had reigned eight years when he renounced the corroding cares attending the imaginary happiness of rule, and withdrew to the monastery of Lindisfarne, where, apart from worldly anxieties, he lived nearly thirty years[2].

Ceolwulf on his abdication was succeeded by his cousin and heir, Eadberht, a brother of archbishop Ecgberht and son of Eata[3], a very able man, fully qualified for the duties of government. Eadberht raised his kingdom to its former estimation, chastised Æthelbald, king of Mercia, who had attacked Northumbria, while he was engaged in warfare with Talorgan mac Fergusa, king of the Picts, and took Cyil in Ayrshire, and the neighbouring lands from Dunnagual, king of Strathclyde, or his father Teudubr, son of Beli mac Elpin (ob. 722). Six years later, in alliance with Ouengus or Unnust, the hated king of the Picts, successor of Talorgan mac Fergusa, who, in the year 750, had fallen in a battle with the Welsh, he took Alcluyd, the capital city of Strathclyde, and reduced that British kingdom under his subjection[4].

---

[1] Sax. Chron. a. 735. [Ecgberht was celebrated for his love of knowledge, and founded a noble library at York. See his Penitential in Anc. LL. and Inst. Alcuini Epist. W. Malm. lib. i.—T.]

[2] Sax. Chron. aa. 737, 760. Sim. Dunelm. a. 764. H. Hunt. lib. iv.

[3] Sax. Chron. Fl. Wigorn. a. 738. Malmesbury calls Ecgberh "fratrem æquivocum."

[4] [In App. ad Bedam, a. 740, it is said, "Aruwini et Eadberctus interempti." This obviously clerical error has not been copied by Simeon, and probably did not exist in the MS. used by him: he says (a. 740), "Arwine filius Eadulfi occisus est," without naming Eadberht.—Of this prince Simeon writes (Hist. Dunelm. ii. 3), "Omnibus adversariis vel sibi subjectis vel bello prostratis, reges circumquaque morantes, Anglorum, Pictorum, Britonum, Scottorum, non solum cum eo pacem servabant, sed et honorem illi deferre gaudebant: cujus excellentiæ fama, ac operum virtutis, longe lateque diffusa, etiam ad regem Franciæ Pipinum pervenit, propter quod ei amicitia junctus, multa ei ac diversa dona regalia transmisit."—T.] App. ad Bedam, a. 750. "Eadberctus campum Cyil cum aliis regionibus suo regno addidit." Cf. Annal. Camb. a. 722, 750, 760.

The Frankish king Pepin sought his friendship, and sent him by his ambassadors costly presents, in which we may discern the respect paid to a powerful prince, and, at the same time, recognise the policy of the Franks, to gain friends in the rulers of North-Britain, and, in the event of a war, allies against the more neighbouring southern parts of the country. But Eadberht grew weary of a glorious, though, according to some accounts, not wholly prosperous sway, and, after a reign of twenty-one years, he also renounced his throne and the world[1]. The other kings of Britain endeavoured to dissuade him from this step, and, it is said, offered to resign to him portions of territory, if he would continue to bear the sceptre[2]. During the ten remaining years of his life he had ample cause not to regret his resolve, or at least to perceive that the anxieties of his predecessors were not groundless. His son Oswulf, to whom he had transferred his crown, was in the following year treacherously murdered by his thanes, when Æthelwald, surnamed Moll, of unknown lineage, was by his faction placed on the throne of Ida[3], the extinction or neglect of whose race brought the most unhappy consequences to the country. One ealdorman after another seized on the government, and held it till his expelled predecessors returned with a superior force, or popular favour and successful treason had raised up a new competitor. The family con-

Annal. Ulton. a. 721. Sim. Dunelm. a. 756. Chron. Mailros. Tigernach, aa. 750, 752.

[1] App. ad Bedam, a. 758, assigns his abdication to causes not easily to be reconciled, "Dei amoris causa et cœlestis patriæ, violentia accepta S. Petri tonsura." H. Hunt. says that, "videns regum prædictorum, Edelbaldi scil. et Sigeberti, vitam ærumnosam et finem infaustum, Ceolwlfi vero prædecessoris sui vitam laudabilem et finem gloriosum, meliorem partem elegit," etc. This cannot, however, be strictly correct, as Ceolwulf did not die till near thirty years after his abdication (764), or nine years after the retirement of Eadberht. Chr. Mailr. more consistently, "tonsura capitis pro Deo accepta, apud Eboracum sub archiepiscopo Egberto factus est canonicus." The Sax. Chron. and Florence place his abdication in 757.—T.

[2] Sim. Dunelm. de Eccl. Dunelm. lib. i.

[3] App. ad Bedam, a. 759. Sim. Dunelm.

nexion, which had hitherto been maintained by marriages
among the Anglo-Saxon princes, ceased, and the subjects of
the usurpers lost not only the friendship and protection of
the once allied states, but found in family hatred, thirst for
restoration and desire of revenge, new and dangerous enemies.
In a battle which lasted three days, at Eadwine's Cliff, or,
according to another account, at Eldun near Melrose, the
ealdorman Oswine was slain[1]. This victory, however, afforded but little security to Æthelwald, who, a few years
afterwards, by a battle fought at Wincanhealh[2], lost his kingdom, though not his life[3], and was succeeded by Alhred[4], a
son of Eanwine, who, it is said, traced his descent from Ida.
Alhred endeavoured to continue the alliance with the Frankish empire, at the moment when Charles the Great was engaged in the Saxon conquest. He not only sent embassies
to the emperor, but was desirous also to use the services of
his countryman Lullus for that object, who, after having faithfully followed Boniface in his self-denying calling, had succeeded him in the see of Mentz[5]. It was to this king that
the Northumbrian Willehad, a friend of Alcwine, applied for
leave to convert the pagan Frisians and Saxons to the Christian faith : whereupon Alhred summoned his bishops and
other ecclesiastics to consult on his request, which, after mature deliberation, was granted. The missionary was recommended to the protection of the Almighty, who did not for-

---

[1] Sax. Chron. a. 761.   Sim. Dunelm.   [2] Pincanhealh?

[3] Fl. Wigorn. "regnum remisit." Sim. Dunelm. "regnum amisit in
Winchanheale." H. Hunt. "coactus dimisit illud" (sc. regnum). Matt.
Westmon. a. 765, "vita decessit:" whence Turner, vol. i. p. 411, "the
tomb received him;" while Lingard (vol. i. p. 110) has, "he resigned in
an assembly of the witan at Finchley."

[4] Sax. Chron. Fl. Wigorn. a. 765.

[5] Othloni Vita S. Bonifacii, lib. i. c. 24. For two letters of Alhred to
Lullus see Magna Biblioth. Patrum, t. xiii. 108. ep. xc. Alhred and his
queen Osgearn write to him : " Nostris quoque, dilectissime frater, legati-
onibus ad dominum nostrum gloriosissimum regem Carl obsecramus consu-
lendo subvenias, ut pax et amicitia, quæ omnibus conveniunt, facias stabi-
liter inter nos confirmari." W. Malm. lib. i. "Lullus, et ipse natione
Anglus," etc.

sake him, but blessed him in the foundation of the bishopric of Bremen, the later archiepiscopal see of Hamburg[1]. After a lapse of some years Alhred, forsaken by his thanes and relations, and driven from York, renounced the throne, and found an asylum with Cyneth, king of the Picts. He was succeeded by Æthelred, a son of Æthelwald Moll[2], who in the fifth year of his reign was compelled to abdicate and forsake his country. Two rebel ealdormen, Æthelbald and Heardberht, had slain Ealdwulf, son of Bosa, the chief commander of the royal army, at Kingscliff, and afterwards his generals Cynewulf and Ecga, in a battle at Hilathirn[3]. Alfwold son of Oswulf, and grandson of Eadberht, then obtained the kingdom[4]. He is praised as a pious and upright king, and adorned with the title of 'friend of God.' But the turbulence of the nobles of his kingdom prevailed over better efforts. The ealdorman Beorn, his chief-justice, was, on account of his rigour, burnt at Silton by the thanes Osbald and Æthelheard, who had assembled a body of forces; and Alfwold himself, after a tumultuous reign of ten years, perished by means of a conspiracy, at the head of which was the ealdorman Siga[5].

Osred son of Alhred now ascended the throne once occupied by his father, but so ill defended it, that when Æthelred, son of Æthelwald Moll[6], returned to the kingdom for-

---

[1] Vita S. Willehadi, c. i., where the king of the Angles is, according to some MSS., called Alachind, in other better ones, Alachrat. In App. ad Bedam, a. 765, he is called Aluchredus. This agreement between the name and race of the king, the native country of the priest (he went in 779 from the Frisians to the Saxons) and the chronology, seems to remove every doubt as to my explanation.

[2] Sax. Chron. a. 774.   [3] H. Hunt. a. 778. Sim. Dunelm.

[4] Sax. Chron. Fl. Wigorn. a. 778. Sim. Dunelm. a. 779.

[5] Sax. Chron. Sim. Dunelm. a. 788. [Alfwold, as we learn from Simeon, was buried in the abbey church of St. Andrew at Hexham, built by Wilfrith, which abbey he describes as excelling in beauty all others in the land of the Angles; its walls were adorned with various colours, and it contained painted histories.—T.]

[6] Sax. Chron. a. 790. Fl. Wigorn. has " Æthelredus *frater* Alfwoldi," instead of "*filius*," and, a. 774, Æthelbertum for Æthelredum.

merly governed also by his father, Osred, betrayed by his
thanes, was declared to have forfeited the crown, was shaven
for a monk and put into a monastery, and afterwards obliged
to seek safety in exile[1]. Æthelred strove to strengthen himself by violent measures. The ealdorman Eardwulf who had
at first governed a part of Northumbria under him, as we
learn from existing coins (an abundant source of Anglo-Saxon
history), but who afterwards opposed him, was seized and
brought to Ripon, where, before the gates of the monastery,
he was, by order of Æthelred, to be put to death. Being left
for dead, his body was by the friars, singing the Gregorian
chant, borne into the church, where in the middle of the night
he was found to be yet living, being reserved for still greater
vicissitudes. The sons of Alfwold, Ælf and Ælfwine, were less
fortunate: being enticed from their sanctuary in the cathedral
of York, they were barbarously murdered at Wonwaldre-
mere[2]. The discontented now again turned their thoughts
to the exile Osred, who had withdrawn to the Isle of Man,
whom they bound themselves by oath to restore to his kingdom; yet scarcely had he landed when, in spite of oaths and
fealty, he was seized and put to death by command of Æthelred. His corpse was buried in the church of Tynemouth.
But Æthelred sought by other means to strengthen his
power: shortly after he had freed himself from his dangerous
rival, he married Ælfflæd, a daughter of Offa king of Mercia[3].

Events such as are here recorded must have been attended
with the saddest effects on the condition of the people; we
accordingly meet with no more distinguished individuals
among the Northumbrians. Agriculture was neglected, famine and its companion pestilence desolated the land. But a
more dreadful scourge than these transient evils was at hand.
In the year 793 the Northmen first landed on Lindisfarne,
plundered the monastery and church, not even sparing the

---

[1] Sax. Chron. Sim. Dunelm. a. 790.   [2] Sim. Dunelm. aa. 790, 791.
[3] Sim. Dunelm. a. 792.

monks, some of whom they slew, some they carried off as slaves, others they sent forth naked, or cast into the sea. In the following year the pirates returned and plundered the monastery at Ecgferthes-mynster (Wearmouth?) : but one of their leaders was slain by the inhabitants, their ships were wrecked in a storm, and the survivors who reached the shore perished by the sword of the Northumbrians[1]. Thus, in accordance with the notions then prevailing, did St. Cuthberht, the patron of that cloister, protect Northumbria from the ravages of the Danes, who were, nevertheless, some years after, destined to destroy not only its peace but its independence. The ruin of that holy edifice made a deep impression over all England, which shows that the destructive spirit of the Northmen was not yet universally known[2].

A few years later Æthelred was murdered by his discontented thanes, among whom the ealdormen Aldred and Wada are especially named as the perpetrators[3]. Many laymen of rank and ecclesiastics now abandoned the realm of internal dissension, which seemed doomed to become the scorn and

[1] Hist. de Cuthberto ap. Sim. Dunelm. p. 69. Here an invasion of the 'Scaldings' after the death of Ecgfrith, and before Ceolwulf's time, i. e. before 729, is supposed, which must be an error, arising possibly from the inroad of the Picts in 710. Cf. Sim. Dunelm. de Rebus gestis Reg. Angl. aa. 793, 794, who is copied by R. Hoveden—" Pagani......princeps eorum ibidem crudeli nece occisus est ab Anglis."

[2] Alcuini Epist. 29, 49, etc. Malmesb. de Pont. lib. iii. ' De Episcopis Lindisfarn.'

[3] Sim. Dunelm. aa. 796, 798. The Sax. Chron. places his murder in 794. Not only does probability speak in favour of the Durham annals, but also the eclipse of the moon on the 28th March, 796, given in both Simeon and the Chronicle as contemporaneous with the accession of Eardwulf. Cf. L'Art de verifier les Dates, in the calculation of eclipses. [The Chronicle gives the eclipse in 795. In a letter to Offa, Alcwine writes that Charles was so incensed against the Northumbrians, in consequence of the murder of Æthelred, that but for his (Alcwine's) mediation he would have done them all the injury in his power, " gentem illam homicidam dominorum suorum pejorem paganis æstimans." W. Malm. lib. i. In this year (798) London was destroyed by fire, and many of the inhabitants perished. Sim. Dunh.—T.]

booty of its neighbours[1]. The ealdorman Osbald, who had been formerly distinguished as the leader of a faction, and had been on terms of close intimacy with Æthelred, was now proclaimed king by his partisans[2], but the returning moon found him a fugitive in the monastery of Lindisfarne, from whence he embarked for the Pictish territory, the usual asylum for Northumbrian exiles. He died about three years afterwards, as an abbot, apparently in his native country[3], and was buried at York. The Northumbrians now recalled the ealdorman Eardwulf, whose life had been so miraculously saved by the monks of Ripon, from exile, that school of the Northumbrian kings, with whom a better state of things seemed to return. A great synod held under his auspices by the archbishop of York at Pincanhealh[4] bears witness to an earnest desire of good. The turbulent nobles again assumed a threatening attitude, and the ever-increasing number of the descendants or relations of deposed kings necessarily laid greater dangers in the path of every succeeding government. The ealdorman Wada was, however, put to flight and slain at Billingahoh[5], near Whalley, together with Alric son of Heardberht, and his faction annihilated[6]. Torhtmund, an ealdorman esteemed for his fidelity and valour, revenged the murder

---

[1] W. Malm. lib. i.

[2] Alcwine (Epist. xxix. Opera, p. 1537) reminds the king Æthelred, the patricius Osbald, and Osbert, "de antiqua amicitia.......de fidei veritate, de pacis concordia, quam habere debetis inter vos ; quia amicitia quæ deseri potest, nunquam vera fuit." This letter cannot have been written long before the murder of Æthelred, as it makes mention of the destruction of the church of St. Cuthberht by the pagans.

[3] Sim. Dunelm. a. 799.   [4] Sim. Dunelm. a. 798.

[5] Here and in *Billingsgate* we meet with the name of the noble race of the Billings. [In the Scôp's Tale (Cod. Exon. p. 320) we are told that, "Billing (weold) Wernum," *Billing (govern'd) the Warni.*—T.]

[6] Sim. Dunelm. a. 799. Alcuini, Epist. xviii. in Oper. p. 1514. In this letter the archbishop of Canterbury, Torhtmund and others are recommended to the hospitality of the emperor Charles. As Æthelheard went to Rome in 799, we may perhaps assume that Torhtmund left his home immediately after the death of Aldred.

of his former master Æthelred on Aldred, one of the perpetrators. The ealdorman Moll, of the family of Æthelwald,
was put to death by order of Eardwulf, as was also Alhmund,
a son of Alhred, who, on his clandestine return with other
exiles, had been seized by the guards of the king. Yet were
his adversaries not disheartened, who, when forced to flee,
found an hospitable hearth and protection with Cenwulf, king
of Mercia. Eardwulf now felt himself strong enough to attack the territory of his treacherous neighbour, the strong
hold of the conspirators: a long warfare which ensued was
ended, through the intervention of the bishops and nobles of
England, by a treaty of peace and friendship between the
two kings sworn on the holy evangelists[1]. Five years afterwards Eardwulf was, however, driven by his subjects into
exile[2]: his determination not to yield to the rebels, who had
once spontaneously sworn fealty to him, and to implore the
aid of the mighty Frankish monarch Charles the Great, as
well as the intervention of the pope Leo the Third, proves
him to have been of a firm and sagacious character. Charles
was not ignorant of the affairs of the north of England;
through his lately deceased friend, Alcwine, they must have
been familiar to him. Eardwulf sought the emperor at Ni-
meguen, and, having forwarded his suit there, hastened to the
holy father at Rome, by whom the desired mediation was
readily undertaken. Accompanied by a papal legate in the
person of the deacon Aldulf, and, on the part of the emperor,
by the abbots Rotfrid of St. Amand, and Nanther of St. Omer,
Eardwulf returned to England, and by the united influence
of the pope and emperor was reinstated in his royal dignity[3].

[1] Sim. Dunelm. a. 801.

[2] Sax. Chron. a. 806. In consequence of an hiatus in Simeon of Durham from a. 803 to 849, we are during that interval nearly without any
accounts of the kingdom of Northumbria.

[3] Einh. Annales, a. 808. Enh. Fuldens. eod. That the expulsion of
Eardwulf was already known to Leo is evident from his letter to Charles
(ap. Bouquet, t. v. p. 602) wherein he says, " quod Eardulphus rex de

Alfwold, a brother probably of king Æthelred, had, during the two years spent in these negotiations, held the reins of government, but offered no long opposition to the restoration of peace. Eardwulf died in the year following, and was succeeded by his son Eanred, who reigned amid intestine dissensions for thirty-three years[1], until the occurrence of events, which will enable us to comprise the entire history of England under one head.

Mercia, towards which we now turn our attention, presents an appearance widely different from that of Northumbria. Long opposition to the introduction of Christianity had been there punished by the absence of the arts and knowledge attending civilization, as well as of institutions conducive to that object. Mercia has left us neither the name of an author, nor even a meagre chronicle. Nowhere was the number of ecclesiastics smaller; and while the other states were divided into dioceses, Mercia proper and Middle Anglia formed together but one bishopric. On the other hand, the energetic measures of Penda had formed valiant soldiers, and created for the posterity of the old sea-heroes a military force alike formidable to the Britons and to the other Germanic states. Placed in the centre of the country, the rulers of Mercia availed themselves of their position to threaten all their neighbours, and obtain the British supremacy or Bretwaldaship.

regno suo ejectus fuisset, jam hoc per Saxones agnoveramus." A messenger from Eanbald, archbishop of York, had not only been sent to Rome but also to the emperor. See the two letters of Leo to Charles in Bouquet, vol. v. p. 601–4. That these letters had reference not only to internal dissensions, but probably to the intention of the king of Mercia not to acknowledge the archbishops and the bishop of Rome, seems evident from the words, " Prædictus Cenulfus rex nec suum archiepiscopum (sc. Cantuariensem) pacificum habet, nec istum Eanbaldum item archiepiscopum," etc. p. 602 c.—" Valde pertimescimus, ne ipse populus acquisitionis sanctæ Romanæ ecclesiæ per quamlibet occasionem et certamen prædecessoris mei, D. Gregorii, beatissimi papæ, quod ipsis in partibus posuit, meis temporibus infructuosum existere videatur, nec mihi in judicio eveniat," etc. p. 604 a. See also Palgrave, vol. i. p. 484.

[1] Sim. Dunelm. de Eccl. Dunelm. lib. iii. c. 5. Matt. Westm. a. 810.

The advantage of some long reigns promoted both its internal tranquillity and the success of its designs against the distracted states around it.

After the death of Wulfhere, his brother Æthelred, who had married Osthryth, a sister of Ecgfrith of Northumbria, succeeded to the throne[1]. In the first year of his reign he made war on Hlothhære (Hlothhæri) king of Kent[2], and ravaged his kingdom, destroying churches and monasteries, and even the episcopal see of Rochester. A few years afterwards he invaded the dominions of his brother-in-law, king Ecgfrith. In this contest, Ælfwine, the brother of Ecgfrith, fell, a youth equally beloved by Mercians and Northumbrians, when the ferocity of both nations, aggravated by this event, threatened the direst consequences. At this conjuncture the wholesome influence and judgement of the archbishop Theodore, who, in pursuance of his calling, to mediate between hostile nations, and with the success which more frequently attends mediators when the passions are at the highest than in earlier stages of the quarrels, prevailed on the Northumbrians to renounce all further vengeance for the death of their prince, in consideration of the payment of the legal wergild, and also to restore to Mercia the province of Lindisse, which had been taken from Wulfhere by Ecgfrith. To the remaining years of his long reign no blame seems to be attached. A great misfortune saddened his later days : the nobles of the northern part of the kingdom, or Southumbria, murdered the queen his consort[3]. He subsequently gave the government of Southumbria to his nephew Cenred, the son of his brother Wulfhere, to whom at length he resigned the entire king-

---

[1] Beda, iv. 21. Sax. Chron. a. 675. Matt. Westm. a. 696, calls her erroneously, " Egfridi regis filiam."

[2] Beda, iv. 12. " Cum Ædilred......adducto maligno exercitu, Cantiam vastaret," etc.

[3] Beda, v. 24, "a Merciorum primatibus interempta." Sax. Chron. a. 697. Fl. Wigorn. a. 696. Matt. Westmon. a. 696, " crudeliter necaverunt."

dom[1], his own sons being yet in their minority. Hence it would appear that the Mercian law of succession, unlike that of Northumbria, where we have seen a boy of eight years succeed to the throne, required from its king, in addition to right by birth, the qualifications indispensable for the duties of that high office. Among those of mature age, the next by birth seems always to have succeeded, and the right of the elder line at the same time to have been preserved. He who had entered on the government was not, however, compelled to resign it on the maturity of the direct heir, whereby all the dangers and calamities of guardianship were prevented: it is, therefore, merely through an error of a comparatively late writer[2] that Cenred is considered as the guardian of Æthelred's son, since he legally and unconditionally possessed for life the kingly power. The son of Penda entered the monastery of Bardeney, took the tonsure, and for many years, as abbot, directed the peaceful avocations of the monks[3]. So soon had the time passed away, when the sons of Woden knew no greater disgrace than to die in a bed! But to the nation the new increasing longing after the cowl was more pernicious than the use of harness[4]. After a few years, passed for the most part in conflicts with the Britons, Cenred also resigned the reins of government to a successor, the young Ceolred, the son of Æthelred and Osthryth, and with Offa of Essex, a prince adorned with all the graces of youth and manners, as well as endowed with every quality befitting a prince, journeyed to Rome, there to take the monastic vow at the hands of pope Constantine, and to fast and pray for the sal-

---

[1] Sax. Chron. aa. 702, 704.

[2] Wallingford (from whom so many errors have found entrance into English history) says (Gale, t. i. p. 527) that Cenred had engaged to Æthelred to resign the crown to his (Æthelred's) son on his majority. That the resignation of Cenred took place before the 13th June, 704, appears from the document in Hickes, t. iii. p. 262. n. 77.

[3] Sax. Chron. Fl. Wigorn. obiit a. 716.

[4] Vita S. Guthlaci in Actis Sanctorum, App. i. vol. ii. p. 39.

vation of the souls of their forsaken consorts, their relations and people, to the end of their earthly course[1]. His successor Ceolred died in the same year as his father.

Ceolred has by later writers, whose accounts are probably derived from the chronicle of some monastery favoured by him, been celebrated, in pompous diction, as the illustrious heir of his father's and his grandfather's virtues; but to us the unfavourable testimony, given by one of his most distinguished contemporaries, the archbishop of Mentz, Boniface, appears more worthy of belief[2]. He seems to have lacked either the valour or the good fortune of Penda, for in the war between him and Ine, the honour of victory at the battle of Wodnes-beorh was claimed by both parties. His young presumptive successor, the clito[3] Æthelbald, son of Alweo, the brother of Penda, who, though remote, was yet his next relative, he persecuted inexorably. Like Penda he was hostile to the church, and gave himself up to sensual pleasures with a recklessness that made him the prey of death during the riot of a feast, thus supplying an historic interpretation to the monkish tradition, that the evil spirit, while conversing with him, had deprived him of life[4].

Æthelbald had hitherto found in the marshes of Croyland, where he afterwards founded the celebrated abbey, not only a shelter, but instruction, with the holy hermit St. Guthlac, who, like the royal house of Mercia, was of the noble race of the Icelings. He was acknowledged as king without opposition. He is described as of vast bodily strength, graceful form and great courage; but pride and sensuality were the

---

[1] Beda, v. 19.   Sax. Chron. a. 709.

[2] Bonifacii Ep. ad Æthelbaldum.   Malmesbury has given us a portion of this letter.

[3] Clito was a title given by the Anglo-Saxons to the members of a royal house, and seems equivalent to ætheling, of which it was probably intended as a translation.

[4] Sax. Chron. a. 716.   Bonifacii Epist. ad Æthelbaldum ap. Malmesb. lib. i.

reproach of his earlier years[1]. While providing by strict justice for the internal peace of the country, for the clergy and the poor, by liberal disbursements, and appearing to execute his public duties, he addicted himself to excesses with married women and nuns, and hurried the thanes of Mercia into the same vortex of corruption and dissoluteness. The affectionate interest with which Boniface ever regarded the fortunes of his native country, the fervour with which he dared to set before the king his transgressions, with a remarkable allusion to the chastity of the Old-Saxons, were not without an effect, which may have been increased by the circumstance, that the scorner of holy wedlock was childless. At a synod held by archbishop Cuthberht, at Clofesho in Oxfordshire, it was attempted, through the prelates and monks, to effect a reformation of the laity[2].

Æthelbald's reign of forty-one years was distinguished by many successful conflicts with the Britons. East Anglia, Kent, and Essex followed his standard without a struggle, and, for a time, Wessex also, against the common enemy. Taking advantage of a change of government he invaded Northumbria, but was driven back by king Eadberht[3]. Nevertheless the haughty Æthelbald maintained the supre-

---

[1] Ingulph. sub init. See the letter already cited of Boniface. Cf. also Felicis Girwii Vita S. Guthlaci in Actis Sanctor. April. xi. c. 3 et 4.

[2] W. Malm. lib. i. c. 4. [The passage relating to the Old-Saxons is worth insertion : "In antiqua Saxonia, ubi nulla est Christi cognitio, si virgo in paterna domo, vel maritata sub conjuge, fuerit adulterata, manu propria strangulatam cremant, et supra fossam sepultæ corruptorem suspendunt; aut, cingulo tenus vestibus abscissis, flagellant eam castæ matronæ et cultellis pungunt, et de villa in villam missæ occurrunt novæ flagellatrices, donec interimant. Insuper et Winedi, quod est foedissimum genus hominum, hunc habent morem, ut mulier viro mortuo se in rogo cremati pariter arsura præcipitet." Malm. l. cit. and De Gestis Pontif. lib. i. c. 4. places the Council of Clofesho in 747. The true date, which is given in the Sax. Chron., is manifest from Æthelbald's charter, beginning "Anno DCCXLII. regni Æthibaldi xxvii. congregatum est magnum concilium apud Clouesho," etc. Cod. Diplom. t. i. p. 105.—T.]

[3] App. ad Bedam, a. 740.

macy in Britain[1], and was able, either by hostile inroads or by fomenting rebellions, so to weaken his most potent rival, Cuthred of Wessex, that he was reduced to submit to the most humiliating oppressions. But excess of disgrace soon re-assembled the disaffected nobles of his realm around the king of Wessex, who was, moreover, much strengthened by a reconciliation with his brave and powerful ealdorman Æthelhun[2], who had unsuccessfully risen in arms against him. The battle at Burford[3] was to the West Saxons a struggle for life and liberty, to the Mercians for the supremacy in Britain. Æthelhun, bearing in his hand the golden dragon, the banner of Wessex, marched in the front of the army, and slew the standard-bearer of the Mercians. The fall of so conspicuous a person struck terror into the enemy, and raised the courage of the West Saxons. A battle of such importance, fought with so much valour and obstinacy, rarely took place between those people. Though no one gave ground, yet no one was more forward than Æthelhun, whose battle-axe, rapid as lightning, clove both armour and body, whose way was marked by death. In like manner did the unconquered sword of Æthelbald cut through armour as a garment, and bones as though they had been flesh. Like firebrands in the opposite arrays they spread destruction around them, when at once the two gigantic terrific forms stood over against each other. A mutual glance, a mutual attack instantly followed, when, strange to relate, yet not without example, strength and courage on a sudden forsook the king, who, while his men were yet bravely fighting, fled at a moment when a single

---

[1] In a charter of 736 he styles himself, " Rex non solum Marcersium, sed et omnium provinciarum quæ generale nomine Sutangli dicuntur : " and signs, "Ego Ætdilbalt, Rex Britanniæ." Cod. Diplom. t. i. p. 96. Smith's Beda, p. 786. Hemingford, t. i. p. 219.

[2] The title of Consul is given to him. H. Hunt. a. 750. So Matt. Westmon. a. 708. " Offerus consul Northamhymbrorum."

[3] Sax. Chron. a. 752. In the account of this battle it will be easy to recognise the pompous diction of Henry of Huntingdon.—T.

stroke might have decided the fate of himself and kingdom. For the one and the other, from that day, the sun of their glory was set. A few years afterwards he fought another battle against Wessex at Secandun[1], where, disdaining flight, notwithstanding the slaughter of his people, he either fell in the field, or was treacherously murdered by his guards, and buried at Repton[2]. Beornred, who had placed himself at the head of the army and government, was obliged in the following year[3] to yield to the superior power and pretensions of Offa, a descendant of the royal house of Wibba, and to retire from the kingdom of Mercia.

The real name of Offa is said to have been Winfrith[4]; his father was an ealdorman named Thingfrith. Though lame, dumb, and blind from his birth, the youth acquired speed of foot, speech, and sight, when the usurper Beornred persecuted his parents and oppressed his native land. Hence he obtained the name of the second Offa, from his resemblance to his ancestor, Offa (Uffo) the son of Wærmund, king of Angeln, who, blind from his birth till his seventh year, and dumb till his thirtieth, yet, roused by the impending shame of being excluded from the succession, through a war threatened by

---

[1] Sax. Chron. a. 755. Florence calls the battle-place Segeswald. Seckington in Warwickshire is supposed to be the spot.—T.

[2] Sim. Dunelm. H. Hunt. "non sine miserabili exercituum ruina, fugam dedignans, occisus est," which has been incorrectly copied by Matt. Westmon. a. 755. "per fugam non declinans ruinam interfectus occubuit."

[3] The Saxon Chronicles are wrong in the year 755, but right in 716, where Æthelbald is said to have reigned forty-one years. Sim. Dunelm. says, a. 757, "Ethelbald.........interfectus est. Eodem vero anno Merci bellum inter se civile inierunt. Bearnred in fugam verso, Offa rex victor extitit." My more definite account is founded on the acts of the Council of Cealchyth in 789, the thirty-first of the reign of Offa. Hickes, t. i. p. 171. The victory over Beornred took place in the autumn of 757, and the coronation of Offa probably only in 758. That the regnal years are not reckoned from the day of the predecessor's death, but from that of the coronation, appears from many passages, as Sim. Dunelm. aa. 758 and 759.

[4] In the Vita Offæ II. he is called Pinefrid, no doubt a repetition of the usual blunder in the Latin chronicles of P for the Anglo-Saxon W (V).—T.

the king of the Saxons, suddenly recovered the use of speech and sight[1].

Such is the account given by the Danish writers, though the author of the Life of Offa II. supposes that the son of Wærmund reigned in England. In the general outline his story is nearly the same as that given in the Danish chronicles, which are, however, not in perfect accordance with each other. It seems, therefore, not improbable that the monkish biographer derived some parts of his narrative from ancient sources with which we are unacquainted, and that between the two Offas there existed some points of similitude sufficient for a foundation to the parallel.

[1] However the several accounts of the genealogies of the Mercian kings may vary with regard to the other names, they all, nevertheless, agree with respect to Wihtlæg, Wermund and Offa. See Nennius, Alfred of Beverley, Saxon Chron. a. 626. This remark holds good also for the same three kings, in the otherwise varying lists of Saxo and that in Eric's Chronicle; though in Svend Aagesen Wiglet (Wihtlæg) is wanting. But in all the three authors, who draw from different sources, we find the same story of Uffo. The Danish or Anglian Uffo, it is true, is not blind, but is the son of the blind Wermund; that he was dumb till his thirtieth year is expressly mentioned by Svend Aagesen. In Beowulf we have Garmund (Wermund), Ongentheow (Angeltheow), Higelac (Icel), all belonging to the genealogy of the Mercian kings. See a saga of Offa in Beow. xxvii. [Cod. Exon. p. 320; also Beow. vol. i. p. 258, and vol. ii. p. xxxii sq. The single combat, in which Uffo revenged the insult offered to his father and himself, took place on an island in the Eider, where a part of the city of Rensburg, called the Altstadt, now stands. Wermund's adversary is said to have been Sigar, a king of Holstein; the name of his son, slain by Uffo, was Hildebrand. See Saxo, lib. iv., and Sveno Aggonis. ap. Langebek.— T.], also Dahlmann's Forschungen, Th. i. p. 233. The story of the two Offas has been written by a monk of St. Albans, and is printed at the end of Watts's edition of Matt. Paris. The account of the elder Offa agrees for the most part with Svend Aagesen's, not only in the general outline, but also in the first speech of Uffo or Offa. Nor is the agreement of the two sagas in the girding of the youth with the sword by the father, as well as the ensuing combat, to be overlooked. It is, however, remarkable that, besides these ' Vitæ,' the date and author of which are unknown, no other ancient English writer mentions the story of the youth of Offa, not even Bromton himself. [The story of the Danish Uffo is well condensed by Suhm, Historie af Danmark, Bd. i., or in Gräter's translation, Bd. i. p. 117. —T.]

At the Council of Clofesho, and on other occasions, the
name of the young patrician Offa appears next in order to
that of the king, at least before those of the other laity. Offa
himself, in two of his charters, mentions his grandfather
Eanwulf, who, in king Æthelbald's time, held land in the
territory of the Hwiccas, where, at Bredon, he had founded
a church[1], and who, if we may hazard a conjecture on the
alliteration of names, so frequent among the Anglo-Saxons,
was either father or brother of the Christian petty kings of
that country, Eanfrith and Eanhere. We must, therefore,
consider him as the nearest relative of the king, though de-
scending in a collateral line from their common ancestor[2], and
ascribe the bloody wars[3] attending his accession to the throne
to the resistance of Beornred, whom we meet with some years
afterwards in Northumbria, where he burnt Catterick, but in
the same year perished himself by fire, as we are told, by the
judgement of God[4].

Offa's dominion does not seem to have been firmly established before the death of Beornred; till then we do not find
him engaged beyond the limits of his kingdom. His first
memorable expedition was against the Hestingas, a people
whose locality, like that of many others among the Saxons, is
not known with certainty. They have been sought for about

[1] See charters in Smith's Beda, pp. 766, 767, and Cod. Diplom. t. i.
pp. 169, 176.

[2] "Offa quinto genu Pendæ abnepos." W. Malm. lib. i. But this is
incorrect, as he descended from Eawa, son of Wibba, the brother of Penda.
Saxon Chron. Fl. Wigorn. a. 755, with which Alfred of Beverley agrees,
"cujus (sc. Ædilbaldi) patruelis, Enulfi nepos Offa." Malmesbury makes
a similar mistake with regard to Cenwulf, the second successor of Offa.
See p. 238.

[3] App. ad Bedam, a. 757. Alcuinus ap. Malmesb. lib. i. c. 4. "Non arbi-
tror quod nobilissimus juvenis Egfertus propter peccata sua mortuus sit,
sed quia pater suus (Offa sc.) pro confirmatione regni ejus multum san-
guinem effudit."

[4] Matt. Westmon. a. 769. Sim. Dunelm., where it is erroneously said,
"Earnredo tyranno............incendio periit, Dei judicio." According to
Malmesbury, Beornred was slain by Offa in 757.

Hastings in Sussex, and most probably inhabited the district around that town to which they gave their name[1]. Some years after Offa fought a bloody battle against his hated enemies, the men of Kent[2], at Otford on the Darent, in which the Mercians gained the victory[3].

In the following year Offa overcame at Bensington in Oxfordshire Cynewulf of Wessex, a prince celebrated for his valour, and took from him the royal town of Bensington[4]. In the wars against the Britons his arms were equally successful. In the early part of his reign he had repulsed them at Hereford[5], and subsequently devastated Deheubarth or South Wales[6]. From the king of Powis he took a considerable tract of his territory, and even his residence Pengwern (Shrewsbury). The flat country at the foot of the eastern sides of the mountains, between the Wye and the Severn, he peopled with Anglo-Saxons, no defence being so efficacious as that of free dwellers on the land, whose settlements may still be traced by their Saxon denominations. To protect the settlers from the sudden inroads and maraudings of the hostile mountaineers, he caused to be constructed a considerable rampart with a ditch[7], from the mouth of the Dee to that of the Wye. This work, known by the name of Offa's dyke, traces of which are yet discernible, so well answered its purpose, that it became the boundary between Britons and Mercians, and afterwards between Wales and England. The

[1] Sim. Dunelm. a. 771. To the town of Hastings there belonged, at a later period, a territory of 500 hydes. See Gale, t. i. p. 748. See also Palgrave, vol. ii. p. cclxxix.

[2] W. Malm. lib. i. (speaking of Cenwulf), "Contra Cantuaritas successivum ab Offa suscipiens odium, regionem illam valide afflixit." Sim. Dunelm. a. 798. Mailros. Hoveden h. a., who copies Simeon.

[3] Sax. Chron. a. 774 (one MS. reads 773). Fl. Wigorn. a. 774.

[4] Sax. Chron. a. 777 (one MS. reads 775). Fl. Wigorn. a. 778. H. Hunt. a. 777. [5] Annal. Camb. Brut y Tyw. a. 760.

[6] Annal. Camb. a. 778. Brut y Tyw. a. 776.

[7] Asser V. Ælfredi. "Offa.........qui vallum magnum inter Britanniam atque Merciam de mari usque ad mare facere imperavit." Giraldus de Illaudabilibus.

last Anglo-Saxon king, Harold, ordered that every Briton who should appear armed on this side of Offa's dyke should have his right hand struck off[1]. If the British language and British customs are met with on this side of the barrier[2], they are to be attributed either to Welsh reduced to a state of complete subjection, or who, at a later period, forsook their desert mountain heights for the fertility of the plain.

Nothing would more raise the wars of Offa above deserving the appellation of battles between the kites and the crows, by which the great epic poet of England has unconsciously eternalized the narrow historic notions of his time[3], than if it could be granted us accurately to ascertain how far they were influenced by the mighty ruler of the Franks, Charles the Great. If any reliance may be placed on the monkish biographer, the kings of Kent, previously to the invasion of that state by Offa, had applied to Charles for his aid and protection[4]. The menacing letters of the emperor were unheeded by the Mercian, and in the course of years their mutual success united the lord of the Germanic insular realm with the chief of the Roman continent. Charles sent to Offa—or, as he himself expresses it, the most powerful ruler of the East to the most powerful ruler of the West—many costly presents, the catalogue of which has been preserved, though not that of the presents sent in return, which to us would have been of far greater interest. From a charter with its seal still in existence, we know, however, that Offa, king of the Mercians, confirmed certain gifts of land near the port of Lundenwyc[5],

---

[1] Joh. Salisbur. Polycrat. lib. vi. See a more particular account of Offa's dyke in R. Higden, Polychron. p. 194.

[2] Asser, x. Camden, edit. Gibson, p. 587. Higden also says, " Sed hodie hinc inde, ultra citraque fossam illam, potissimum in provincia Cestriæ, Salopiæ, Herfordiæ, Wallici cum Anglicis passim sunt permixti."

[3] " Such bickerings to recount, met often in these our writers, what more worth is it than to chronicle the wars of kites or crows, flocking and fighting in the air ?" Milton, Hist. of England.—T.   [4] Vita Offæ II.

[5] This remarkable charter, dated April 5, 790, together with those of other English kings in favour of St. Denis, exist in the Trésor des Chartes, in the Hôtel Soubise at Paris.

made by one of his subjects to the abbey of St. Denis. The
same highly favoured cloister received from another of Offa's
vassals, the ealdorman Berhtwald of Sussex, with the confirmation of the king, the church of Rotherfield, and his ports
of Hastings and Pevensey[1]. Charlemagne promised not only
to pilgrims, but also to merchants from England, his immediate protection[2], which last concession may, perhaps, be
regarded as an extension of the privilege granted by Dagobert
to the Anglo-Saxons attending the fair at St. Denis, and may,
therefore, have been the immediate cause of the above-mentioned donations. A dangerous misunderstanding took place,
however, between the two monarchs on the following occasion.
Charlemagne had demanded for his son Charles the hand of
one of Offa's daughters, which the latter would grant only on
condition that to his own son Ecgferth (Ecgfrith) should be
given in marriage Berhta, the beloved daughter of Charlemagne, who was afterwards secretly married to Angilbert,
the learned abbot of St. Riquier, and is celebrated by her
contemporaries as the softened resemblance of her father in
mind, voice, aspect, and bearing[3]. Gerwold, abbot of St.
Wandrille or Fontenelle, of a distinguished family, and
formerly chaplain to queen Bertrade, but who had been appointed to the administration of the customs in the northern

---

[1] Charter of 792 ap. Du Chesne. Monast. Angl. t. vi. p. 1077.

[2] See the letter of Charles to Offa in Wilkins, Conc. t. i. p. 158, in Alcuini Oper. t. ii. App. p. 618, and an extract of it in Malmesbury, Leland
Collect. t. i. p. 402. Cf. Privilege of Pepin, a. 753, ap. Bouquet, t. v. p. 227.
As in this letter he speaks of the death of pope Hadrian I., which took
place in Dec. 795, and mentions Æthelred of Northumbria, who died on
the following 18th of April, as still living, the date of it is fixed with
tolerable accuracy. According to this letter the emperor, besides other
presents, sends to Offa a Hunnic sword and belt, and two silken mantles;
a circumstance greatly in favour of the genuineness of the letter, as Charles,
in the beginning of the year 796, distributed many presents from the treasures taken from the Huns. See Einh. Annal. a. 796. Chron. Moissac.
Sim. Dunelm. a. 795. " Karolus.........Hunorum gentem subegerat.........
sublatis inde xv. plaustris auro argentoque palliisque holosericis preciosis
repletis."

[3] See Helperich's or Angilbert's ' Carolus Magnus,' v. 219 sq.

towns and ports of France, particularly at Quentawic, was frequently sent with commissions from the emperor to king Offa, with whom he had become very intimate. He was, nevertheless, unsuccessful in his endeavours to lower the proud pretension of the descendant of Woden, and to induce him to abandon a demand, which had so greatly incensed the invincible emperor of the Franks, that it required all his exertions to prevent the closing of the French sea-ports against the merchants of England[1]. According to other accounts, the decree was already carried into effect, a similar interdict was also issued by Offa in the English ports, and Alcwine, the friend of both princes, was destined to appease a quarrel arising from disappointed ambition[2]. We are made acquainted with the restoration of peace by an earlier document than the before-mentioned letter to Offa, namely, by a letter of intercession in favour of some Mercian exiles, to Æthelheard, archbishop of Canterbury[3].

The notion of Offa's great influence at this time, entertained by pope Hadrian, was grounded more on the suspicion that the king of Mercia was desirous to instigate the Frankish monarch to cast him from the papal chair[4] than on the splendour attending many victories over his countrymen. That a hostile disposition might have arisen between Offa and the pope is, considering the pretensions raised by the latter at every opportunity, exceedingly probable. While the small kingdom of Kent, which had already been under subjection to his ancestors, possessed the first primacy of the Anglo-

[1] Chron. Fontanel. in Monum. Hist. Germ. t. ii. p. 291, according to which this event took place about the year 788.

[2] Epist. Alcuini ad Colcum Lectorem in Scotia. Bouquet, t. v. p. 607; also W. Malm. lib. i. c. 4.

[3] Wilkins, t. i. p. 154. Alcuini Epist. lxi. `Æthelheard became archbishop in 791. [These exiles were probably those who had sided with Beornred against Offa. There seems little doubt that they had been harboured by Charles for hostile purposes.—T.]

[4] Hadriani Epist. ap. Bouquet, t. v. p. 589.

Saxon church, and the one next in rank was placed in the
rapidly declining state of Northumbria, Offa felt the want, in
his own more powerful realm, of a prelate independent of
both Canterbury and York. He had long vainly endeavoured
to persuade Jaenberht, archbishop of Canterbury, to transfer
his see to Lichfield. The archbishop was now accused of
having promised aid and shelter in his diocese to the Franks,
in the case of their effecting a hostile landing in England[1];
which reason, together with others, such as that Offa was
desirous of founding an archiepiscopal see near the spot where
he had humbled his enemies, being considered valid, it was
resolved, in a synod held at Cealchyth, under the legate of
Hadrian, to establish a separate archbishopric for the kingdom
of Mercia, which should be conferred on the hitherto bishops
of Lichfield, and first in the person of Aldulf[2], the successor
of Higeberht. That this new ecclesiastical arrangement, notwithstanding the ready compliance yielded to the formidable
Offa, must have been a source of heartburning among the
neighbouring kingdoms, already in a state of irritation from
so many other causes, may be easily imagined, the effects of
which were manifested in the early abolition of the archiepiscopal see of Lichfield.

Offa acquired greater renown to himself and greater power
to his state than had ever been possessed by any Anglo-Saxon
king or kingdom[3]. His firmness and his valour are incon-
testable. His delight in reading is also celebrated by his
contemporaries[4]. For the better administration of his dominions he provided by the formation or collection of a code of

[1] W. Malm. lib. i. Vita Offæ II. p. 21.

[2] W. Malm. lib. i. and De Gestis Pont. lib. iv. Vita Offæ. Rad. Dicet.
Abbrev. Chron. a. 787, where the limits of the new archbishopric are given.
Sim. Dunelm. a. 786.

[3] See charters of 780 in Cod. Diplom. pp. 167, 169. Smith's Beda,
p. 767. "Ego Offa, Dei gratia concedente, rex Merciorum simulque na-
tionum in circuitu."

[4] Alcuini Opera, fol. 1554.

Mercian laws, the loss of which is deeply to be lamented[1]. Yet were these estimable qualities, by means of which he had founded his power, stained with crime which stands in singular contrast to the better part of his character. No deed has excited greater horror than the murder of Æthelberht[2], the young and accomplished king of the East Angles, of which he is accused. In the hope of obtaining the hand of Æthelthryth, the daughter of Offa, this unfortunate prince had, by the advice of his council, though in opposition to the will of his mother, set out on a journey to the Mercian court. On arriving at the border he sent forward a letter to Offa, together with valuable presents, and in return received an invitation couched in the warmest terms, with an assurance of security. By Offa he was received in the most hospitable and splendid manner; but after he had retired to his apartment for the night, a message was brought to him by an officer of the palace named Wimberht, that Offa was desirous of conferring with him on business of moment. The unsuspecting guest followed the messenger, but when passing through a dark passage he was attacked and basely murdered by assassins posted there for the purpose. By the monk of St. Albans the guilt of this foul murder has been transferred from the head of the founder of his abbey to that of the queen Cynethryth[3]; but, in such a case, privity to the deed is as criminal as the deed itself, especially when, as in the instance of Offa, who soon rendered himself master of the kingless state, the fruits of the perfidy must inevitably fall to the accomplice. Offa affected great sorrow for this atrocious crime,

---

[1] See Laws of Alfred in Ancient Laws and Institutes, p. 27, fol. edit.

[2] Sax. Chron. a. 792.

[3] So not only the Vita Offæ II., but also Fl. Wigorn. a. 793. [" Offæ ....detestanda jussione, suæque conjugis Cynethrithe reginæ nefaria persuasione, regno vitaque privatus est capititis abscissione." The Sax. Chron. Ethelwerd, H. Hunt., W. Malm., place the event in 792, and agree as to the decapitation. By R. Wendover we are told that the queen caused her victim to fall into a pit prepared under his couch, where he was smothered by the attendants. See Fl. Hist. t. i. p. 250.—T.]

and raised a stately monument over the remains of his victim in the church of Hereford, on which he bestowed rich donations. In the same year Ælflæd, another daughter of Offa, was married to Æthelred king of Northumbria.

Among those events recorded of Offa's life of which the authenticity is very questionable, is a journey to Rome which he is said to have made towards the latter part of his reign. His munificence to the churches and pious establishments in that city is highly extolled; and though it is difficult to ascribe to Offa other than ambitious motives[1], yet, if we consider the age in which he lived rather than the individual, a pilgrimage in expiation of the murder of Æthelberht appears by no means improbable. But though Offa himself may not have visited Rome, the accounts of his liberality to the Saxon school there[2], and of the donation or confirmation of Romescot for the benefit of that foundation, seem not undeserving of credit.

Offa during eight-and-thirty years had toiled indefatigably for the aggrandizement of his dominion, when he was seized by the hand of death[3] only a few years after the murder of Æthelberht, which had called down upon him the execration

[1] The monk of St. Albans is perhaps more trustworthy than he has hitherto been considered. The inmate of a monastery founded by Offa, he has, no doubt, placed many actions of the founder in a different light from that in which others have regarded them; yet he may have had the use of documents inaccessible to others. Many of his accounts agree accurately with those of Florence, W. of Malmesbury and others; if, therefore, he is not older than these, but has made use of them, the circumstance of having availed himself of such sources speaks in favour of his general credibility. He is not therefore to be altogether rejected, but in cases only when, for particular reasons, he is to be regarded with suspicion.

[2] Vita Offæ II. W. Malm. lib. ii. c. ii. Among the traditions concerning Offa a German one may be noticed, viz. that Opho, rex Angliæ, the maternal uncle of St. Willibold, first bishop of Eichstädt, erected the monastery of Schüttern, in the year 703 or 717. See Appendices in Chron. Montis Sereni, ed. Mader, pp. 282, 289.

[3] Sax. Chron. 29 July. Sim. Dunelm. 26 July a. 796. Fl. Wigorn. erroneously, 794.

of Europe.   Seldom do we see the hand of the avenging
Nemesis so manifest as in the destinies of the house of the
perfidious Offa.   Cynethryth, of whose ambition and presumption a tangible proof still exists in the coins which she
alone of all the Anglo-Saxon queens caused to be stampt with
her own image, was, three months after the deed which has
branded her, thrown by robbers into her own well; a manner
of death which, if void of truth, may, nevertheless, serve to
show what her contemporaries wished and thought of her.
Tradition will not even acknowledge her as an Anglo-Saxon,
but represents her as a Frank, who for some atrocious crime
had been sent out to sea in an open boat, and having been
found by the youthful Offa, had seduced him to conduct her
to his home[1].   While the sanctity of the pious Æthelberht
was working numerous miracles, the bones of his murderer
were washed by the sweeping floods of the Ouse out of their
consecrated earth[2].   His son Ecgferth, whom in the year 785
he had caused to be crowned king[3], died of disease only a
few months after the death of his father[4]; in him the male
line of Offa was extinguished.   Of his daughters, Æthelthryth,
the affianced of Æthelberht, ended her days in solitude and
sorrow in the abbey of Croyland.   Of Eadburh, the aban-

---

[1] Vita Offæ.   Bromton, a. 752.

[2] Offa was buried in a chapel just without Bedford. R. Wend. t. i.
p. 262.—T.

[3] H. Hunt. says king of the province of Kent ; but this is not only inconsistent with Malmesbury and other authorities, by whom we are informed
that Alric, son of Wihtræd, and the last of the Æscings, reigned in Kent
till 794, but is unsupported by the oldest testimonies, which state merely
that Offa associated his son with him in the kingdom of Mercia, making no
mention whatever of Kent.   Sax. Chron. a. 785. "And Ecgferth was consecrated king."   Fl. Wigorn. "Egferthus rex est consecratus."   W. Malm.
lib. i. "Egfertum filium, ante mortem suam, in regem inunctum."   R.
Wendover, t. i. p. 247. "In illo quoque concilio (Cealchyth) Offa rex Merciorum potentissimus in regem fecit solemniter coronari Egfridum, filium
suum primogenitum, qui deinceps cum patre.........usque ad finem vitæ
ejus regnavit."   See also charters of Offa in Cod. Diplom. Nos. 152, 165,
where Ecgferth signs himself ' rex Merciorum.'—T.

[4] Ingulphus.

doned consort of Beorhtric king of Wessex, we shall speak hereafter. The remaining daughter, Ælflæd, lost father, brother and husband in the same year.

The rich inheritance of Offa, dominion, authority, treasures, fell after the short reign of Ecgferth, which was not such as to justify any very sanguine hopes[1], to Cenwulf, a descendant of Cenwealh, a son of Wibba, and consequently brother of Penda. Cenwulf was endowed with the kingly qualities of Offa, but he knew also how to maintain his power by justice and clemency as well as by valour. So at least sings the praise bestowed on him almost unanimously by the ecclesiastical chroniclers of the middle age, in whose hands were placed the golden keys of earthly immortality and undying renown. The prosperity of his reign, which was followed by no similar one in Mercia, is undeniable. The arts of peace begun to be more steadily and, therefore, more successfully cultivated. Almost the only art which has left behind it unquestionable monuments of its time, the coinage, proves that, first under Offa, and subsequently under Cenwulf, it yielded the best impressions which Mercia could produce.

The Æscings who had worn the crown of Kent, though under the supremacy of Mercia, were now extinct, and Cenwulf formed the plan of uniting that kingdom still more closely with his own. He found an opponent in Eadberht, surnamed Præn, who held the sovereignty of Kent for three years. This prince, who seems to have been collaterally connected with the Æscings, and also related to Ecgberht king of Wessex, had formerly been an ecclesiastic[2]. The Mercian

---

[1] So it may be inferred from Alcwine's letter to him (No. xlviii.).

[2] Sax. Chron. a. 794. Fl. Wigorn. Thorne, p. 2238. Wallingford, p. 530, confounds Eadberht Præn with the eldest son of Wihtræd, who, according to the Sax. Chron. and Fl. Wigorn., died in 748. That he was an ecclesiastic appears from a letter of pope Leo (Anglia Sacra, t. i. p. 460), where it is said, "De illa epistola, quam Æthelhardus (archiep. Cantuar.) nobis transmisit.........reddimus responsum, quia nos de *clerico illo apostata*, qui ascenderat in regnum, similem illum reputantes Juliano Parabatæ, ana-

overcame his rival by the sword, as well as by the equally
efficient aid of spiritual weapons. He offered to abolish the
archbishopric of Lichfield, an act which could not fail to
dispose in his favour all the higher clergy of England, and
was especially calculated to gain over to the king of Mercia
the archbishop of Canterbury and all whose interests immediately depended on that dignity. The pope, Leo the Third,
declared also his willingness to abolish the new archbishopric, and to excommunicate the apostate churchman who had
usurped the throne of Kent. Cenwulf, after having laid the
Kentish territory waste as far as the marshes, took the king
Eadberht prisoner, led him bound into Mercia, having caused
the eyes of his captive to be put out and his hands ampu-
tated[1]. He did not, however, deprive him of life, but, after
some time, on the occasion of the consecration of the church
founded by him at Winchelcomb, which was conducted with
extraordinary pomp, and at which splendid gifts were bestowed both on ecclesiastics and laymen, he restored him to
liberty[2].

themizantes objicimus," etc.   Other particulars concerning him have been
preserved only by H. of Huntingdon : " Populos Cantiæ......rex Egbricht
in dominium suscepit, quos prius *cognatus suus* Pren injuste amiserat.
Edbriht Pren regnavit III. annis."

[1] Sax. Chron. a. 796.   Sim. Dunelm. a. 798.   Neither Ethelwerd nor
Florence mention the mutilation. "quem vinculis oppressum duxerunt
usque ad Merce." Ethelw. a. 796.   "ligatum in Merciam secum duxit."
Fl. Wigorn.—T.

[2] Malmesbury gives a glowing account of Cenwulf's munificence and
clemency at this ceremony : "Apud Winchelcumbam, ubi ecclesiam Deo
exædificaverat, ipsa dedicationis die regem captivum ad altare manumittens,
libertate palpavit, memorabile clementiæ suæ spectaculum exhibens [!].
Aderat ibidem regiæ munificentiæ applausor Cuthredus, quem ille Cantua-
ritis regem præfecerat.   Sonabat basilica plausibus, platea fremebat dis-
cursibus, eo quod ibi in conventu tredecim episcoporum, decem ducum,
nullus largitatis pateretur repulsam, omnes suffarcinatis marsupiis abirent ;
nam præter illa xenia quæ magnates susceperant, inæstimabilis scilicet
pretii et numeri, in utensilibus, vestibus, equis electissimis, omnibus, qui
agros non habebant, libram argenti, presbyteris marcam auri, monachis
solidam unum, postremo toti populo multa erogavit."—T.

The arms of Cenwulf were also fortunate against the Welsh. In the first year of his reign the battle of Rhuddlan in the Vale of Clwyd was fought, when they were driven back over Offa's dyke.   In another battle Caradoc, king of Gwynedd, perished.   In his latter years his army penetrated to Snowdon, and devastated the country adjacent [1].

The government of Kent was assigned by Cenwulf to his brother Cuthred [2]; but the suppression of the Mercian archbishopric was delayed for some years, until, at a synod held by the primate of Canterbury and his twelve suffragans at Clofesho [3], it was carried into effect.   We read not without surprise in what contemptuous terms the decree of the synod mentions the schemes of Offa, through which the see of the holy Augustine had been prejudiced in its rights, and afterwards learn from the same source that archbishop Æthelheard himself had made a journey to Rome for the purpose of prevailing on the pope to suppress the new archbishopric, and restore to its integrity the foundation of his glorious predecessor Gregory the Great.   Pure good-will towards Æthelheard seems to have moved the pope to this remarkable act of compliance in his favour; the papal court could derive from it no advantage.

Æthelheard died shortly after the completion of his object. Between Cenwulf and Wulfred, the new archbishop, a quarrel soon arose, in which the violence and avarice of the former are bitterly complained of.   For six years the king prohibited the primate from exercising the archiepiscopal duties; and, on his return from Rome, where he had obtained a favourable decision of his cause, Cenwulf declared in a council, that, unless he surrendered certain lands, and paid a certain sum of money, he should be expelled from the kingdom, and that no decrees of the pope nor solicitation of the emperor Charle-

[1] Annal. Camb. aa. 796, 798, 816, 818.   Brut y Tyw. a. 819.
[2] Ob. A.D. 805.
[3] A.D. 803.   See Wilkins, Conc. t. i. pp. 163, 167.   Smith's Beda, p. 787.

magne should ever effect his return. To both demands the
archbishop at length yielded, but the promised restoration of
its privileges to the church of Canterbury was unfulfilled[1].

The foregoing particulars of the life of Cenwulf seem, as
we have already remarked, inconsistent with the praise so
liberally bestowed on him by the chroniclers, who, moreover,
inform us that, after a reign of twenty-six years, he passed to
the reward of his numerous good deeds, and was buried at
Winchelcomb[2].

Cenwulf was succeeded by his son Cenhelm, a child of
seven years, who, at the instigation of his sister Cwenthryth,
was basely murdered in a wood by Æsceberht, his tutor.
Ceolwulf, a brother of Cenwulf, then succeeded to the throne,
from which he was driven two years afterwards by the usurper
Beornwulf, a Mercian without any pretensions by birth[3].
Mercia now rapidly approached its fall.

The history of the smaller states contributing to form what
by later writers has commonly, though erroneously, been
called the Heptarchy, is almost wholly lost. Even the genealogies of their kings, which among those people constituted
the chief basis of their annals, is, soon after the introduction
of Christianity, defective, and only the stories or rather legends of a few pious nuns, according to the usual pattern,
and in the customary strains of praise, were composed. What
beyond this is known of their kingdoms, consists in accounts
of the victories of their more powerful neighbours, and isolated traces of resistance on the part of the weaker.

None of these states excites the curiosity of the historical
inquirer so much as that of East Anglia, which, inhabited
by Germans probably before the time of Hengest and Horsa,
entirely surrounded by German neighbours, in no contact
with the Britons, must necessarily have presented a most
faithful picture of Teutonic antiquity. Even at the present

---

[1] Evidentiæ Eccles. Cantuar. ap. Twysden, p. 2213.

[2] Sax. Chron. a. 819. [H. Hunt. lib. iv. "Cenwlf regnavit xxvi annis
pacifice, et mortuus est communi morte."—T.]   [3] Fl. Wigorn. Ingulph.

day in no other part of England do so many well preserved
German names of places declare who were their ancient lords
or founders. Many remarkable traditions, though hitherto
not sufficiently investigated and sifted for use as materials of
history, are preserved relative to this district. Its position
was particularly favourable to an intercourse with the Old-
Saxons, and we may regard not only London, in those remote
times, but also the East Anglian ports Lynn, Yarmouth and
Dunwich, as resorts for Frisic, Saxon and Gallic mariners
and members of the several commercial guilds or 'hansen.'

This connexion with Germany declares itself in the legends
of East Anglia, according to which Eadmund, who reigned
there in the ninth century, was a son of Alcmund, a king of
Saxony, and born at Nüremberg. The land itself bore for
the most part a close resemblance to the opposite marshy
coasts of Holland and Friesland, and it was only after the
lapse of many ages that the drained fens of Cambridgeshire,
or of the so-called isle of Ely, begun to yield to the inmates
of the several cloisters there the blessing of the land of Go-
shen. As Offa against the Welsh, so had the first kings of
East Anglia raised a vast rampart, defended by a ditch,
against Mercia, which bore the name of the Recken-dyke,
though known at a later period among the common people
as St. Edmund's, sometimes the devil's, and lastly as Cnut's,
or Henry the First's[1]. We have already seen that this dyke
was no safeguard against the powerful Penda; such artificial
defences tending generally to the restraint of intercourse in
times of peace, and, in times of danger, to the injury of the
people, by a delusive appearance of security. It long continued, however, to define the limit of the authority of the
nominal kings of the country, and afterwards of the peaceful
jurisdiction of the crosier of Norwich.

After the kings Sigeberht and Ecgric had fallen in battle
against Penda, Anna, the son of Æne, a brother of the Bret-

---

[1] Fl. Wigorn. a. 905. "Limes S. Eadmundi." Cf. Sax. Chron. h. a.

walda Rædwald, shared the same fate. He was succeeded
by his brother Æthelhere, who, compelled to submit to the
formidable conqueror, was in the following year slain with
him in the memorable battle against Oswiu of Bernicia[1]. It
does not appear that Anna left any male offspring. Of his
four daughters, Sexburh, married to Earconberht king of
Kent, and Æthelthryth to Ecgfrith of Northumbria, died
abbesses of Ely; Æthelburh was abbess of Faremoustier en
Brie, and Wihtburh a nun at Ely[2]. Æthelhere was succeeded
by his brother Æthelwald[3], who was followed by Ealdwulf[4],
a son of his brother Æthelhere, who, after a reign of forty-
nine years, was succeeded by his brother Ælfwold[5]. This
prince seems to have been the last of the direct line of the
Uffings, as after his death we find East Anglia divided between Beonna and Æthelberht or Alberht[6], who were followed by Æthelred, the father, by his queen Leofrun, of
Æthelberht, the unfortunate victim of Offa and Cynethryth.

The history of no Anglo-Saxon state is so defective as that
of the East Saxons. At an early period in subjection to the

[1] Sax. Chron. a. 655.
[2] Beda, iii. 8, iv. 19. Fl. Wigorn. Geneal.   [3] A.D. 655.
[4] A.D. 664.   Fl. Wigorn. and Geneal.   Ealdwulf was present at the
Synod of Heathfield; his mother was Hereswith, a sister of St. Hild.
Beda, iv. 17, 23. He died, according to the Ann. Lauresh., in 713. See
Literary Introduction, p. xxxvi. note[3].
[5] A letter of his to archbishop Boniface is extant. See Max. Bibl.
Patrum, t. xiii. ep. lxxvi.
[6] Sim. Dunelm. a. 749. " Elfwald rex Orientalium Anglorum defunctus
est, regnumque Hunbeanna et Albert sibi diviserunt." So Chron. Mailr.
In the belief, however, that the first-mentioned of these personages never
existed, I feel no scruple in eliminating the name from the list of East
Anglian kings. Simeon's original was apparently some Saxon chronicle,
where two words were joined, as æᵹᵗeꝼ hımbeanna ꝼenᵹ ᵗo ꝼıce, *after
him Beanna (Beonna) succeeded*; out of which, misled by the near resemblance in Saxon manuscript of ım to un, he formed the name of Hunbeanna. Florence (Geneal.) says, " regnante Offa Beorna regnavit in East
Anglia, et post eum Æthelredus," etc. In ' Beorna ' the final vowel appears very suspicious, while Beonna (written also Beanna and Bynna) is a
common Saxon name. This mistake has undoubtedly arisen from the slight
difference in Saxon MS. between n and ꝼ.—T.

kings of Kent, they subsequently fell under that of Mercia,
or perhaps together with Mercia, under that of Northumbria.
Some battles with Wessex in which, about the year 617, their
kings Sexred, Sæward and Sigeberht were slain, indicate a
short interval of independence. To these succeeded Sigeberht, surnamed the Little, a son of Sæward, who was followed by Sigebert the Good, the son of Sigebald and friend
of Oswiu, at whose instance he turned to the Christian faith
and received baptism. He was assassinated by two brothers,
who, as we are told, hated him for his merciful disposition.
He was followed by his brother Swithhelm, also a convert to
Christianity[1]. It is probable that the East Saxons were conquered by Penda, though the chroniclers have not conde-
scended to record the event; but who, as a matter far more
important, inform us that king Sebbe (Sebbi) assumed the
tonsure, and lived till the year 694; and afterwards that the
youthful Offa also abdicated the throne and made a pilgrimage
to Rome[2]. His successor was Selred, who was slain, but
whether in battle or otherwise we are not informed[3].

Though under subjection to Mercia, the old race of the
Offings continued to rule, whose genealogy, though not altogether clear, yet sufficiently shows the legitimate succession.
From the reign of Sleda it seems to have been observed as
a family law, during a period of two hundred and fifty years,

[1] A.D. 660.   Beda, iii. 22.   Fl. Wigorn. Geneal.

[2] A.D. 709.   Beda (v. 19) says of him, "Offa juvenis amantissimæ
ætatis et venustatis," but styles him merely "filius Sigheri": hence it
would seem that he had never assumed the reins of government. The
charter in Thorne (ap. Twysden, p. 2219) issued by "Offa rex Anglorum,"
in the 38th year of his reign, is not of 690, but a century later, and is a
charter of Offa of Mercia. [See the document in Cod. Diplom. t. i. p. 191,
where it is marked as spurious.—T.]

[3] Sax. Chron.   Fl. Wigorn.   H. Hunt. a. 746. This prince has by
some writers, following a blunder of the Chron. Mailros., rather than the
authority of Florence, been placed among the rulers of East Anglia, while
his name alone would have been sufficient to show the race to which he
belonged.—T.

that the names of their kings should begin with the same letter. To these probably a king Sigebald belonged, who endeavoured to prevail on Boniface to become the spiritual guide of his people[1]. Even of London itself, the most important place in Essex, we find scarcely any accounts beyond the names of some ecclesiastics: it must with its environs at an early period have fallen under subjection to Mercia[2].

Kent, though probably not the oldest of the Germanic states in Britain, had, through the valour of its first kings and leaders, as well as by its earlier connexion with the Frankish realm, and its adherence to the continental church, acquired a certain eminence and even precedence over the other insular kingdoms. Soon, however, after the death of Æthelberht, under his son Eadbald, Kent sank into a condition more commensurate with its physical strength, although the sister of Eadbald was married to the powerful Eadwine of Northumbria, and himself, now reclaimed from his criminal passion for his step-mother, had espoused Emma, a Frankish princess[3]. Eadbald was succeeded by Earconberht[4], his son by Emma, who guilefully supplanted his elder brother Eormenred, the eldest son of Eadbald. Like his father, Earconberht reigned a round number of twenty-four years. His ecclesiastical regulations are mentioned with praise, and for him was reserved the total destruction of idols. His son Ecgberht succeeded to the throne, on which, as long as his two cousins, Æthelred and Æthelberht, the sons of his father's eldest brother, Eormenred, were alive, he felt no security. A thane

---

[1] Bonifacii Epist. xlix.

[2] W. Malm. lib. i. " Londonia cum circumjacentibus regionibus, Merciorum regibus, quamdiu ipsi imperitaverunt, paruit."

[3] For the date of his death (20 June) see Literary Introduction, p. xxxvi. note[3]. It is also given by Thorne, p. 1769, though not by the older writers. Emma's name appears in a charter of Eadbald a. 618. See Smith's Beda, p. 694 [and Cod. Diplom. t. i. p. 8, where it is marked as spurious]. Emma was probably a daughter of the Austrasian king Theudebert II. Langhorne, Chron. Reg. Angl. p. 155. Pagi, a. 640.

[4] Beda, iii. 8. Sax. Chron. a. 640.

named Thunor, either divining the wish or obeying the command of his master, murdered the innocent princes[1]. According to the beautiful legend, to which history itself will not refuse a space, their bodies were buried by the murderer in the king's palace, under the royal seat; but a heavenly light was seen to shine over their resting-place, which led to the detection of the foul misdeed. The guilty king gave to Eormenbeorh[2], a sister of the murdered princes, a space of land as blood-fine (manbôt); thus making atonement to the secular, as he did afterwards to the ecclesiastical law, by a public supplication and the founding of a monastery in the Isle of Thanet. The course of a hind during a day determined the extent of the land; and the murderer Thunor was swallowed by the gaping earth. Of the daughters of Earconberht, by his wife Sexburh, a daughter of Anna king of the East Angles, we find that Earcongote became abbess of Faremoustier; Eormengild was married to Wulfhere of Mercia.

Eadric, the son of Ecgberht[3], was deprived of his throne by his uncle Hlothhære (Hlothhæri), with whom he seems, however, to have for some time reigned conjointly. With the help of the South Saxons Eadric at length overcame his faithless kinsman in a battle, who died of his wounds[4]. After a reign of about a year and a half, Eadric was carried off by a violent death[5], when Kent, as we shall presently see[6], became a prey to invaders, and the seat of a war with Ceadwealla of Wessex, until, at the expiration of nine years, the legitimate succession was restored in the person of Wihtræd son of Ecgberht[7], with whom, at least in the early part of his reign,

---

[1] Sax. Chron. a. 640. Sim. Dunelm. h. a., whose narrative of the murder is particularly circumstantial and florid. Malmesbury merely alludes to it. See also Thorne, p. 1906.

[2] Called also Domneva. Sim. Dunelm. Fl. Wigorn. She was married to Merewald, a son of Penda, king of the West Hecanas.—T.

[3] Ob. A.D. 673.

[4] Beda, iv. 26. Sax. Chron. Fl. Wigorn. H. Hunt. a. 685.

[5] Beda, iv. 26. W. Malm. lib. i.   [6] See p. 260.

[7] Sax. Chron. a. 694. This date can apply only to his becoming sole

a certain Swæbheard or Wæbheard appears to have been associated. After a reign of thirty-three years, Wihtræd was succeeded by his sons, Eadberht[1], Æthelberht II.[2]—six years before whose death the capital suffered by fire—and Alric[3], in whom, after a reign of thirty-four years, the race of the Æscings became extinct. Eadberht seems to have had a son Eardulf[4], who for some years reigned with his uncle, but died before him. It was Alric who yielded to the superior power of Offa in the battle of Otford. The state of Kent in the following times is extremely obscure. The small territory was often divided between two or more dependent kings[5], and served as an appanage for the sons of the Mercian or West Saxon sovereigns. Of Eadberht Præn we have already made mention under Cenwulf of Mercia. The see of Canterbury imparted to this little kingdom a greater degree of integrity than it could else have enjoyed in existence with the

possessor of the kingdom, as we find him in 692 already reigning conjointly with Swæbheard. See Beda, v. 8.—T.

[1] Ob. A.D. 748. A charter of donation to the church of Canterbury (Thorne, p. 2209), purporting to be granted by Eadbrith Eating, is without doubt a forgery of comparatively recent date, by one who confounded Eadberht of Kent with the Northumbrian king Eadberht the son of Eata. —T.

[2] Ob. A.D. 760. As characteristic of the age may be noticed Æthelberht's request to the venerable archbishop Boniface, that he would send him some hawks. Bonif. Ep. xl. His mother, the consort of Wihtræd, was named Æthelburh (Aedilburg). See fac-simile charter of 697 in the Antiquarian Repertory, vol. ii. p. 133, also Cod. Diplom. t. i. p. 50.

[3] Beda, v. 23. Sax. Chron. a. 725.

[4] A charter of Eardulf, dated 762, is extant in the Textus Roffensis (Cod. Diplom. t. i. p. 115) of a donation to the church of St. Andrew at Rochester. The date is evidently a clerical error which may be corrected by the substitution of v for x, making it cclvii. instead of cclxii. A donation of Eardulf without date is given in Twysden, p. 2220. See also a letter from him to Lullus archbishop of Mentz (Ep. Bonif. xxxvi.) written conjointly with Eardulf bishop of Rochester.

[5] See charter, dated 762, of Sigiræd king of Kent of donation to Rochester, signed also by " Eadberht rex Cantiæ ; " and another of about the same date, signed by " Eanmund rex." Charters of Ecgberht are also extant, dating from 779 to 791, in one of which a " Heahberht rex " appears among the signatures. See Cod. Diplom. t. i.—T.

powerful states of Northumbria, Mercia, and Wessex. To the more universal civilization of Kent it is probably owing, that the earliest Anglo-Saxon laws extant are those enacted under the kings of that country, viz. Æthelberht, Hlothhære and Eadric, and Wihtræd.

Sussex, the kingdom of Ælle, the first Bretwalda of Anglo-Saxon tradition, sank soon after the death of that prince into a state bordering on nonentity. When we consider its small extent in comparison with the neighbouring kingdoms, as well as its position, unfavourable even at the present day to purposes connected with navigation, and too remote from the centre of the country for political influence, we can ascribe the part it acted under the sway of Ælle only to the personal character of that chieftain, and to the valour, displayed also at a later period, of its rugged inhabitants. This virtue of the South Saxons is conspicuous on almost every occasion where their name occurs in history; as in the deadly conflict with Ceolwulf of Wessex, in their wars with his successor Ceadwealla, as well as in instances hereafter to be mentioned. The late conversion of the South Saxons, and the wild state of the country have been already noticed. To these circumstances, and to the necessarily consequent lack of literary ecclesiastics, it is to be ascribed, that we do not possess even a meagre series of their rulers, much less any circumstantial details concerning them. They were the vassals sometimes of Wessex, sometimes of Mercia. Æthelwealh, the first Christian king of Sussex, received from Wulfhere, king of Mercia, the investiture of the Isle of Wight, and of the mægth[1] or tribe of the Meanwaras in Hampshire; we, nevertheless, regard him as the vassal of Wessex, as well as his successors, whether under the denomination of heretogas (duces), kings, or under-kings. In the latter days of Æthelwealh occurs the aid, already noticed, afforded by Sussex to Eadric king of

[1] Tribe, territory, so denominated from its inhabitants being all of the same race or tribe.

Kent. Æthelwealh, we are informed, was succeeded by Eadric, who, like his predecessor, fell in a battle against Ceadwealla of Wessex[1]. At a later period the conquest by Offa of the territory around Hastings is recorded without any mention on the occasion of a king of Sussex[2]. It is the echo of Ælle's name alone to which Sussex is indebted for a place in the Anglo-Saxon Heptarchy; a denomination equally accurate or inaccurate with most similar expressions adopted for the purpose of generalizing the particular facts of history.

More desirable than showing that the usually so-called greater kingdoms did not always subsist in a state of independence[3], it would be to give some account of the smaller ones, all traces of which have insensibly, and at an early period, almost vanished from the page of history. To these belong—Middel-Seaxe (Middlesex), which owes this appellation both to its position with regard to Essex and to the temporary neighbourhood of the West Saxons, through the conquest of Ceolwulf, but which subsequently passed to the Mercians; Suthrige (Surrey)[4]; the Jutish state on the Isle of Wight; Magesetania, or the land of the Magesætas or Hwiccas (Worcestershire) and of the Hecanas (Herefordshire): Middel Engle; Elmet[5]; the Lindisfaras (Lindsey), who were in later times governed by under-kings, and, when that title fell into disuse, by heretogas and ealdormen or gerefas;—and, without doubt, many others, whose history may yet receive illustration both from local tradition and the

[1] W. Malm. lib. i.

[2] After the rulers mentioned in the text we meet with the names of Huna, Numa (Nunna), Nothelm, and Wattus, as governing under the supremacy of Ine; and at a later period, Osmund, Æthelberht and Sigeberht are named as kings of the South Saxons. A charter of Nothelm is subscribed by "Cænredus, Rex West Saxonum:" this was, no doubt, the father of Ine. See Palgrave, vol. ii. p. cclxxiv.—T.

[3] Some of the elder chronicles, omitting Essex and Sussex, speak often of five Anglo-Saxon kingdoms. Chron. Angliæ MS. Hamburg.

[4] Fl. Wigorn. a. 823.

[5] See p. 148. Beda (ii. 14) speaks only of the Silva Elmete.

use of hitherto neglected records.   At present we can speak
of the greater number of these districts only with uncertainty,
though some others may with confidence be specified, as the
extensive territory of the Pecsætas (Peakland in Derbyshire) ;
of the East and West Wilsætas (Wiltshire); the Ciltern-
sætas ; Spalda (Spalding)[1] ; the South and North Gyrwas[2].
We know, however, from the accounts transmitted to us relative to the most important of these small states, the Hwiccas,
that they were generally held by branches of the greater royal
houses in hereditary succession, and were sometimes in the
joint possession of two or more brothers.   Of this territory
the first princes, whose names are recorded, seem to be Eanhere and his brother Eanfrith, whose daughter, as we have
already seen, was married to Æthelwealh, king of the South
Saxons. These were probably succeeded by Osric[3] (supposed
to be a nephew of Æthelred of Mercia) and Oswald[4], the
former ruling over Gloucestershire, the other over Worcestershire.   Their follower Oshere[5] was succeeded by his sons
Æthelheard, Æthelweard and Æthelric[6], and these by the
brothers Eanberht, Uhtred and Aldred[7].   Under or after

[1] In a charter of 736 mention is made of the Husmeri on the banks of
the Stour. Smith's Beda, p. 786.

[2] Considerable information concerning the territorial partition of England
before the division into shires might be derived from the ancient notices in
Gale, t. i. p. 748, were they not unfortunately too incorrectly written or
printed to admit of our founding even a conjecture on the greater part of
them : e. g. to the South Saxons, whose territory is estimated by Beda
(iv. 13) at 7000 hides, it assigns no less than 100,000 hides.   See also
Ellis's Introd. to Domesday, vol. i. p. 145.

[3] Beda, iv. 23. " provinciam Huicciorum cui rex Osric præfuit." Charter
a. 676, in Cod. Diplom. t. i. p. 16, granting 100 manentes to the abbess
Bertana for the founding of a convent near Hat Bathu.

[4] Monast. t. i. p. 541.

[5] Charter aa. 680 and 693 ? in Cod. Diplom. t. i. pp. 22, 41.

[6] Charter 704–709, 706, in Cod. Diplom. t. i. pp. 60, 64, 65, 96.   Hickes,
t. i. pp. 169, 170.   Smith's Beda, p. 786.

[7] Chart. from a. 757 to 780 in Cod. Diplom. t. i.   Hickes, t. i. p. 170 sq.
Smith's Beda, p. 767.   This charter is perhaps not spurious, but for v we
should read x, making the date 761 instead of 756.

these princes, who all bore the title of king, we meet with others styled ealdormen (principes, duces), of whom little more is known than the names[1].

It now remains for us to turn our attention to Wessex, and to consider what were the circumstances which favoured this land more than the other states, and, for some centuries, caused it to be especially regarded as England. A solution of the problem will be found in the circumstance, that when Northumbria was compelled to renounce all thoughts of further aggrandizement, when the hostile neighbours of Mercia were confined within their own limits by Offa's dyke, Wessex, though defended neither by natural barriers nor early success in arms, always found not only a field for warfare, but also land to bestow on the valiant, both on the Severn and in Cornwall, the land of the strangers : hence martial discipline, legitimate succession, and a tranquil state of possession were rendered so permanent in the country, that it became enabled to adopt gradual improvements, till, in one of its princes, it found a clear-sighted and energetic man, who united the descendants of the invading hordes into closer connexion, and brought them, as far as newly occurring impediments permitted, to a higher degree of political culture.

The successor of Ceolwulf, Cynegils (Cynegisl), and latterly jointly with him his son Cwichelm[2], conducted the war against the Britons with hereditary success. The boundaries of the very small state were thus gradually enlarged, which had hitherto comprised only the districts forming in later

[1] Palgrave, vol. ii. p. cclxxxix. We find a. 800 a dux Merciorum Æthelmund, whose father Ingeld must have borne the same title under Aldred. See charter in Hickes, l. cit. " dux et prefectus regis." Oshere also says (Cod. Diplom. p. 41), " consentiente comite meo Cutberhto." The title of princeps was frequently borne by ealdormen. See Hickes, l. c. 171.

[2] Fl. Wigorn. aa. 614, 628, 636, 648 ; also Alfred of Beverley. Malmesbury indeed says (lib. i. 2), " filii Celrici, Cinegislus et Quicelmus ;" though he afterwards calls Cuthred, the son of Cwichelm, the fratruelis of Cenwealh, the son of Cynegils. The cause of the confusion is probably that the son died before the father.

times the shires of Hampton, Berks, Wilts, Gloucester to
the Severn, and a part of Oxfordshire.   These kings penetrated far into the territory of the South Britons, who were
defeated at Beamdûn (Bampton).   Seized with a panic at the
sight of their well-appointed foes, of their gleaming battle-
axes, and the magnitude of their spears, the Britons took to
flight, leaving two thousand and sixty-two of their countrymen dead on the field[1].   The two kings were equally successful against Essex, which lost three kings, the sons of Sæberht,
in a bloody battle from which very few escaped, flight being
impeded by the heaps of slain and torrents of blood[2].   Penda
made war on them, though in the battle of Cirencester[3] he
did not overcome them.   It was only in the contest with
Eadwine of Northumbria that they lost a part of their possessions, and the murderous attempt made on the life of that
prince, at the instigation of the exasperated Cwichelm, led to
a defeat[4], which does not, however, seem to have been followed up by Eadwine.   Cynegils, at the instance of Oswald
of Northumbria, became a convert to Christianity, and was
baptized by bishop Birinus.   Cwichelm also received baptism
and died in the year following[5].

The succeeding years passed on quietly in settling the new
ecclesiastical arrangements.   Cenwealh, the second son of
Cynegils, had married a sister of Penda, by which connexion
a most dangerous enemy or neighbour—the expressions were
in those days synonymous—seemed conciliated.   Cenwealh,
on the death of his father, inherited his throne[6], but not his
principles.   He rejected Christianity, repudiated his wife, and
married Sexburh, who survived him.   Penda avenged the

---

[1] Sax. Chron.   Fl. Wigorn.   H. Hunt. a. 614.

[2] In this and similar descriptions Henry of Huntingdon is easily to be
recognised.   [3] Sax. Chron. a. 628.

[4] Beda, ii. 9.   Sax. Chron. a. 626.   W. Malm. lib. i.

[5] Beda, iii. 7.   Sax. Chron.   Fl. Wigorn.   H. Hunt. aa. 635, 636.

[6] Sax. Chron.   Fl. Wigorn.   H. Hunt. a. 643.   Three MSS. of the Chron.
read 641.

injury of his sister by driving Cenwealh from his throne, who found an asylum at the court of Anna, king of the East Angles, with whom he passed three years, and by whose counsel and example he was converted to the Christian faith. With the assistance of Cuthred, the son of Cwichelm, he was reinstated in his kingdom, and rewarded his nephew by the resignation in his favour of a third part of his dominions, or, according to other accounts, with a grant of three thousand hydes at Æscesdûn[1]. This little state bordered on Mercia, and was probably Ashdown in the south of Berkshire.

The reign of Cenwealh is important on account of the aggrandizement of Wessex. He defeated in several battles the Britons of Dyvnaint and Cernau, who had endeavoured to throw off the Saxon yoke[2], first at Wirtgeornesburh, afterwards, with more important results, at Bradenford (Bradford) on the Avon in Wiltshire[3], and again at Peonna (on the hill of Pen in Somersetshire), where the power of the Britons melted like snow before the sun, and the race of Brut received an incurable wound, when he drove them as far as the Pedrede (the river Parret)[4]. A consequence of this augmentation of territory was the establishment of a second bishopric in his kingdom, at Winchester, where he also founded a monastery and a church, famed, even at its first erection, for its magnificence[5].

Though the conduct of Cenwealh towards Agilbert, of which mention has already been made, may appear unjust, it seems, nevertheless, to have chiefly resulted from the ardent zeal of the new convert; nor perhaps ought we to blame in

[1] Sax. Chron. aa. 648, 661. Fl. Wigorn. a. 648.

[2] W. Malm. lib. i. " Britannos antiquæ libertatis conscientiam frementes, et ob hoc crebram rebellionem meditantes, bis omnino protrivit; primum in loco qui dicitur Wirtgernesburg; secundo juxta montem qui dicitur Pene."—T.

[3] Sax. Chron. a. 652, where it is merely stated that Cenwealh fought at Bradford.—T.

[4] Sax. Chron. Fl. Wigorn. H. Hunt. a. 658.   [5] W. Malm. lib. i.

him the wish to possess a bishop speaking his mother-tongue,
the only one intelligible to him[1]; while to other distinguished
dignitaries of the Anglo-Saxon church, as in the instance of
Benedict Biscop, the founder of the monastery at Wearmouth,
he gave frequent proofs of good will[2]. The new ecclesiastical
organization was the more important, as the general administration of the Anglo-Saxons had reference chiefly to the
military constitution, and could not be regarded as a moral
bond of union, such as the erection of the see of Winchester must necessarily have been in a very high degree.
The old British ecclesiastical establishments were not disturbed, but rather cherished by the conqueror; and we are
not ignorant of the donation by which the monks of Glastonbury were induced, even on the grave of Arthur himself, to
pray for the eternal salvation of the Germanic intruder[3].

More dangerous to Cenwealh was the contest which now
took place with the king of Mercia, Wulfhere, the brother of
his first consort; for although, in the beginning of the campaign, the latter sustained an overthrow, and was probably
made a prisoner in the territory of Cuthred, at Æscesdûn,
where he appears as the assailing party[4], yet, in the same
year, Cenwealh lost two valuable friends in his nephew
Cuthred and Cenberht, another under-king. The Mercians
too pressed forward, or were successfully supported by their
southern friends, in return for the cession by Wulfhere of the
Isle of Wight, and of the Meanwara mægth or tribe, a portion of Hampshire, to his ally Æthelwealh, the apparently
new king of Sussex.

After a reign of more than thirty years Cenwealh died

[1] Beda, iii. 7. " Rex, qui Saxonum tantum linguam noverat, pertæsus
barbaræ loquelæ, subintroduxit in provinciam alium suæ linguæ episcopum,
vocabulo Vini."

[2] Bedæ Vita S. Benedicti. "cujus (sc. Coinwalh) ante non semel amicitiis
usus, et beneficiis erat adjutus."

[3] Malmesb. de Antiq. Glaston. Eccl. ap. Gale, t. i. p. 308.

[4] Sax. Chron. a. 661.   Ethelw. lib. ii. 7.   H. Hunt.

suddenly[1] without children or lineal descendants. He had, however, provided for the administration of his kingdom by committing it to his queen Sexburh. The talents displayed by this princess, both at the head of the army and of the state, have been extolled in terms which show how great must have been the impression made on her countrymen by a phenomenon so rare as a reigning queen[2]. Nevertheless, within a year the energies of Sexburh proved inadequate to the cares and anxieties of the male dignity, which were not a little aggravated by the illegality of her pretensions. On the death or expulsion of Sexburh[3], two under-kings of Wessex, Æscwine[4], a lineal descendant of Ceolwulf, and Centwine, the brother of Cenwealh,—who appears to have been the only rightful heir, and whose exclusion by Sexburh seems inexplicable,—governed the state, either in succession or jointly, for several years. The obscurity attending these reigns is further increased by the account, that the immediate successor of Sexburh was Cenfûs, the father of Æscwine[5]. Even Beda, whose early years fell in this period, knew little of the ten years' anarchy in the kingdom of Wessex. The existence of Æscwine himself as king would probably, like that of his father, have afforded matter of doubt,

---

[1] Sax. Chron. a. 672. Bedæ Vita S. Benedicti. "immatura morte præreptus." [2] W. Malm. lib. i.

[3] W. Malm. lib. i. "plus quam fœmineos animos anhelantem vita destituit, annua vix potestate perfunctam." [R. Wendover, p. 162, however, says that she was expelled, "indignantibus regni magnatibus expulsa est a regno, nolentibus sub sexu fœmineo militare."—T.] So also Matt. Westm. a. 672.

[4] Malmesbury says, " Escuinus, regali prosapiæ proximus, quippe qui fuerit Cinegisli ex fratre Cuthgislo abnepos." I follow Fl. Wigorn. a. 674, and Geneal.; also Sax. Chron.

[5] Sax. Chron. Fl. Wigorn. a. 674 ; but in Geneal. Regum W. Sax. he says, "Deinde Kenfus duobus annis, secundum dicta regis Ælfredi, juxta vero Chronicam Anglicam, filius ejus Æscwinus fere tribus annis regnavit." The latter account only is noticed by Florence in his Chronicle, and on the authority of the ' Anglica Chronica Occidentalium Saxonum.'

had not a great battle which he fought against Wulfhere of Mercia, who had advanced to Bedwin in Wiltshire, gained for him a hero's fame. This bloody conflict was sufficiently important to influence the accounts of it in a manner agreeable to the local feelings of the narrators. While the chronicler of Middle England strives to secure the honours of a hard-earned victory for the king of Mercia, he of Wessex—in whose favour the retreat of the Mercians loudly speaks—entertains no doubt of his defeat[1]. By the death of Æscwine, which followed soon after, Centwine appears as sole ruler of the West Saxons.

The wars of the Anglo-Saxons with each other excited in the Armoricans the hope of recovering the home of their fathers from the hand of the stranger. The absence of the British king Cadwaladyr, who had departed on a pilgrimage to Rome, and left his son Yvor to the care of the king of Armorica, Alan the Second, encouraged the ambitious views of that prince ; and a landing effected under the guidance of Yvor and his cousin Inyr led to the conquest of the old British country to the south of the Avon. Centwine led a powerful army against the invaders, but a battle was prevented by an amicable arrangement, according to which Yvor was invested by Centwine with the principality of Dyvnaint and Cernau, and, it is said, obtained the hand of Æthelburh, a niece of the king of Wessex, and, at a subsequent period, his kingdom also.

According to these and other Welsh narratives, Yvor appears completely identical with Ine, the second successor of

---

[1] Sax. Chron. Fl. Wigorn. a. 675. Late writers follow H. Hunt.—
"Rex vero Mercensis, patria et avita virtute usus, aliquantulum præstantior pugna fuit ; uterque tamen exercitus terribiliter contritus est," etc.—
and overlook W. of Malmesbury, who says, "ille (Escuinus) Mercios anxia clade perculit." [The Saxon Chron. and Florence say nothing of the result of the conflict ; the latter's silence seems certainly to be in favour of the W. Saxons.—T.]

Centwine; as the story of Yvor's father resembles that of the predecessor of Ine[1]. The part assigned to the king of Armorica in this expedition accords in no respect with the weakness of character ascribed to him in other accounts[2]. It must indeed be confessed that our knowledge of the history of Wessex, derived from Anglo-Saxon sources, is highly unsatisfactory; we must, therefore, have occasional recourse to the Welsh traditions, where, in consequence of the proximity of the two states, much latent history may reasonably be supposed to exist[3]. If in this respect too little regard has been shown to Jeffrey of Monmouth, on the other hand, care must be taken not to overrate his contemporary Caradoc of Llancarvan, though criticism has hitherto but seldom directed its shafts against the latter, an accumulation of quotations from whom imparts a show of deep research to some modern historic productions. In most instances, however, of such conflicting narratives, it may be assumed that the Welsh historians adopted the policy of purloining from a successful enemy, and skilfully transferring to his British contemporaries, if not to imaginary personages, the object and reward of his battles, the glory and lastingness of his individuality in history. The case before us leads also to the remark, that a similarity of names sometimes occurs between the West Saxons and the Britons, to be accounted for only by the supposition of early alliances between both nations. With regard to the name of Ceadwealla, it may not be unimportant, for the genuineness of Anglo-Saxon history, to remark, that this name, as in use among the old Germanic tribes, is to be found in Cæsar, and perhaps in Tacitus[4].

---

[1] Caradoc of Llancarvan, p. 13 sq.

[2] Daru, Histoire de Bretagne.

[3] That a war like the above-mentioned was carried on may be inferred from Florence a. 682, where it is said, " Centwine, rex West-Saxonum, *occidentales* Britones usque ad mare in ore gladii fugavit." The Sax. Chr. and other authorities state merely that Centwine drove the *Britons* to the sea.

[4] Cæsar (B. G. vi. 31) informs us that a prince of the Eburones, a people

While Centwine maintained or restored the supremacy of
Wessex in the south of his kingdom, he extended its influence
also over the Britons of Gwent on the northern side, who had
endeavoured to cast off the Germanic yoke[1]. But more than
by external enemies, the tranquillity of Centwine was disturbed by his nearest relative, Ceadwealla, a bold aspiring
youth of the race of Cynric, and son of Cenberht, a sub-king,
whose territory is not mentioned[2]. Ceadwealla had been
banished by Centwine, but the flower of the warlike youth
gathered round the exile, who found a harbour in the forests
of Andredeswald and Chiltene on the boundary of Sussex.
With this valiant band he subdued that kingdom, and slew
its king Æthelwealh[3]; but Ceadwealla was subsequently expelled by two ealdormen of Sussex, Berhthun and Æthelhun,
who through him had lost their former power and influence[4].
At this juncture Centwine, it seems, abdicated the throne.
That this sickly and aged prince named Ceadwealla as his
successor, who had till then been the object of his persecution[5], is one of the many improbabilities with which the

near Liege and Aix-la-Chapelle, was called Cativolcus, which is, no doubt,
identical with Ceadwealla. The name in Tacìtus (Ann. ii. 62), if correctly
recorded by him, is rather that of the British Cadwaladyr than of the king
of Wessex : " Erat inter Gothones nobilis juvenis nomine Catvalda."—T.

[1] Malmesb. de Pont. t. i. p. 349. Wharton, Anglia Sacra, t. ii. 14.

[2] In the Sax. Chr. a. 661 he is styled " Cœnbyrht cyning." Fl. Wigorn.
" Cenbriht subregulus." Beda calls Ceadwealla merely " de regio genere
Geuissorum." The authorities agree as to his descent, with the exception
of Malmesbury, who calls him " Ceaulini ex *fratre* Cuda pronepos," where
the last word shows that, for " fratre," we should read " filio."

[3] A.D. 685. Beda, iv. 15. Care should be taken not to confound Æthelwealh, king of Sussex, with Æthelwald (written in the charters Ecguald),
a vassal king under Ceadwealla. Wendover (t. i. p. 182) erroneously calls
the former Athelwoldus.—T.

[4] Fl. Wigorn. a. 685. H. Hunt. lib. iii. "qui prius regnaverunt." [Very
probably a mistake for Beda's " qui deinceps regnum provinciæ tenuerunt."
—T.] Æthelhun is by Beda called " Andhunus ;" in Ælfred's version,
" Hune."

[5] Malmesb. de Gestis Pont. lib. v. 1. The Saxon Chronicle a. 685 does
not say that Centwine died in that year, but that " Ceadwalla began to

ecclesiastics have sought to embellish the life of their convert. Ceadwealla was the nearest in succession, and had been converted to Christianity by Wilfrith, the banished bishop of York, whom he had attached to himself in Sussex.

The first enterprise of Ceadwealla was to take vengeance on Sussex. Berhthun was slain in battle, also Eadric, the successor of Æthelwealh[1], and Sussex was partitioned into several small states or kingdoms, under the supremacy of the king of Wessex.

A hard fate befell the Isle of Wight, which, only a few years before, had, by Wulfhere of Mercia, been severed from Wessex and ceded to Sussex, though governed by its own prince, Arwald. The twelve hundred families, dwelling on the island—the only Anglo-Saxon territory, to our knowledge, which had not yet embraced Christianity—were nearly all slaughtered by the yet unbaptized Ceadwealla, in fulfilment

contend for the kingdom." Malmesbury's words are, " Kentwinus morbo et senio gravis, Cedwallam regii generis juvenem successorem decreverat." The same writer afterwards adduces a charter dated in August 688, in which the name of Centwine appears : " consilio et confirmatione Kentuuini regis." If, therefore, this document be.genuine, Centwine was then not only living, but had retained the kingly title, and had, perhaps, after the resignation of Ceadwealla, been required to give his sanction to a donation. That Centwine abdicated and entered a cloister, having transferred his kingdom to Ceadwealla as the next heir, appears from a disregarded poem of Aldhelm in Alcwine's works (edit. Quercetan. f. 1675 sq.), where, instead of ' Entuuini,' we should no doubt read ' Centwini.'

> ...." Entuuini filia regis,
> Qui primus imperium Saxonum rite regebat.
>
> ......rexit regnum plures feliciter annos,
> Donec conversus cellam migravit in almam.
> Inde petit superas meritis splendentibus arces.
> Post hunc successit bello famosus et armis
> Rex Ceadualla, potens regni possessor, ut hæres......
>
> Tertius accepit sceptrum regnator opimum
> Quem clamant In incerto cognomine gentes,
> Qui nunc imperium Saxonum jure gubernat."

[H. Hunt. a. 686 says, however, Centwino " Occidentalium rege defuncto, Cedwalla post eum regnans."—T.]

[1] A.D. 685.   W. Malm. lib. i. 2.

of a vow, that, if he took the island, he would devote to Christ the fourth part both of the land and the spoil, and which he performed by assigning it to Wilfrith, who happened to be present, for religious purposes; by him the same was transferred to his nephew Bernwine, who, assisted by a priest named Hiddila, effected the conversion of the island. Two young brothers of Arwald fled from the enemy to the adjacent Jutish province, and sought a refuge at Stoneham, where, being betrayed to Ceadwealla, they were condemned to death. On receiving this intelligence, Cyneberht, abbot of Hreutford (Redbridge), besought the king, who had retired to that neighbourhood for the cure of the wounds he had received in the conflict with Arwald, that, if it were absolutely necessary to slay the youths, he might be previously allowed to instil into them the mysteries of the Christian faith. The pious office being fulfilled they readily submitted to their fate [1], and the anniversary of the young martyrs was celebrated by the church during many centuries[2]. From hence, accompanied by his brother Mul, he proceeded into Kent, which he laid waste, no resistance being offered by the inhabitants, who fled on his approach[3].

The rapid success which had crowned the enterprises of Ceadwealla, and the internal dissensions which prevailed in Kent, seduced him to allow his brother Mul to invade and ravage that kingdom a second time. On this, as on the previous occasion, towns and villages were abandoned by their inhabitants, who retired on the advance of the enemy; when Mul, who is represented as endowed with all the qualities constituting the old Germanic pagan prince and warrior,— elegance of figure, grace of manners, liberality, and valour bordering on ferocity,—having with twelve attendants only

---

[1] Beda, iv. 16.

[2] The anniversary of the "Fratres Regis Arwaldi MM." was on the 21st of August.—T.

[3] Sax. Chron. Fl. Wigorn. H. Hunt. a. 686. W. Malm. lib. i.

entered a house for the sake of plunder, was discovered by the country people and burnt to death. A bloody vengeance for the death of his brother was taken by Ceadwealla, whose devastations ceased not while any objects of rapine or slaughter were to be found in the devoted province[1].

Influenced apparently by the exhortations of his revered friend Wilfrith, Ceadwealla, after a successful reign of two years only, resolved to renounce his crown in favour of his cousin Ine (Ini)[2], and make a pilgrimage to Rome, for the purpose of receiving baptism at the hands of pope Sergius. On his way he was most honourably welcomed by Cunibert, king of the Lombards, who had espoused Hermelind, an Anglo-Saxon princess[3]. He was baptized on Easter-day, and assumed the name of Peter in honour of the chief of the apostles; but before he had laid aside the white garb of baptism, he was seized with a malady which terminated in death on the twentieth of April, eight days only after the ceremony, in the thirtieth year of his age. He was interred in the church of St. Peter, where an epitaph, placed by order of the pontiff, recorded, during many ages, the sanctity of the Anglo-Saxon king[4].

The early history of Ine is involved in obscurity. That the Britons have identified him with their Ivor or Ynor has been

[1] Sax. Chron. Fl. Wigorn. H. Hunt. a. 687. W. Malm. lib. i.

[2] On the 19th Aug. 688 he issued a charter of donation. Malmesb. de Pont. lib. v. [Cod. Diplom. t. i. p. 32. Kemble questions the authenticity of this document.—T.]

[3] The remarkable connexion of this Lombard prince, as well as of his father Bertari, with the insular Saxons, has been already noticed. From the first part of her name we might be induced to seek for the kindred of Hermelind among the kings of Kent. Cf. Paul. Warnef. lib. vi. c. 15.

[4] Beda, v. 7. The sepulchral inscription on Ceadwealla by S. Benedictus Crispus, archbishop of Milan, was discovered in the 15th century, according to Johannes de Deio ' de Successione S. Barnabæ,' p. 23, but has since disappeared. It is given by Beda l. cit. The Britons make their Cadwaladyr die at Rome on the same day (xii. Kal. Maii) of the year 689. Galf. Monom. lib. xii. 18. Brut y Tyw. a. 681 also says he died at Rome, but Annal. Camb. a. 682 that he died of pestilence in his own country.

already noticed, and even the English accounts of his descent are inconsistent with each other ; still there appears no valid reason for rejecting the testimony of the oldest authorities, which represent him as the son of Cenred, a sub-king, and, like his predecessor, a descendant of Cutha, the son of Ceawlin[1].

The first years of Ine's reign must have been passed in disquietude, though we are not informed against what foe, foreign or domestic, he had to contend. Not till after a lapse of five years does he appear to have been able to wield the sword of vengeance against the people of Kent for the murder of his kinsman Mul[2], when the Kentish king Wihtræd deemed it prudent to avoid an unequal contest, and to appease him by the payment of thirty thousand pounds[3], the wergeld or legal price of the prince, who it was considered had not fallen in open warfare, but had been treacherously murdered.

Impelled by hereditary hatred, Ine is stated to have di-

[1] The title " subregulus " is found in Fl. Wigorn. Geneal. Cf. Asseri Vita Ælfredi. Sax. Chron. a. 855. Fl. Wigorn. a. 688. The varying genealogy in Malmesbury, lib. i. 2, "Ina, qui Cinegisli ex fratre Cuthbaldo pronepos," might excite scruples in a modern historian, being similar to that in the Chronicle a. 688, but which is not to be found in all the manuscripts, and is at variance with the other one, a. 855. Cynegils, otherwise known as the son of Ceolric, gets thereby another father, and Cuthwine, the father of Ceolwald or Cuthbald, becomes, instead of a grandson, a son of Ceawlin. In Malmesb. de Pont. lib. ii. Ine's father is named Cissa, and so again in lib. v. (ap. Wharton, t. ii.), though the edition of this work in Gale (t. i. p. 346) gives the name according to the charter there printed, " Cisi, Cenred, pater Inæ." [In the preamble to his laws he says, "I Ine, with the counsel of Cenred my father."—T.]

[2] According to one MS. of the Sax. Chr. and Fl. Wigorn. a. 694, Mul was a brother of Ine as well as of Ceadwealla. Probably Ine and Mul had the same mother. [R. Wendover, t. i. p. 187, calls him " cognatus;" Ethelwerd, " propinquus" (Inæ).—T.]

[3] The Sax. Chron. a. 694 says 30,000 pounds. W. Malm. lib. i. " nundinantur pacem triginta millibus auri mancis." Florence has 3750 pounds (libras), which, reckoning eight mancuses to the pound, agrees with Malmesbury. Ethelwerd's account is, that it was " 30,000 solidi, per singulos constanti numero sexdecim nummis."

rected his arms against East Anglia, which he ravaged, having previously expelled the nobility from the country[1].

During the long reign of Ine hostile collisions with the Britons were inevitable : among these the most memorable is the war against Geraint, king of Cernau, conducted by Ine and his kinsman Nunna, which ended in the flight of the British prince[2].

A power next to the king's was possessed, from the days of Centwine, in the southern parts of Wessex, by a king or sub-king Baldred, whose influence and importance, though apparent from other sources, is rendered more manifest by the circumstance, that the Welsh assign to a prince of Devon and Cornwall living at the time the Saxon name of Baldrich[3].

The hardest conflicts were, however, those of the Anglo-Saxons among themselves, in which they engaged with all the ardour and ferocity of their forefathers, for martial glory and supremacy in their loosely bound confederation. In the year 715 a battle was fought between the armies of Mercia and Wessex, in which it was unknown on which side the slaughter was most appalling. The scene of this engagement was Wodnesbeorh (Wenborough in Wiltshire), a spot which from its position either natural, or perhaps strengthened by art as a protection to a temple of Woden, had already been strewed with the corpses of the slain in former conflicts.

[1] W. Malm. lib. i. "Nec solum Cantuaritæ, sed et Orientales Angli hæreditarium exceperunt odium, omni nobilitate primo pulsa, post etiam bello fusa." [2] Sax. Chron. Fl. Wigorn. a. 710.
[3] W. Malm. de Antiq. Glaston. p. 308, a. 681 : " Baldred rex......Kenwine etiam consentiente dedit," p. 309. "Lanctocay......Kenwino etiam et Baldredo consentientibus dedit." Ibid. p. 311. " Privilegium regis Inæ, a. 725. Ina......hortatu Balddredi et Athelardi subregulorum."—"Baltrec." Ine continues, "a predecessoribus meis Kenewalchio, Kenwino, Cedwalla, Baldredo confirmatum." At the end, "Ego Baldredus rex confirmavi. Ego Adelard frater reginæ consensi." Cuthred also in a charter a. 744 calls Baldred his predecessor, and places him between Centwine and Ceadwealla. In a letter of Aldhelm, written about 701, he is called "patricius Baldredus." Ib. 347. By the Britons, " Baldrich;" see Caradoc, edit. Wynne, p. 17.

But not alone for his warlike achievements, which almost exclusively occupy the chronicles of the time, has the name of Ine been celebrated. A collection of the laws of Wessex, made by his command, is, with the exception of those of the Kentish kings, the earliest known to us among the Anglo-Saxons. These laws, seventy-six in number, have special reference to theft, murder or manslaughter, feuds, and pecuniary compensations (bôta), with others applicable to the British subjects (Wealas), who are placed on a footing nearly equal to that of their Germanic conquerors.

Ine also improved the ecclesiastical administration of his kingdom, by detaching from the diocese of Winchester, after the death of bishop Hedde in 703, a new bishopric, the see of which was established at Shireburn[1]. Among his numerous praiseworthy services in the founding and endowment of monasteries, the rebuilding and enlarged endowment of the old British abbey of Glastonbury, for the repose of the soul of his murdered kinsman Mul, is the most memorable[2]. But we feel more particularly induced to ascribe to the actions and views of Ine a nobler character, when we know that his friend and counsellor was the excellent bishop Aldhelm (Ealdhelm), a man on whom no brighter lustre can be shed by the royal descent assigned to him by his rank-adoring countrymen, and whose merits we unhesitatingly place on a level with those of the Venerable Beda[3]; for though in comprehensiveness of knowledge he may not, perhaps, have been his equal, yet as a Latin poet he stood higher, merited greater praise for the cultivation of his mother-tongue, left him far

[1] Malmesb. de Pont. lib. ii.

[2] Malmesb. de Antiq. Glaston. ap. Gale, t. i.

[3] Aldhelm ob. a. 709. See W. Malm. lib. i. Also the 5th book of Malmesbury, De Gestis Pontificum, published in Savile and Gale, also in Wharton's Anglia Sacra, which is a biography of Aldhelm. An edition of his Latin poems as well as of his work ʻDe Septenario et de Re Grammatica ac Metrica ad Alfridum regem Northumbrorum' is in Maii Classici Auctores e Vat. Codd. ed. t. v.

behind in knowledge of the canon and Roman law, and greatly excelled him in influential, practical activity. For his extensive knowledge of the Greek and Latin tongues he was indebted to the school of Canterbury, more especially to Hadrian[1], abbot of the abbey of St. Augustine in that city, who did not come to England till Aldhelm was near thirty years old; though his earlier instruction, particularly in dialectics, he owed to the abbey, founded by a Scot of Maildulfesburh, the modern Malmesbury[2], a celebrated monk of which, William of Malmesbury, has raised an honourable biographic monument to this most renowned scholar, and subsequently abbot of his cloister. In enumerating and characterizing the works of Aldhelm, no observation is more descriptive both of him and his nation, even in our days, than that which distinguishes pomp as a leading quality[3].

An individual, around whose name a still brighter glory shines than even that around Aldhelm's, may not here be totally passed over in silence. Winfrith, more generally known under his assumed name of Boniface, was a contemporary of Ine, and, previously to his triumphs over paganism in Germany, had been employed by that prince on a mission to the archbishop of Canterbury, a choice equally illustrative of the discriminating sagacity of the monarch, and honourable to the future apostle of our continental brethren. As the record of the greater and holier acts of Boniface belongs not to our history, we must, though reluctantly, limit our notice of him to this little more than simple mention of his name[4].

The latter years of Ine's reign were less prosperous than most of the earlier ones. Under the year 721 it is recorded

---

[1] Beda, iv. 1, v. 20.　W. Malm. lib. i.　See p. 181.

[2] Beda, v. 18, and Smith's note.

[3] Malmesb. de Pont. ap. Gale, p. 342.　" Græci involute, Romani splendide, Angli pompatice dictare solent.　Quem (Aldhelmum) si perfecte legeris, et ex acumine Græcum putabis, et ex nitore Romanum jurabis, et ex pompa Anglum intelliges."

[4] See Vita S. Bonifacii.

that the ætheling Cynewulf was slain by Ine[1], the cause of
which act can only be sought for in a rebellion raised by the
former.   The flame once kindled seems, however, not to have
been quenched with the blood of Cynewulf.   The insurgents
had made themselves masters of Tantûn (Taunton) in Somersetshire, a town built by Ine; but his queen wrested it from
their hands and razed it to the ground.   While Ine was car-
rying on a successful war against Sussex, and apparently a
less successful one against the Britons in Cornwall and Glamorgan, who, under the king of that country, Rodri Mal-
wynog, and Ivor with other chieftains, had taken advantage
of the disturbed state of Wessex[2], Ealdberht, also an ætheling,
fled from Wessex, after the loss of Taunton, at the head of the
insurgents, and wandered about in Surrey in all the misery
of exile, but found afterwards support in Sussex.   He was at
length overcome and slain by Ine[3].

Shortly after these successes, and when he had reigned
thirty-seven years, Ine resolved to renounce the sceptre and
the world[4].   The wish by which this step was preceded must
have been occasioned by the cares of royalty and the turbulence of those over whom Ine had perhaps already reigned
too long; but the manner in which it was brought to maturity
by the queen Æthelburh is too characteristic to be passed
over in silence.   A sumptuous entertainment had been given

---

[1] Sax. Chron.   Fl. Wigorn.   If faith is to be placed in Malmesbury,
Ine had no domestic enemy : " Domi gratiam, foris reverentiam mercabatur.
Adeo annis duobus de quadraginta potestate functus, sine ullo insidiarum
metu securus incanuit, sanctissimus publici amoris lenocinator." [For
'quadraginta,' the reading of five MSS. cited by Mr. Hardy, Savile's text
has 'sexaginta.'. According to Beda (v. 7), Ine reigned thirty-seven years.
—T.]   [2] Annal. Camb. a. 722.   Brut y Tyw. a. 721.

[3] Sax. Chron. a. 725.

[4] Sax. Chron.   Fl. Wigorn. a. 728.   This date is unquestionably incorrect.   The Chronicle is, moreover, inconsistent with itself, giving to Æthelheard, the successor of Ine, a reign of fourteen years, and placing his death
in 741 (some MSS. 740).   According to App. ad Bedam he died in 739.
[In four MSS. of the Chronicle, Ine's departure is correctly given in 726.
—T.]

at one of the royal villas. On the following day, after the departure of Ine and his queen, the superintendent, by order of the latter, defiled the palace with the dung of cattle and heaps of rubbish, and placed in the bed, where the royal pair had passed the night, a sow which had recently farrowed. When they had already proceeded more than a mile on their way back, Ine, for reasons assigned by his queen, was induced to return to the villa. On arriving there, and seeing the change it had undergone, he turned his inquiring eyes towards his consort, who hereupon took occasion to expatiate on the vanity of human life. The resolve of the deeply affected monarch was no longer delayed; he resigned his crown to the brother of his wife, the under-king Æthelheard, of the race of Cerdic[1], and went, accompanied by Æthelburh, as a pilgrim to Rome, where, rejecting every vestige of earthly pomp, and declining to lay aside his hair, but clad in a homely garb, he passed the remainder of his years in privacy and devotion. His wife, who had prompted him to this step, was his companion and comfort to the last[2].

Ine left also another relative in the male line, the ætheling Oswald, to whom he had destined a share of his kingdom[3]. The struggle between the two competitors lasted some years, till the death of Oswald, when his party, though powerful, desisted from further opposition to Æthelheard. Attacks from without rendered this union extremely necessary; though the victories which the Britons ascribe to themselves over Adelrad of Wessex, in Wales and Cornwall, by which name Æthelheard seems to be intended, are mentioned as having taken place in the years 720 and 722, consequently during the reign of Ine, and are, therefore, extremely doubtful. At the same time a leader could reckon on no dependents and no

---

[1] Fl. Wigorn. a. 728. W. Malm. lib. i.   [2] W. Malm.
[3] Beda, v. 7. "ipse, relicto regno ac juvenioribus commendato......profectus est." Later writers mention only the final succession of Æthelheard.

renown if he had not been victorious over the refractory
Welsh, who it is certain had about this time, that is, after
the abdication of Ine, succeeded in great measure in casting
off the Saxon yoke[1]; and equally certain it appears that
Æthelheard had to answer for this disgrace to his subjects.
More formidable, however, for Æthelheard was the preponderance gained over all the Anglo-Saxon states as far as the
Humber by the Mercian king Æthelbald, who, having assembled a formidable army, invested Sumertûn (Somerton),
the chief town of the Sumersætas, which, the inhabitants
being unable to offer any efficient resistance from within, and
cut off from external succour, he reduced under his subjection[2].   After a reign of fourteen years Æthelheard died, and
was succeeded by his kinsman Cuthred[3].

It was the lot of Cuthred to pass the greater part of his
reign in warfare with Æthelbald of Mercia, which led to no
beneficial result for either of the contending parties.   The
Britons, on the other hand, taking advantage of the discord
prevailing among the Anglo-Saxons, had so greatly increased
in strength, that both the hostile monarchs united their forces
for the purpose of quelling them.   In this undertaking, owing
to the superior number and the emulation of their men, they
were so successful that the honour of victory was indisputably
on the side of the Anglo-Saxons[4].   On the occasion of a new
quarrel between Cuthred and Æthelbald, the Britons took
part with the former, who with their aid is said to have gained
a victory over the Mercians near Hereford, but was, nevertheless, unable to protect his new allies from the vengeance
of Æthelbald[5].   In this war the ætheling Cynric, the son of
Cuthred, fell, a youth famed both as an undaunted warrior

---

[1] Fl. Wigorn. a. 731. "Britones magna ex parte Anglorum servitio
mancipati fuere."   [2] Sax. Chron. H. Hunt. a. 733.
    [3] Sax. Chron. Fl. Wigorn. a. 741.
    [4] Sax. Chron. Fl. Wigorn. a. 743.   H. Hunt. Caradoc also seems to
speak of this battle, though, instead of Cuthred, he names Æthelheard.
    [5] Caradoc, p. 17.

and a hunter: he seems to have perished in a sedition among his followers, who, unable to face the dangers into which he would urge them, saw no other escape than in the murder of their leader[1].

The supremacy which Mercia had in the course of these contests gained over Wessex became at length so oppressive, that Cuthred resolved to take the field once more against Æthelbald and his ally Oengus or Unnust, king of the Picts[2], when a dangerous rebellion broke out in his kingdom, at the head of which was Æthelhun, an ealdorman renowned for his valour, who, with far inferior forces, was yet able for a considerable time to maintain the field against his sovereign; but having received a wound, victory at length declared itself on the side of Cuthred[3], who used it with generosity, and restored Æthelhun to favour. Two years afterwards a decisive victory, owing chiefly to the valour of Æthelhun, was gained over the Mercians at Burford[4], which freed Wessex from all further aggression on the part of the other Anglo-Saxon states. From that glorious day the West Saxon dynasty rapidly rose to the supremacy over all the other insular states, which it maintained during a period of three centuries, when it sank under the resistless attacks of a barbarous enemy.

The year following the humiliation of Mercia, Cuthred turned his arms against the Britons, who, weakened apparently by the victories which the Dalriads had obtained over them[5], and unable to offer effectual resistance, lost great numbers in their flight[6]. Soon after these events Cuthred died

---

[1] H. Hunt. Sax. Chron. a. 748.   [2] App. ad Bedam, a. 750.   Sim. Dunelm.
[3] Sax. Chron. H. Hunt. a. 750.   [4] Sax. Chron. a. 752. See p. 226.
[5] "Congressio Dalriada et Britonum in lapide qui vocatur Minvirce, et Britones devicti sunt." Tigern. a. 717.
[6] Sax. Chron.   Fl. Wigorn.   H. Hunt. a. 753.   According to Geffrei Gaimar, v. 1803, Cuthred was beaten by the Welsh:

"Dous anz apres, Gudret li reis   descunfiz fu, mes bien guari,
    se combati contre Gualeis: ne gueres del son ni perdi."

In this he is not, however, copied even by Bromton.

childless[1], and too early to witness the rising prosperity of his nation.

Cuthred was succeeded by his kinsman Sigebyrht, the son of an under-king Sigeric, two names which remind us of the kings of Essex[2], who were nearly allied to the race of Cerdic. The prosperity of his predecessor had so blinded this prince, that he treated his subjects in the most injurious manner. The exhortations of his faithful counsellors, to preserve the laws inviolate and maintain justice, only served to instigate the tyrant to greater acts of violence. At the beginning of the second year of his reign, in an assembly of the nobles and people[3], Sigebyrht was formally deposed and banished from the kingdom, the government of which was intrusted to Cynewulf, another descendant of Cerdic, Hampshire alone remaining under the authority of Sigebyrht, from whence he was, however, soon compelled to flee, for having in his anger murdered the faithful ealdorman Cumbra[4], who had ventured to give him some wholesome counsel. Like his predecessor Ceadwealla, he fled to Andredeswald, though, unlike him, not again to leave it. A faithful swineherd of Cumbra discovered him, and avenged with his spear the blood of his murdered master.

The long reign[5] of Cynewulf is remarkably barren of events of which any memorial has been preserved. He engaged in several hard-fought though successful conflicts with the Britons, but at what place and in what year we are not informed[6]. One memorial regarding this prince has, however,

---

[1] Sax. Chron. Fl. Wigorn.

[2] Fl. Wigorn. Geneal. Cf. Sax. Chron. a. 823.

[3] H. Hunt. a. 755. "Congregati sunt proceres et populus totius regni."

[4] "Consul nobilissimus." H. Hunt. In a charter of Cuthred, a. 744 (Cod. Diplom. p. 112), Cumbra signs himself, "præfectus regis."

[5] The Chronicle and other ancient authorities assign to Cynewulf a reign of thirty-one years, while they place his accession in 755, and his murder in 784.—T.

[6] Sax. Chron. H. Hunt. a. 784. In the latter years of this prince, several of the Frisian family of the Fortemanni are said to have served the king of England. See Ocka Scharlensis Chronicke van Frieslandt, fol. 18.

been preserved in the form of a grant of lands to the church of Wells in expiation of his sins, and of the severities which he had exercised towards his Cornish enemies[1]. The letter which, in conjunction with his bishops and nobles, he addressed to Lullus, archbishop of Mentz, shows that considerable intercourse existed between the Anglo-Saxon and the German church[2]. A conflict with Offa, the powerful king of Mercia, ended, unfortunately for the people of Wessex, who lost Bensington (Benson) in Oxfordshire to the conquerors[3].

The death of Cynewulf though late was violent. He had ordered into banishment Cyneheard, the younger brother of his predecessor, who, instead of yielding to the mandate, having learned that the king with a slender retinue was gone to visit a female at Merton to whom he was attached, surrounded the house with his followers, when the inmates were wrapt in sleep. On discovering that the place was beset, the king, seizing his weapons, rushed to the door of his apartment and offered a stout resistance to his assailants, when, perceiving the ætheling, he wounded him severely, but was himself immediately overpowered and slain. At this moment the attendants of Cynewulf, who were lodged in the neighbourhood, roused by the cries of the female, hastened, though too late, to their master's succour. Cyneheard's offers of life and rewards they received with scorn, and desperately fighting were all slain with the exception of one, a British hostage, who was sorely wounded.

On the following morning the king's friend, the ealdorman Osric, and Wigferth his faithful thane, with all the thanes who had remained behind, having heard what had taken place, immediately rode to Merton, where they found the gates closed against them. On their attempting to force an

---

[1] Charter a. 766 in Monast. Angl. [Also in Cod. Diplom. t. i. p. 141, where its genuineness is questioned.—T.]   [2] Epist. Bonifacii, xcii.
[3] Sax. Chron. a. 775 (777). Fl. Wigorn. a. 778.

entrance, the ætheling promised them money and lands at
their own discretion if they would receive him for their king,
at the same time intimating to them, that many of their kindred were with him who would not forsake him.   But the
faithful band declared unanimously that no kinsman could be
dearer to them than their lord, and that they would never
follow his murderer.   They then called upon their relations
who were with Cyneheard to leave him while they were yet
safe and unhurt; but these also answered that they had made
a similar offer to those who were yesterday with the king,
which was not listened to; they could not, therefore, accept
that now made to themselves.   A conflict then ensued before
the gates, which being soon forced, the ætheling with his followers, to the number of eighty-four, were slain, one only,
the godson of Osric, escaping with life, and he was covered
with wounds.   The corpse of Cynewulf was buried with those
of his forefathers at Winchester; that of the ætheling at
Axminster[1].

The next in succession to the vacant throne, as far as our
knowledge of the line of Cerdic enables us to judge, was
Ealhmund, king of Kent, a great grandson of Ingild, the
brother of Ine, whose pretensions, either from disregard to
the strict line of succession, provided the individual were of
the race of Cerdic, or from some other to us unknown cause,
seem to have been passed by, and another member of the
royal house, Beorhtric, of whose right it is merely said that
he was descended from Cerdic, was by the witan chosen for
king.   Beorhtric justified the confidence which had called
him to the throne.   For the internal security of his realm he
provided by the expulsion of Ecgberht, the son of Ealhmund;
and against the inroads of foreign foes, whether Britons or
other Anglo-Saxons, he also rendered himself secure.   The
peace of the land was, moreover, not a little confirmed by his
alliance with Offa of Mercia, whose daughter Eadburh he had

[1] Sax. Chron. a. 784.   Ethelwerd.

espoused[1]. Ecgberht, who until this event had found shelter among the Mercians, and cherished hopes of one day obtaining the crown of Wessex, now fled to the court of the Frankish emperor.

This reign was remarkable for the first landing of the Northmen in England, which took place on the coast of Dorsetshire from three ships. On being apprised of the event the king's reeve (gerefa), named Beaduheard[2], who resided at Dorchester, supposing them to be contraband traders rather than pirates, rode hastily to the port and commanded that they should be forcibly conducted to the king's town; whereupon he was assailed by the Northmen and slain with all his retinue.

To the influence of the queen Eadburh, a daughter of that Cynethrith whose memory the murder of the young king of East Anglia has stained with everlasting infamy, may probably be ascribed the indifference with which Beorhtric seems to have regarded the increasing power of Mercia over Kent. Through the fond weakness of her consort, this woman had imperceptibly acquired an absolute dominion in all the internal concerns of the kingdom. Those towards whom Beorhtric evinced an attachment, or who were opposed to her baneful caprices, she found means to destroy, either by false accusations or, failing in them, by poison. A young ealdorman named Worr, distinguished both on account of his high birth and amiable character, was the favourite of Beorhtric, and consequently an object of hatred to his wife. Accusations against him proving ineffectual, she had recourse to her usual alternative of poison. Her purpose was effected, but her husband also partook of the deadly cup and perished with his friend. In their utter detestation of this abandoned woman, the West Saxons resolved that no future consort of

[1] Sax. Chron. a. 787.
[2] Ethelwerd, lib. iii. Procem. Fl. Wigorn. Sax. Chron. a. 787, where it is said that the Northmen came out of " Hæretha lande."

a king should be permitted to occupy a royal throne by the
side of her husband, or to bear the title of queen[1].

After this event, finding that her presence could no longer
be tolerated in Wessex, Eadburh fled with her treasures to
the court of Charlemagne, who, on her presenting him with
various costly gifts, jocosely said to her, " Choose, Eadburh,
between me and my son, who stands there in the saloon[2],
which you will have." To which she thoughtlessly answered,
" If I may be allowed to choose, I will have your son as being
the younger." " If you had chosen me," replied Charles
laughing, " you should have had my son ; but having chosen
my son, you shall have neither me nor him." Charles, however, bestowed on her a considerable monastery, in which for
a short time she exercised the duties of abbess, but being con-
victed of criminal intercourse with one of her own countrymen, as well as with others, she was by the emperor's order
expelled from the convent. Attended by a single slave, the
daughter of Offa and wife of Beorhtric, after various wanderings, died a beggar in the city of Pavia[3].

---

[1] Sax. Chron.   Fl. Wigorn. a. 800.   Asser.   Sim. Dunelm.   W. Malm.
From that time the consort of the king usually bore the title of ' hlæfdige,'
lady.—T.

[2] " Elige, Eadburgh, quem velis inter me et filium meum, qui mecum in
solario isto stat." Asser.—T.

[3] A.D. 802.   "Uno servulo comitata." Asser, a. 856.   Sim. Dunelm.
a. 802. [Asser informs us that he had the story of Eadburh from Ælfred's
own mouth : " a domino meo Ælfredo, Angulsaxonum rege veridico, etiam
sæpe mihi referente audivi, quod et ille etiam a veridicis multis referentibus,
immo ex parte non modica illud factum commemorantibus, audierat."—T.]

ADDITIONAL NOTES.

Page 11, note [2].—The characters of the runic alphabet are also named chiefly after natural objects, some of them from trees, as *oak, birch, thorn*; and like the bardic alphabet it consisted originally of sixteen letters.—T.

P. 48.—The following passage from the Codex Eberbrard Clusanus of the Gesta Treverorum is rather curious : "Hujus Marcelli (episc. Treverici) et prædecessoris Naviti per Angliam facta prædicatione, ipse rex Britanniæ fidem Christi suscepit, et baptizatus est ab eodem Marcello anno Dñi cclxxxvi."

Pp. 79, note [3], and 97, note [4].—That the Jutes landed in England where they occupied Kent, the Isle of Wight and part of Wessex, is, I believe, generally admitted. That they were under a leader, or (as was usual among the Danes) two leaders, may also be believed, without exposing the believer to the imputation of being over credulous : nor can I found any disbelief or doubt on the circumstance, that the one leader was named Hengest, the other Horsa.

In addition to the testimonies of Nennius, Beda, and the

Saxon Chronicle, the following extracts may be adduced in favour of the existence of Hengest, Fin, etc.

1. From the Geographer of Ravenna, who is supposed to have lived in the seventh century. See p. 88, note [4].

2. From the Scôp or Scald's Tale. (Cod. Exon. p. 320; Kemble's Beow. vol. i. p. 229.)

. . . . (weold)	. . . . .
Fin Folcwalding	*Fin Folcwalding (rul'd)*
Fresna cynne	*the Frisian race*
. . . . .	. . . . ·.
Hnæf Hocingum.	*Hnæf the Hocings*[a].

3. From the Battle of Finnesburh. (Kemble's Beow. vol. i. p. 239.)

Ordlaf and Guðlaf,	*Ordlaf and Guthlaf,*
and Hengest sylf	*and Hengest himself*
hwearf him on laste	*follow'd in his track*
. . . . . .	. . . . . .
. . . . . .	. . . . . .
þonne Hnæfe guldon	*then for Hnæf paid*
his hægstealdas.	*his followers.*

4. Beowulf. Hnæf prince of the Hocings, and Hengest the Jute, vassals of the Danish king Healfdene (the Haldanus of Saxo), are sent to invade the Frisian territory, at that time governed by Fin, the son of Folcwalda, and husband of Hildeburh, the daughter of Hoce. A battle is fought, in which Hnæf, together with all the children, brothers, and almost all the thanes of Fin, is slain. During a truce which ensues, the bodies of Hnæf and the rest of the slain are burnt. Hengest remains with Fin, but at the same time meditates vengeance for the death of Hnæf and his followers, which he subsequently wreaks, Fin being slain, and his queen Hildeburh borne off to Denmark. The entire episode follows :

---

[a] The Hocings are supposed by Zeuss to be identical with the Chauci. See Ettmüller, Scôpes Vidsidh, p. 16, and Cod. Exon. p. 515.

XVI.

Ðær wæs sang and sweg	*There was song and sound*
samod ætgædere	*at once together*
fore Healfdenes	*before Healfdene's*
hilde-wísan,	*warlike chiefs,*
gomen-wudu greted,	*the wood of joy was greeted,*
gid oft wrecen,	*the lay oft recited,*
ðonne heal-gamen	*when the joy of hall*
Hroðgares scóp,	*Hrothgar's bard,*
æfter medo-bence,	*after the mead-bench,*
mænan sceolde	*should recount*
be Finnes eaferum,	*concerning Fin's offspring,*
þa hie se fær begeat ;	*when them peril o'erwhelm'd ;*
hæleð Healfdenes,	*when Healfdene's hero,*
Hnæf Scyldinga,	*the Scyldings' Hnæf,*
in Fres-wæle	*in Frisian slaughter*
feallan sceolde.	*was doom'd to fall.*
Ne huru Hildeburh	*Not Hildeburh at least*
herian þorfte	*had need to praise*
Eotena treowe :	*the faith of the Jutes :*
unsynnum wearð	*she was of her innocent*
beloren leofum	*beloved ones depriv'd*
æt þam lind-plegan,	*at the linden-play,*
bearnum and broðrum :	*of her children and brothers :*
hie on gebyrd hruron,	*they in succession fell,*
gare wunde.	*by the dart wounded.*
Ðæt wæs geomuru ides :	*That was a mournful woman :*
nalles holinga	*not without cause*
Hoces dohtor	*Hoces daughter*
metodsceaft bemearn,	*the Lord's decree bemourn'd,*
siððan morgen com,	*after morning came,*
þa heo under swegle	*when she under heaven*
geseón meahte	*might see*
morþor-bealo maga,	*the slaughter of her kinsmen,*
þær heo ǽr mæste heold	*where she ere had most possess'd*
worulde wynne.	*of worldly joy.*

Line numbers: 10, 20, 30

5. i. e. the harp.
13. MS. Healfdena.
22. conject. Kemble, MS. hild-p. of the lime, or linden tree.

11. be, added from conjecture.
20. unsynnigum ?
So called from the shield being made
34. MS. he.

Wig ealle fornam	*War destroy'd all*
Finnes þegnas,	*Fin's thanes,*
nemne feaum anum ;	*save a few only ;*
þæt he ne mihte	*so that he might not*
on þam meþel-stede	*on the battle-place*
wið Hengeste	*against Hengest*
wiht gefeohtan,	*at all contend,*
ne þa wea-lafe	*nor the sad remnant*
wige forþringan	*by war protect*
þeodnes þegne ; 10	*from the king's thane ;*
ac hie him geþingo budon,	*but they to him conditions offer'd,*
þæt hie him oðer flet	*that they to him another dwelling*
eal gerymdon,	*would wholly yield,*
healle and heah-setl ;	*a hall and high seat ;*
þæt hie healfre geweald	*that they half power*
wið Eotena bearn	*with the sons of the Jutes*
agan moston,	*might possess,*
and æt feoh-gyftum	*and at the money-gifts*
Folcwaldan sunu	*Folcwalda's son*
dogra gehwylce 20	*every day*
Dene weorþode,	*the Danes should honour,*
Hengestes heap	*Hengest's band*
hringum þenede,	*with rings should serve,*
efne swa swiðe	*even as much*
sinc-gestreonum	*with costly treasures*
fættan goldes,	*of rich gold,*
swa he Fresna cyn,	*as he the Frisian race,*
on beor-sele	*in the beer-hall*
byldan wolde.	*would adorn.*
Ða hie getruwedon, 30	*Then they confirm'd,*
on twa healfa,	*on the two sides,*
fæste frioðu-wære,	*a fast peaceful compact,*
Fin Hengeste	*Fin to Hengest*
elne, unflitme,	*earnestly, without dispute,*
áðum benemde,	*by oath enjoin'd,*
þæt he þa wea-lafe,	*that he the sad remnant,*

6. MS. wig.   10. i. e. Hengest.
11. hie, *they,* i. e. the Danes and Jutes.
15. hie, *they,* i. e. the Frisians.   23. MS. wenede.
27. he, i. e. Hengest.
29. gibelde, *ornavit,* inscrip. in Nero D. 4, MS. Cott.

weotena dome,	*by his witan's doom,*
árum heolde,	*piously should hold,*
þæt ðær ænig mon,	*that there no man,*
wordum ne weorcum,	*by words or works,*
wære ne bræce,	*should break the compact,*
ne þurh inwit-searo	*nor through guileful craft*
æfre gemændon,	*should they ever complain,*
þeah hie hira beag-gyfan	*though they their ring-giver's*
banan folgedon,	*murderer followed,*
þeodenlease, 10	*lordless,*
þa him swa geþearfod wæs;	*since they were so compel'd ;*
gyf þonne Frysna hwylc,	*but if of the Frisians any one,*
frecnan spræce,	*by audacious speech,*
þæs morþor-heteś	*this deadly feud*
myndgiend wære,	*should call to mind,*
þonne hit sweordes ecg	*then it the edge of sword*
sweðrian sceolde.	*should appease.*
Að wæs geæfned,	*The oath was completed,*
and icge gold	*and moreover gold*
ahæfen of horde. 20	*rais'd from the hoard.*
Here-Scyldinga	*Of the martial Scyldings*
betst beado-rinca	*the best of warriors*
wæs on bæl gearu :	*on the pile was ready :*
æt þam áde wæs	*at the heap was*
eð-gesyne	*easy to be seen*
swatfah syrce,	*the blood-stain'd tunic,*
swýn eal gylden,	*the swine all golden,*
eofer iren-heard,	*the boar iron-hard,*
æþeling mænig	*many an ætheling*
wundum awyrded, 30	*with wounds afflicted,*
sume on wæle crungon.	*(some had in the slaughter fall'n).*
Het þa Hildeburh,	*Bade then Hildeburh,*
æt Hnæfes áde,	*at Hnæf's pile,*
hire selfre suna	*her own sons*
sweoloðe befæstan,	*be to the fire committed,*

8. For þeah I suspect we should read þæt.
17. MS. syððan.
19. icge is very questionable.
22. betst b.-r., i. e. Hnæf.
34. MS. sunu, i. e. her sons who had been slain.

bán-fatu bærnan,	*their carcases be burnt,*
and on bæl dón	*and on the pile be reduced*
earme on axe.	*the miserable ones to ashes.*
Ides gnornode,	*The woman mourn'd,*
geomrode giddum;	*bewail'd in songs;*
guð-rinc astah,	*the warrior ascended,*
wand to wolcnum,	*wended to the clouds,*
wæl-fyra mæst	*the greatest of death-fires*
hlynode for hlawe;	*roar'd before the mound;*
hafelan multon, 10	*their heads were consum'd,*
ben-geato burston;	*their wound-gates burst;*
ðonne blód ætspranc	*then out sprang the blood*
láð-bíte lices:	*from the corpse's hostile bite:*
lig ealle forswealg,	*flame swallow'd all*
gæsta gifrost,	*(greediest of guests,)* [*bereft.*
þara ðe þær guð fornam.	*those whom war had there of life*
Bega folca wæs	*Of both people was*
hira blæd scacen.	*their flower departed.*

XVII.

Gewiton him ða wigend	*The warriors then departed*
wica neosian, 20	*their villages to visit,*
freondum befeallen,	*of their friends deprived,*
Frysland geseón,	*Friesland to see,*
hamas and hea-burh.	*its dwellings and high burgh.*
Hengest ða-gyt	*Hengest yet*
wælfagne winter	*the death-hued winter*
wunode mid Finne,	*remain'd with Fin,*
unflitme,	*without strife,*
eard gemunde,	*his home remember'd,*
þeah þe he ne meahte	*although he might not*
on mere drifan 30	*on the sea drive*
hringed-stefnan.	*the ringed prow.*
Holm storme weol,	*Ocean boil'd with storm,*

3. MS. eaxle.

6. i. e. *Hnæf ascended* (*in flame and smoke*), like the Ger. (in Feuer und Rauch) aufgehen.   So also Homily, MS. Bibl. Pub. Cantab. p. 282. MS. þæt ceaf he forbærnð......forðan ðe ðæra mánfulra smíc astihð on ecnysse.   10. So Beow. 4646, bolda selest bryne-wylmum mealt.

21. *deprived through their having fallen.*   26. MS. Finnel.

27. MS. unhlitme.   29. ne, added.

won wið winde,	war'd against the wind,
winter yþe beleac	winter lock'd the wave
ís-gebinde,	with icy band,
oðþæt oðer com	till that came the second
gear in geardas.	year to the courts.
Swa nu gyt deð	So now yet do
þa ðe singale	those who constantly
sæle bewitiað,	watch a happy moment,
wuldor-torhtan weder.	gloriously bright weather.
Ða wæs winter scacen, 10	When winter was departed,
fæger foldan bearm,	earth's bosom fair,
fundode wrecca,	the stranger hasten'd,
gæst of geardum.	the guest from the courts.
He to gyrn-wræce	He on wily vengeance
swiðor þohte	was more intent
þonne to sǽ-láde,	than on a sea-voyage,
gif he torn-gemót	if he a conflict
þurhteon mihte ;	could bring to pass ;
þæs he Eotena bearn	for he the sons of the Jutes
inn-gemunde, 20	inwardly remember'd,
swa he ne forwyrnde	so he refus'd not
woruldrædenne,	worldly intercourse,
þonne him Hunlafing,	when he Hunlafing,
hilde leoman,	the flame of war,
billa selest,	the best of falchions,
on bearm dyde ;	in his bosom placed ;
þæs wæron mid Eotenum	for with the Jutes there were
ecge cuðe,	men fam'd for sword-play,
swylce ferhð-frecan.	also of spirit bold.

7. MS. singales.   8. MS. sele.   13. MS. gist.

14. gyrn = gryn.

14. *wily vengeance,* i. e. the fæhð or deadly feud for the death of Hnæf and the others.   19. MS. þæt.   19. *the slain ones.*

23. Hunlafing is apparently the name of Hengest's sword, which had probably been the property of Hun, king of the Hætweras (Scôps Tale, p. 320, 22). The terminations laf, *a relic, legacy,* and ing are commonly applied to a sword; thus Beow. eald laf, *an ancient sword:* so Tyrfing, Miming, Hrunting, names of celebrated swords. See Kemble's Glossary to Beowulf, *v.* Laf. Hunlaf occurs, however, as a man's name among the Anglo-Saxons.

26. So Beow. l. 4382 : sweord......þæt he on Biowulfes bearm alegde : *sword......that he in Beowulf's bosom laid.*

Fin eft begeat	*Fin afterwards o'erwhelm'd*
sweord-bealo sliðen,	*cruel misery from the sword,*
æt his sylfes hám,	*at his own dwelling,*
siðþan grimne gripe	*when the grim one with gripe*
Guðlaf and Oslaf,	*Guthlaf and Oslaf,*
æfter sǽ-siðe,	*after a sea-journey,*
sorge mændon,	*grievously upbraided,* [*woes:*
ætwiton weana dæl :	*reproach'd for his part in their*
ne meahte wæfre mód	*he might not his wavering soul*
forhabban in hreþre. 10	*in his breast retain.*
Ða wæs heal hroden	*Then was the hall beset*
feonda feorum,	*with foemen,*
swilce Fin slægen,	*also Fin slain,*
cyning on corþre,	*the king amid his people,*
and seo cwen numen.	*and the queen taken.*
Sceotend Scyldinga	*The Scyldings' warriors*
to scypum feredon	*to their ships bore*
eal in-gesteald	*all the house-chattels*
eorð-cyninges,	*of the earth-king,*
swylce hie æt Finnes hám 20	*such as at Fin's dwelling*
findan meahton,	*they could find,*
sigla, searo-gimma.	*of jewels and curious gems.*
Hie on sǽ-láde	*They on the sea-road*
drihtlice wíf	*the princely woman*
to Denum feredon,	*to the Danes bore,*
læddon to leodum.	*to their people led.—T.*

Page 91, note [2].—For the near resemblance between the Northumbrian and East Anglian dialects, see Lufa's Testament in Analecta Anglo-Saxonica, p. 119.—T.

Page 203, note [4].—The publication of "The Poetry of the Codex Vercellensis, with an English translation, by J. M. Kemble, M.A. Part I. The Legend of St. Andrew, for the Ælfric Society," induces me to add a few words to the above-cited note relative to my own connexion with the Vercelli Poetry. In 1834 Mr.

5. 'Ordlaf,' Batt. of Finnesb. perhaps more correct than Oslaf.

7. mændon. In Homily, MS. Bibl. Pub. Cantab. p. 217, the verse of Luke there quoted (xviii. 15) has 'bemændon' where the editions of the Gospels have ' ciddon,' *rebuked.*

17. MS. scypon.

Cooper, then Secretary to the Record Commission, sent me a transcript of the manuscript, requesting me to report on its contents. On inspection I found that, besides Homilies, the volume contained the several poetic pieces since known as the ' Vercelli Poetry.' Having stated my opinion of these poems to Mr. Cooper, their communication to the world was resolved on : they were printed accordingly as one of the Appendices to that gentleman's intended Report on Rymer's Fœdera, though, in consequence of the dissolution of the Commission, not published. Soon after the formation of the Ælfric Society I suggested the publication of these relics to the Council, though, regarding them as Government property, not until I had ascertained from Lord Langdale (under whose control they had been placed) that he had no objection to their publication by the Ælfric Society.—T.

GENEALOGY OF THE SONS OF WODEN.

From the Sax.	From Snorra Edda.
Chron. a. 855.	edit. Rask.
Noe.	Sif.
Sceaf.	Loride.
Bedwig.	Henrede.
Hwala.	Vingethor.
Hathra.	Vingener.
Itermon.	Moda.
Heremod.	Magi.
Sceldwa.	Cespheth (Sefsmeg).
Beaw.	Bedvig.
Tætwa.	Atra (*nobis* Anna).
Geat.	Itrmann.
Godwulf.	Heremod.
Finn.	Skialldunn (*nobis* Skiöld).
Frithuwulf.	Biaf (*nobis* Biar and Bavr).
Frealaf[1].	Jat.
Frithuwald.	Guthólfr.
	[Finnr.]
𝔚𝔬𝔡𝔢𝔫.	Fiarlef (Frialafr) (*nobis* Frithleif).
	Vothinn (*nobis* Othinn).

Wecta,	Bældæg.	Casere,	Seaxneât,	Wægdæg,	Wihtlæg,	Winta,
ancestor of the kings of Kent.	Brond.	ancestor of the kings of E. Anglia.	ancestor of the kings of Essex.	ancestor of the kings of Deira.	ancestor of the kings of Mercia.	ancestor of the princes of the Lindisfaras.

Frithogar,	Beornd (Beonoc),
ancestor of the kings of Wessex.	ancestor of the kings of Bernicia.

[1] Three MSS. for Frealaf read Freawine, and omit the following Frithuwald. In the Bernician list (S.C. a. 547) Frealaf is called Freotholaf.

GENEALOGY OF THE KINGS OF KENT.

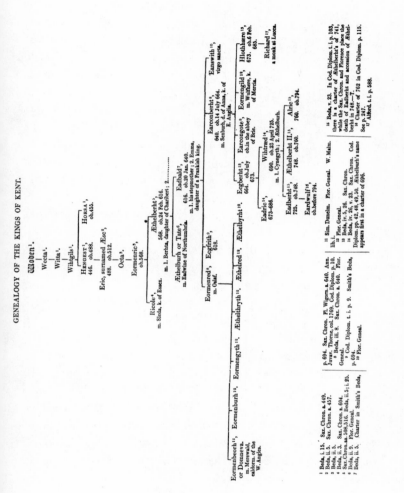

Wóden[1].

Wecta[1].

Witta[1].

Wihtgils[1].

Hengest[1], 446. ob.488.   Horsa[1], ob.455.

Eric, surnamed Æsc[2], 488. ob.512.

Octa[1].

Eormenric[3], ob.568.

Æthelberht[3], 568. ob.24 Feb. 616. m. 1. Bertha, daughter of Charibert; 2. ....

Ricole[4], m. Sleda, k. of Essex.

Æthelburh or Tate[5], m. Eadwine of Northumbria.

Eadbald[7], 616. ob.20 Jan. 640. m. 1. his stepmother; 2. Emma, daughter of a Frankish king.

Eormenred[6], m. Oslaf.   Egfrith[6], 618.

Earconberht[6], 640. ob.14 July 664. m. Sexburh, d. of Anna, k. of E. Anglia.   Eanswith[10], virgo sancta.

Eormenbeorh[11], Eormenburh[12], Eormengyth[12], Æthelred[16], Æthelbryht[16].

Eormenbeorh[11], or Domneva, m. Merewald, ealdorm. of the W. Angles.

Earcongote[8], ob.in the abbey of Brie.   Ecgberht[13], 664. ob.July 673.   Eormengild[12], m. Wulfhere, k. of Mercia.   Hlothhære[12], 673. ob.6 Feb. 685.   Richard[17], a monk at Lucca.

Wihtred[14], 690. ob.23 April 725. m. 1. Cynegyth; 2. Æthelburh.

Eadric[14], 673-686.

Eadberht[15], 725. ob.748.   Æthelberht II[15], 748. ob.760.   Alric[15], 760. ob.794.

Eardwulf[16], ob.before 794.

1 Beda, i. 115.   Sax. Chron. a. 449.
2 Beda, ii. 5.   Sax. Chron. a. 457.
3 Beda, ii. 5.
4 Beda, ii. 3.   Sax. Chron. a. 604.
5 Sax.Chron.aa. 508,516. Beda, ii. 5; i. 25.
6 Beda, ii. 9.   Flor. Geneal.
7 Beda, ii. 5.   Charter in Smith's Beda, p. 694. Sax. Chron. Fl. Wigorn. a. 640. Ann. Juvav. Thorpe, col. 1769. Cod. Diplom. p.10.
8 Beda, iii. 8.   Sax. Chron. a. 640.   Flor. Geneal.
9 Cod. Diplom. t. i. p. 9.   Smith's Beda, p. 694.
10 Flor. Geneal.

11 Sim. Dunelm.   Flor. Geneal.   W. Malm. lib. i.
12 Flor. Geneal.
13 Beda, iv. 5, 26.   Sax. Chron.
14 Beda, iv. 26, v. 23.   Sax. Chron.   Cod. Diplom. pp. 42, 48, 49, 50. Æthelburh's name appears first in a charter of 696.

15 Beda, v. 23.   In Cod. Diplom. t. i. p. 103, there is a charter of Æthelberht's of 741, while the Sax. Chron. and Florence place the death of Eadberht and accession of Æthelberht in 748.—†.
† Charter of 762 in Cod. Diplom. p. 115.
16 See p. 247.
17 Alford. t. i. p. 588.

GENEALOGY OF THE KINGS OF WESSEX, FROM WODEN TO EGBERHT.

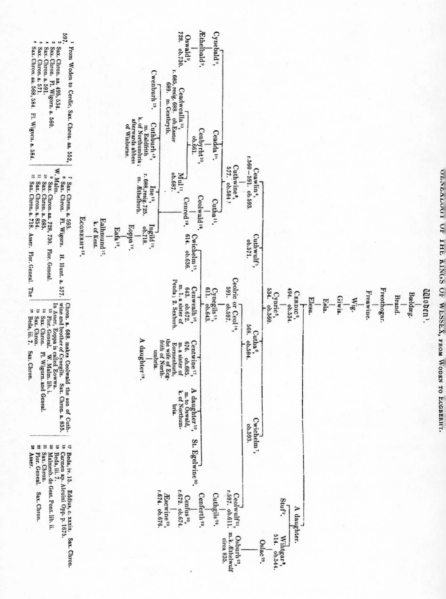

GENEALOGY OF THE KINGS OF EAST ANGLIA.

Woden[1].
|
Casere.
|
Tytmon.
|
Trygils.
|
Hrothmund.
|
Hryp.
|
Wilhelm.
|
Wewa or Wehha.
|
Wuffa[2].
|
Tytila[2].

OF UNKNOWN LINEAGE.

Sigeberht,
brother of Eorpwald
on the mother's side.
r. 631, resig. 634.   ob.635.

Ecgric,
kinsman of Sigeberht.
r. 634.   ob.635.

Rædwald[2], 593.   —617.   **Æne**[4].

Eorpwald[2], r. 617.   ob.628.   **Ræginhere**[3], ob.617.   **Anna**[4], r. 635.   ob.654.   **Æthelhere**[5], r.654.   ob.655.
m. Hereswith,
d. of Hereric.
ob.20 Sept. ...   **Æthelwold**[6], r. 655.   ob.664.   *Edric*[7].

Ealdwulf[8], r.663.   ob.713.   **Alfwold**[9], r. 713.   ob.749.   **Iurwine**[10].

Elric[7].   **Eadburh**[10], abbess of Repton.

Sexburh[11], m. Earconberht k. of Kent. ob.abbess of Ely, 6 July after 679.   **Æthelburh**[11], abbess of Brie in France. "Filia naturalis."   **Æthelthryth**[12], m. 1. Tunberht, ealdorm. of the S. Gyrwas; 2. Ecgfrith, k. of Northumberland. ob.23 June 679, as abbess of Ely.   **S. Wihtburh or Wihtgyth**[13], a nun at Ely.

---

[1] From Woden to Wewa, Flor. Geneal.
[2] Beda, ii. 15.   Flor. Geneal.
[3] Beda, ii. 12.   Flor. Geneal.
[4] Beda, iii. 18.
[5] Beda, iii. 24.
[6] Beda, iii. 22.
[7] Nennius, App., the only authority for this prince's existence.

[8] Beda, iv. 17.   See Literary Introd. p. xxxvi. *note* [3].
[9] W. Malm. lib. i.   Sim. Dunelm. a. 749.
[10] T. Eliens. Hist. Eliens. ap. Wharton, A. S. t. i. p. 595.   Felix, Vita S. Guthl. iv. 33.
[11] Beda, iii. 8, iv. 19.
[12] Beda, iv. 3, 19, 20.
[13] Flor. Geneal.

GENEALOGY OF THE KINGS OF ESSEX.

𝕎𝕠𝕕𝕖𝕟[1].

Seaxneât[1].

Gesecg[1].

Antsecg[1].

Sweppa[1].

Sigefugel[1].

Bedca[1].

Offa[1].

ÆSCWINE or ERCENWINE[1],
a. 527.

Sleda[2],
587. m. Ricole, sister of Æthelberht,
k. of Kent.

Sæberht[3],
ob.616.

Seaxbald[10].

Scaxred[4],
ob.soon after 616.

Sæward[4],
ob.soon after 616.

Sigeberht[4],
ob.soon after 616.

Sigeberht the Good[11],
653. ob.660.

Swithhelm.

Sigeberht the Little[5],
617. —653.

Sebbe[6],
reg. 665, resig. ... ob.694.

Selred[12],
r. 709. ob.746.

Sigehere[8],
m. S. Osyth, d. of
Frithewald, k. of Surrey,
and Wilburh d. of Penda.

Sigeheard[7],
r. after his father,
694.

Swæfred,
r. after his father,
704.

Offa[9],
resig. 709.
died a monk at Rome.

[1] Flor. Geneal.   H. Hunt. who makes Antsecg the son, and Gesecg the grandson of Seaxneât, and calls Sigefugel Sigewlf.
[2] Beda, ii. 3.   Sax. Chron. a. 604.
[3] Beda, ii. 5.
[4] Fl. Wigorn. Geneal.   W. Malm. lib. i.
[5] Beda, iii. 22.   Flor. Geneal.   W. Malm.

[6] Beda, v. 30.
[7] Beda, iv. 11.   W. Malm.
[8] Beda, iii. 30.   Rad. de Diceto, Abbreviat. a. 641.
[9] Beda, v. 19.   W. Malm.
[10] Flor. Geneal.
[11] Beda, iii. 22.
[12] Sax. Chron.   Fl. Wigorn. a. 746.   W. Malm. lib.

Woden¹.
Baeldeag.
Brand.
Beorn.
Beornd.
Waegbrand.
Ingebrand.
Alusa.
Angengeat.
Ingengeat.
Aethelbryht.
Oesn.
Eoppa.
Ioa³, 547. ob.559. m. 1. Bearnoch; 2. concubine.

Woden⁹.
Baeldeag.
Brand.
Beonoc.
Aloe.
Angenwit.
Ingui.
Esa.
Eoppa.
Ida.

Sons of Ida:
Glappa⁴, r. 1 yr. — Adda⁴ — Æthelric⁴, r. 8 yrs. r. 588–592. — Theodric⁴, r. 4 yrs. — Frithuwald⁴, r. 7 yrs. — Hussa⁴, r. 7 yrs.

Æthelfrith³; 593. ob.617. m. 1. Bebbe; 2. Acha, sister of Eadwine.
Theodbald⁶.

Offa⁸. Oswudu⁸.
Ebbe¹², abbess of Coldingham.

Eanfrith⁷, m. a d. of the k. of the Picts. ob.634.
Oslac⁸. Oslaf⁸.
Oswald⁹, born 604. ob.5 Aug. 642. m. of Cyneglsa the k. of Wessex.
Æthelwald¹⁰, k. of Deira.
Oswiu¹¹, r. 642. ob.15 Feb. 670. m. 1. Rieanmelth; 2. Eanfled, d. of Eadwine.
Ælfwine²⁰, born 661. ob.679.
Ælfled²⁸, born 634. ob.713, abbess of Whitby.

Tolargain, or Talorgan¹⁴, k. of the Picts. ob.656.
Ecgfrith¹⁵, born 645, r. 670. ob.20 May 685. m. 1. Æthelthryth, d. of Anna, k. of E. Anglia; 2. Eormenburh, sister of the qu. of Centwine, k. of Wessex.
Osthryth¹⁵, m. Æthelred of Mercia. ob.697.
Ealdfrith¹⁷, r. 685. ob.705. m. Cuthburh, sister of Ine.
Osred¹⁸, born 697, r. 705. ob.716.

Ealhfrith¹³, m. Cyneburh, d. of Penda.
Ealhflæd¹⁴, m. Peada, s. of Penda. ob.653.
Osric¹⁹, r. 718. ob.9 May 729.
Oslac³¹.
Adlsing³¹.
Echun³¹.
Oslaf³¹.

Cenred²⁴, r. 716. ob.718.
Ceolwulf²⁵, r. 729, resig. 737. became a monk.
Cuthwine²².

Eadberht³⁰, r. 737, resig. 758. ob.20 Aug. 768.
Egbert³³, archb. of York. ob.766.

Oswulf³², r. 758. ob.24 July 759.

Alfwold³¹, r. 779. ob.23 Sept. 788.
Ælf³², ob.791. Ælfwine³³, ob.791.

Right branch:

2. Ecca⁴. 2. Oswald⁴. 2. Sogor⁴. 2. Sogorthere⁴.
2. Alric⁴.
Oeca⁴. Blaecman²⁶. Bofa²⁶.
Ealdhelm²². Byrnhom²⁶.
Eegwald²³. Ealhwine²⁶.
Leodwald¹³.

Cuthwine⁹².
Ealhred²⁷, r. 765. ob.774. m. Osgearn, or Osgifu.
Ealhmund¹⁸, ob.800.

Osred³⁰, r. 788. ob.792.

Osgearn, or Osgifu²⁷, m. Balred. 768.
Eata²⁷.

Footnotes:

¹ This list to Ida is from Florence Geneal., which I have preferred, not so much because it is more complete than that in the Chronicle, but rather, judging from the orthography, from its being probably derived from a Northumbrian source.—T.

² This list is from the Sax. Chron. a. 547, which Florence has copied in his Chronicon.

³ Sax. Chron. a. 547. Fl. Wigorn. Sim. Dunelm., who assigns a reign of eleven years only to Ida. Nennii App.

⁴ The names of the sons of Ida are from Simeon and the Chronol. ap. Wanley and Petrie. Instead of Glappa, Frithuwald and Hussa, Florence and others have Bealric, Theodhere and Osmær. See p. 119.

⁵ Sax. Chron. Fl. Wigorn. Nennius. Beda, iii. 6.

⁶ Beda, i. 34.

⁷ Beda, iii. 1. Annal. Utton. p. 53.

⁸ Flor. Geneal.

⁹ Beda, iii. 9, 7.

¹⁰ Beda, iii. 14.

¹¹ Beda, iii. 14, iv. 5, iii. 15. Nennii App.

¹² Beda, iv. 19, 25. Vita S. Cuthb. c. x. Eddii Vita S. Wilf. c. xxxviii.

¹³ Beda, iii 14, 21.

¹⁴ Beda, iii. 21.

¹⁵ Beda, iv. 21. Sax. Chron. a. 697.

¹⁶ Beda, iv. 19, 26. Eddius, c. xxxix.

¹⁷ Beda, v. 18. Sax. Chron. a. 705. W. Malm.

¹⁸ Beda, v. 18, 22.

¹⁹ Beda, v. 23, and Smith, ib. Sax. Chron. a. 729. The descent of Osric seems uncertain.

²⁰ Beda, iv. 21.

²¹ Nennii App.

²² Beda, iii. 24. Acta SS. t. ii. p. 178.

²³ Sax. Chron. aa. 729, 738. Flor. Geneal.

²⁴ Sax. Chron. a. 716.

²⁵ Sax. Chron. aa. 729, 731, 737.

²⁶ Flor. Geneal.

²⁷ Sax. Chron. a. 765. Flor. Geneal. Sim. Dunelm. a. 768. Chron. Mailr. Bonifacii Epist.

²⁸ Sim. Dunelm.

²⁹ Sax. Chron. a. 738. Flor. Geneal.

³⁰ Sax. Chron. aa. 738, 757, 768.

³¹ Sax. Chron. Fl. Wigorn. a. 789.

³² Sax. Chron.

³³ Sax. Chron. aa. 738, 766.

³⁴ Annal. Ult.

Woden[1].

Wægdæg.

Sigegar.

Swæbdæg.

Sigegeat.

Sæbald.

Sæfugel.

Seomel.

Wæcerta.

Westerfalcna.

Wilgils.

Uscfrea.

Yffe.

Ælle, 559. ob.588.

'Acha[4],' m. Æthelfrith, k. of Bernicia.

Eadwine[5], born 585. r.616. ob.14 Oct. 633. m.1.Cwenburh, d. of Ceorl, k. of Mercia; 2. Æthelburh, d. of Æthelberht of Kent.

Ælfric[2].

Osric[2], r. 633. ob.634.

Oswine[3], r. 644. ob.20 Aug. 651.

Osfrith[8], ob.14 Oct. 633.

Eadfrith[8], ob.after 633.

Eanflæd[9], born 626. m. Oswiu of Bernicia.

Æthelhun[10], ob.at York.

Æthelthryth[10], ob.at York.

Wuscfrea[8], ob.after 634 in France.

Individual not named.

Hereric[6], m. Beorhtswyth, poisoned in Elmet before 616.

Hild[7], born 614. ob.15 Dec. 680. Abbess of Whitby

Hereswyth[7], m. Anna, k. of E. Anglia.

[1] The line from Woden to Ælle is from the Chronicle, aa. 560, 588, and Florence. The names of Swerta and Seomel do not appear in the Chronicle.

[2] Beda, iii. i.

[3] Beda, iii. 14. Sax. Chron.
[4] Beda, iii. 6.
[5] Beda, ii. 20, ii. 14,9.
[6] Beda, iv. 23. Flor. Geneal., where Hereric as a son of Eadfrith and grandson of Eadwine. Florence has, no doubt,

rendered Beda's words, "nepos Æduini regis," erroneously.
[7] Beda, iv. 23.
[8] Beda, ii. 20.
[9] Beda, ii. 9, iii. 15.
[10] Beda, ii. 14.

Woden[1].
Wihtlæg.
Wærmund.
Offa.
Dan, surnamed Mykillati[3], k. of Denmark.

Angeltheow.
Eomer.
Icel.
Cnebba.
Cynewald.
Creoda.
Wybba.

Woden[2].
Weothelgeat.
Waga.
Wihtlæg.
Wærmund.
Offa.
Angengeat.

Ceorl, a kinsman of Wybba. r. 596. ob.606.
Cwenburh, m. Eadwine, k. of Deira.

Eawa[6], ob.5 Aug 642.

Penda[3], r. 626. ob.655. m. Cyneswyth, or Cynewise.

Cenwealh[7], Cuthwealh[91], Centwine[91], Centreou[91], Bassa[91], Cuthberht[91], descendant in the 5th degree of Cenwealh.

Cenwulf[94], r.796. m. 1. Cynegyth; 2. Ælfthryth.
Cuthred[30], k. of Kent. ob.805.
Ceolwulf[31], r.819. ob.821.
Ælfled[32], m. Wigmund, s. of Wiglaf, k. of Mercia.

Wistan[32], ob.850.

Cynethryth[33], Cenhelm[55], ob.17 July 819. Burgenhild[33].

Osmod[94].
Eanvulf[94].
Thingferth[24], m. Marcellina.
Offa[24], r.757. ob.10 Aug. 796. m. Cyne-thryth.

Eadburh[25], 787. m.Beorhtric, k. of Wessex.

Ælfthryth[26], betrothed to Æthelberht, k. of E. Anglia.
Eogferth[28], ob.796.

A daughter[4], m. Cenweah, k. of Wessex.

Merewald[10], ealdorm. of the W. Hecanas. m. Eormenburh of Kent.
Merchelm[11], or Mercelin.

Wilburh[15], m. Frithwold, under-king of Surrey.
Cyneburh[13], m. Ealhfrith of Northumberland.
Cyneswyth[14].

Mildburh[90], Mildthryth[90], Mildgyth[90], Merewine[90], Alweo[93].

Æthelbald[93], r.716. ob.757.
Heardberht[93].

Æthelred[10], r.675, resig. 704. ob.4 May 716. m. Osthryth, d.of Oswin.

Ælfled[26], m. Æthelred, k. of Northumbria.

Peada[8], ob.Easter 656. m. Ealhflæd, a d. of Oswin.
Wulfhere[9], r. 656. ob.675. m. Eormengild of Kent.

Cenred[16], r.704, resig. 709.
Werburh[17], Beorhtwald[18], 686, a sub-king.
Ceolred[19], 709, ob.716. m. Werburh. ob.702 as an abbess.

1 The line from Woden to Penda is according to the Sax. Chron. a. 626.
2 This list is according to Florence, having two additional names, and Angengeat for Angeltheow.
3 Saxo Gramm. lib. iv. p. 175, t. i. ed. Müller.
4 Beda, iii. 7. Flor. Geneal.
5 Beda, iii. 21.
6 Sax. Chron. a. 716. Nennius. Ann. Camb. a. 644.
7 Flor. Geneal.
8 Beda, iii. 21, 24.
9 Beda, iii. 24. Sax. Chron. a. 675.
10 Sax. Chron. Beda, iii. 11, iv. 21. Sim. Dunelm. Flor. Geneal. W. Malm.
12 W. Malm. Flor. Geneal.
13 Beda, iii. 24.
14 Flor. Geneal. W. Malm.
15 Rad. de Diceto, Abbrev. a. 641. Vita S. Osithæ, in Smith's Beda, p. 129.
16 Beda, v. 24.
17 W. Malm. i. ii.
18 Eddii Vita S. Wilfr. c. xxxix. Malmesh. de Pont. lib. v. ap. Gale, p. 345, and charter a. 686 ib.
19 Beda, v. 24. Sax. Chron. a. 782. Sim. Dunelm. a. 783.
20 Flor. Geneal. W. Malm.
21 Flor. Geneal.
22 Sax. Chron. a. 716. Flor. Geneal.
23 Charter in Smith's Beda, a. 786. Hemming, t. i. p. 219.
24 Sax. Chron. a. 755. Flor. Geneal.
25 Sim. Dunelm. Sax. Chron. R. Wendover, t. i. p. 250. According to the Vita Offæ II., Drithe was a Frank, called also Petronilla, a relation of the emperor Charles.
26 Sax. Chron. Flor. Geneal.
27 Flor. Geneal.
28 W. Malm.
29 Sax. Chron. Cod. Diplom. t. i. pp. 214, 238.
30 Sax. Chron. a. 805.
31 Sax. Chron.
32 Flor. Geneal.
33 Fl. Wigorn. a. 850, and Geneal. W. Malm.

GENEALOGY OF THE PRINCES OF THE LINDIS-FARAS, OR INHABITANTS OF LINDSEY, THE TERRITORY ABOUT LINCOLN.

𝕴𝖂𝖔𝖉𝖊𝖓[1].
|
Winta.
|
Cretta.
|
Cweldgils.
|
Cædbæd.
|
Bubba.
|
Beda.
|
Biscop[2].
|
Eanferth.
|
Eatta.
|
Ealdfrith.

[1] This list is from Fl. Wigorn.
[2] This is apparently Benedict Biscop, surnamed Baducing, the founder of Wearmouth abbey. See p. 174. It is singular that the name of Blecca does not appear in the above list, of whom see p. 153.—T.

END OF VOL. I.